CW01639226

Photographic Memories
of
The Heart of England

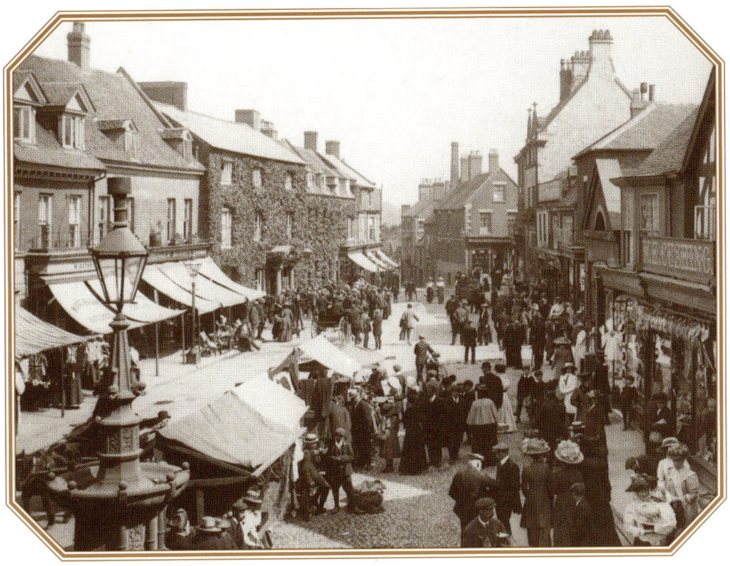

Front cover picture:
Corporation Street, Birmingham, 1890 (B100002)

Above:
Market Day, Market Drayton, 1911 (63338)

FRANCIS FRITH AND HIS UNIQUE ARCHIVE

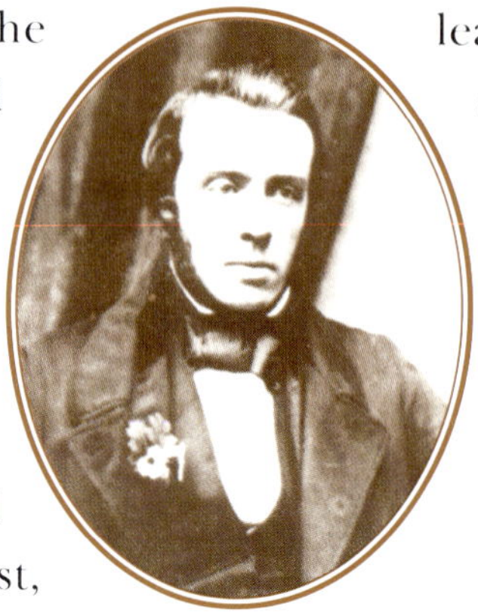

In 1860, Francis Frith, the Quaker son of a Chesterfield cooper, was 38 years old. He had already sold a massive grocery business he had built up, for a small fortune. Like Livingstone and Stanley, Frith was fired with a romantic Wanderlust, and the Victorian deep passion for travelling and exploring. Between 1857 and '59 he made several pioneering photographic journeys to remote regions of the Nile that brought him considerable fame.

After his marriage in 1860, he confined his wanderings a little closer to home and began a series of photo trips around Britain. His aim was to make his pictures available to the greatest number of people possible - life was hard and drab for millions of Victorians, and Frith believed his 'view souvenirs' of seaside resorts, beauty spots and town and village scenes would help keep their rare days out alive in their memories. He was right: by 1890 he had created the largest photographic publishing company in the world!

As well as thousands of views of high streets around Britain, Frith's growing archive included beautiful scenes of leafy glades, dusty lanes, rocks and coastlines, and the boats and riversides, beloved of Victorian wanderers like Jerome K Jerome - whose 'Three Men in a Boat' had struck a strong chord with the public.

Life in the Frith family was never dull. The family went with him on many trips, and the highlights were recorded by his wife, Mary Ann, in her journal. In 1872 she tells of a relaxing three week expedition to Ilfracombe in North Devon. Whilst such trips may have been something of a holiday for his wife and children, Francis Frith found no time to put his feet up. He was up and down the coast photographing Barnstaple and Lynton, hiring carters to carry him out to remote locations, and boatsmen to row him round the bay to view and photograph spectacular cliff formations.

After Francis Frith died in 1898 his sons carried on the business for many years with great success, specialising in postcards and other prints. So impressive is the archive he started that **The Financial Times** called it '*a unique and priceless record of English life in the last century*'.

PHOTOGRAPHIC MEMORIES

OF

THE HEART OF ENGLAND

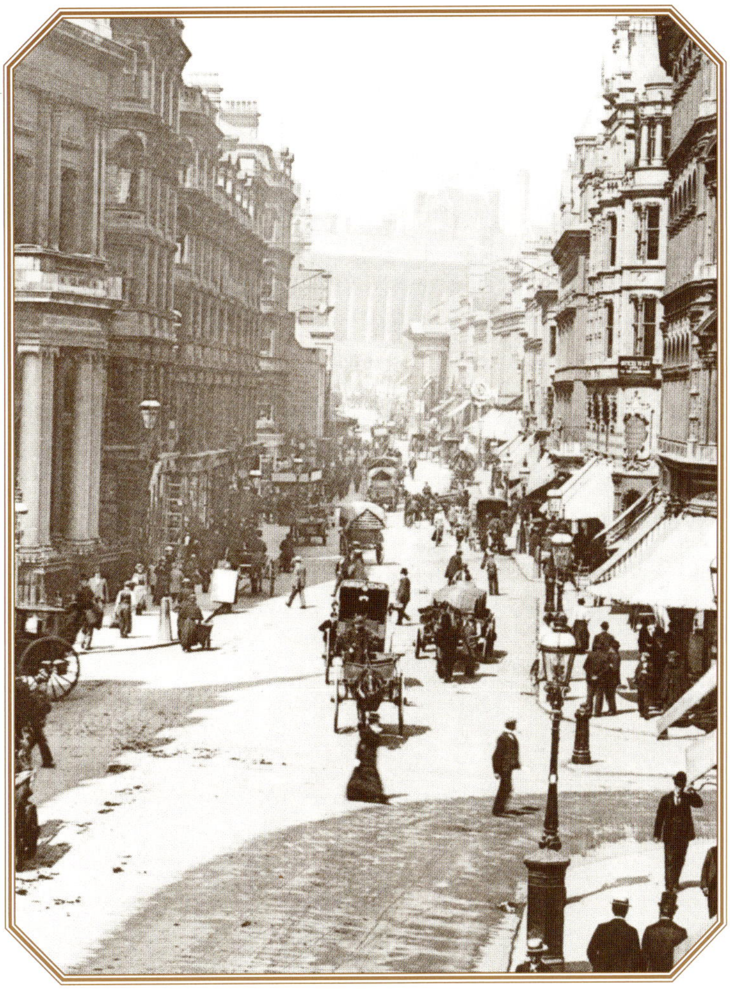

THE FRANCIS FRITH COLLECTION

A Century of Change in the Midlands

This edition published by
The Francis Frith Collection exclusively for
Selectabook Ltd., Roundway, Devizes,
Wiltshire SN10 2HR

First Published in 1996

ISBN 1 85937 022 5

Printed in Italy by Imago Publishing

Reproductions of all the photographs in this book are available as framed or mounted prints from The Francis Frith Collection at the address below. Please quote the town, full title and negative number shown in brackets.

The Francis Frith Collection
The Old Rectory, Bimport, Shaftesbury, Dorset SP7 8AT
Tel: 01747 855669 Fax: 01747 855065

CONTENTS

OXFORD. 'The noble cluster of famous towers and spires always arouse in me an indescribable thrill of pride and love and enthusiasm. There is nothing like Oxford.' The Victorian curate, Francis Kilvert, expresses the sentiments of generations of romantics, scholars and writers who have come to this ancient university town and fallen in love with its architectural gems and the sanctuary of its quadrangles and gardens.

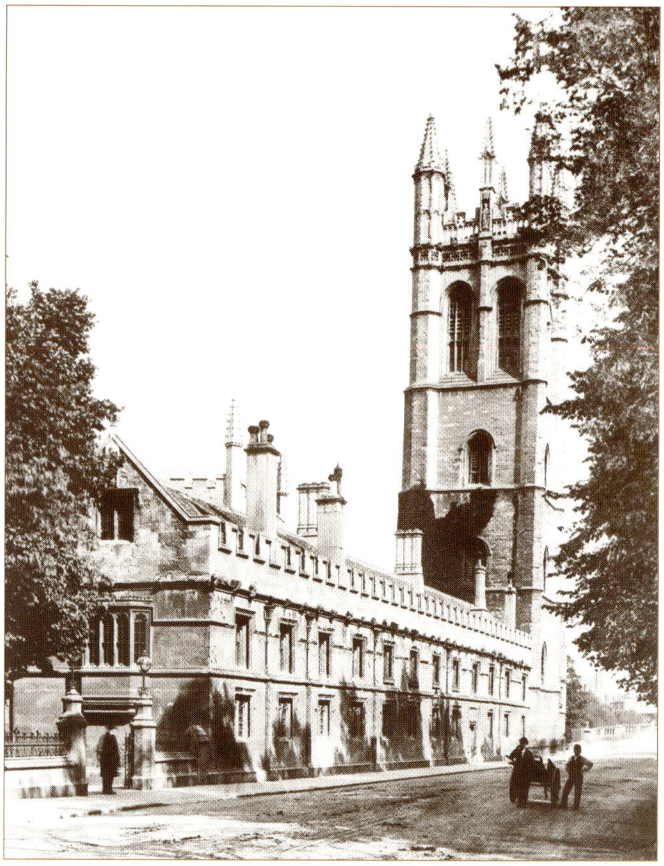

Right: Magdalen College, Oxford, 1890 (26822). Its magnificent bell tower, the finest in Oxford, rises over the eastern gate to the city. Its choristers sing their Latin hymn at dawn on May-day morning.

Below: High Street, Oxford, 1900 (45181). The High, with its graceful sweep, is the most elegant street in the city, with a clutch of fine buildings. The majestic tower of St Mary the Virgin rises in the distance. On the right is the classical facade of Queen's College, and then the Gothic glories of All Soul's. Hansom cabs ply for trade.

Opposite: On the River, Oxford, 1922 (72057).

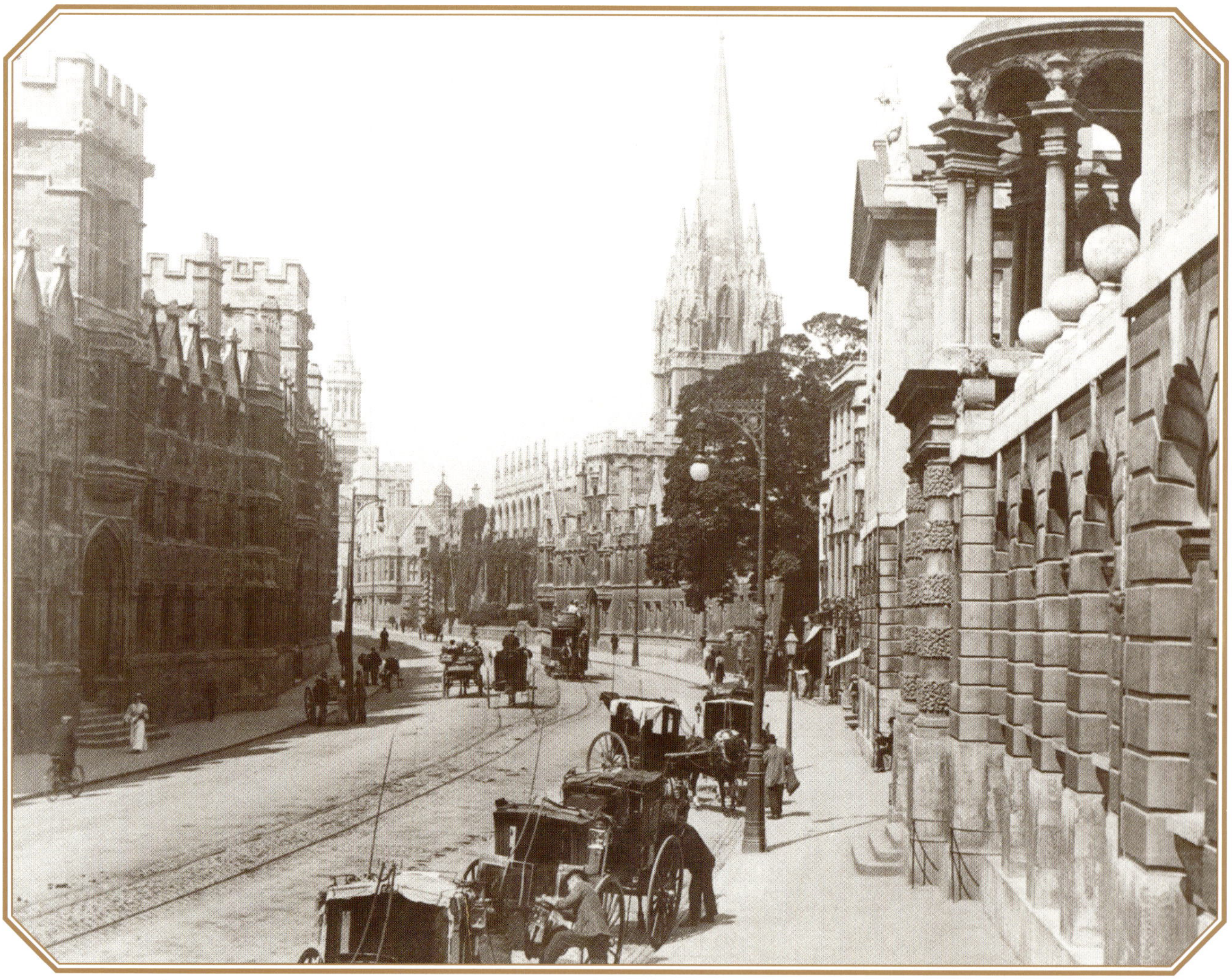

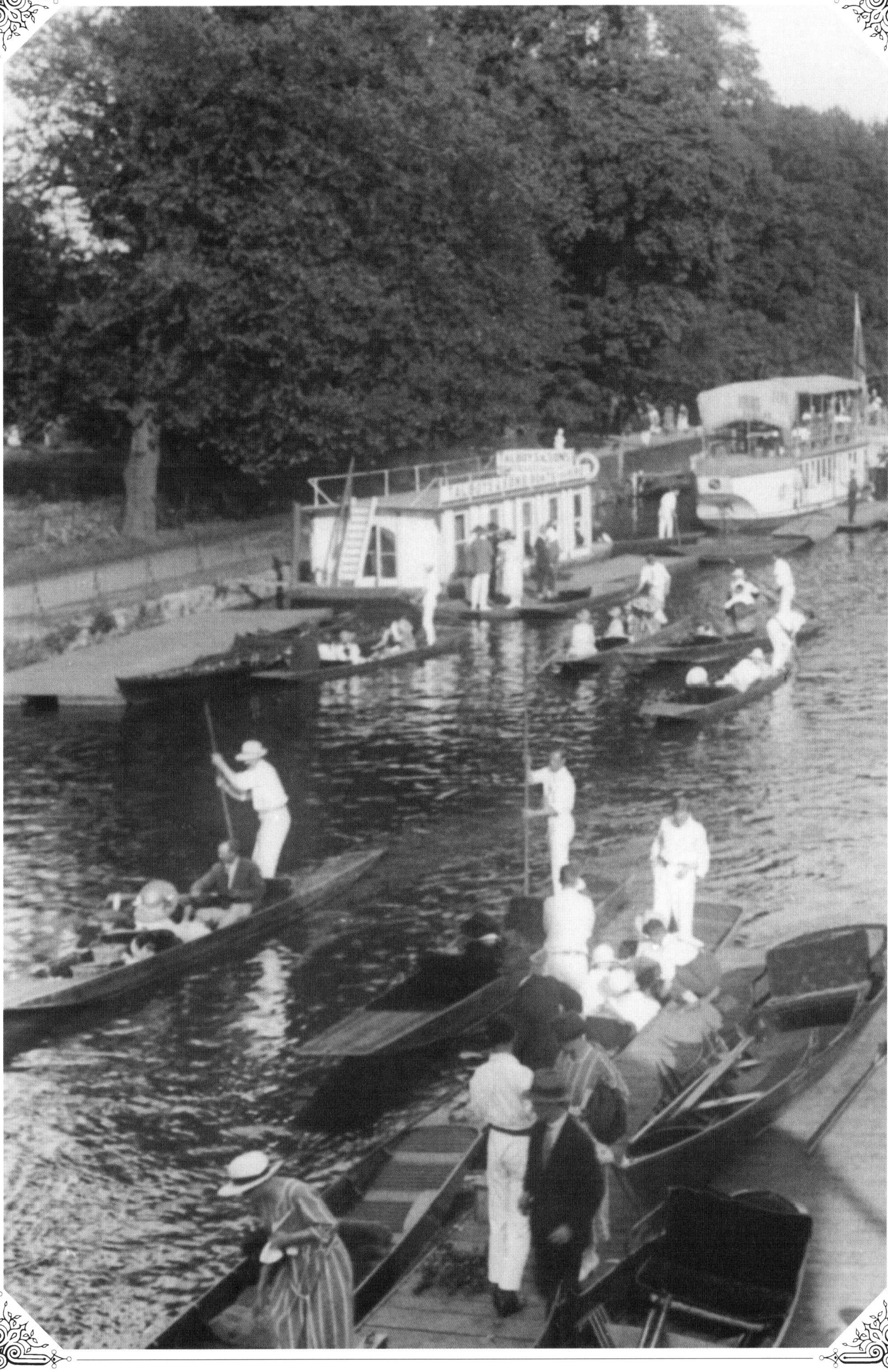

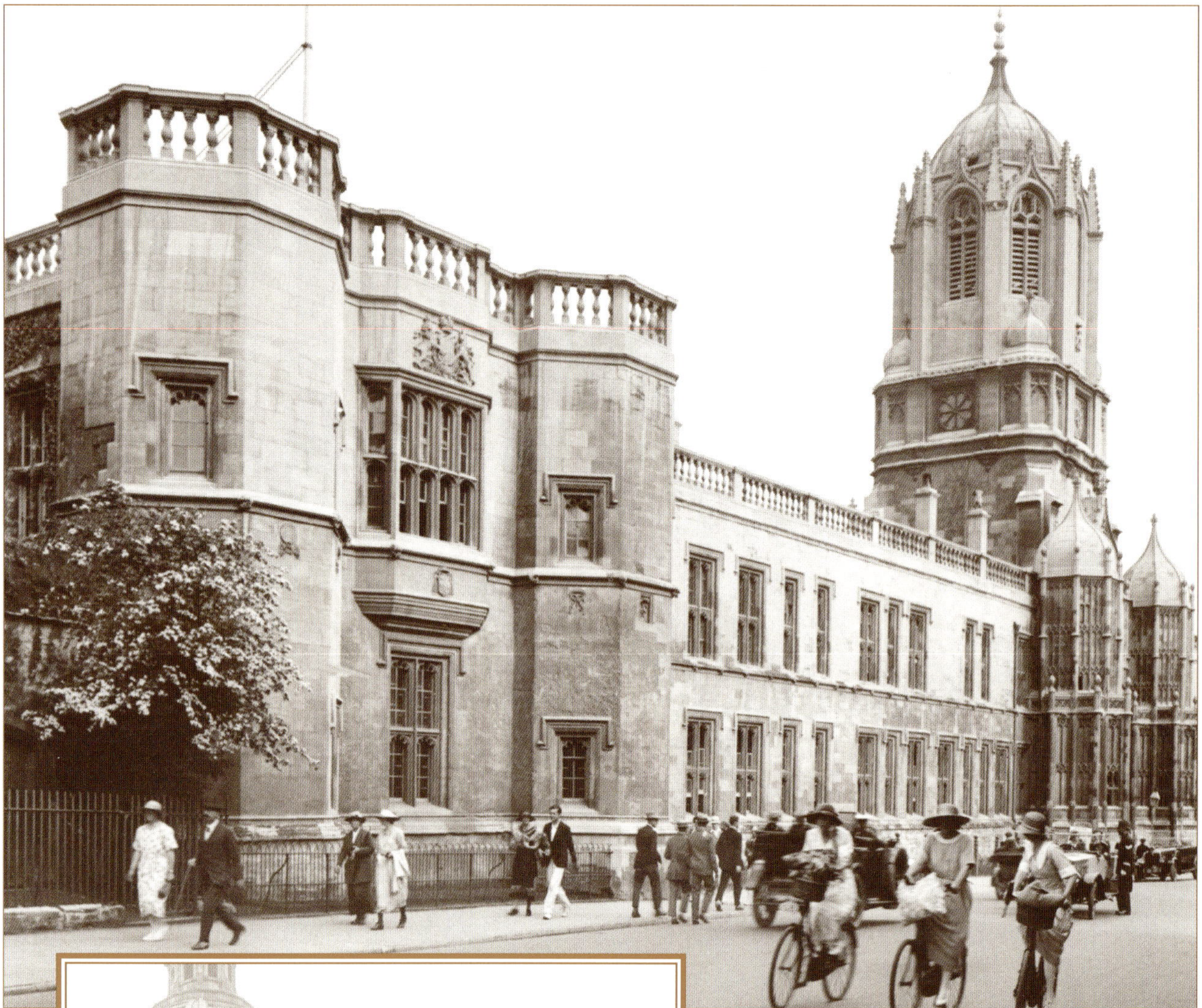

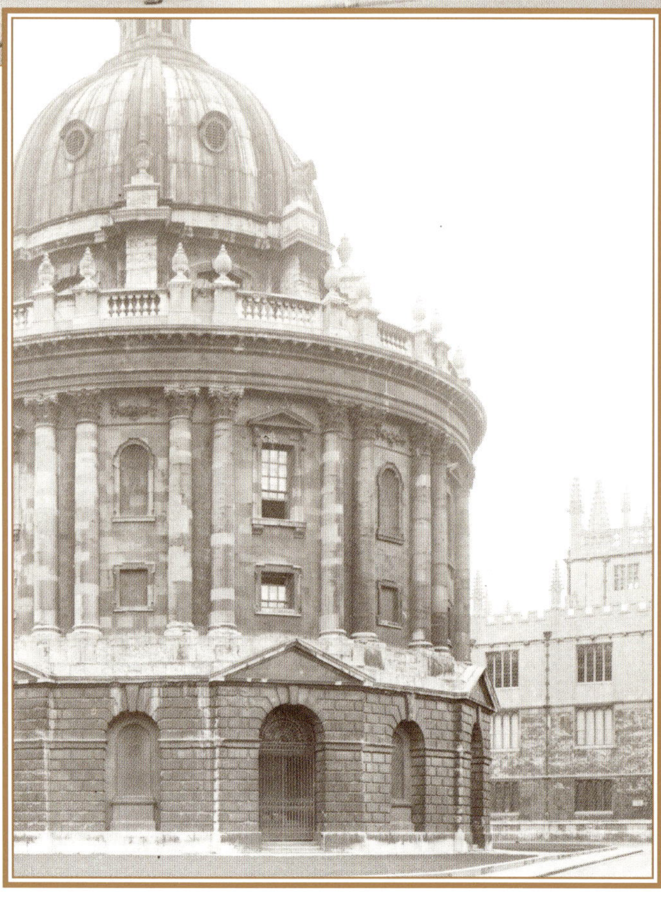

Above: Christ Church, Oxford, 1922 (72009). Many illustrious men have strolled in its quiet quadrangle below Wren's Tom Tower, away from the bustling street of St Aldates. They include Lewis Carroll and John Wesley. Here three women are getting around the city in the most practical way possible - by bicycle. Scholars in flannels dawdle between tutorials. This scene is reminiscent of the Oxford of Evelyn Waugh's "Brideshead Revisited".

Left: Radcliffe Camera, Oxford, 1937 (88079). Built in 1737 as a Physic Library by James Gibbs, this superb domed rotunda is now a reading room for the Bodleian Library. Inside the dome, around the gallery, generations of students have scratched their names on the windows.

Opposite top: Magdalen College, Oxford, from the Bridge, 1920 (71999).

Opposite below: The Oxford Eights, 1922 (72061). Hotly contested, these bump races are run from Folly Bridge.

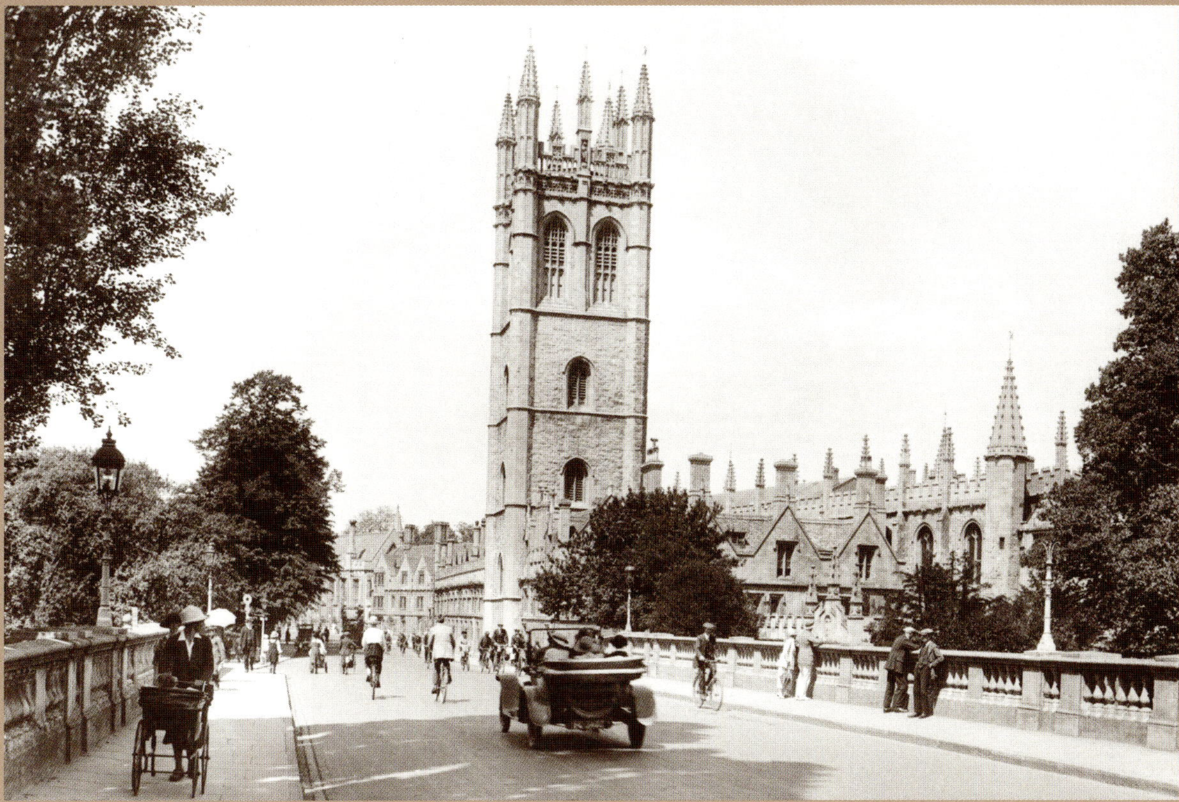

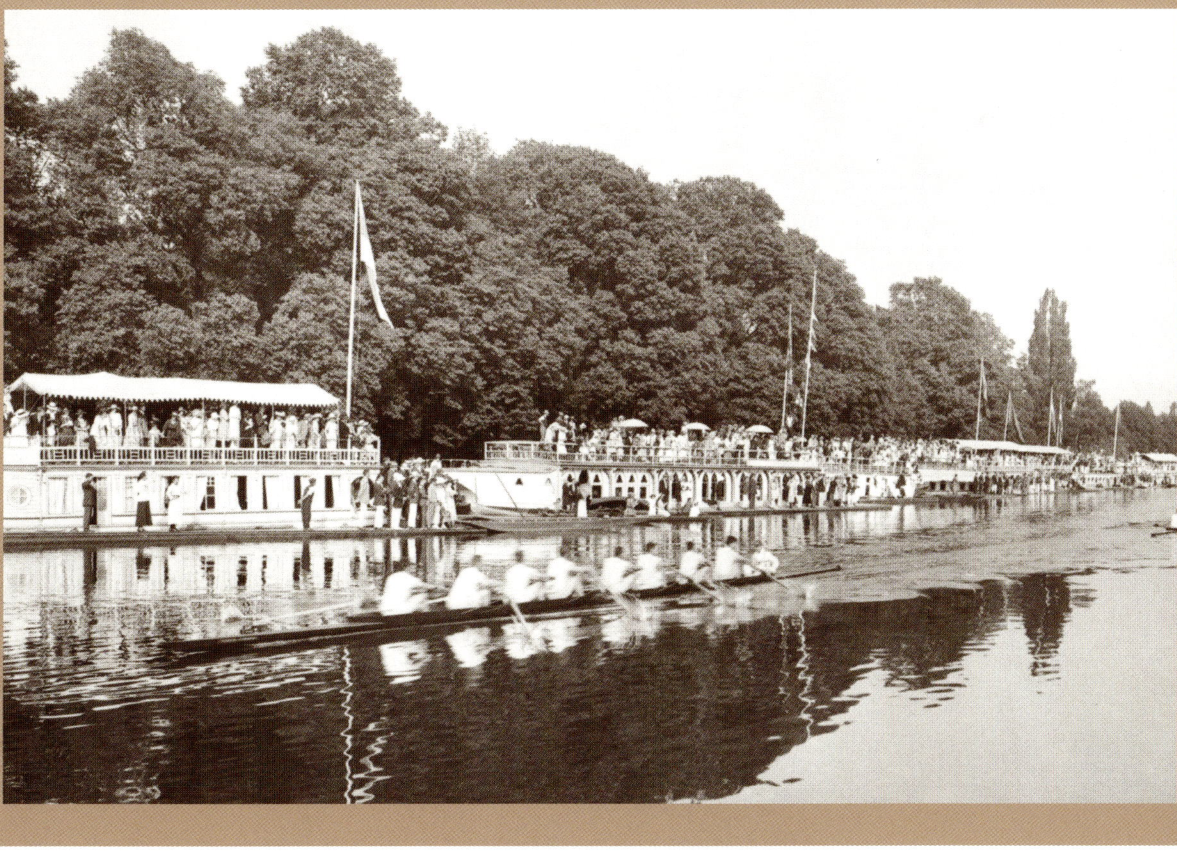

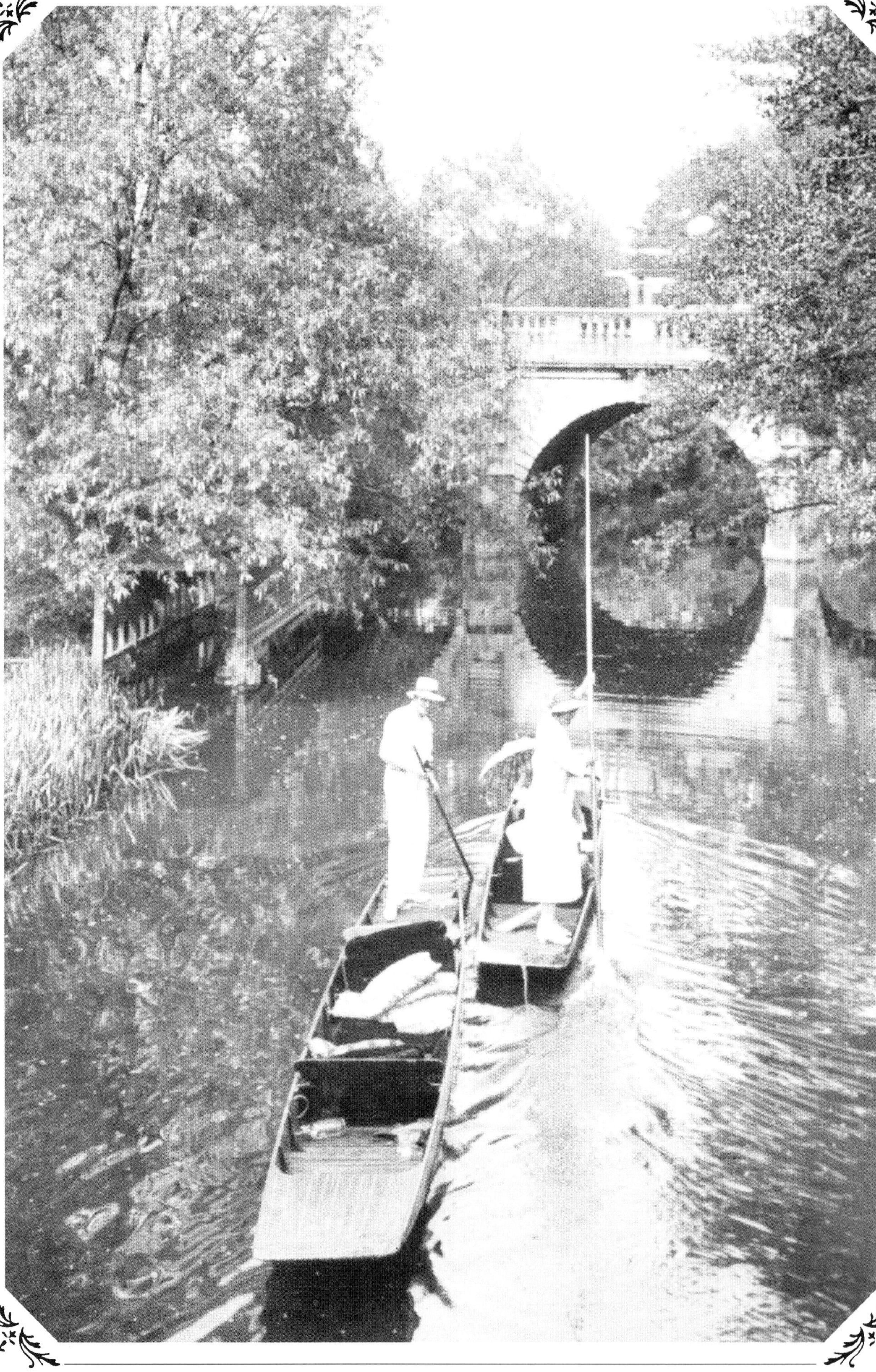

Opposite: On the Cherwell under Magdalen Bridge, Oxford, 1922 (72007) Jerome K Jerome did not recommend hiring a boat at Oxford. In his 'Three Men in a Boat' he says how the one he was offered looked like 'an antediluvian chunk of wood... recently dug out of somewhere and dug out carelessly'. These two plucky punters look happy enough, though.

Right: On the Cherwell, Oxford, 1906 (72053) You couldn't always rely on a peaceful afternoon out on the sunlit water under the shade of the willows. Things could get fraught and very busy, with collisions and altercations at every turn.

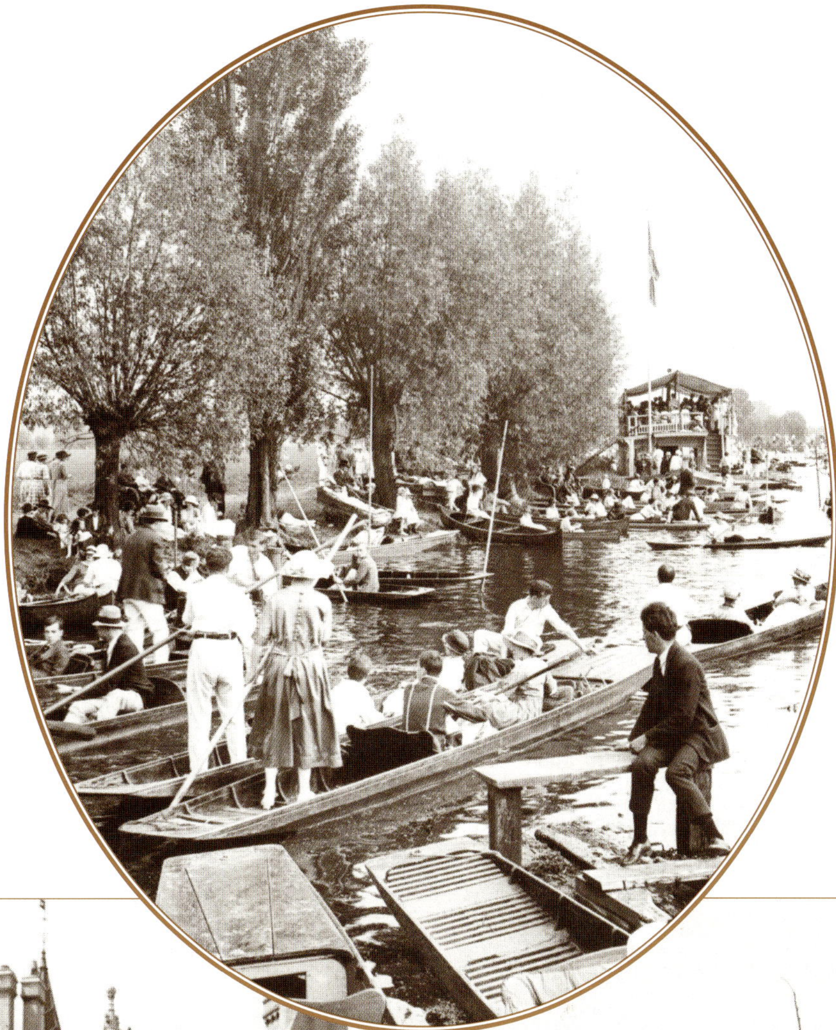

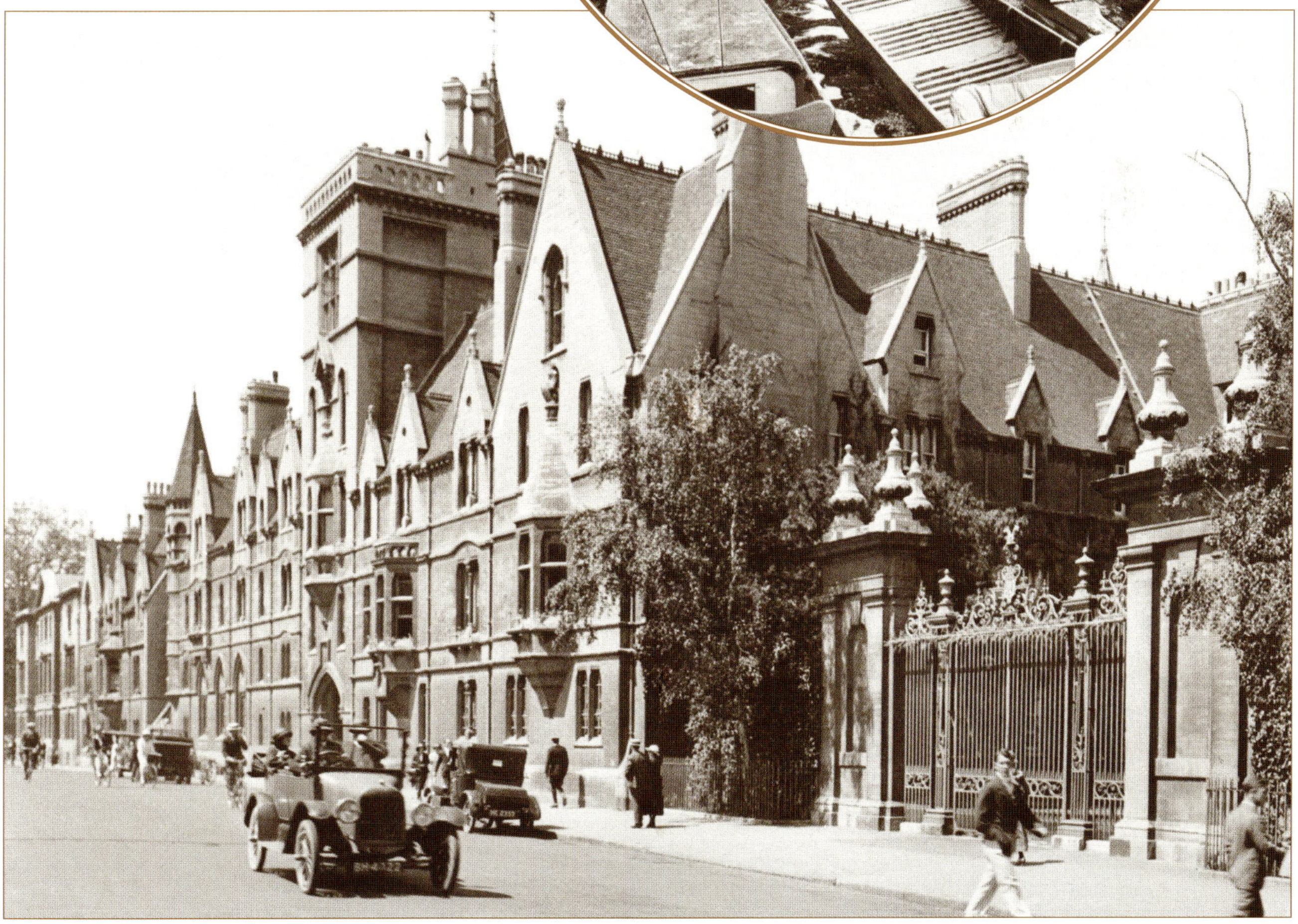

Above: Balliol College, Oxford, 1922 (72020) This monumental Victorian frontage is set along the north side of the city's spacious thoroughfare, Broad Street. Apart from Swinburne and Matthew Arnold, one of its most illustrious graduates was Lord Peter Wimsey, hero of Dorothy Sayers' detective novels. **Overleaf: Oxford from Magdalen Tower, 1890** (26802) The poet and writer, Edward Thomas, 'felt the mysterious pleasure of being in an elevated Oxford chamber at night', and described the city's 'sea of roofs and horned turrets and spires... speaking strongly and clearly, pompous as Latin, subtle as Greek'.

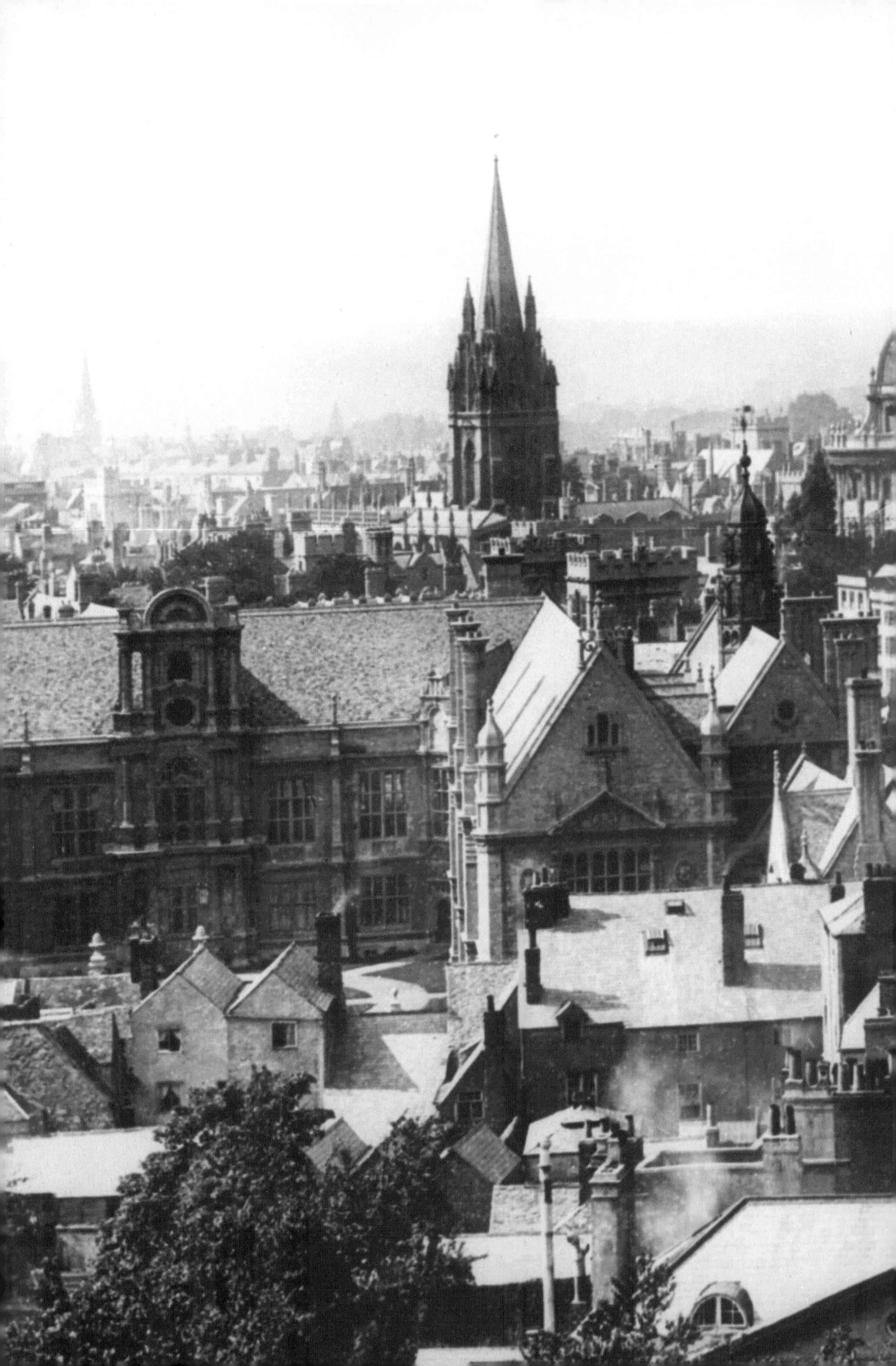

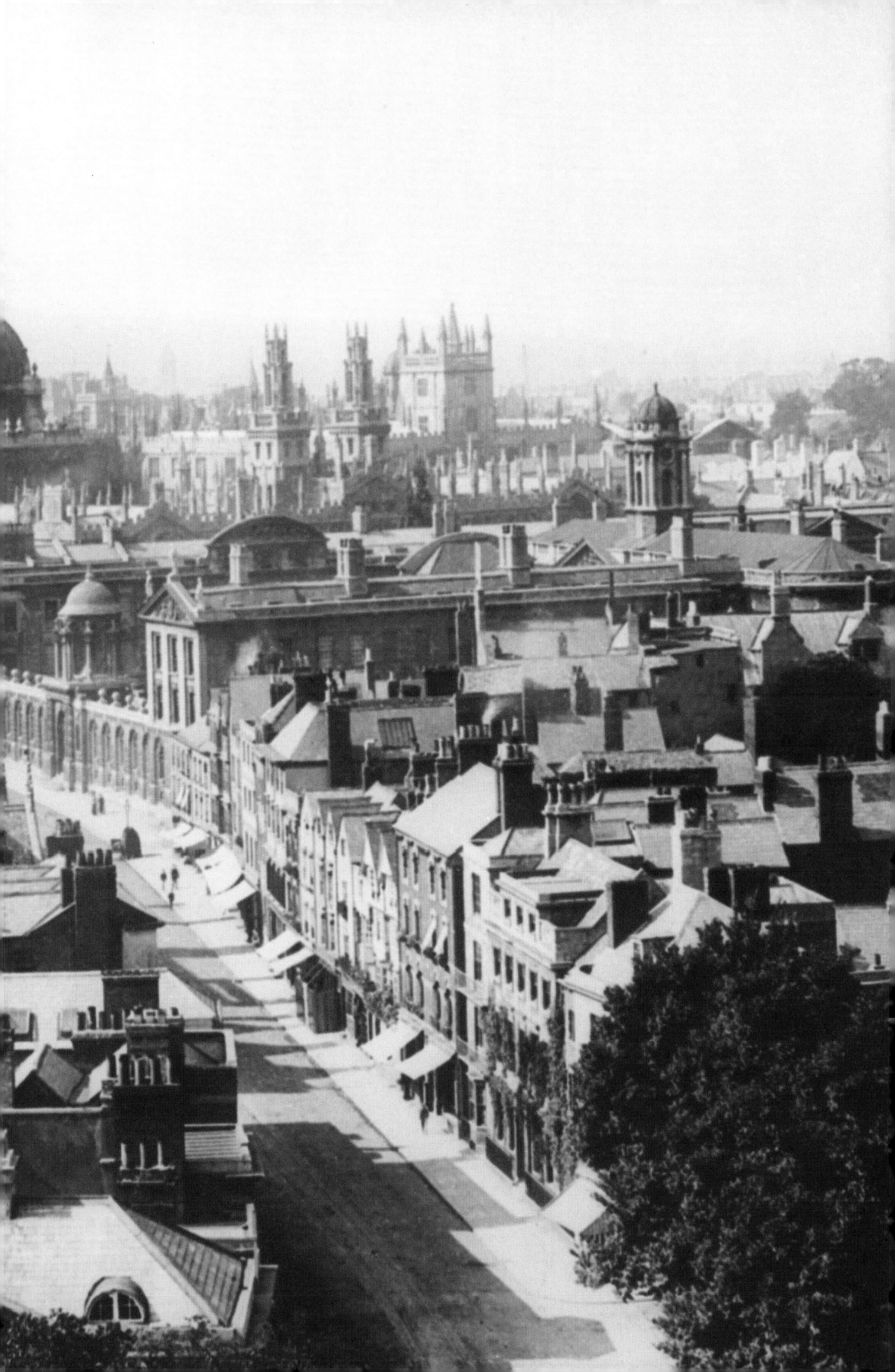

BANBURY. This old market town is renowned for more than its children's rhyme. Banbury cakes - delicious flakey pastry and currants - are traditional fare in the town, and its old inns have been hosts to travellers down the centuries. Flora Thompson, who wrote the idyll of vanished country life 'Lark Rise to Candleford' just a few miles to the east of the town, must have come often to the bustling market.

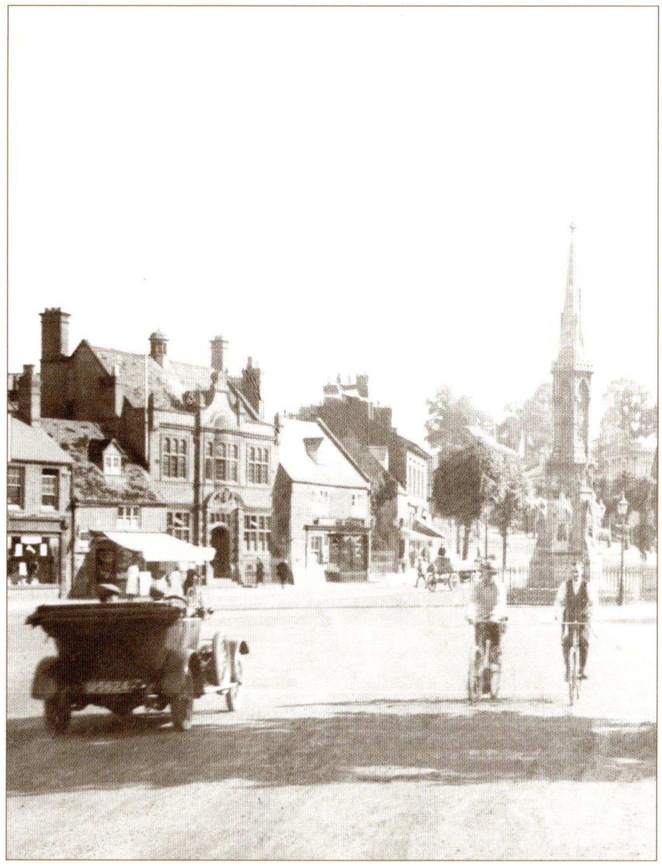

Right: Banbury Cross, 1921 (70582)
This busy market town had an ancient cross in medieval times, but it was destroyed by the Puritans in 1602. The Gothic cross dominating the centre of the Horsefair is a Victorian creation, celebrating the 'fine lady' of the famous rhyme.

Below: Banbury Market in 1922 (72067)
In the foreground a weary drover has finally got his cow to market. A boy has hitched a ride on a cart and, in front of the Town Hall, a thick throng of farmers, clutching their sticks, are busy looking over the animals.

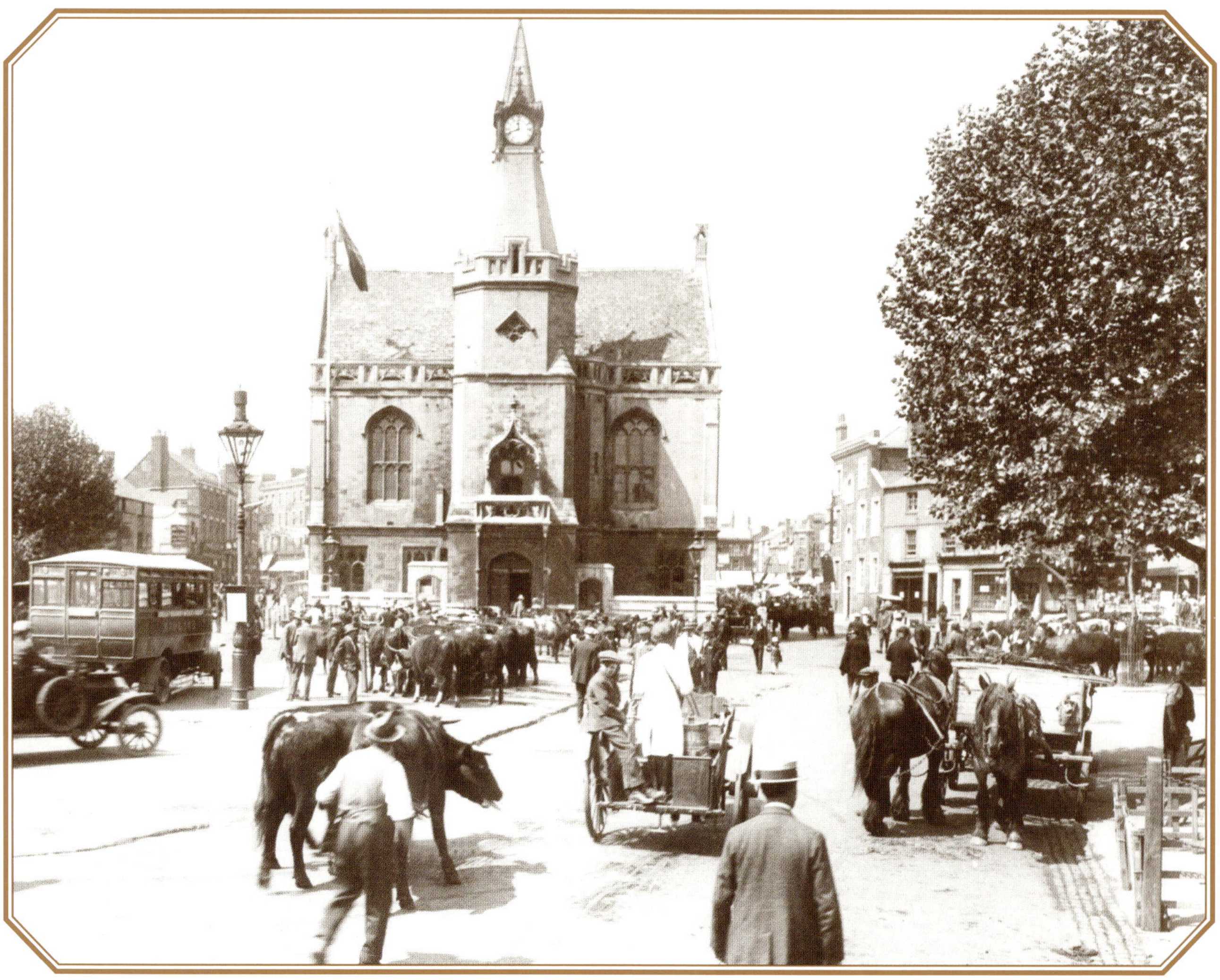

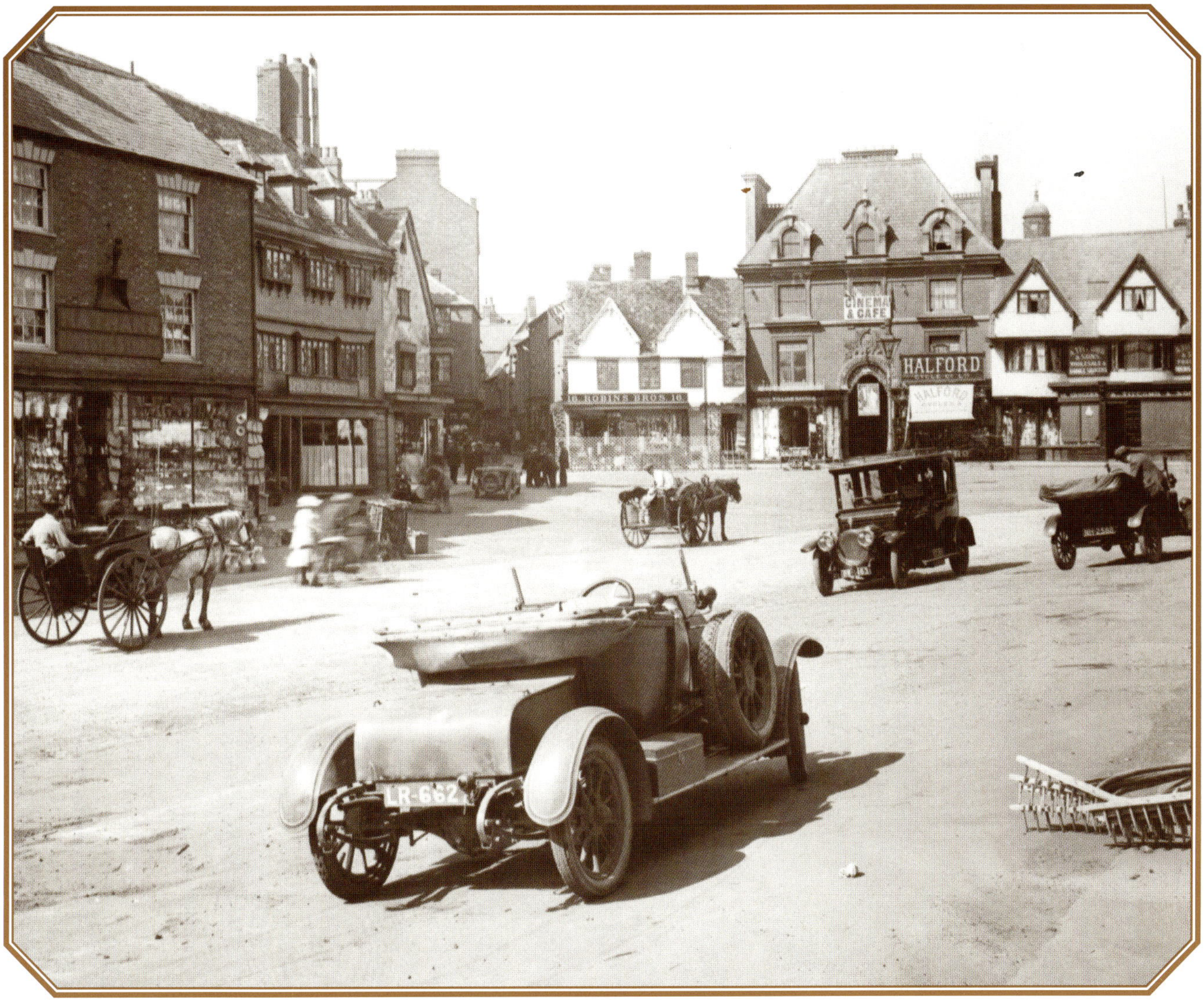

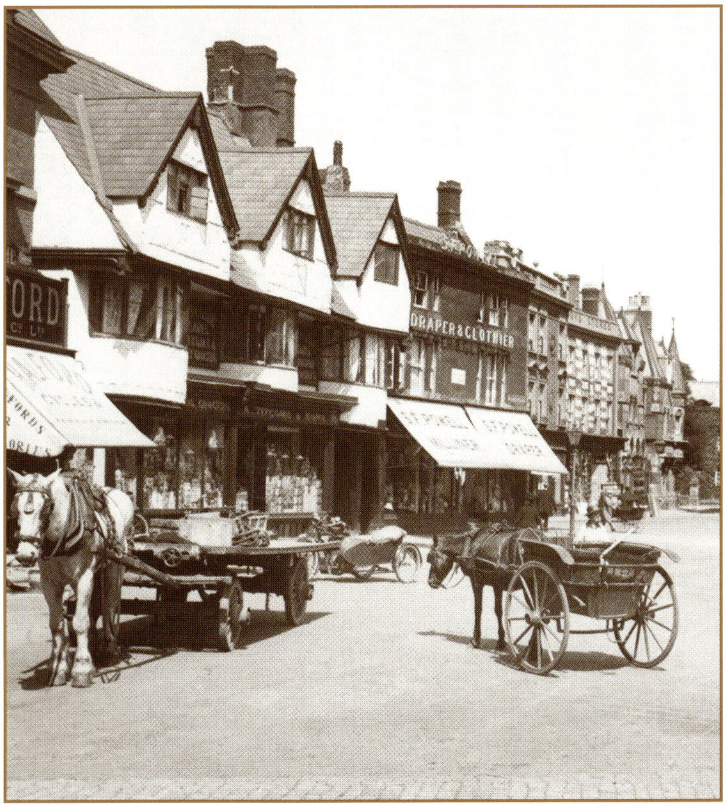

Above: Market Place, Banbury, 1921
(70572) We couldn't park like this today! Here, cars are abandoned haphazardly as if they were left where they happened to come to rest. Dotted around the broad square are unsold items from the market - hay rakes and other agricultural tools. The buildings are a hotch-potch of styles, with Victorian buildings filling the gaps between the older ones.

Left: Market Place, Banbury, 1921
(70571) Here is a sign of the times: on the extreme left is one of the earliest of the chain stores that spread rapidly throughout our towns in the first two decades of the century. Halfords are offering cheap cycles to the citizens of Banbury. The blinds are down, and it is a hot, stuffy afternoon. Horses wait patiently in the sunlight for their drivers.

Overleaf: Banbury Market, 1921 (70569)
Market day as it has been for centuries. Crowds cluster round the stalls, and the shops have taken advantage of the road to use as vital extra selling space.

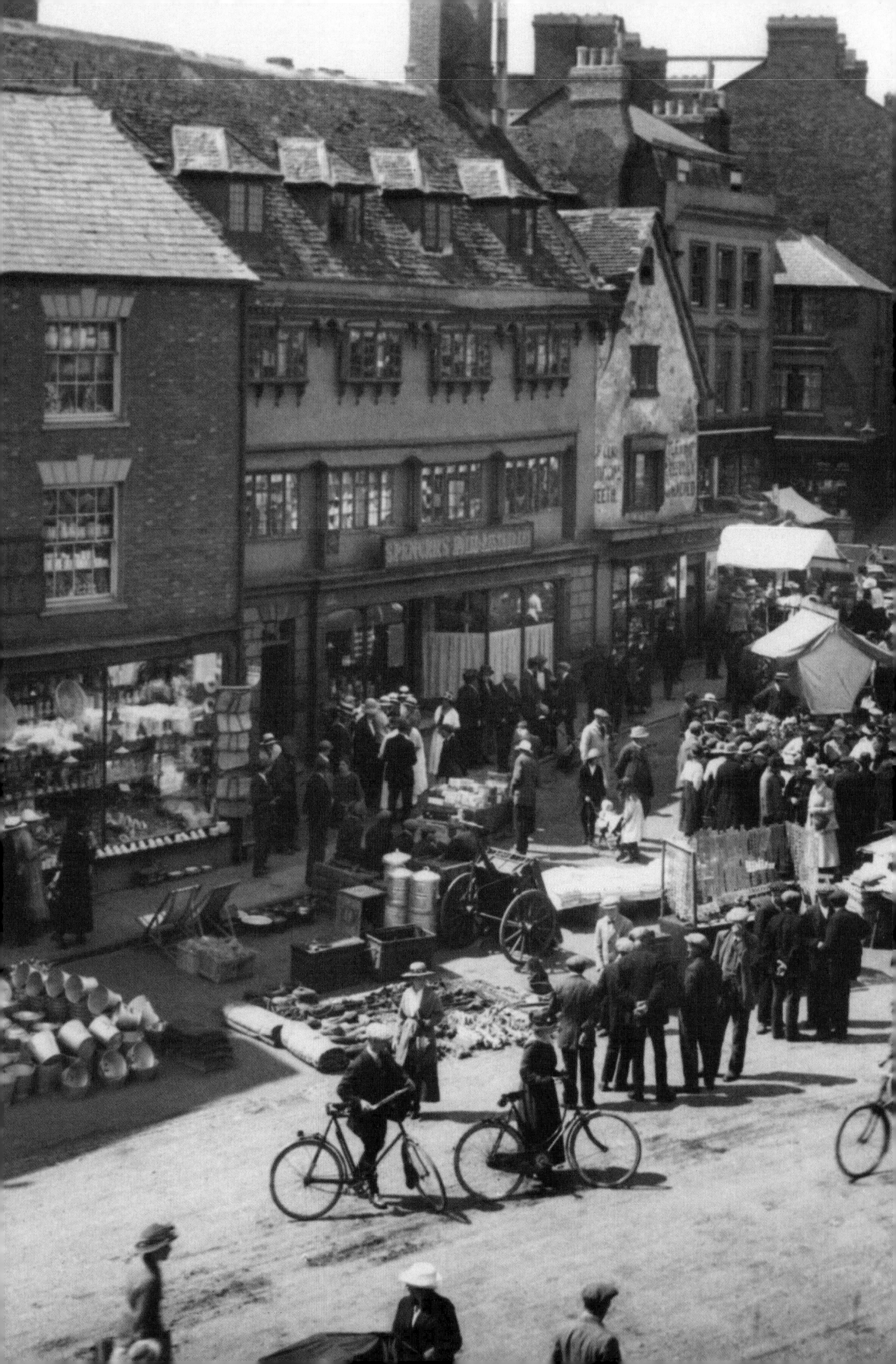

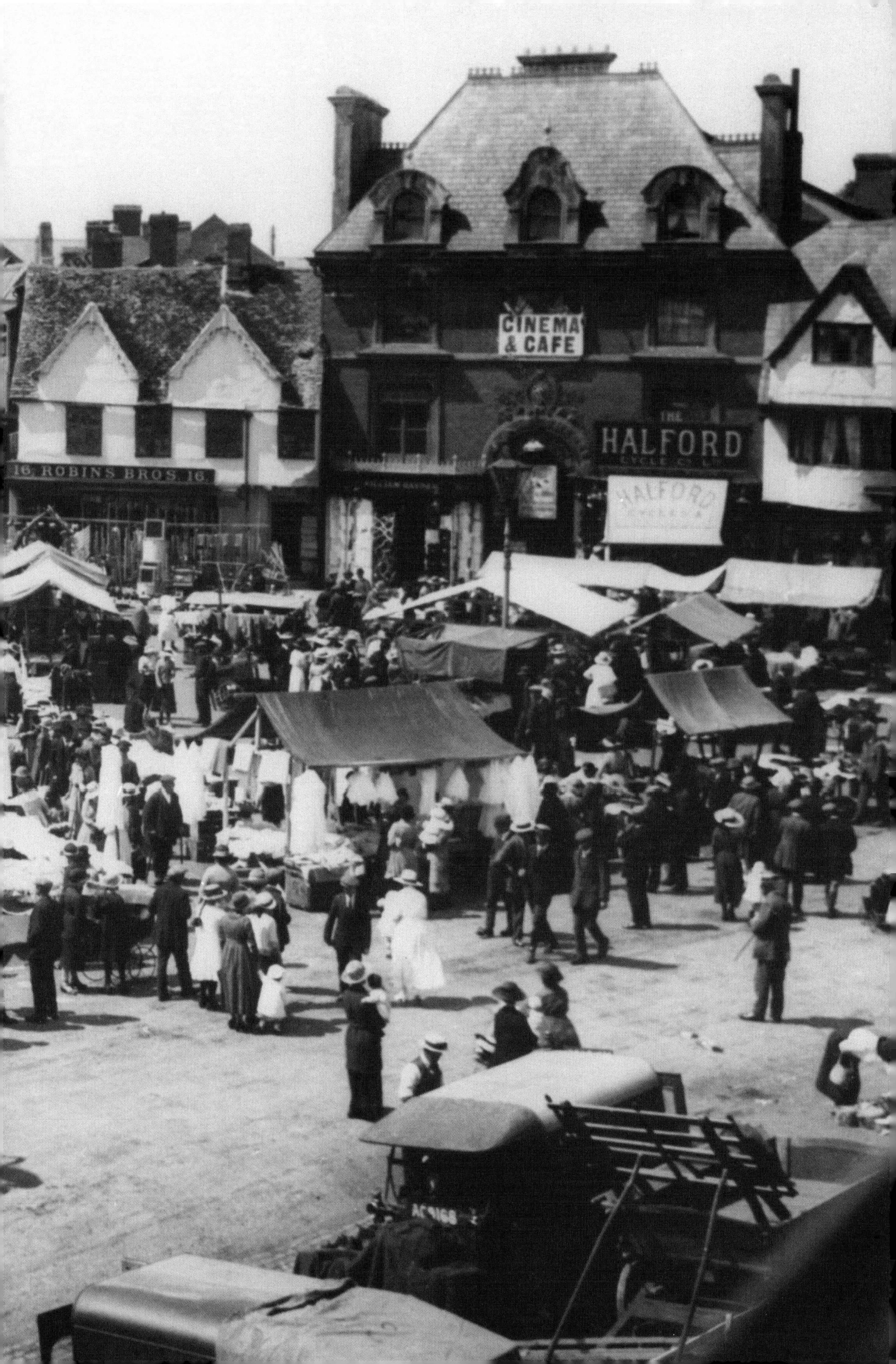
CINEMA
& CAFE
THE
HALFORD
16. ROBINS BROS. 16.
HALFORD

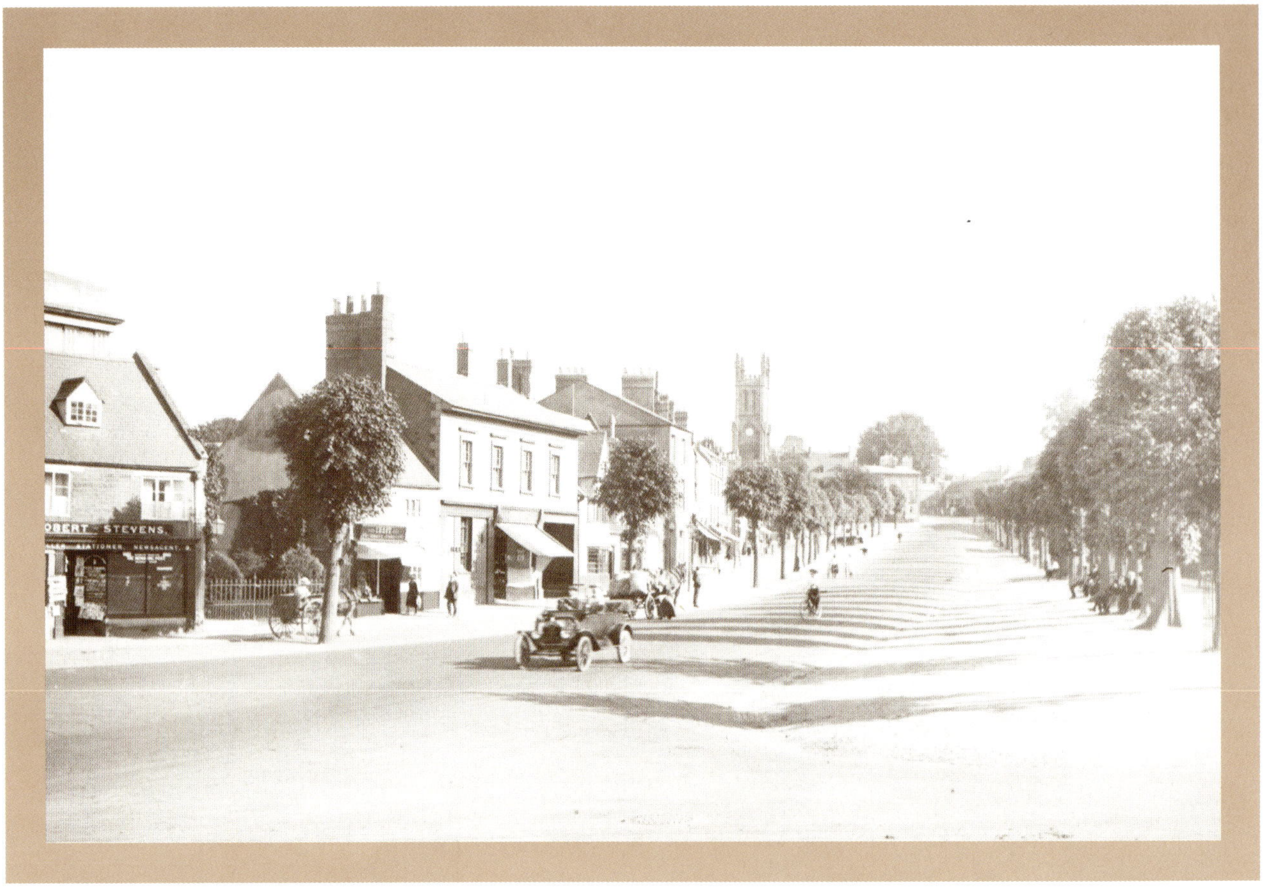
STEVENS.
STATIONER, NEWSAGENT

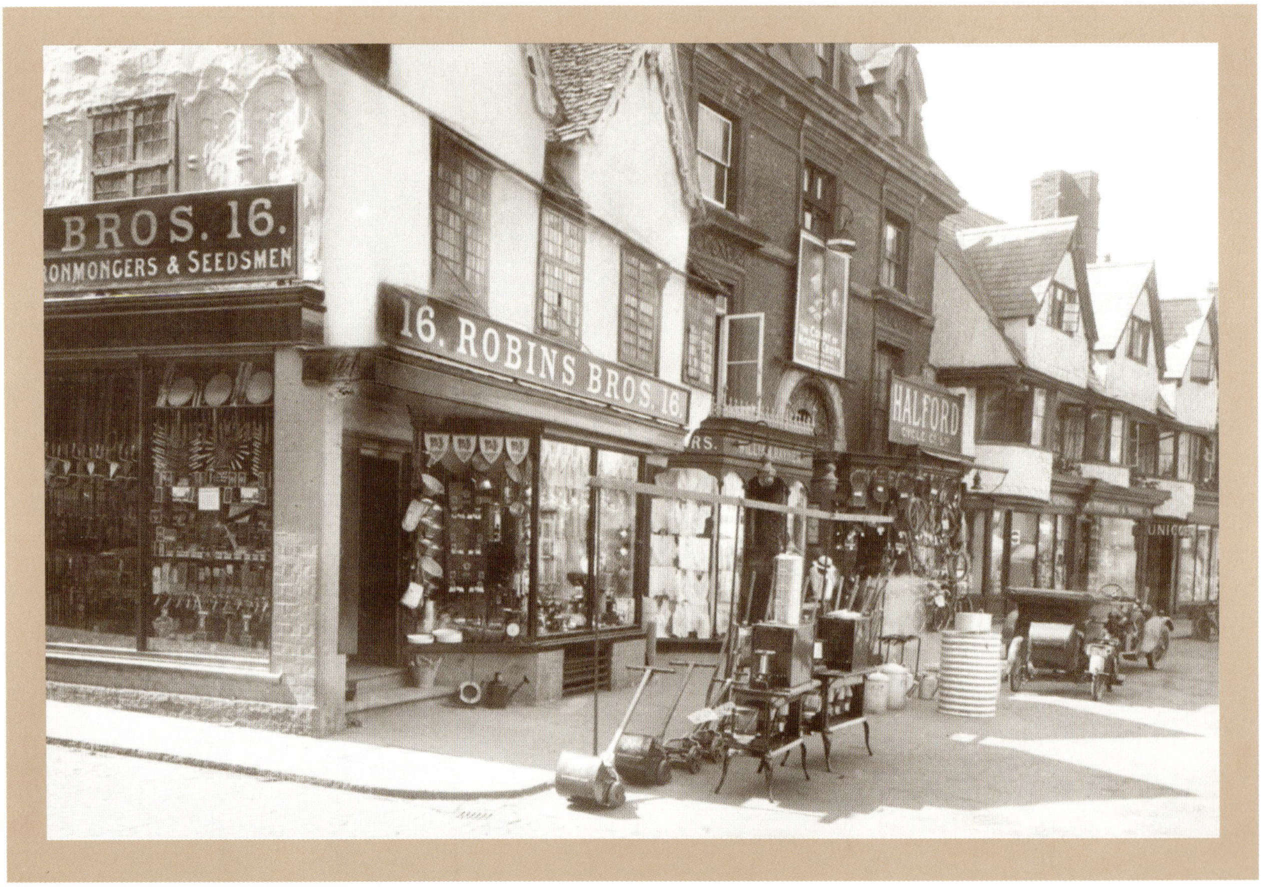
BROS. 16.
RONMONGERS & SEEDSMEN
16. ROBINS BROS. 16
HALFORD

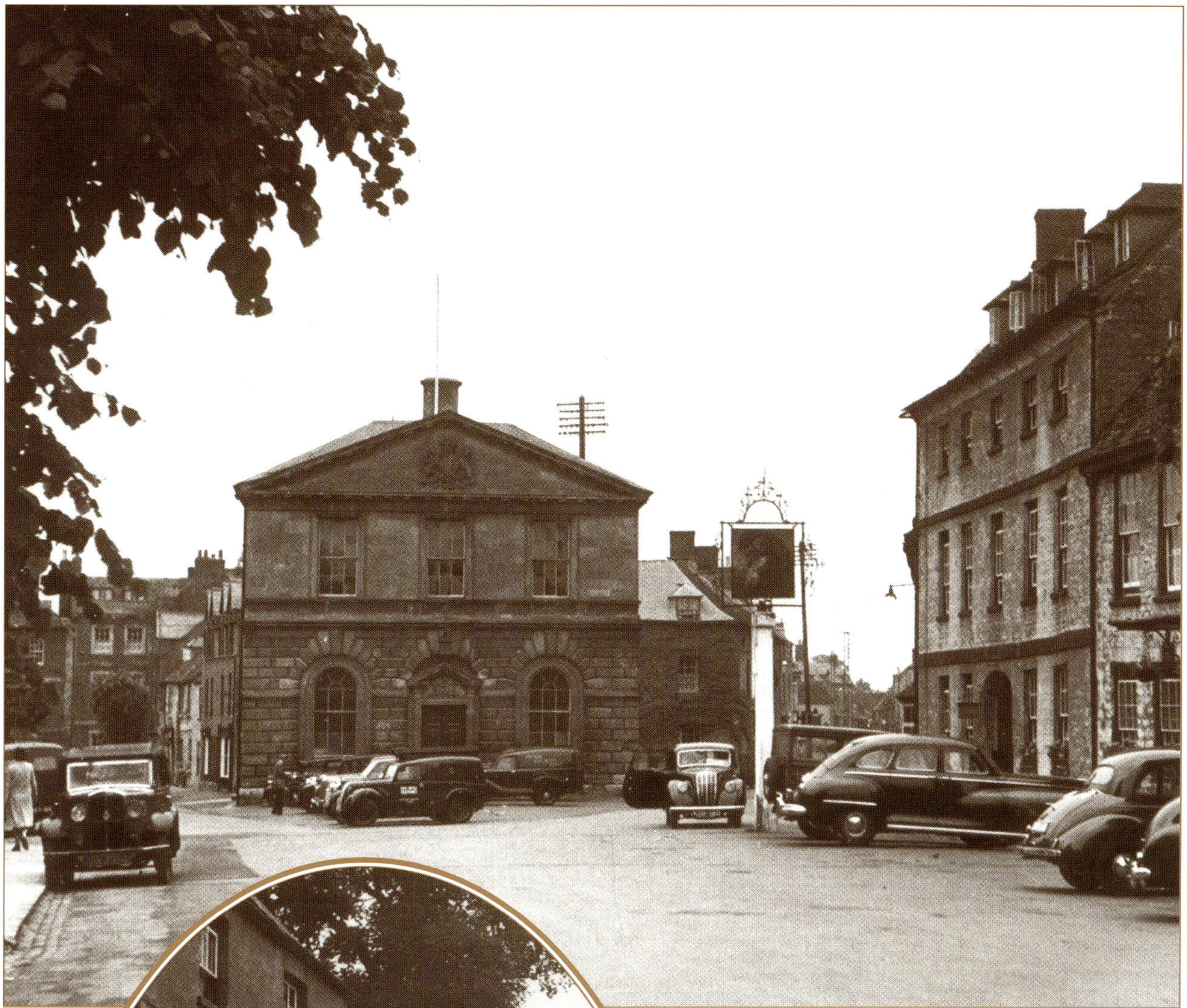

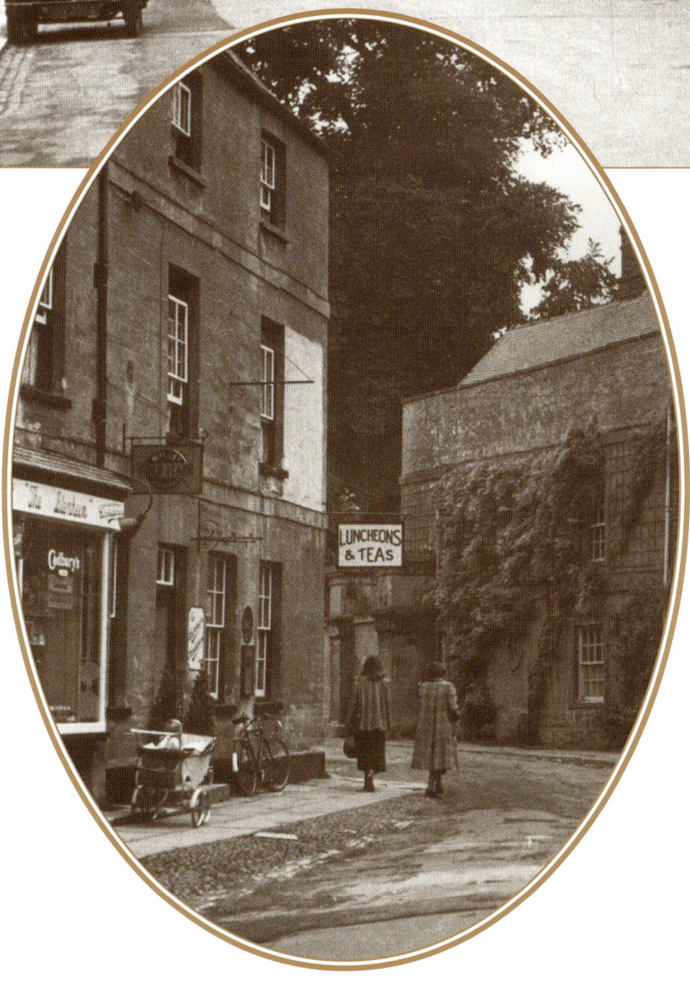

Above: Market Square, Woodstock, c1955 (W285016) When we think of Woodstock we think of Blenheim Palace. Yet the Bear Inn is much older, and far more steeped in history. Local tradition dates it as far back as the 13th century. The elegant classical Town Hall was built by James Gibbs in 1766.

Left: Park Street, Woodstock, c1955 (W285015) A quiet corner of the town with the house where Chaucer is said to have stayed.

Opposite top: South Bar, Banbury, 1921 (70579) A broad, pleasing thoroughfare fringed with pollarded limes.

Opposite below: Market Place, Banbury, 1922 (72090) An outstanding view of Robins Bros hardware emporium. Lined up in the road outside is a convoy of early lawnmowers. The windows are stuffed with pots, pans and metal utensils.

BIDFORD ON AVON. 'Drunken Bidford' Shakespeare called it, in a scrap of doggerel he is said to have penned after a bout of ale drinking at the Falcon Inn.

With its ancient eight-arched bridge over the meandering Avon and its beautiful streets packed tight with fine old cottages Bidford shows itself in these photographs as quintessentially English.

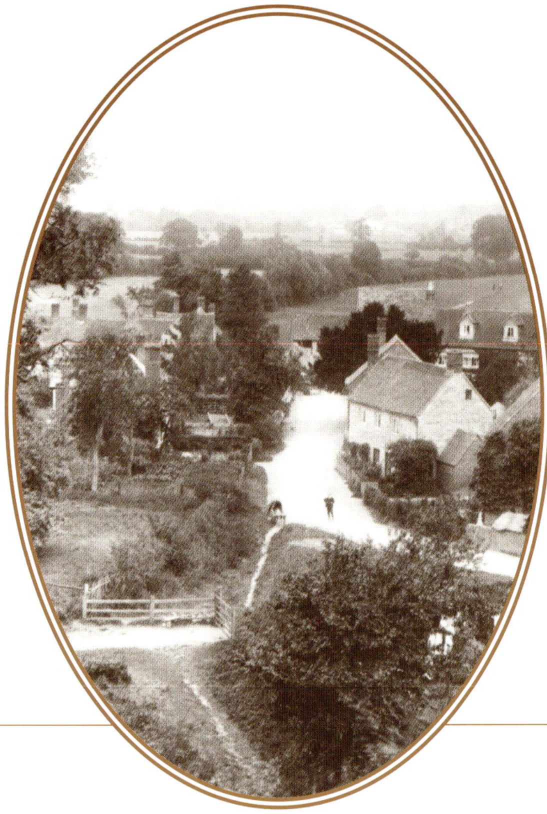

Right: Marlcliffe, Bidford on Avon, 1910 (62639) A pleasing panorama of thatch, burgeoning trees, field paths and cottage gardens.

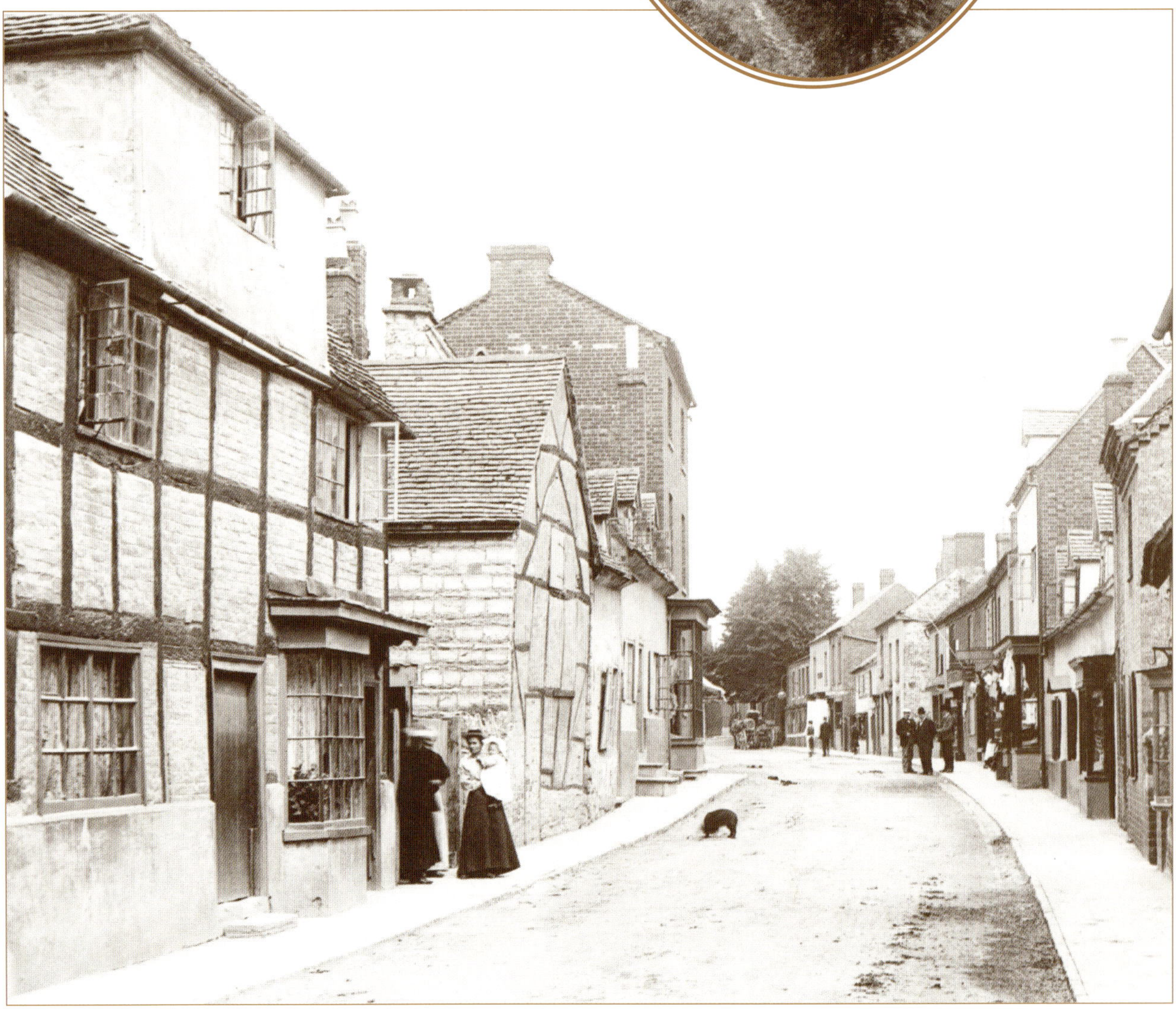

Above: High Street, Bidford on Avon, 1899 (44132) A picturesque scene of a peaceful village street, rich in buildings of all shapes and sizes, styles and materials. Some are timber-framed houses with projecting bay windows that were probably once shops, others simple cottages of lime plaster render. In some houses the walls are clad with stone masking earlier timber construction. There is plenty of time to stand and stare, to chat with neighbours, and to show off the new addition to the family.

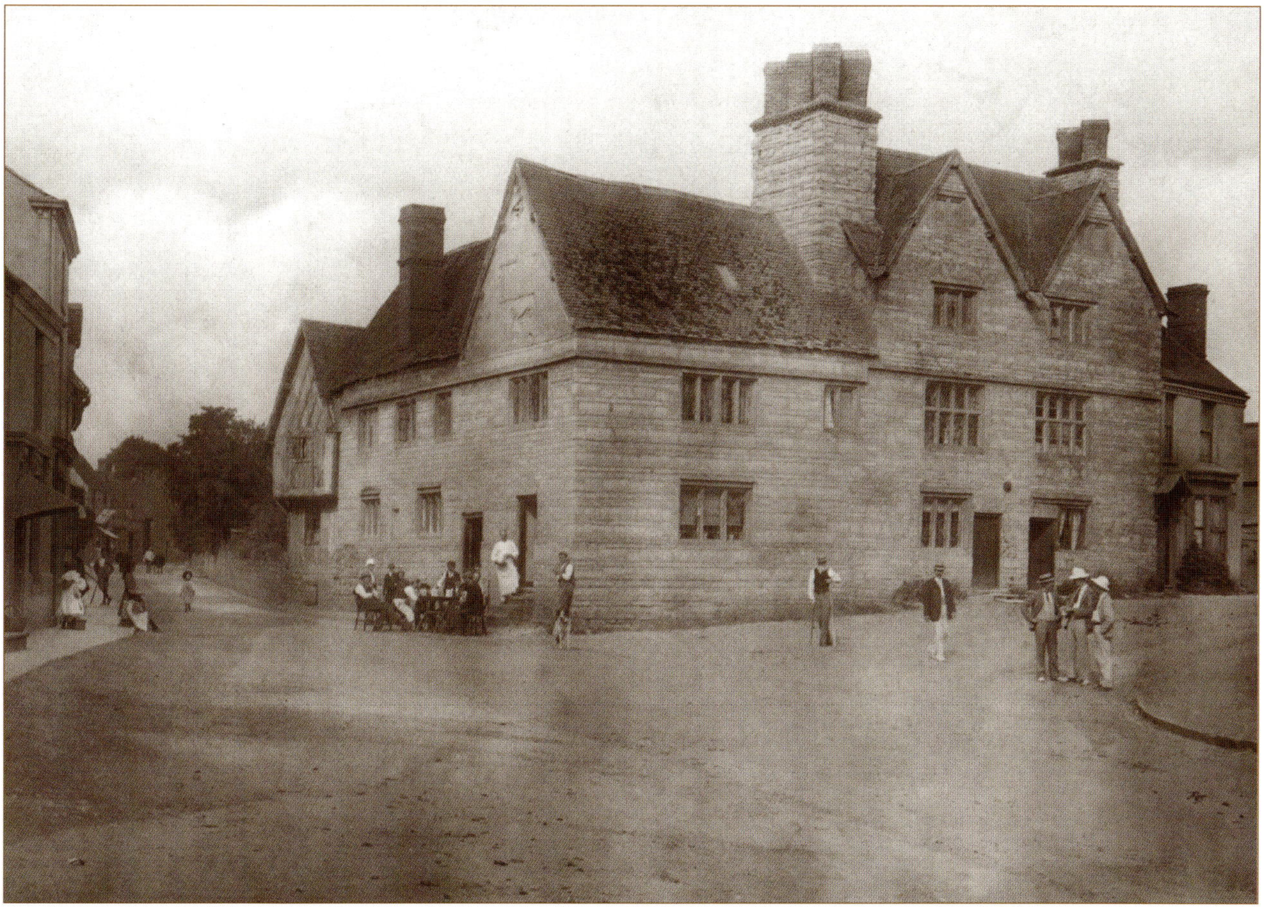

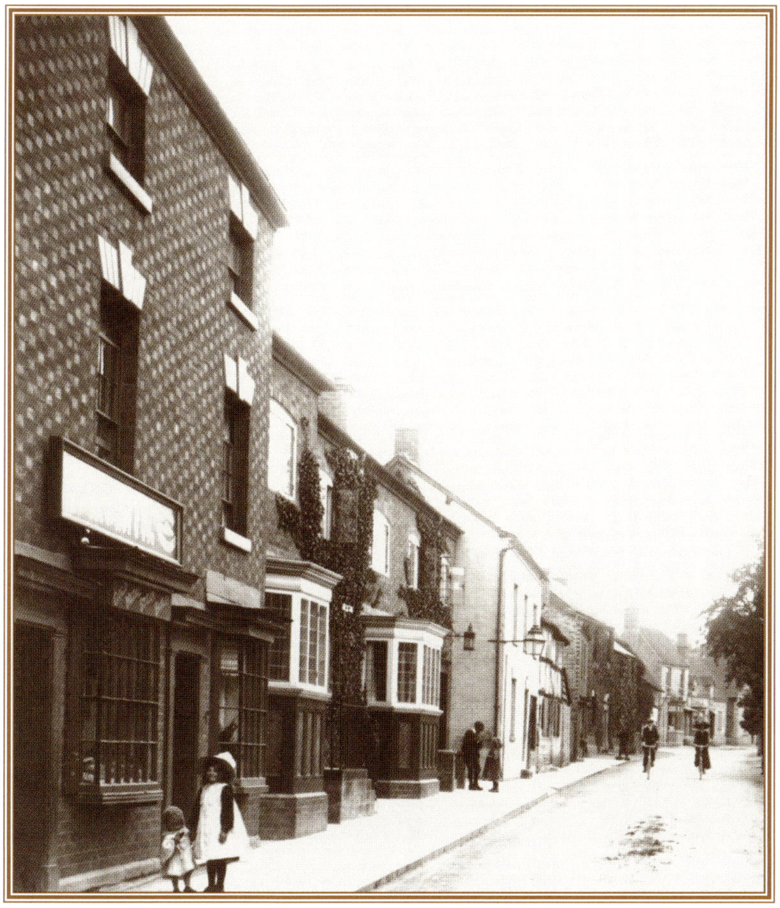

Above: Ye Old Falcon Inn, Bidford on Avon, 1901 (47340) Maybe Shakespeare was right about Bidford being drunken. There is a party of what look like very serious drinkers sitting at a table laden with brimming pewter pots outside this old building, once a famous inn. At this time it was probably the workhouse, so the revellers may be the poor of the village enjoying a rare treat on the parish.

It is said that after his merry making the Bard reeled home to Stratford and then died, but as with almost everything about his life, there is no convincing evidence whatsoever.

The old tavern dominates the village centre, with its fine 16th-century exterior of coursed Cotswold stone.

Left: Bidford on Avon, 1910 (62642) Another charming view of the village street. Note William Smith's fine shop facade with its patchwork of vitrified, coloured brick headers.

STRATFORD ON AVON. Set close by the ancient Watling and Fosse ways and Icknield Street, and home of our most celebrated playwright, Stratford is truly at the very heart of England. Cradling the town is the Avon, the river that threads its way from the Northamptonshire uplands down to lovely Tewkesbury in the south.

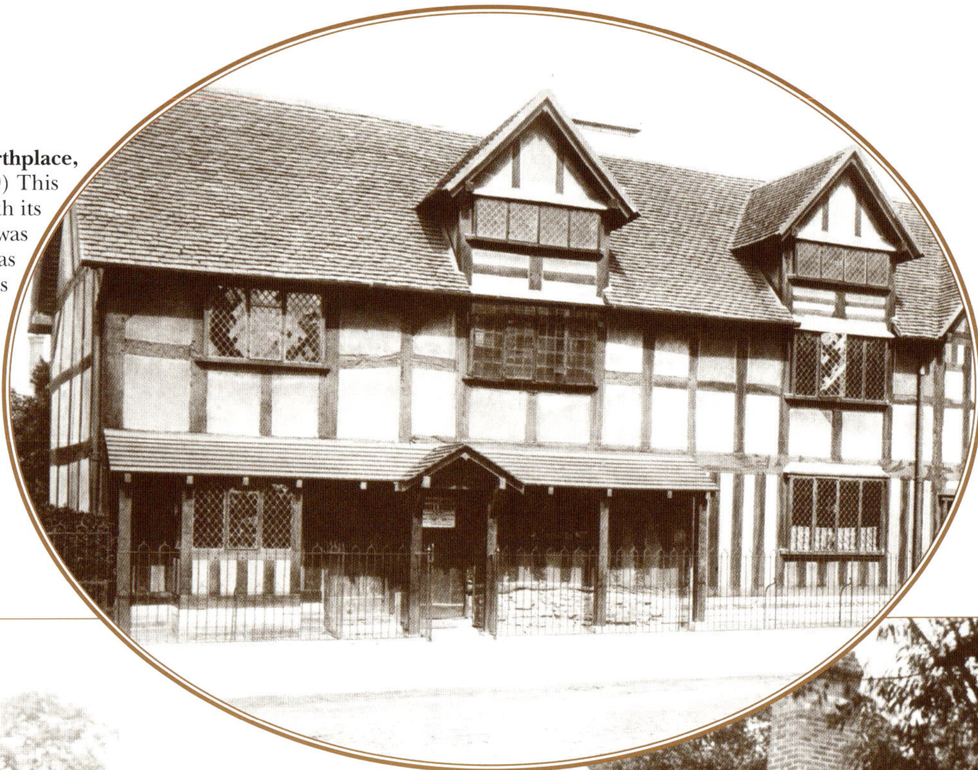

Right: Shakespeare's Birthplace, Stratford, 1892 (31059) This timber-framed house, with its miniature leaded lights, was where Shakespeare was born. The building was given a complete overhaul in the late 1850s, the rooms preserved, gables added, and the shop where the poet's father worked as a glover restored.

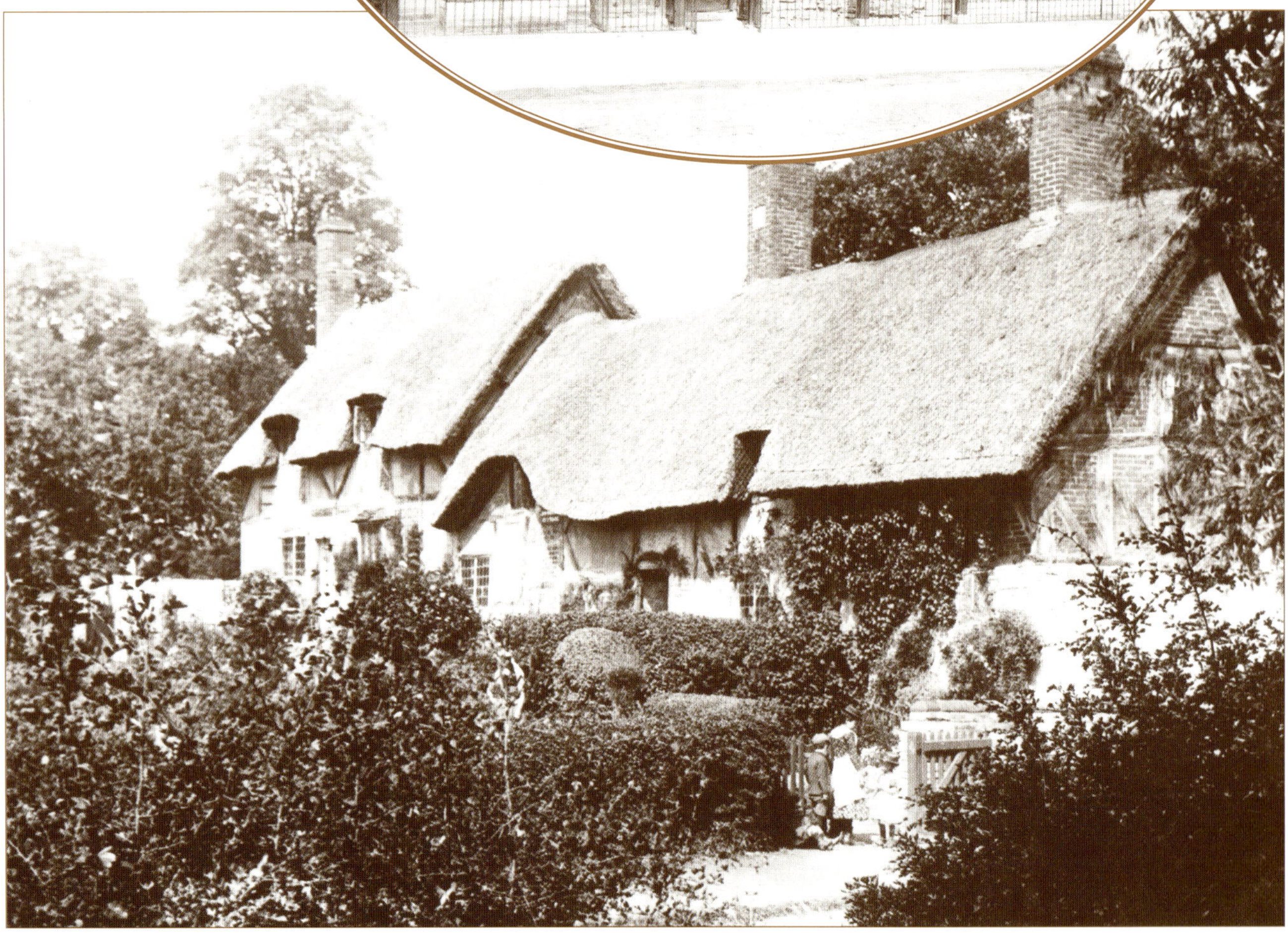

Above: Ann Hathaway's Cottage, Shottery, 1892 (31084) A mile away across the fields, in this lovely old Elizabethan farmhouse, Shakespeare courted Anne Hathaway. He must have drawn inspiration from its tumbling thatch roofs and the profusion of English cottage garden plants. **Opposite: The Memorial Theatre, Stratford, 1922** (72392) This great theatre opened in 1879 but was destroyed by fire in 1926. The river was always a fashionable venue for boating. The Victorian novelist, Marie Corelli, scandalised local opinion by lazing away the afternoons in a real Venetian gondola, serenaded by a real Venetian gondolier.

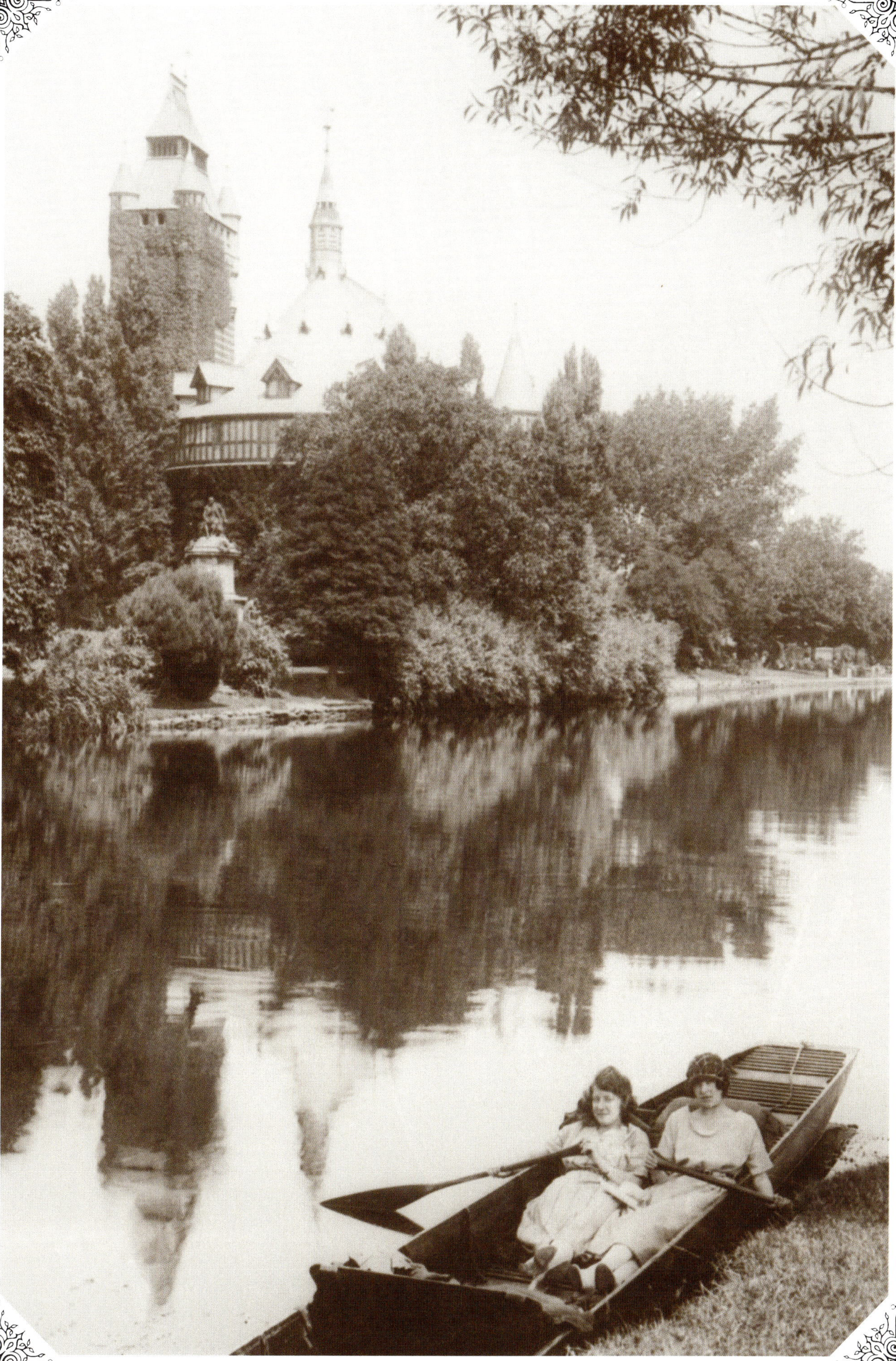

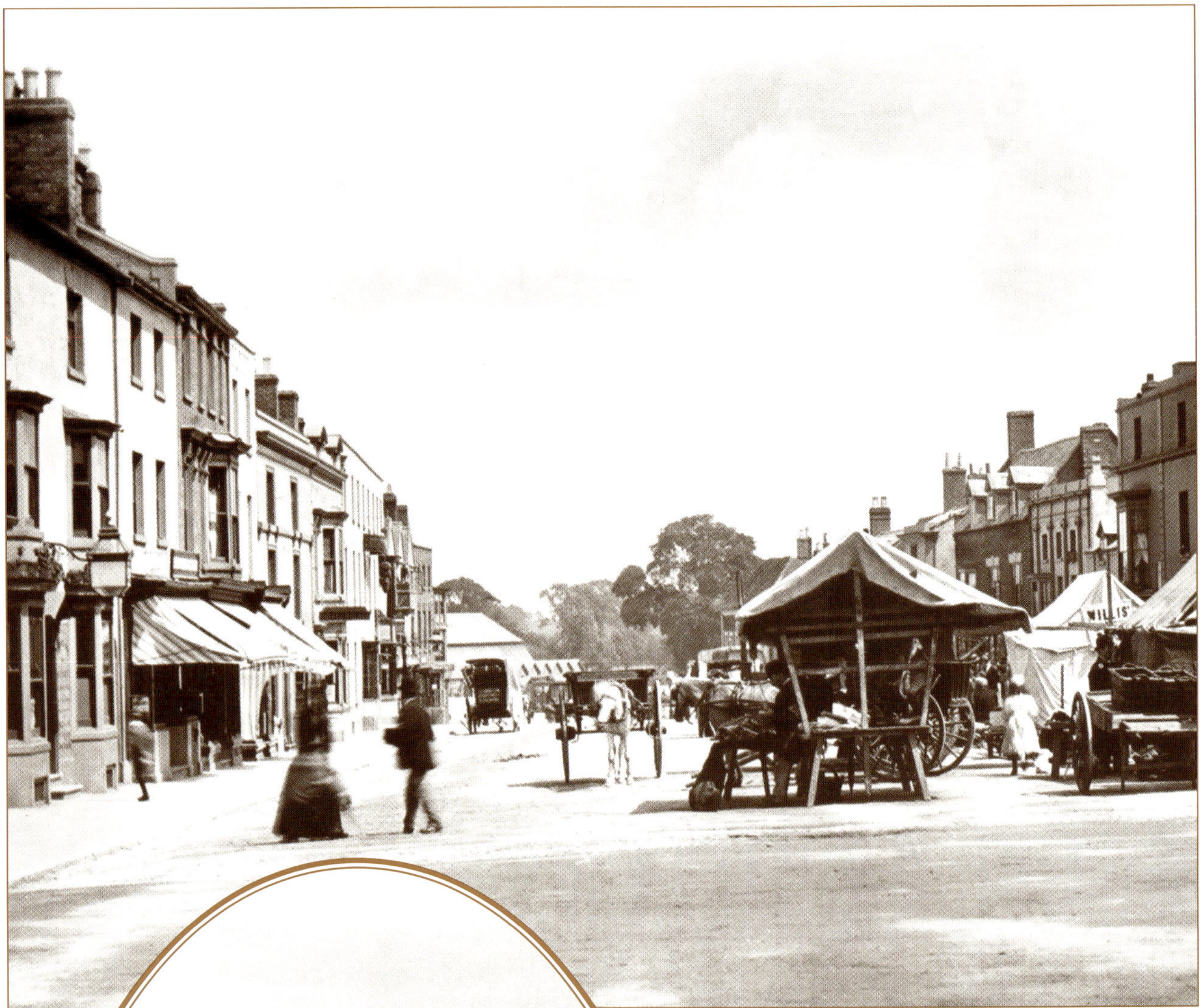

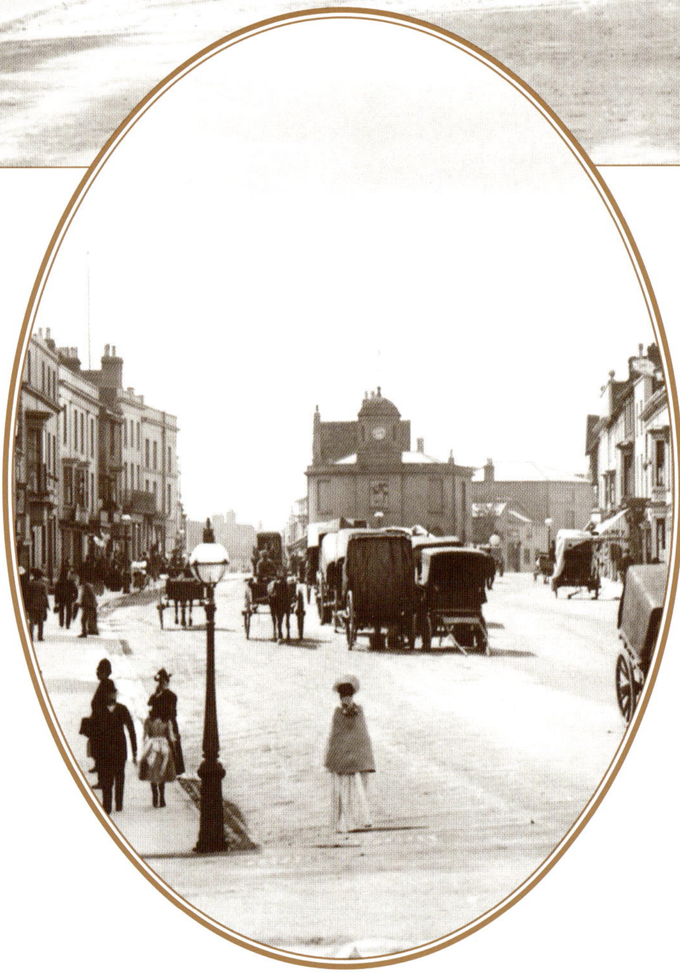

Above: The Market Place, Stratford, 1892 (31073) The market is in full swing, with its jumble of stalls and booths. It had been in existence for centuries. Shakespeare must have enjoyed the town's annual Mop Fair, when farmworkers and apprentices offered themselves for hire and the streets were filled with dancers, travelling players and jugglers. Many of them surely found their way into his plays.

Left: The Market Place, Stratford, 1892 (31075) Carriers' carts and carriages are parked in the centre of the dusty street, their horses whiling away the hours in the stables of the local inns.

Opposite top: The Guild Chapel, Stratford, 1892 (31071) Beyond the Shakespeare Hotel is the old Guild Chapel. The shadow from its tower would have fallen over the playwright's garden.

Opposite below: Harvard House, High Street, Stratford, 1922 (72383)

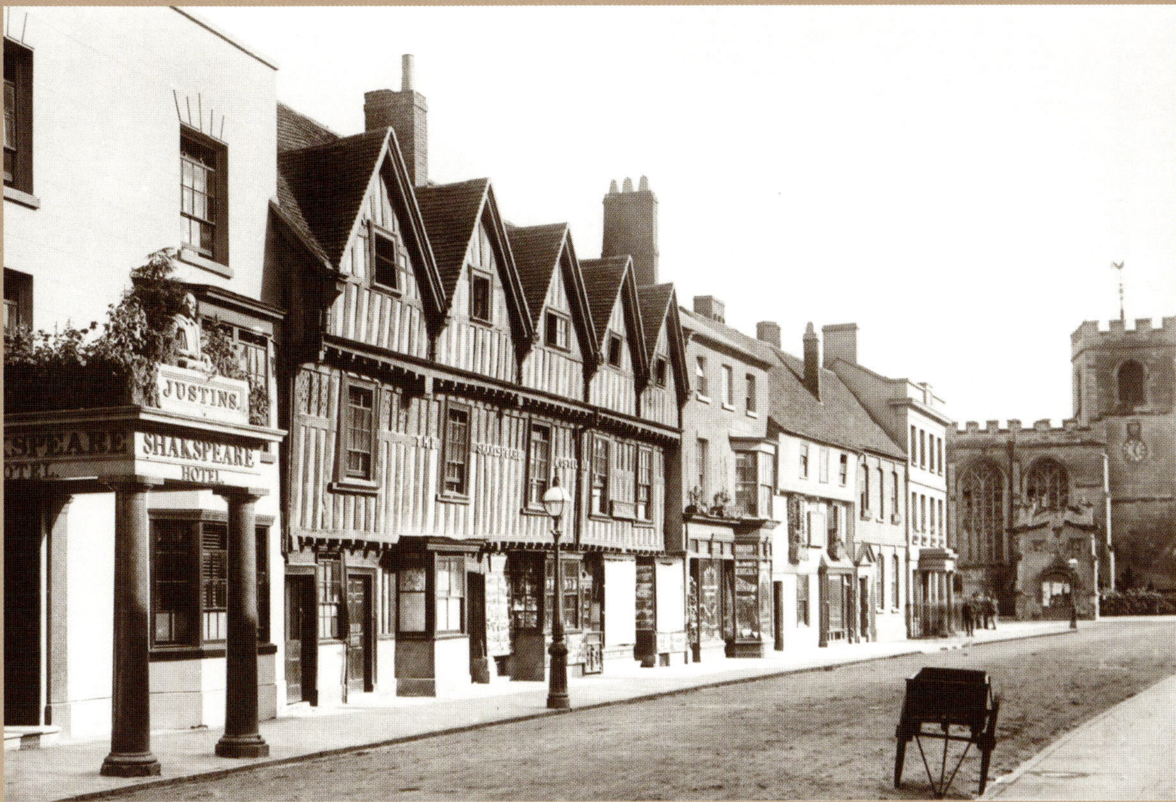
JUSTINS
KSPEARE
HOTEL
SHAKSPEARE
HOTEL

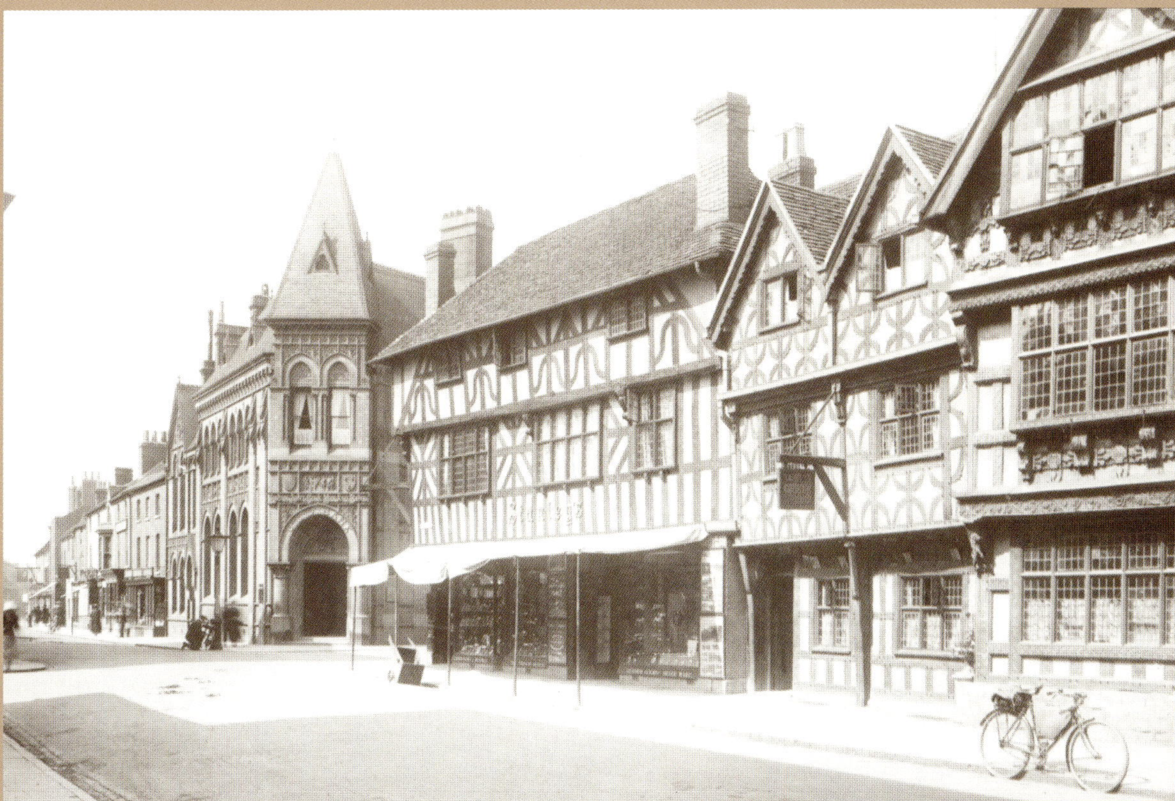

Right: Shakespeare's House, Stratford on Avon, 1922 (72387) It was to these beautiful gardens that Shakespeare came to retire after he had gained fame and fortune in the London theatre. It was here, too, that he died, but all that can be seen of his old house are the foundations, preserved amidst the roses and marguerites.

Below: Shottery, 1922 (72399) This quiet hamlet of thatched cottages with roses clambering over their walls would have never come to the attention of the world had it not been for Shakespeare. Now it is one of the most visited places in the country.

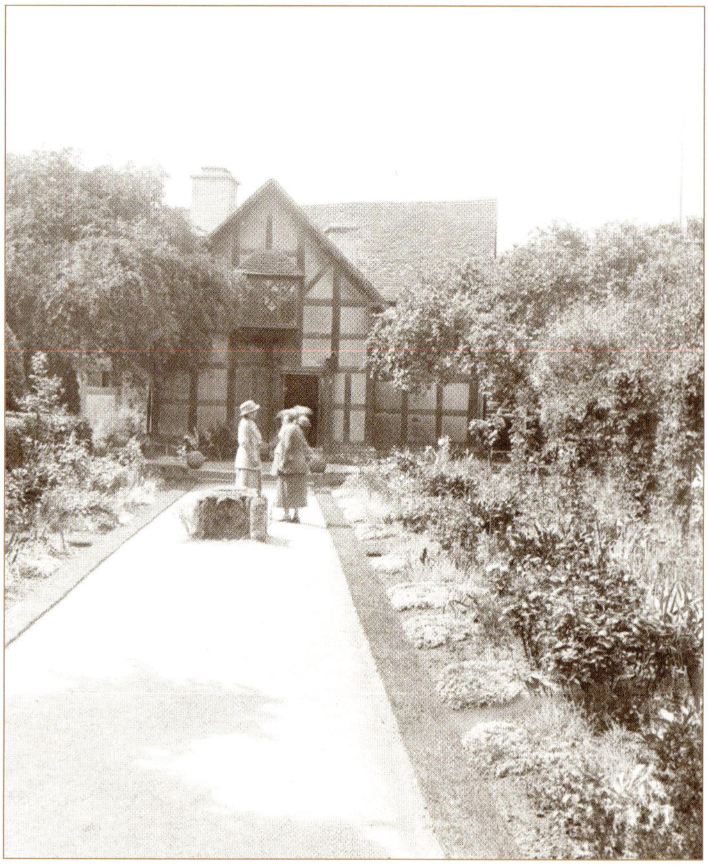

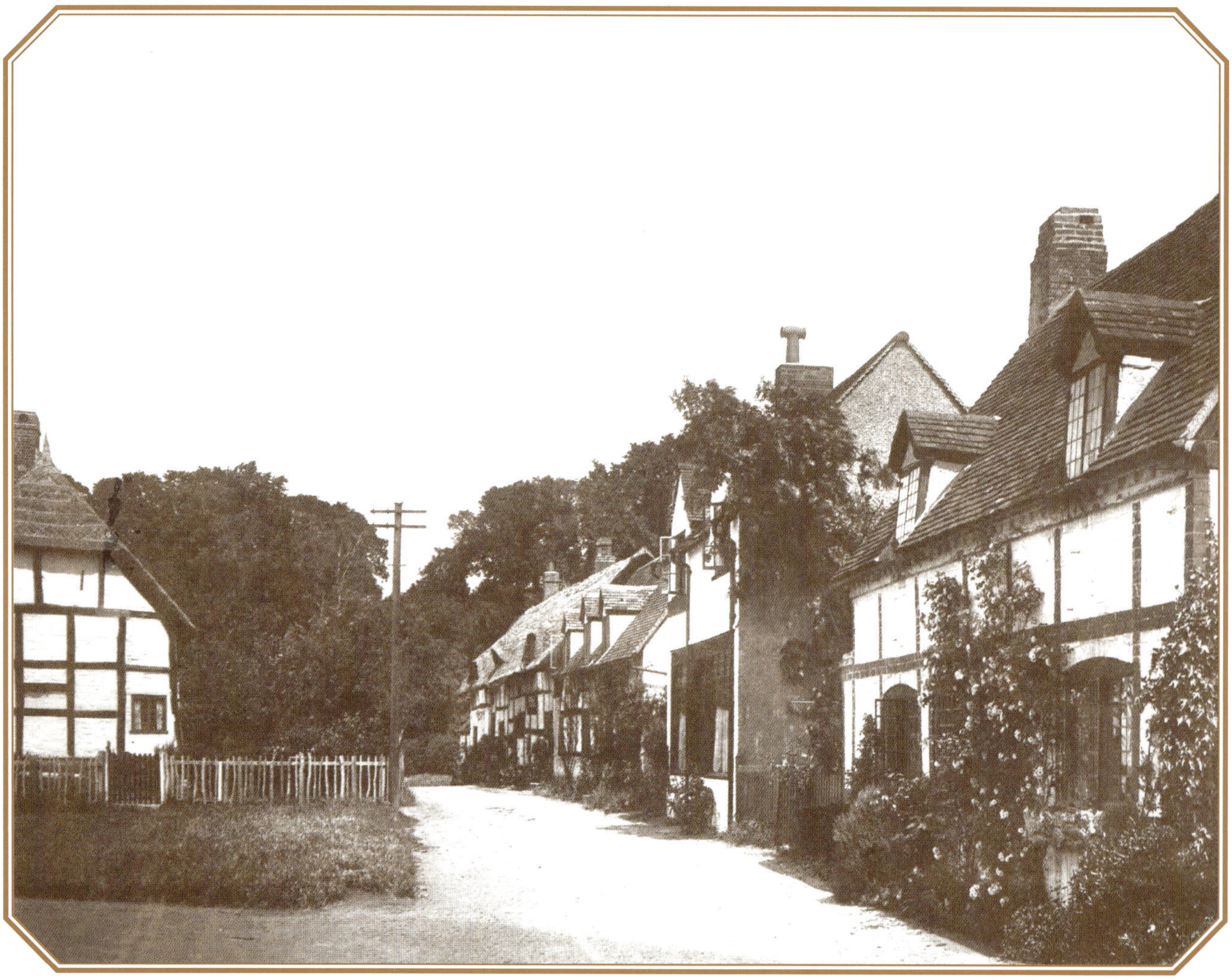

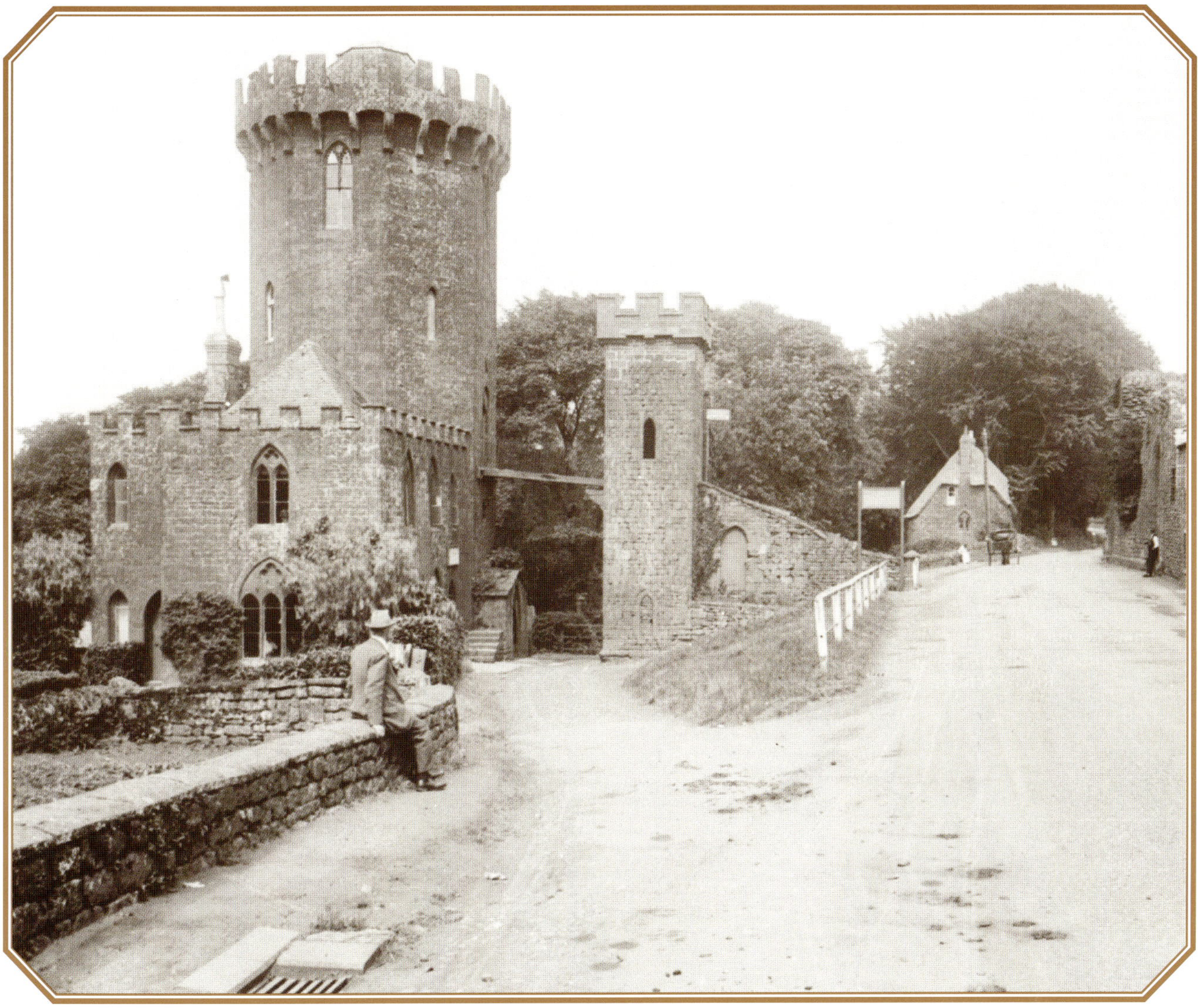

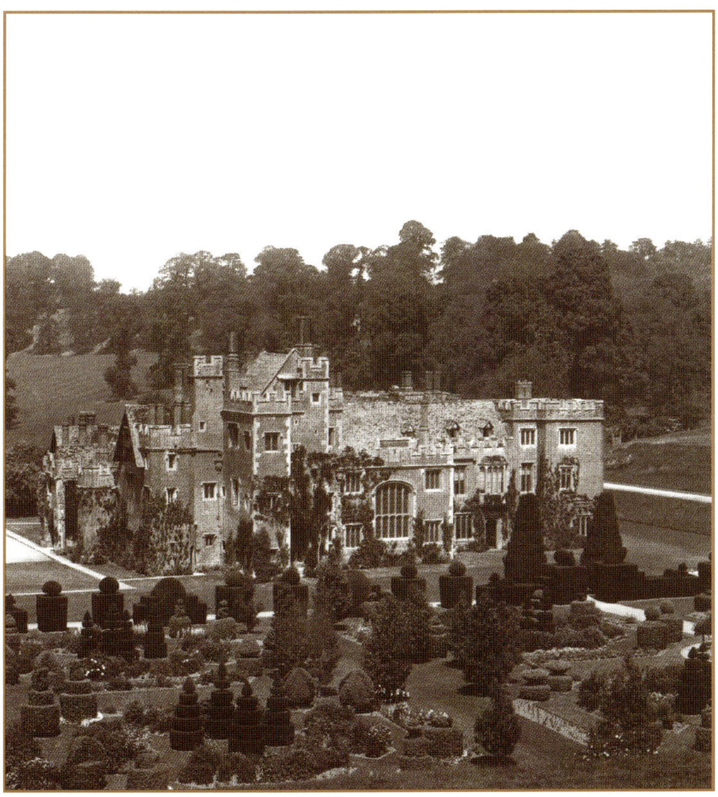

Above: Edge Hill, 1922 (72072) Now a part of the Castle Inn, the castellated Radway Tower was built as a folly in the 18th century by Sanderson Miller. Offering a breezy panorama for tourists, it is reputed to stand on the precise spot where King Charles raised his standard to signal the start of the first battle of the Civil War on 23rd October 1642. The battle was long and bloody, and by the end of the day 4,000 men had died.

Left: Compton Wynyates, near Edge Hill, 1922 (72096) This gem of a Tudor house is set in a deep, spacious hollow, amidst a green panorama of parkland and lawns. Built in stone and rose pink brick, with turrets, dormers, oriels and twisting chimneys, and surrounded by its extraordinary topiary garden, it conjures up a unique fantasy of timeless English country life. The strange shapes of the painstakingly clipped yews rise up from among the roses, casting their long shadows over the lawns. One is in the form of an old man with a top hat.

WARWICK. The county town of Shakespeare country. English history is crowded into the small space within its two ancient gates. The oldest parts of the town are on the fringes - in 1694 a fire raged throughout the town, destroying so much of the centre that most had to be rebuilt. There is much to see: the old Leycester hospital, the majestic castle ruins, the beautiful church of St Mary, the Court House, and many fine old timbered houses.

Right: East Gate, Warwick, 1892 (31029) One of the town's great medieval gates, a glory of architecture in this peaceful scene but an awkward obstacle in our own car-dominated century. On the right is the 15th-century birthplace of the poet Walter Savage Landor. His tempestuous and quarrelsome nature had him expelled from Rugby School.

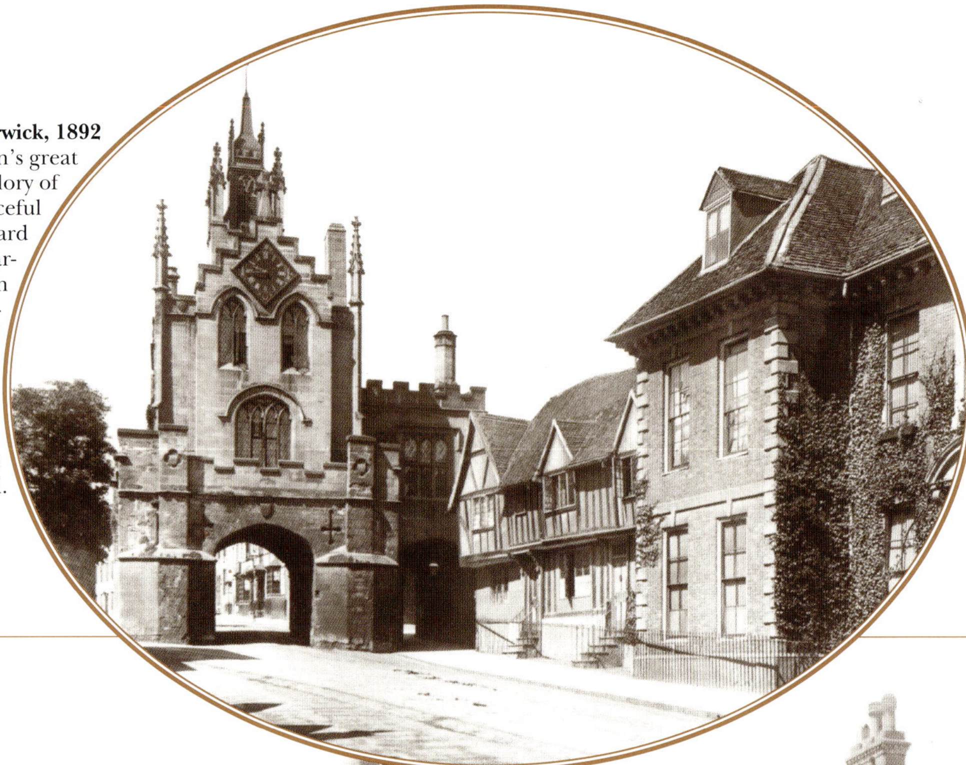

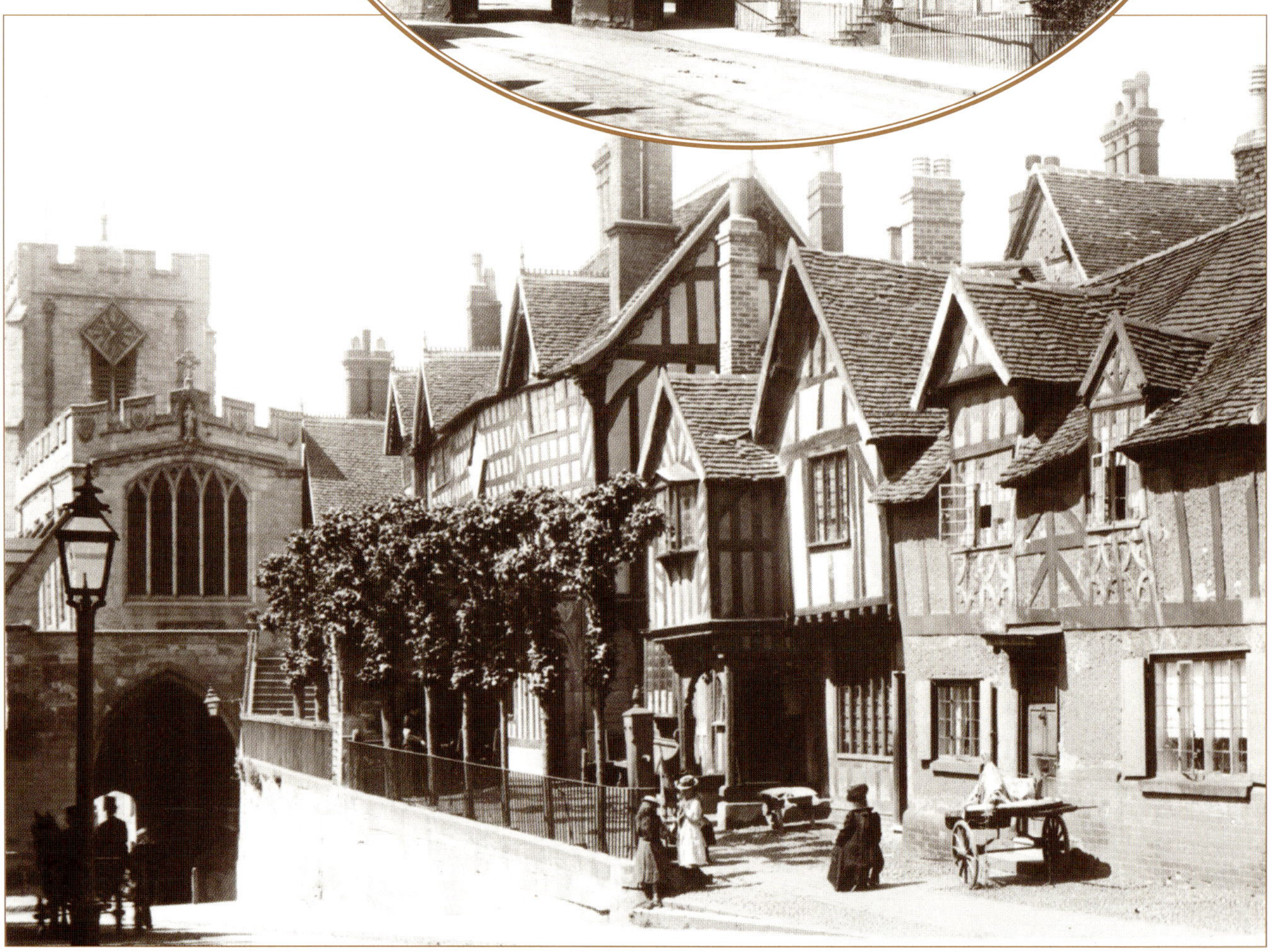

Above: the Leycester Hospital, Warwick, 1892 (31022) Close by the town's West Gate, this spectacular timbered, many gabled building, studded with crests and heraldic shields, was originally the Guild House of St George. It was transformed in 1571 into a hospice and almshouses for disabled soldiers and their wives by the Earl of Leicester. Overwhelmingly picturesque and atmospheric, it has always been a favourite spot for artists. Other photographs in the Frith archive show them at work at their easels.

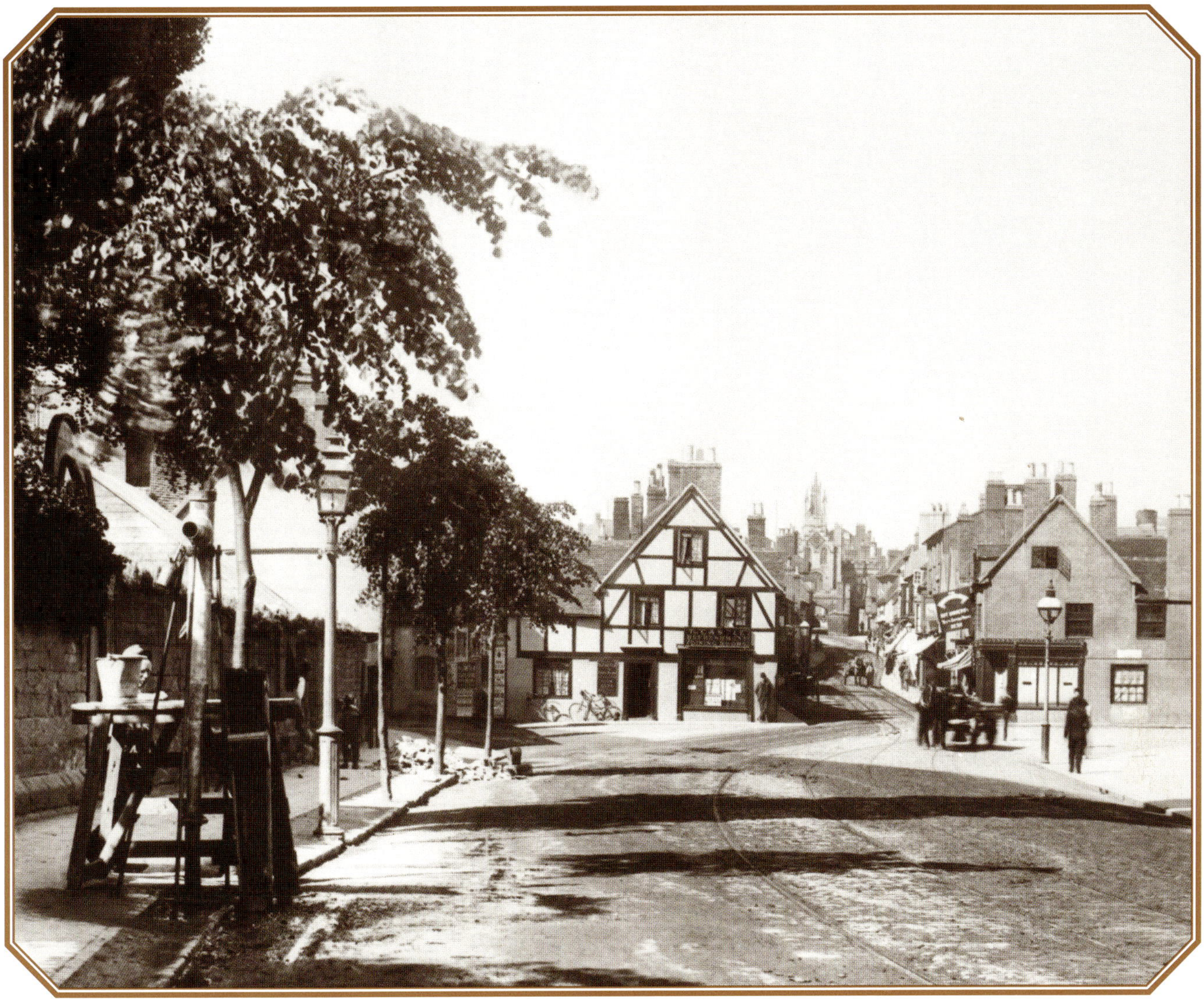

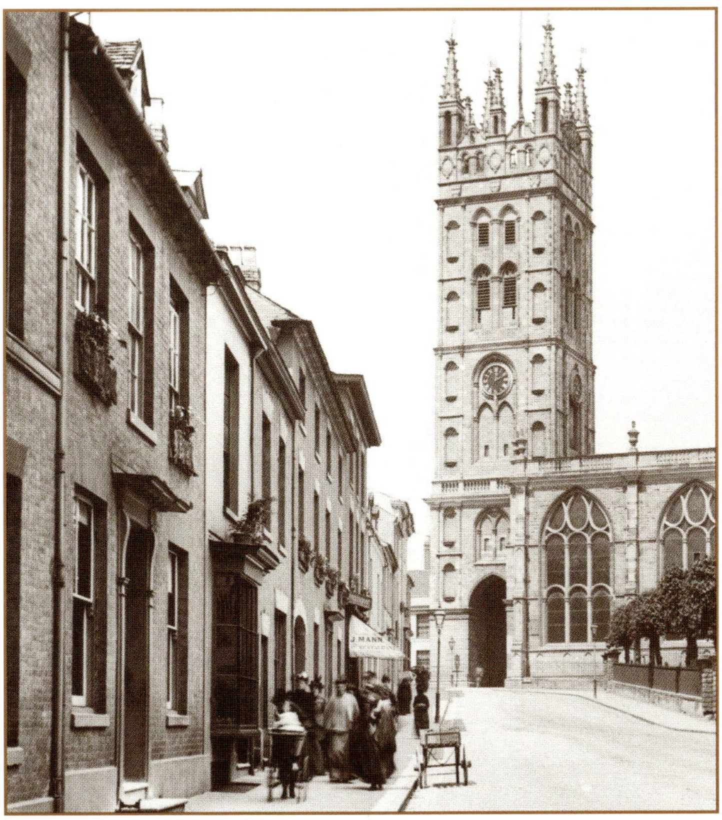

Above: Coten End, Warwick, 1892 (31031). On the left is one of the town water pumps, where residents could catch up on gossip with their neighbours while filling the bucket. Already there are horse-drawn trams in the town - you can see the tracks running along the centre of the street.

Left: St Mary's Church, Warwick, 1892 (31015) Perched on Warwick's highest point, this massive 174-foot tower with its sixteen decorative pinnacles is a landmark for miles around. Light and spacious, the old church harbours many fine tombs. The original tower, nave and aisles were destroyed in the great fire of 1694, which burned down over 250 buildings in the town. Note the window boxes all along the street. Maybe it is a festival day.

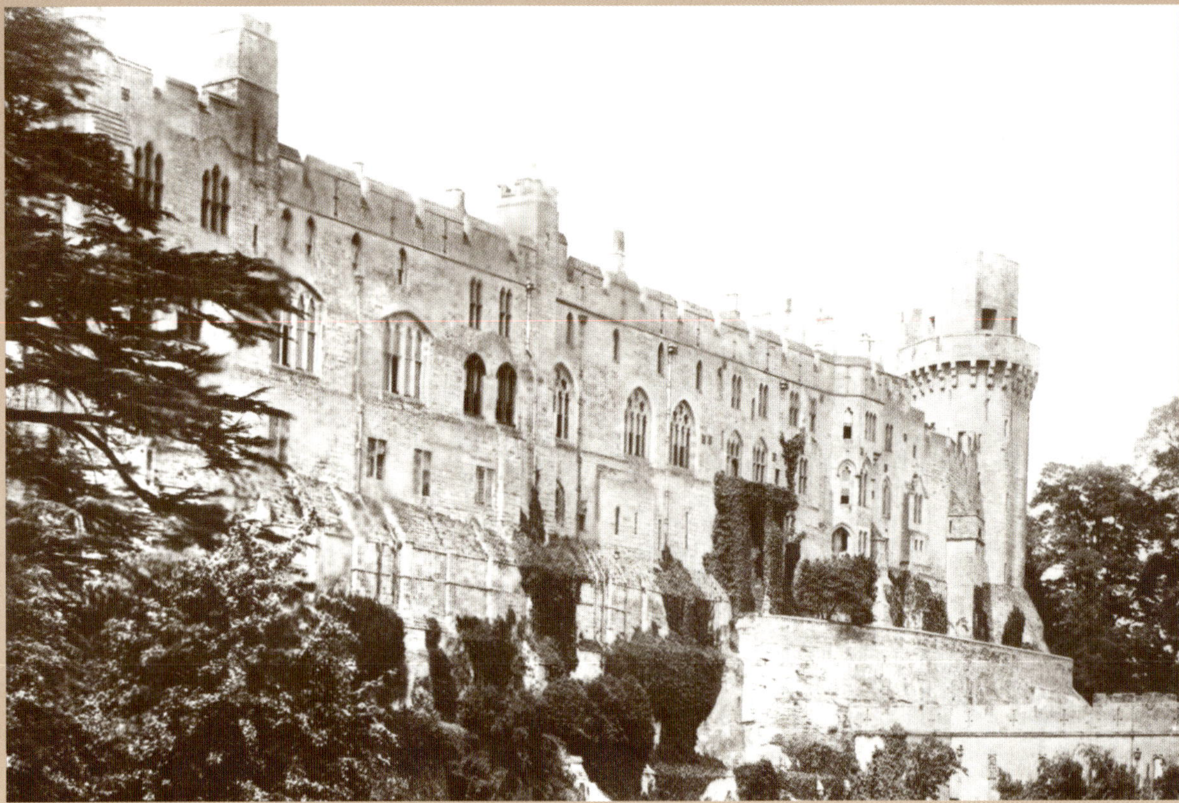

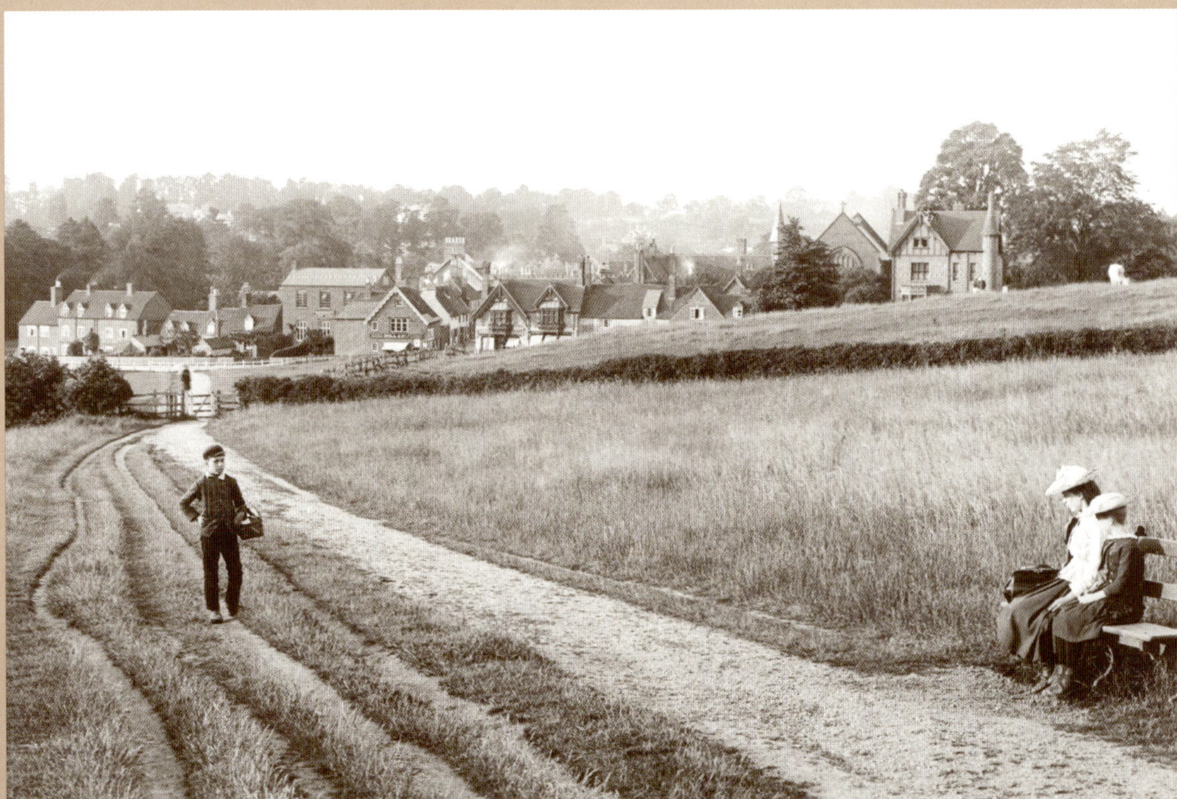

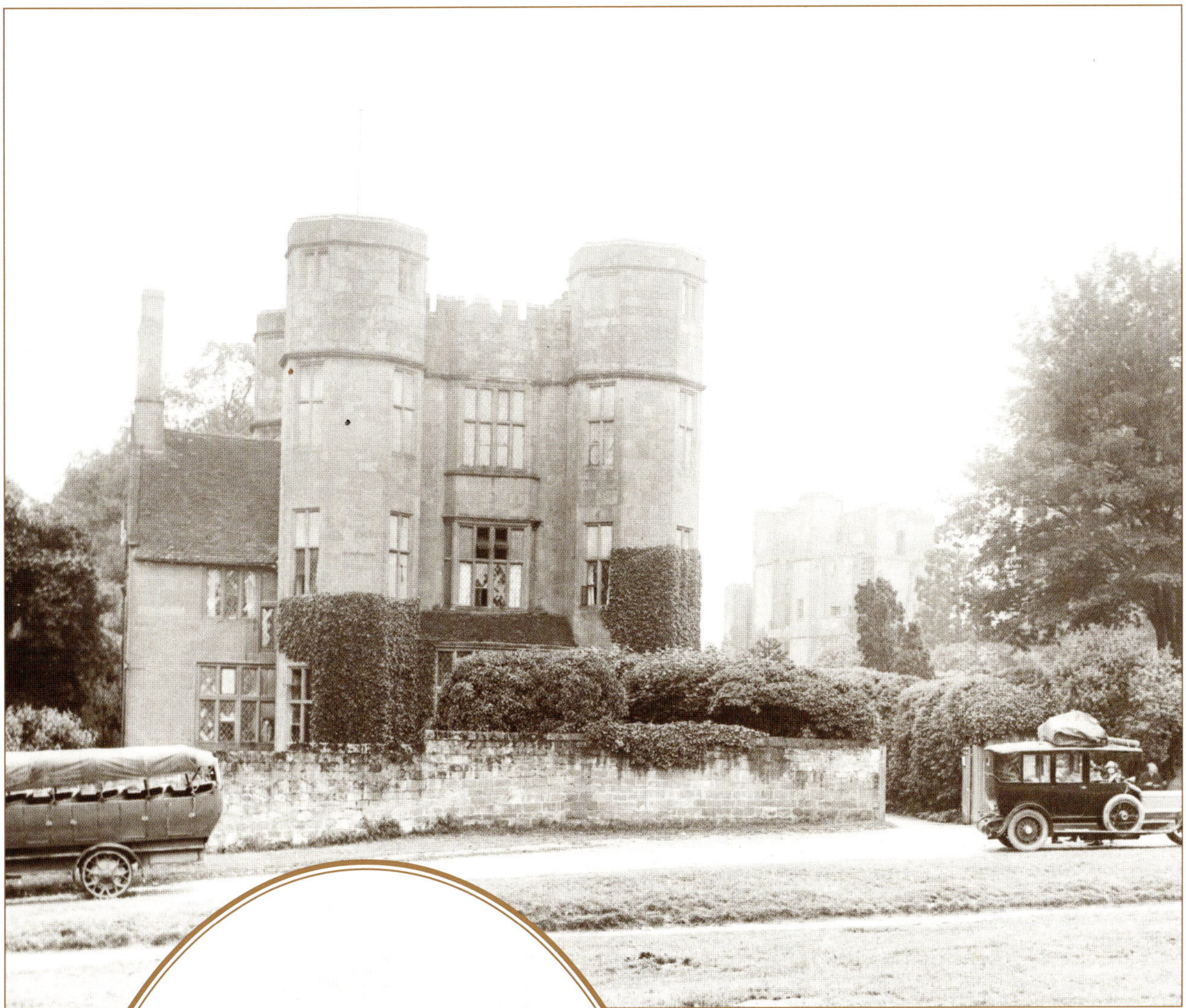

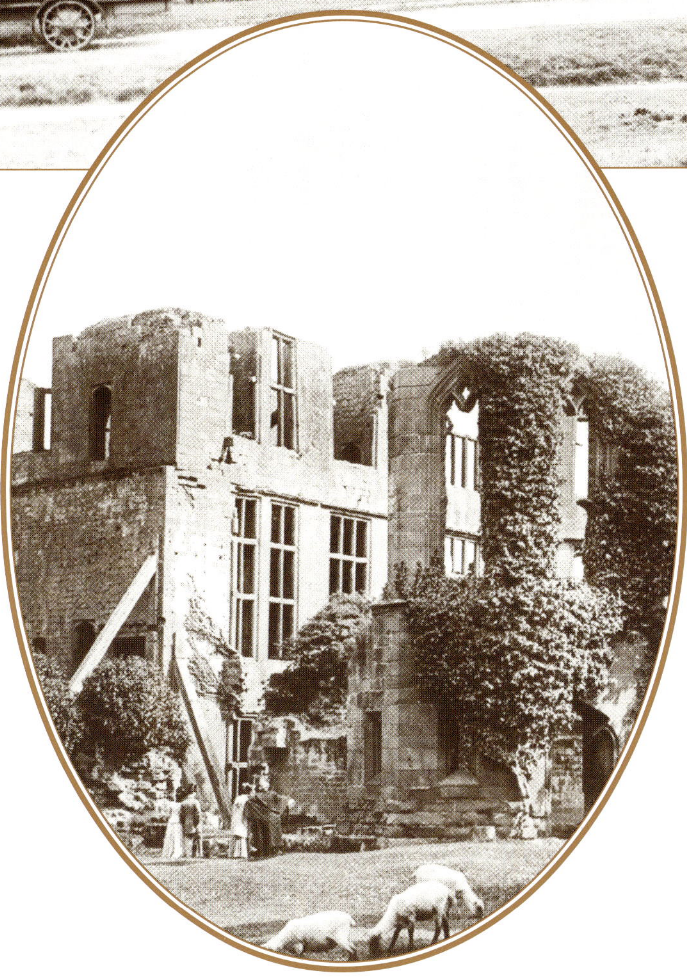

Above: Kenilworth Castle, 1922 (72405) A charabanc has already deposited the first visitors of the day to this gaunt red-walled ruin, believed by many to be the greatest of its kind in England. Unequalled in its prime for lavish pageantry and splendour, Kenilworth was visited regularly by Elizabeth I, who on one occasion enjoyed seventeen days of feasting, revelry and fireworks. It was finally pulled to pieces by Cromwell's soldiers.

Left: Kenilworth Castle, 1892 (30935) A sad prospect: sheep graze among the ruins and huge wooden buttresses support what is left of the walls.

Opposite top: Warwick Castle, 1892 (30998).

Opposite below: Kenilworth Village, 1892 (30945) Smoke rises from cottage chimneys in the distance. A young boy is on his way back from the village shop to an outlying farm. It must be a popular spot for a stroll - a public seat has been provided.

LEAMINGTON SPA is one of the most handsome towns in the Midlands, with tree-shaded streets and a profusion of public gardens. It was a fashionable Royal health resort in Victorian times, and many illustrious men and women have been helped back to health after taking advantage of its healing waters. Charles Dickens describes a memorable visit to the Pump Room in *Dombey and Son.*

Right: The Royal Pump Room, Leamington Spa, 1922 (72443) Set in spacious gardens with lime and rhododendron walks, Henry Jephson's elegant colonnaded Pump Room dates from 1814, but was rebuilt three years after this photograph. Many famous men and women came to take its waters, including the writer and critic John Ruskin.

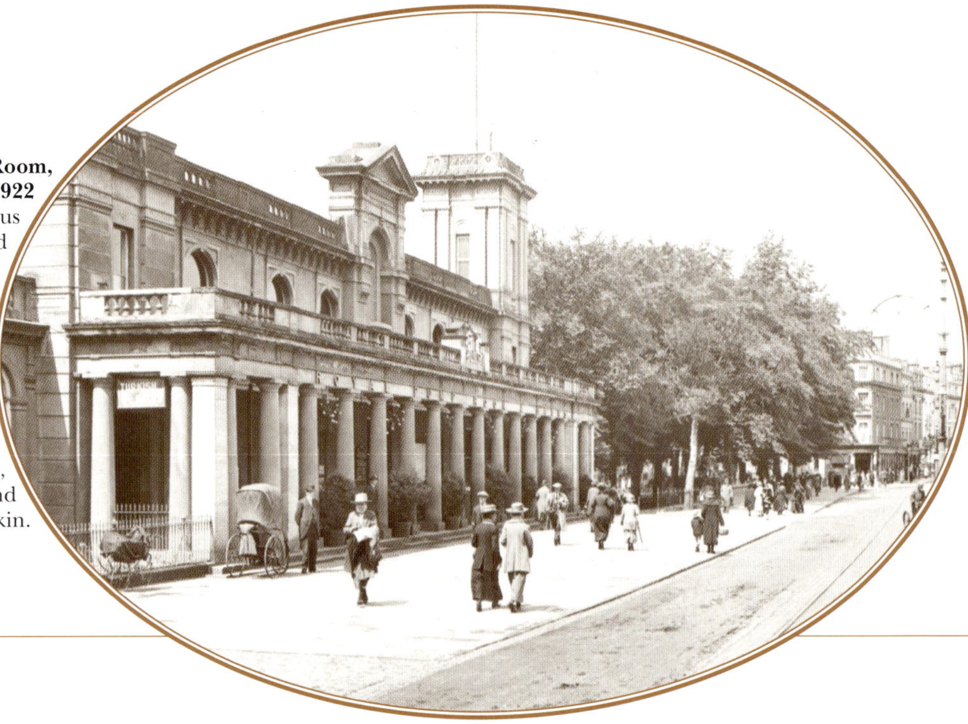

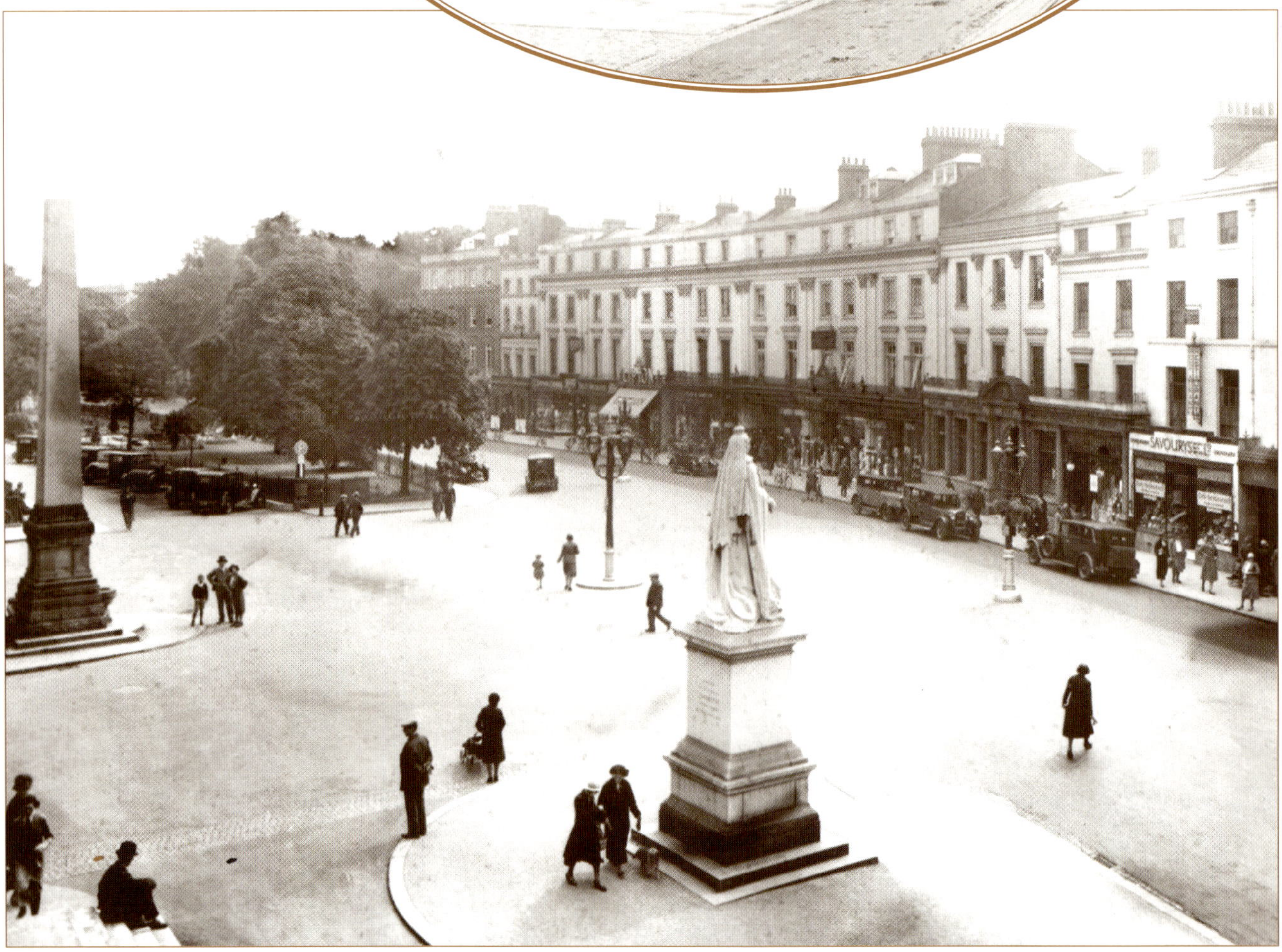

Above: Leamington Spa, 1932 (85204) Although a modern town compared with historic Warwick or Stratford, Leamington offers visitors a sophisticated melange of smart shops and fine Regency buildings. Here, in front of the Town Hall, is the supremely dignified statue of Queen Victoria, underlining the town's strictly respectable and regal image. Grand cars are parked alongside the shops. You can almost sense the town's civic pride in its broad, airy spaces - there is nothing medieval or cluttered about this spa town.

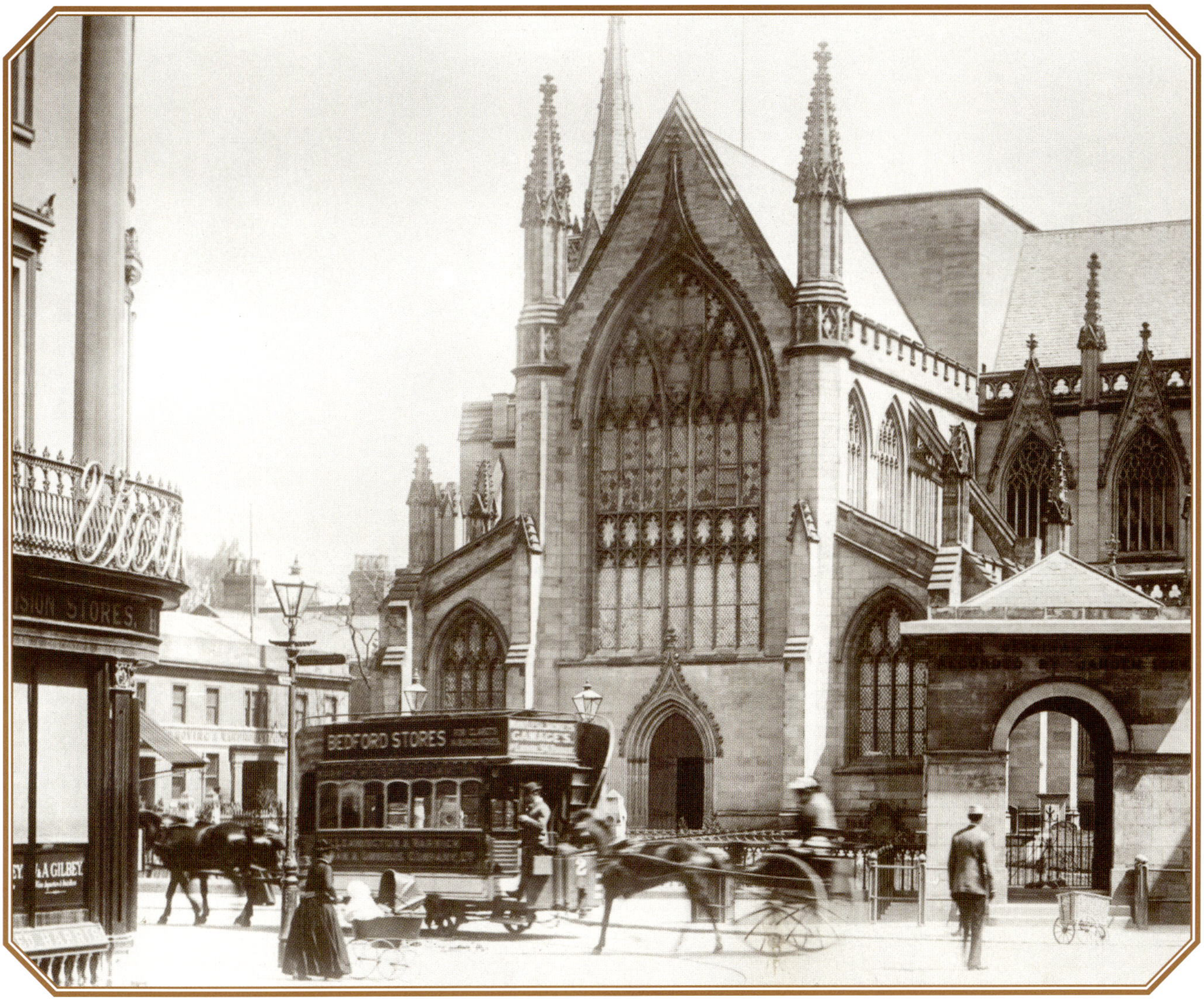

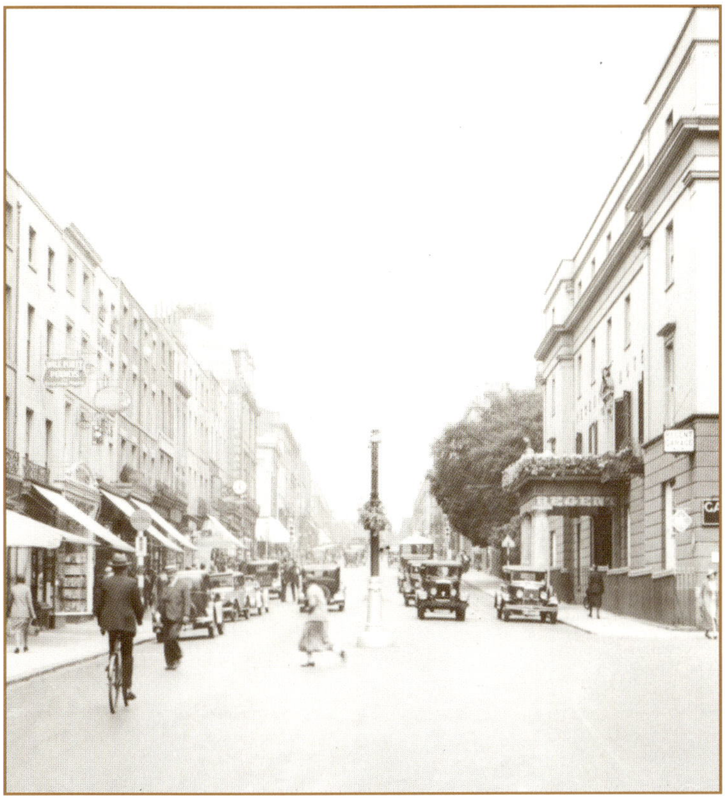

Above: All Saints Church, Leamington Spa, 1892 (30961) This handsome church was built in the French style in the 1850s - note the flying buttresses and fussy Gothic detailing. A lofty tower was added ten years after this photograph was taken. A horse-drawn bus looks as if it is about to be overtaken by a woman driving a gig - she is travelling too fast for the Victorian camera to capture her and is little more than a blur.

Left: Regent Hotel and Parade, Leamington Spa, 1932 (85200) This smart hotel was the biggest in England when it opened in 1819. It was originally called the William Hotel after its owner - but only for a month; the Prince Regent graced the new building with his royal presence whilst on his way to Warwick. Not slow to capitalise on this timely celebrity event, the owner immediately changed the name to the Regent. Such a strategic move can have done no harm whatsoever to business.

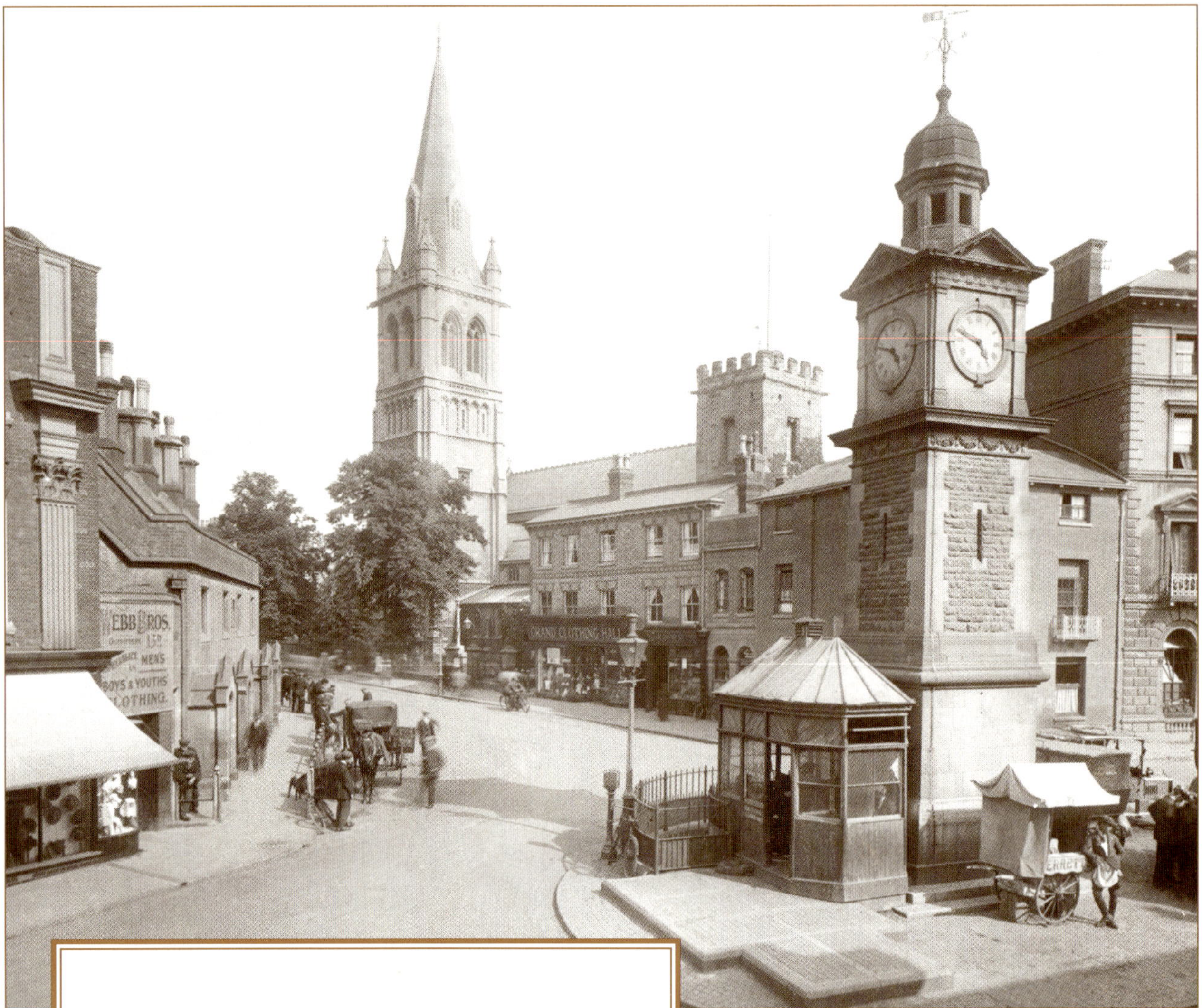

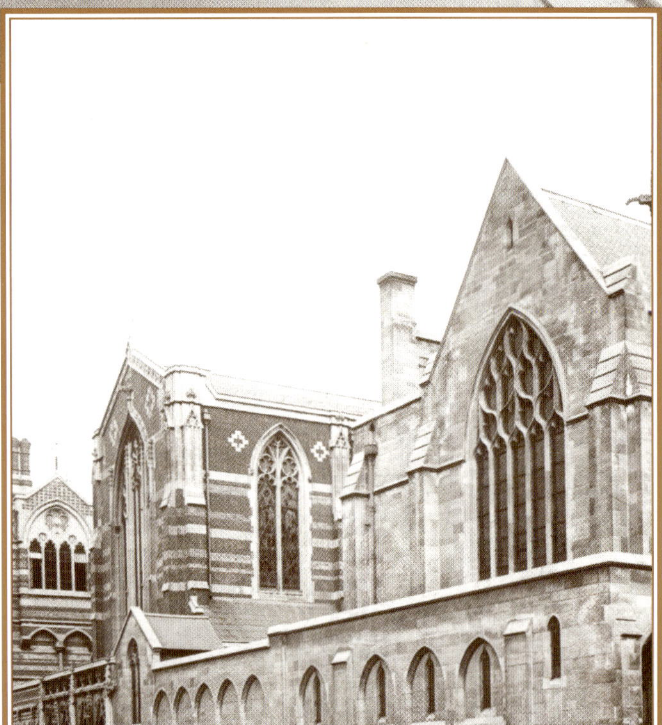

Above: The Clock Tower, Rugby, 1922 (72125) Cab drivers chat between fares at their rank. No one seems to be at all interested in buying what the street vendor is selling from his stall. He slouches disconsolately in his apron. In the background is The Grand Clothing Hall, offering suits and dresses to all and sundry. In the forground on the left is the opposition: Webb Bros have an equally impressive looking frontage and window display.

Left: Rugby School and Chapel, 1932 (85186) Dr Thomas Arnold gave this school its prestigious reputation. He is said to have 'changed the face of education in the public schools of England'.

Opposite top: Regent Street, Rugby, 1922 (72129)

Opposite below: Market Place, Rugby, 1932 (85177) Here are some very fine period shopfronts, with shaped fascias, high quality embossed glass and ornate wrought iron.

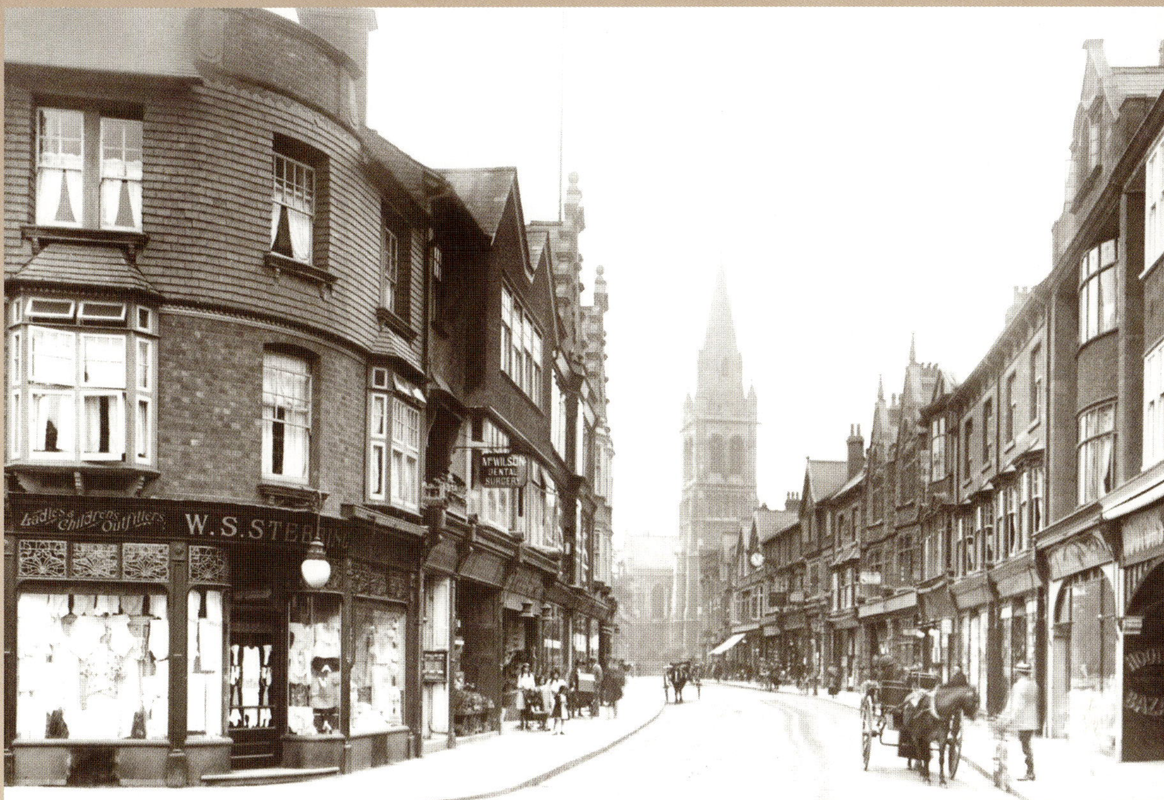
Ladies & Childrens Outfitters
Mr WILSON DENTAL SURGERY

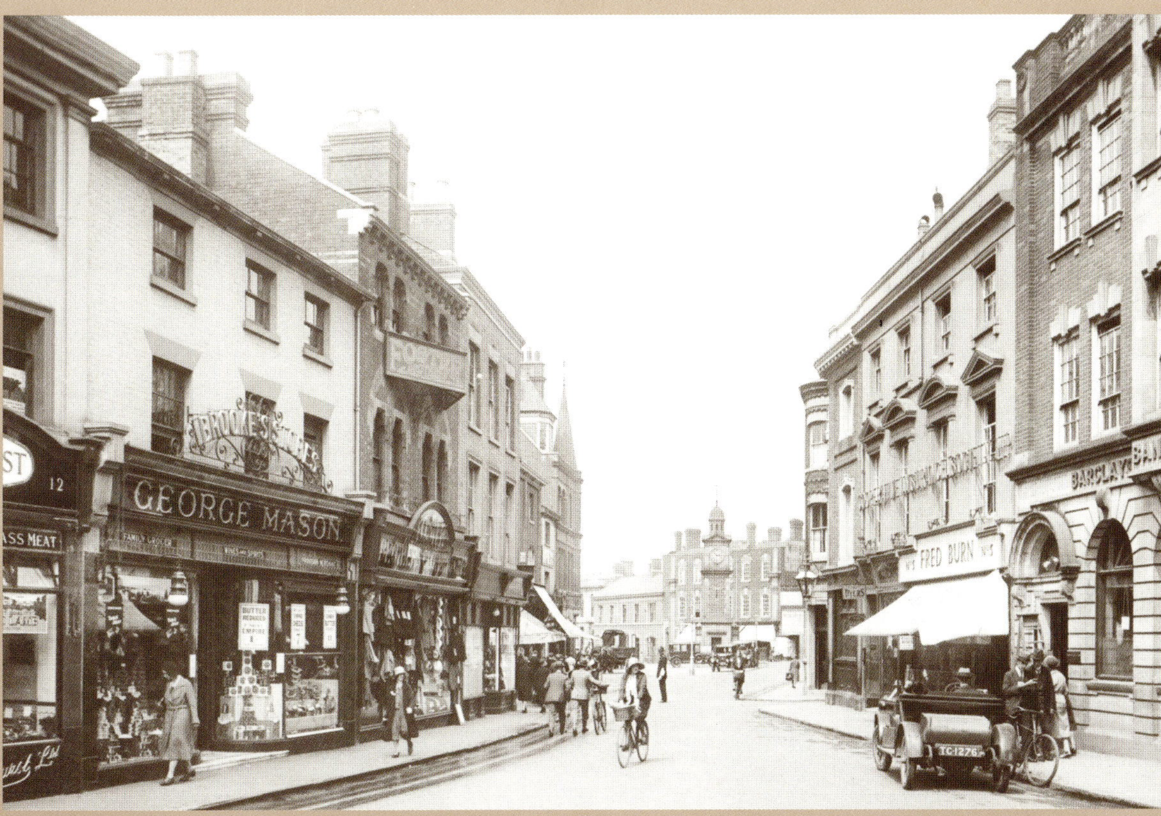
GEORGE MASON
FRED BURN

NORTHAMPTON. The 17th-century traveller Celia Fiennes described this old Anglo-Saxon market and cloth centre as ' a large town well built'. She saw it just after its reconstruction - it suffered an appalling fire in 1675. By the beginning of our century it was much more than just a regional market, and had become a world centre for boot and shoe making.

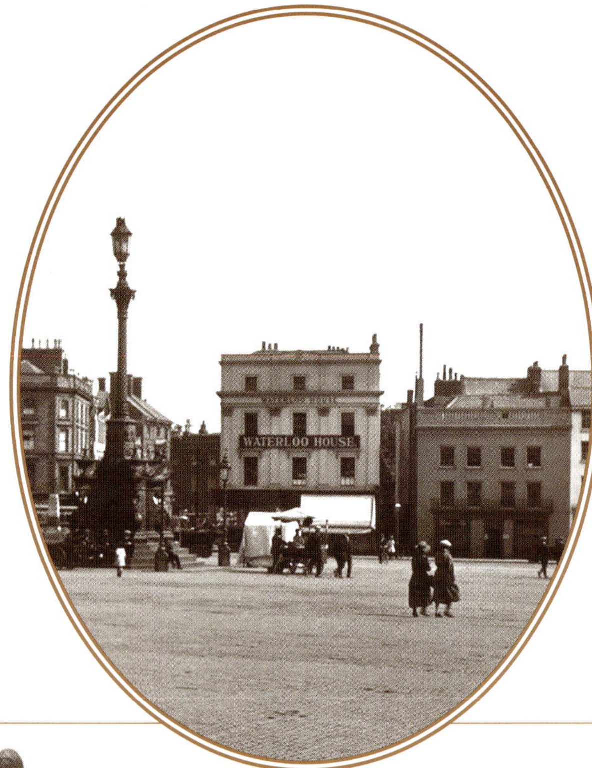

Right: The Market Place, Northampton, 1922 (72169) A broad, pleasing prospect, thought to be the largest market place in England, with many fine buildings.

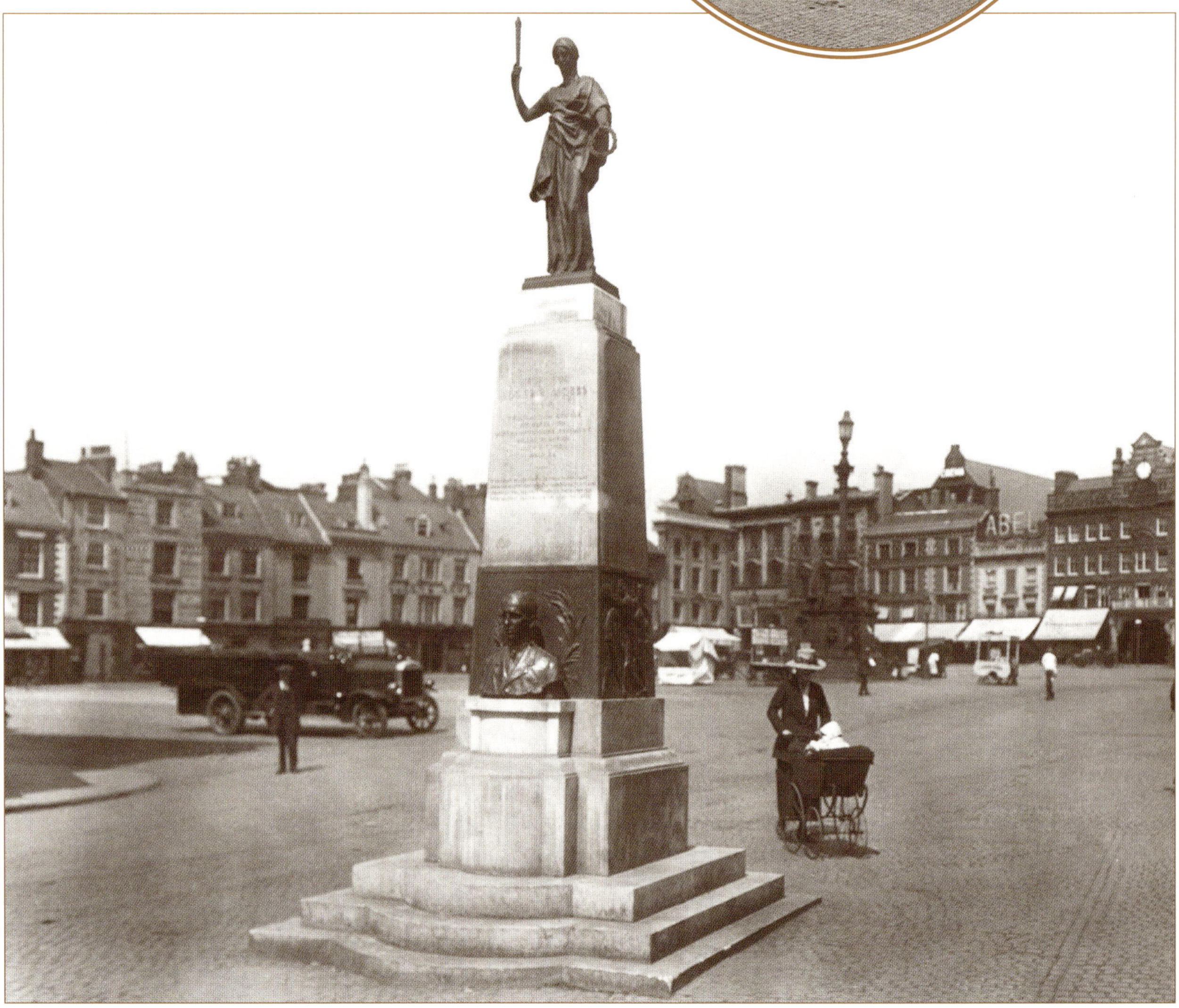

Above: The Market Place, Northampton, 1922 (72168) It was enlarged after a disastrous fire in 1675. At the heart of the old town is this vast cobbled area, which is filled to bursting point on market days with stalls that are a riot of colour with their bright striped awnings and throngs of shoppers and bargain hunters. One notable building that survived the ravages of the fire is the Welsh House, decorated with heraldic shields and obelisks. Not satisfied with this huge market area, the Victorians built the highly decorated Emporium Arcade at one end, which is a warren of tiny shops.

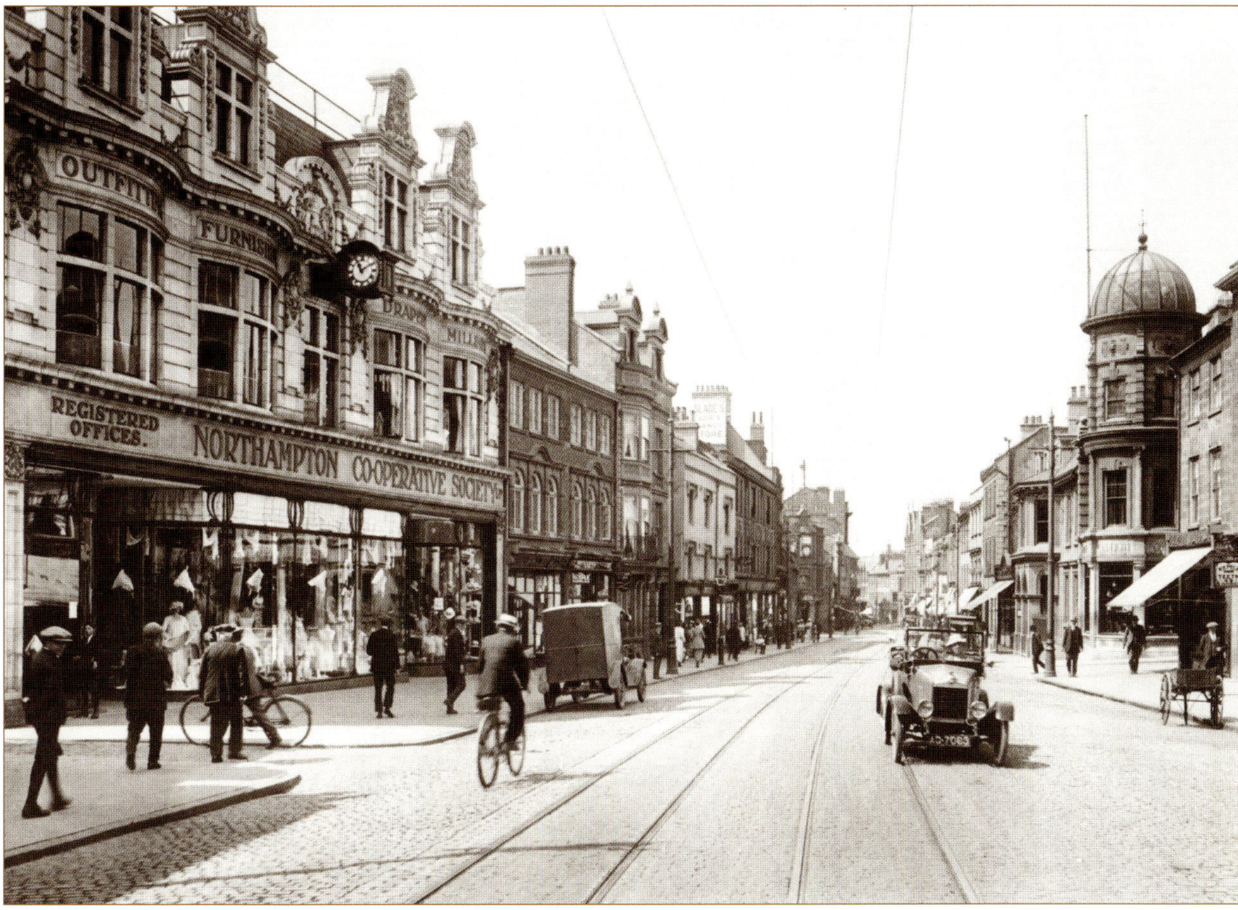

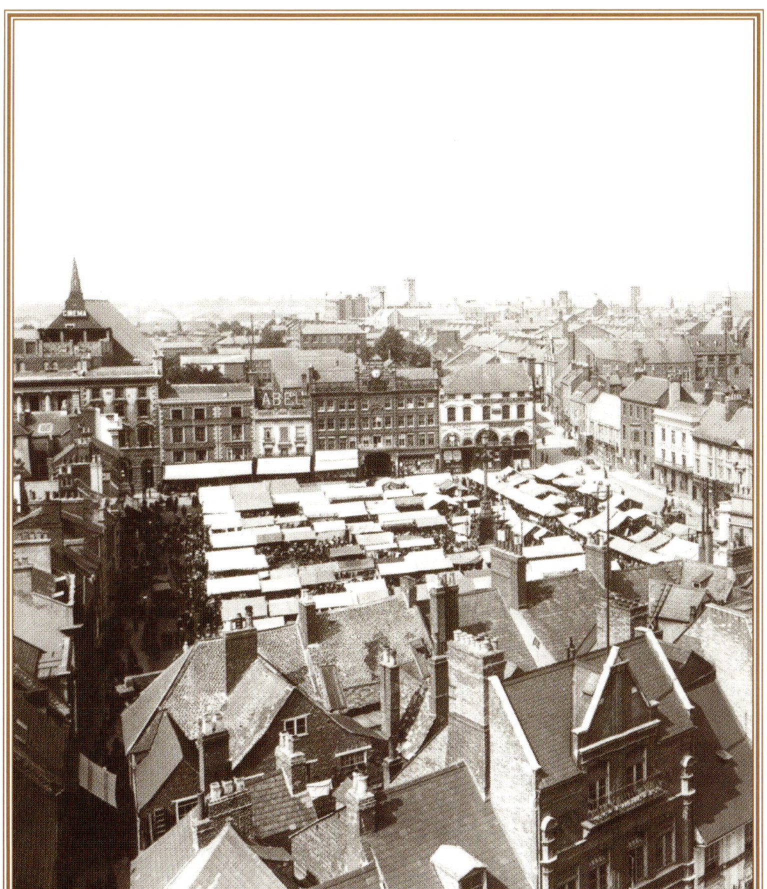

Above: Abington Street, Northampton, 1922 (72171) Leading out of the Market Square this thriving shopping thoroughfare heads out of the town in a north-easterly direction. On the left is the prestigious premises of the Northampton Co-operative Society, with terracotta detailing and fake rustication. They were outfitters, furnishers and drapers, and aimed at offering the local people cheap products through their special savings scheme.

Left: Northampton, from All Saints Church, 1922 (72166) An impressive panorama from the church tower, showing the roofs surrounding Mercers Row and a sea of market awnings. In the far distance, out of sight, are the red brick terraced houses of the workers in the town's important shoe industry. The medieval tower of All Saints is all that survived the fire. The church was rebuilt in the Wren style. Charles II gave 1,000 tons of timber towards the rebuilding.

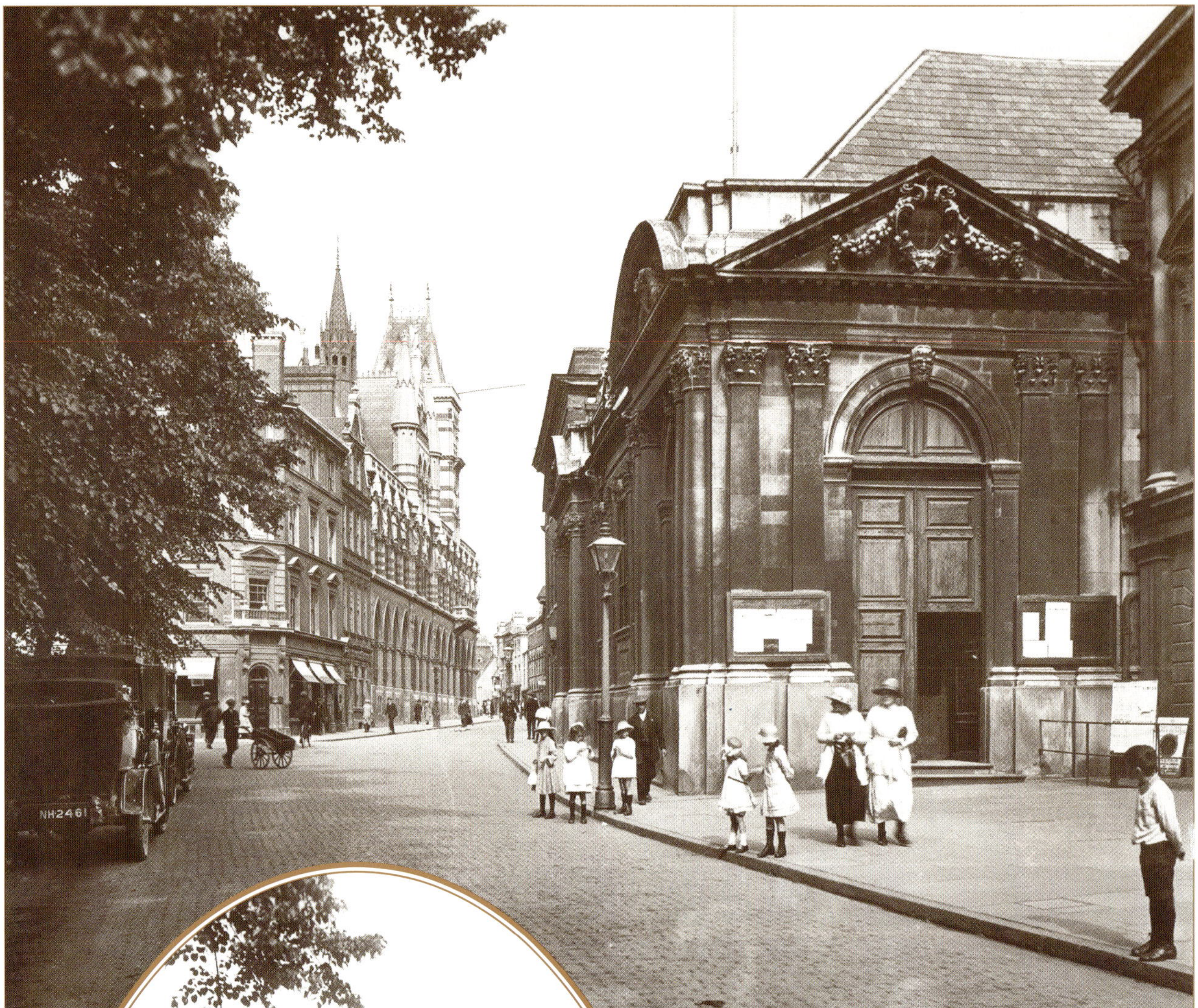

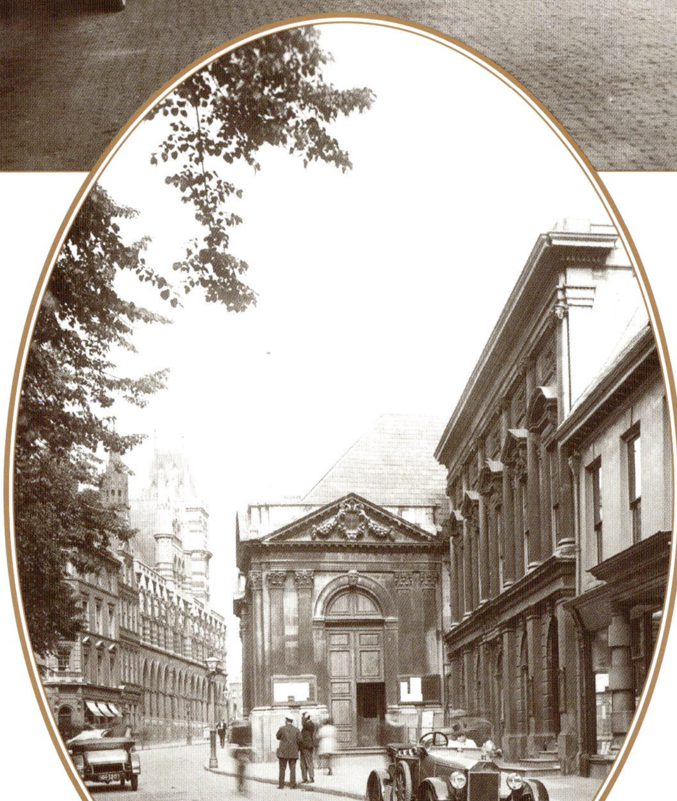

Above: George Row, Northampton, 1922 (72179) In the centre is the handsome classical style Sessions House, with its balustrade, hipped roof, and Corinthian columns.

Left: George Row, Northampton, 1922 (72178) Another view showing this leafy cobbled street. Drivers and passengers must have suffered a bone-shaking ride in their open-top cars.

Opposite top: Drapery, Northampton, 1922 (72174) This broad shopping street and tram route runs along the west side of the market square. The street facade was almost entirely reconstructed in the two decades before this picture was taken. Victorian big business had no qualms in pulling down traditional buildings and replacing them with the most fashionable and monumental designs of the day.

Opposite below: The Town Hall, Northampton, 1922 (72181) A typical Victorian Gothic extravaganza.

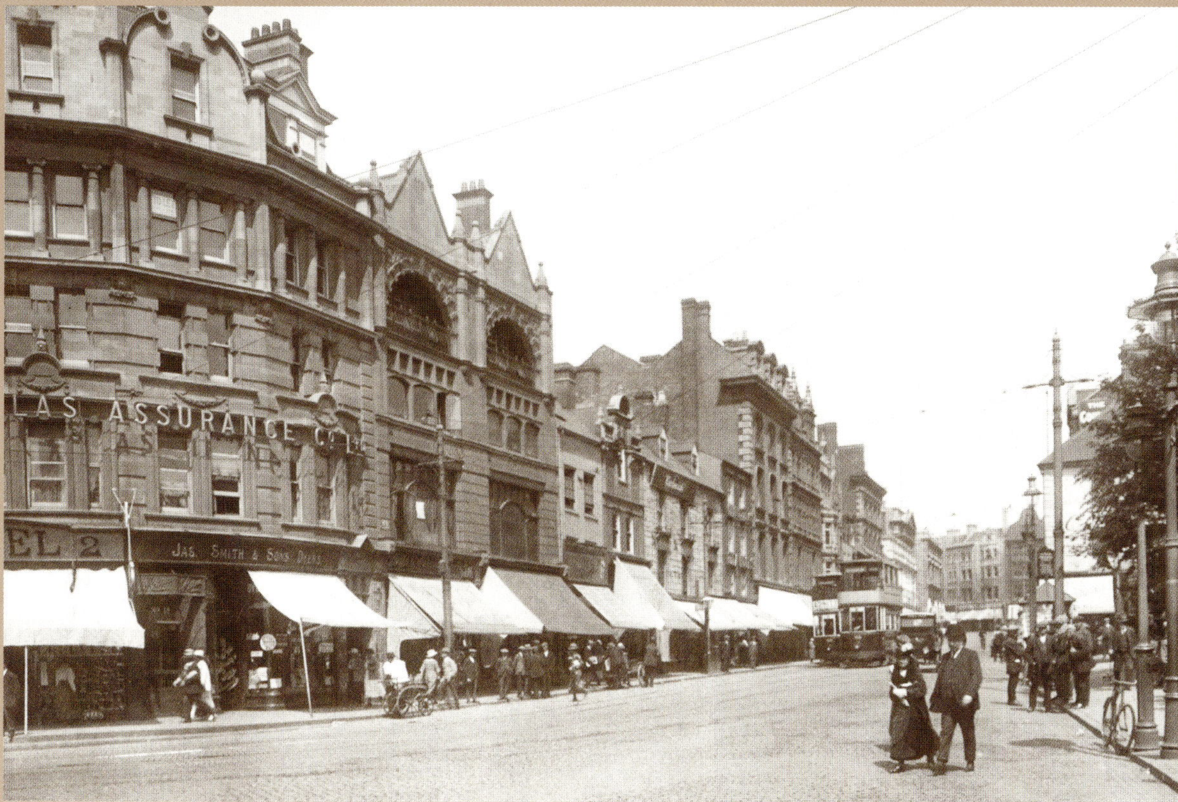
LAS ASSURANCE Cº Lᵀᴰ
EL 2
JAS. SMITH & SONS

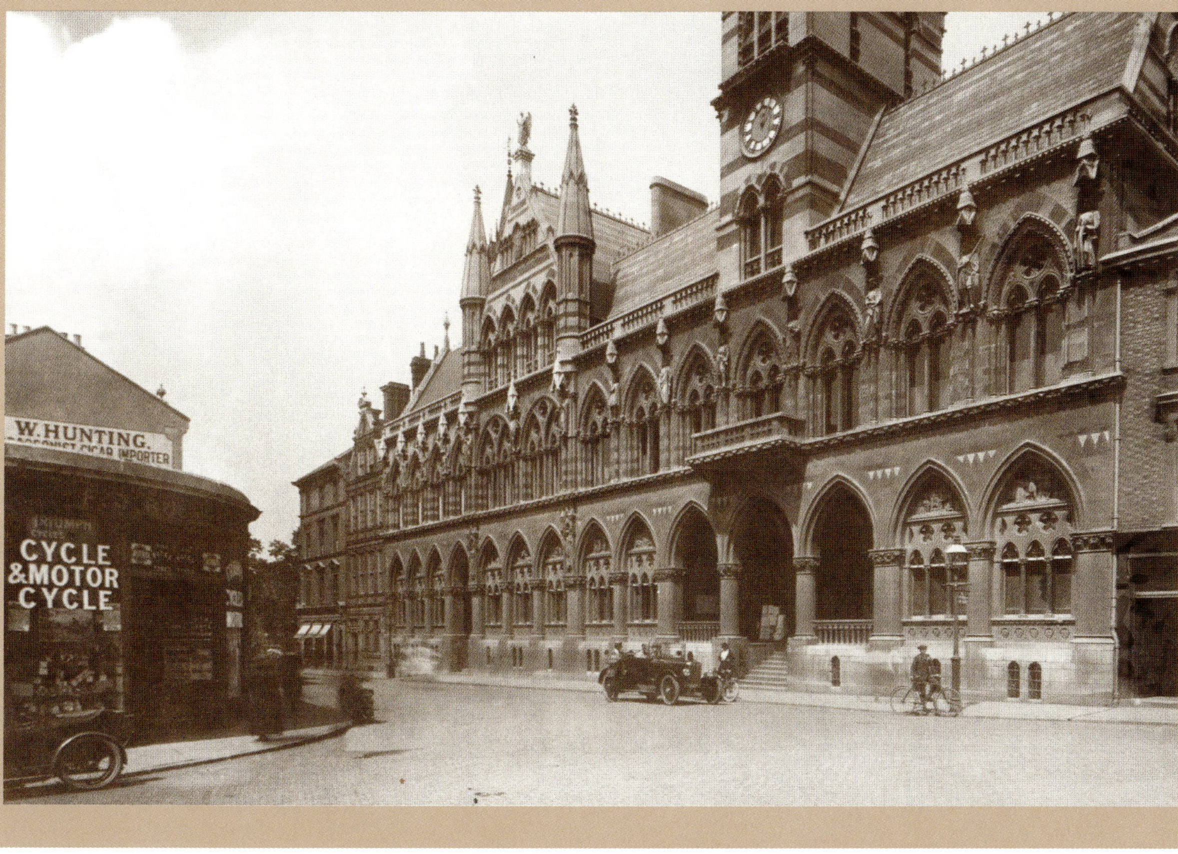
W. HUNTING.
CIGAR IMPORTER
CYCLE
&MOTOR
CYCLE

Right: Castle Ashby, 1922 (72221) This stately home is set in rich parkland spreading over a square mile, created by the famous and fashionable 18th-century landscape designer, Capability Brown. On this occasion he did not stint - there are seven ornamental lakes! Much of the house is 16th century, built for the Earl of Northampton, but it was added to in the 1700s when the wings were joined with a classical screen with pediments, by Inigo Jones. Note the ornate octagonal towers. The lawns extend almost up to the walls, separated only by the balustraded gravelled walk, so that the ladies did not get their feet wet. The formal decorative clipped shrubs must have needed an army of gardeners.

Below: The Terrace Gardens, Castle Ashby, 1922 (72223)

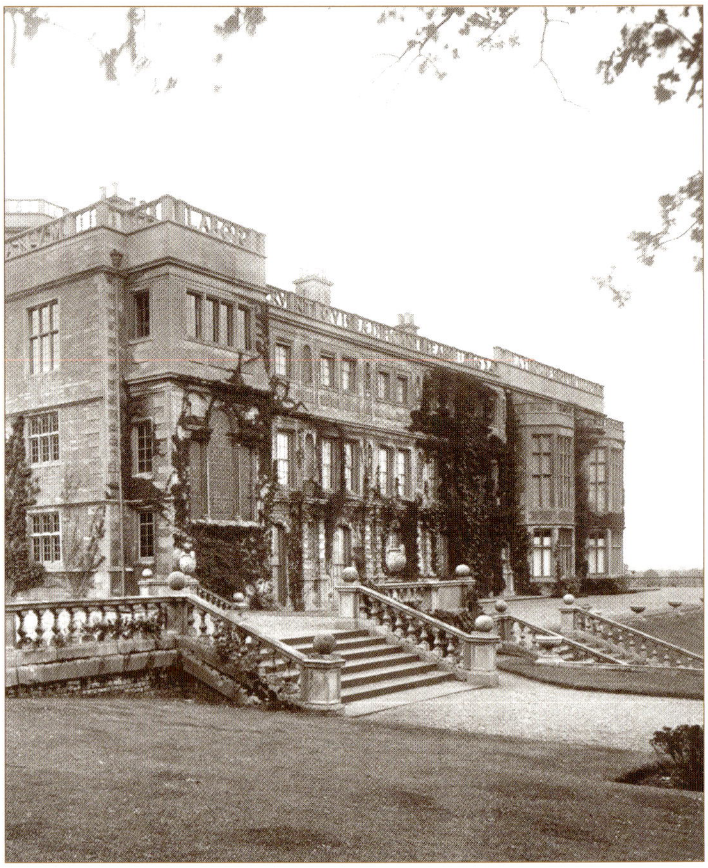

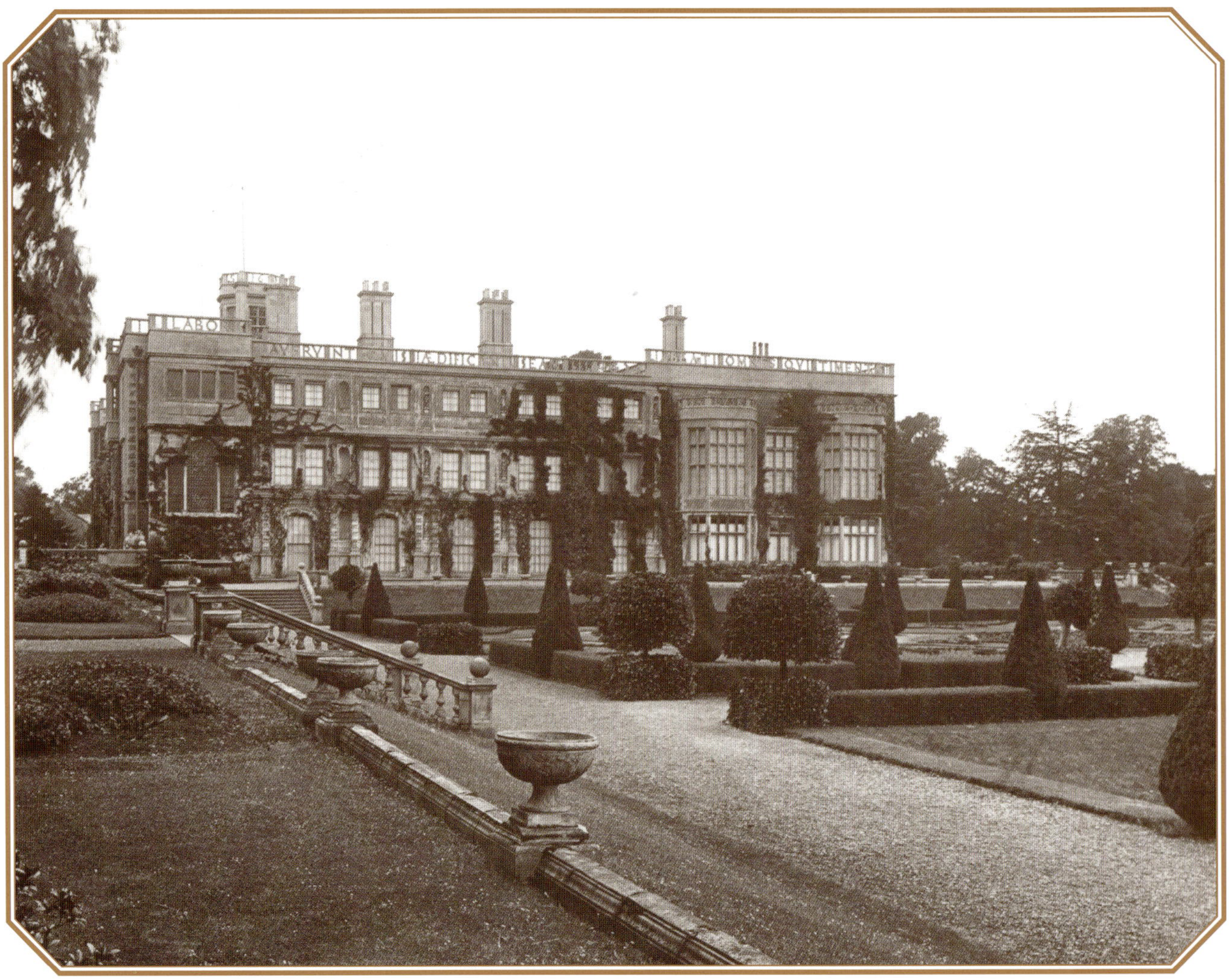

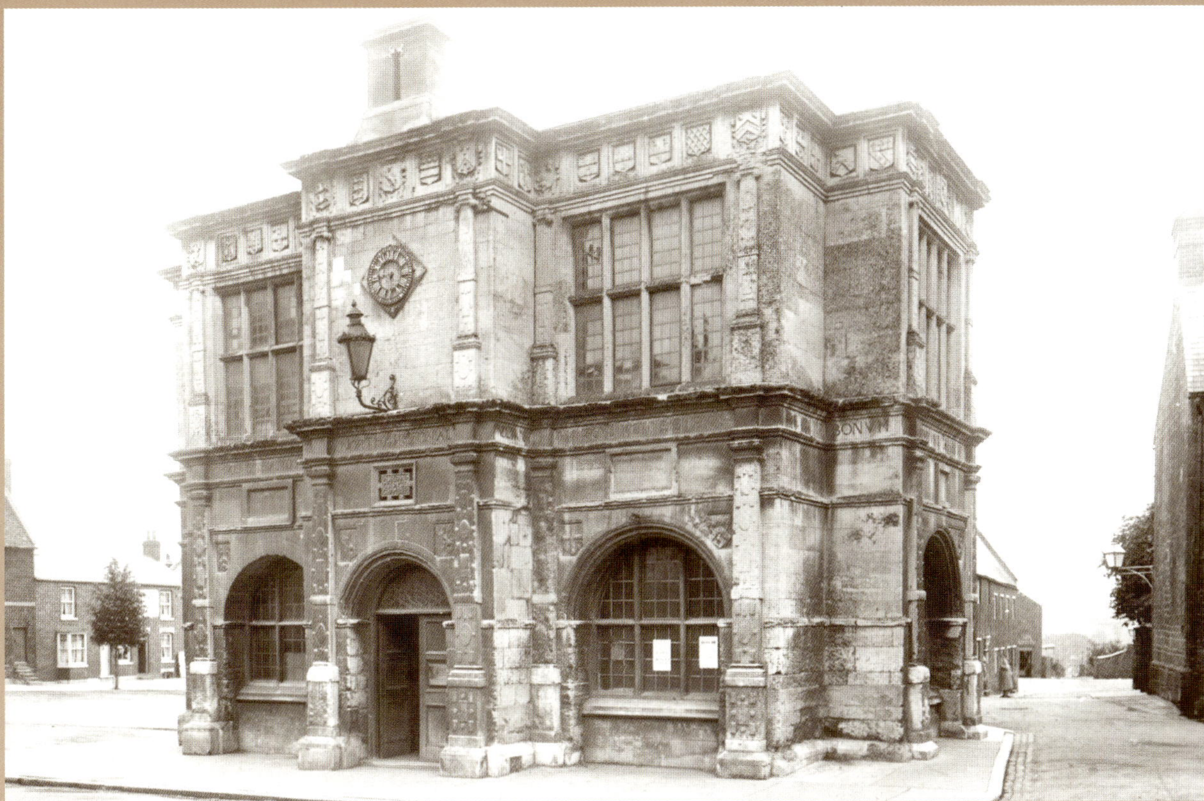

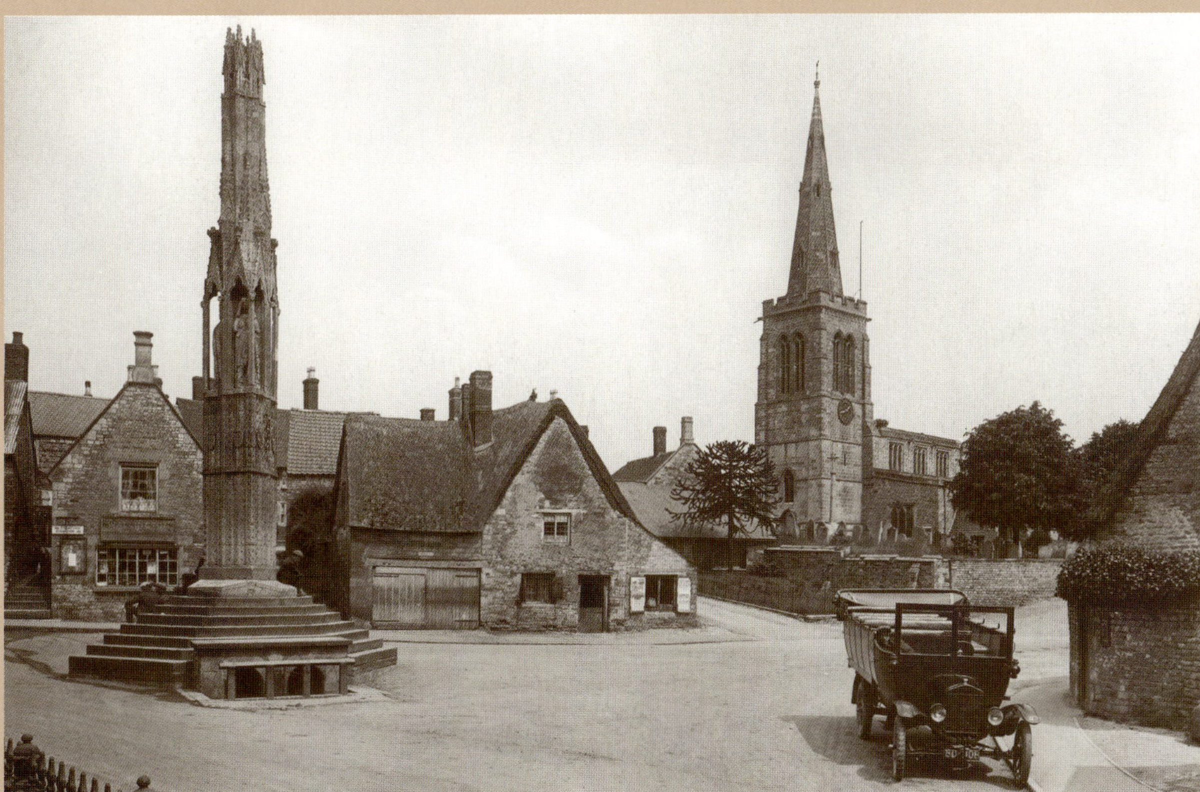

Top: The Old Town Hall, Rothwell, 1922 (72249) This old industrial town was a centre for the shoe making industry. Rothwell's exceptional Town Hall was built by Sir Thomas Tresham in 1580. The decorative frieze incorporates the heraldic shields of many local landowners. **Above: Geddington 1922** (72253) A charming village cradled in wooded countryside. The finely-carved Eleanor Cross was one of the many erected by Edward I to commemorate the places where the coffin of his queen was rested during its journey to Westminster Abbey. Note the charabanc, doubtless carrying visitors to see the lovely old thatched cottages and medieval bridge.

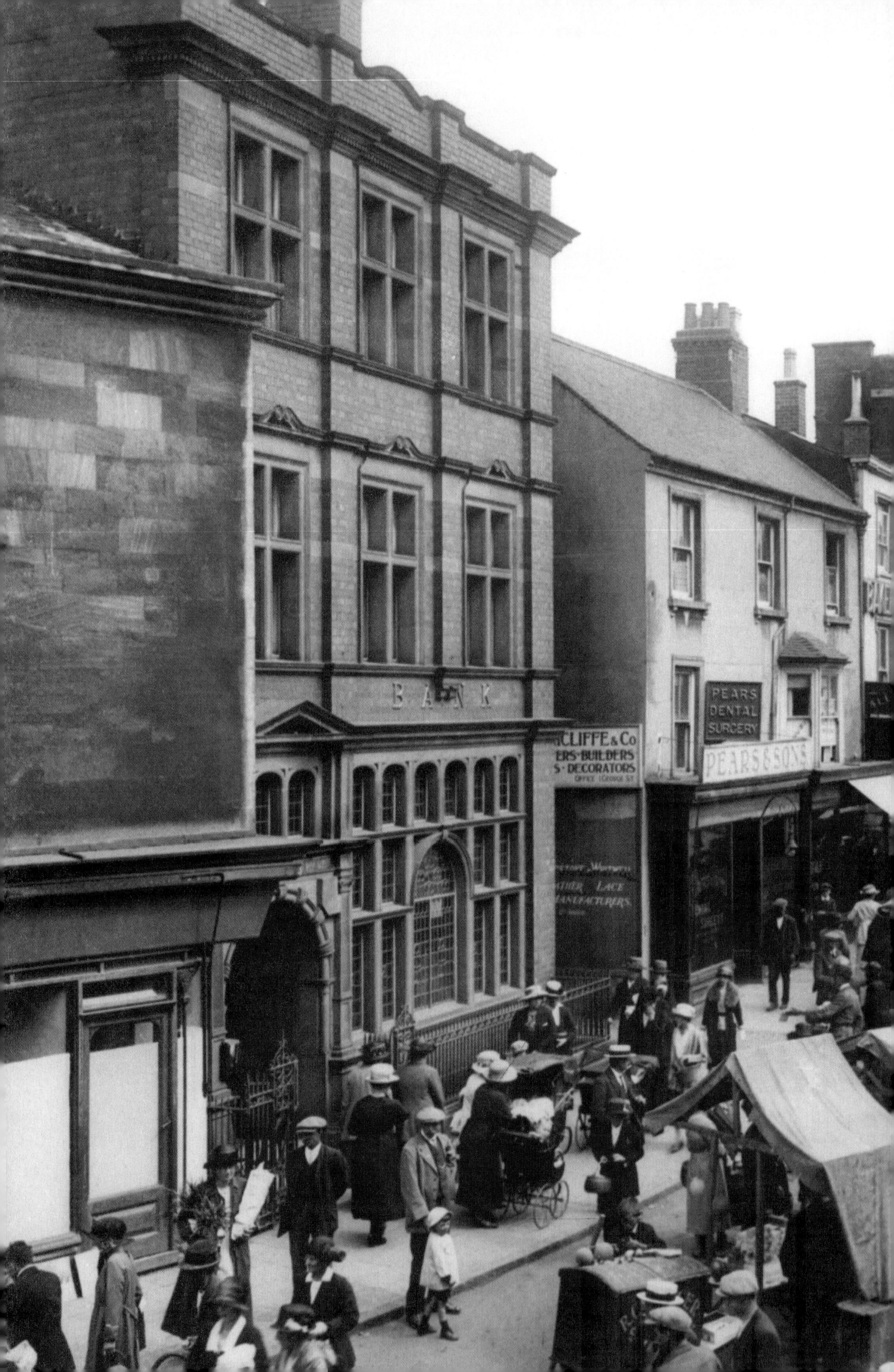
BANK
CLIFFE & Co
PEARS
DENTAL
SURGERY
PEARS & SONS

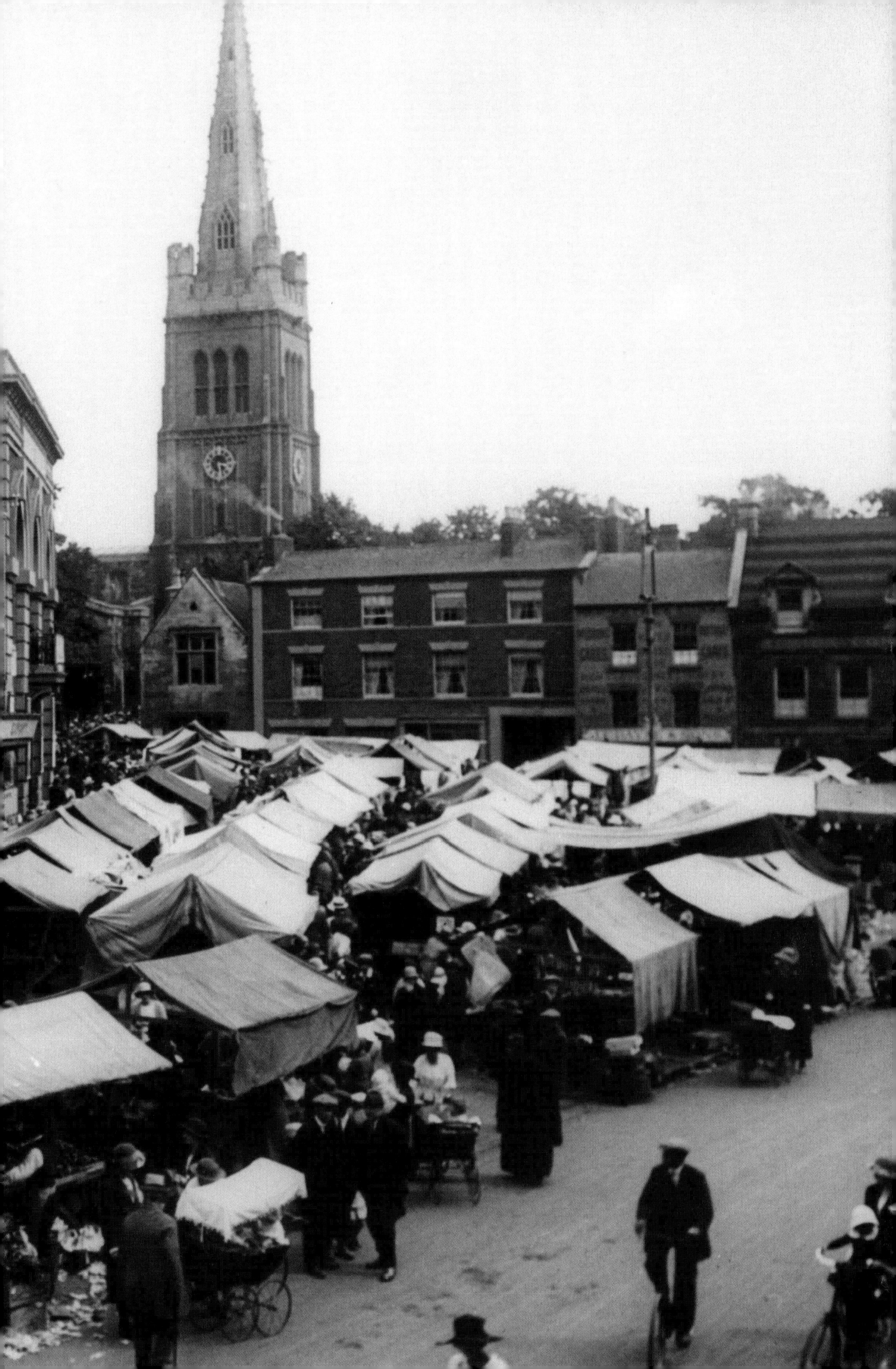

KETTERING had been a small market town serving the local countryside since its market charter was granted in 1227 by Henry III. It expanded rapidly into a sizeable industrial centre in late Victorian times. Boots and shoes were the main industry.

Previous pages: Kettering Market, 1922 (72232) A busy market scene. Beyond the bank on the left are the workshops of Stone & Whitwell, leather and lace manufacturers, and just beyond is Pears' dental surgery. In the background is the Albion Hotel.

Right: The parish church of St Peter and St Paul, Kettering, 1922 (72239) The ornate tower of this ancient limestone church soars over the town, its walls shrouded in greenery.

Below: High Street, Kettering, 1922 (72229) Another view of the High Street. Two workmen are repairing Hepworth's signboard.

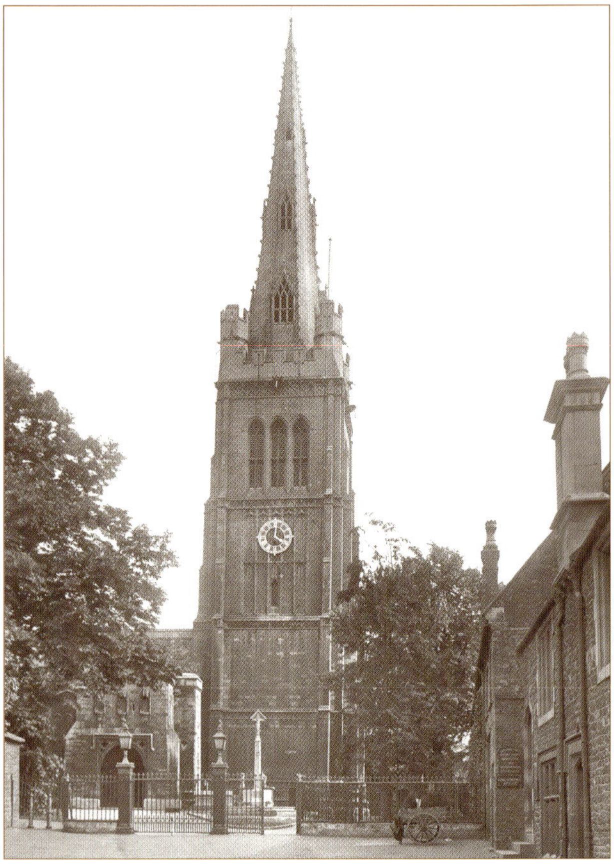

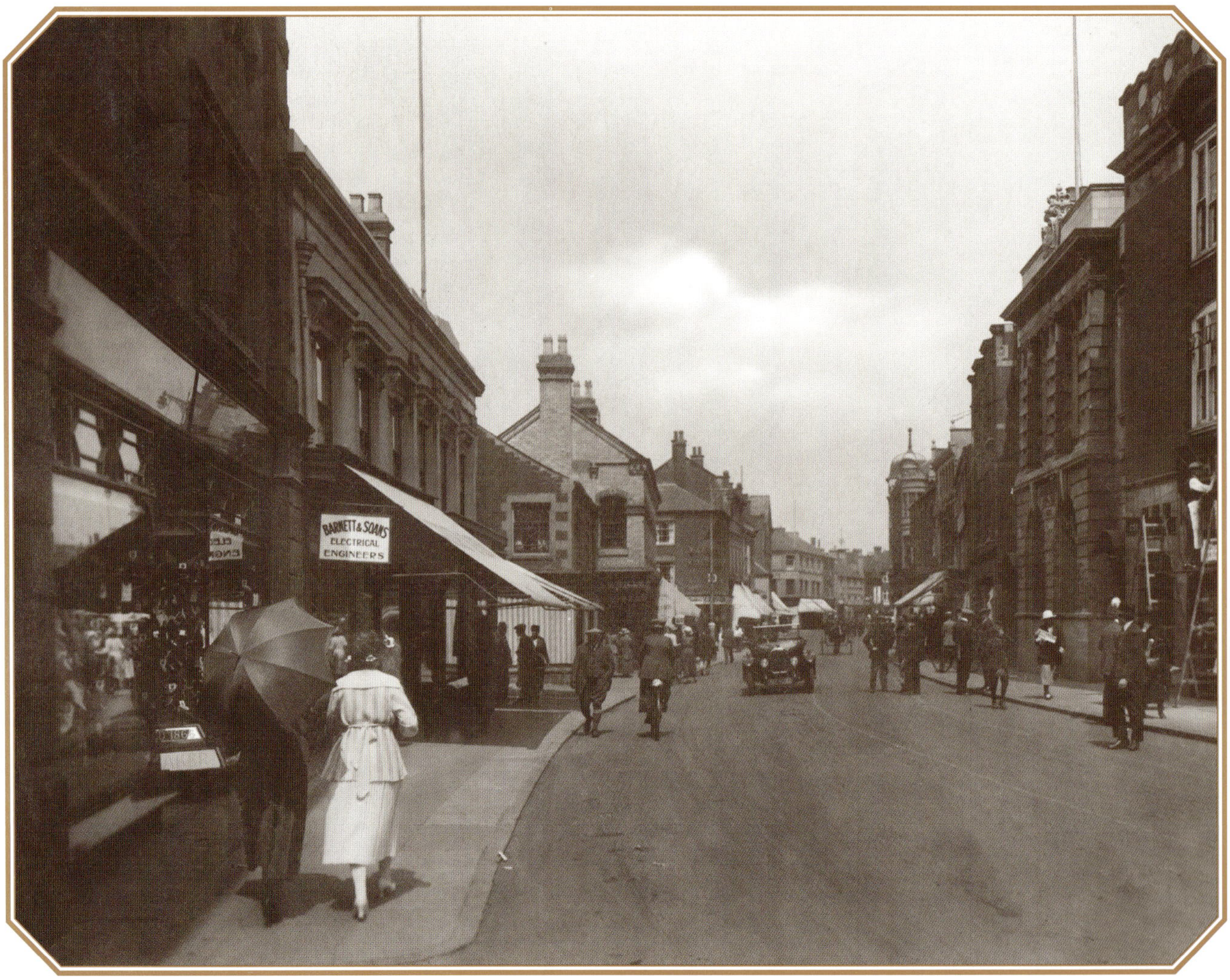

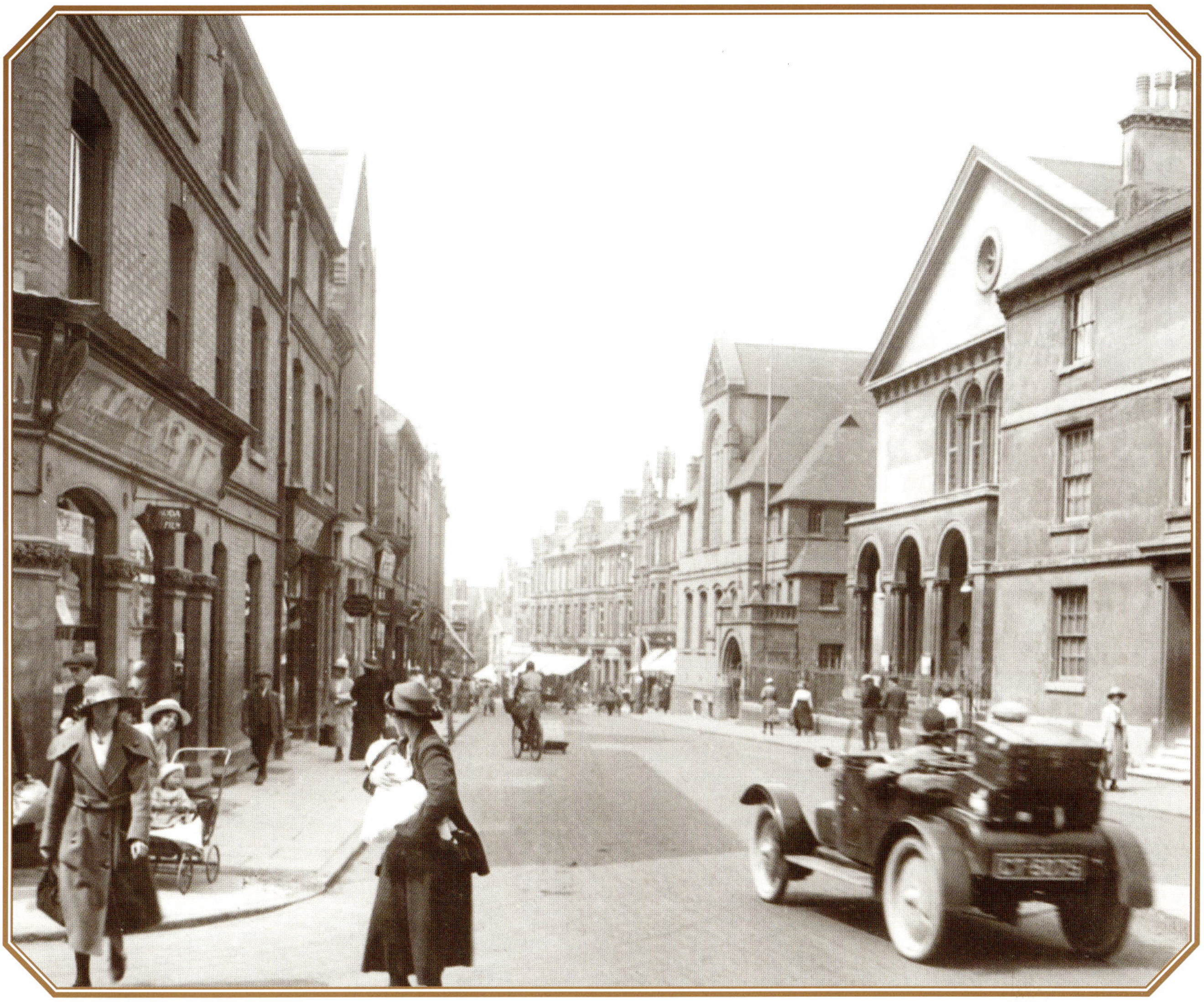

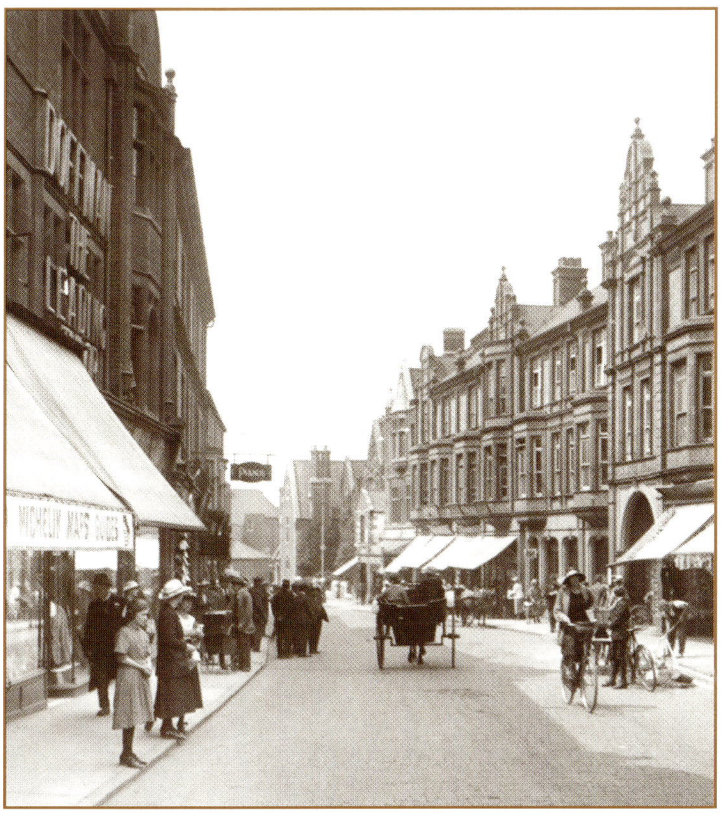

Above: Gold Street, Kettering, 1923 (72230) The narrow high street twists its way through the town. Kettering grew rapidly in Victorian times as a result of its expanding industries, with many terraces of simple dwellings to house the many workers. The line of the street is broken continually by Victorian buildings.

Left: Gold Street, Kettering, 1922 (72231) The bookshop on the left is offering Michelin guides and maps. A workman to the right of the cyclist is replacing the pavement kerbing. The country people are still travelling to the market in horse-drawn carts and traps, even though the car was beginning to take over the streets of Britain.

Overleaf: Newland Street, Kettering, 1922 (72235) The North Rubber Company proudly announces that it is the 'finest house in the country for all sport'. The windows and fascia are decked with rubber rings and tennis rackets. Two policemen are enjoying a short lull in the traffic flow.

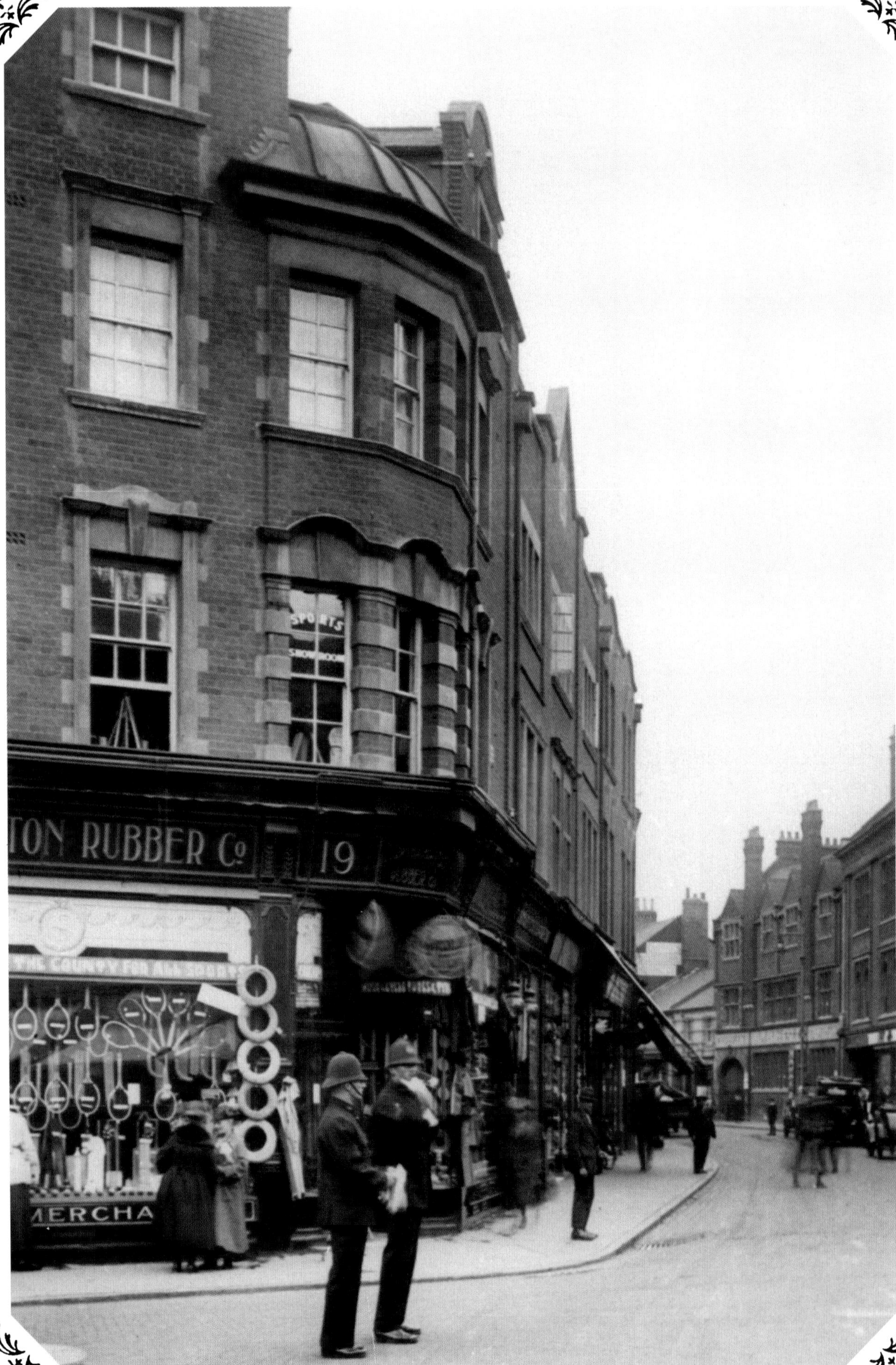
TON RUBBER Co
19
SPORTS
SHOWROOM
MERCHA

Right: High Street, Kettering, 1922 (72228) On the left is the Royal Hotel.

Below: Kettering Market, 1922 (72233) Open markets were held three times a week in the broad central square. Mr Bernstein's stall is swathed in flowing net curtains. In the foreground crocks are piled high. On the extreme right is the Variety cinema. The market was of supreme importance to local people right up to the 1950s. Local shops until the first decade of our century had sold mainly local produce. Things only changed when chainstores came to our small towns, quickly displacing local shops with their much wider, more exciting product ranges. And they were cheaper, too. It was almost impossible for local people to resist the temptation.

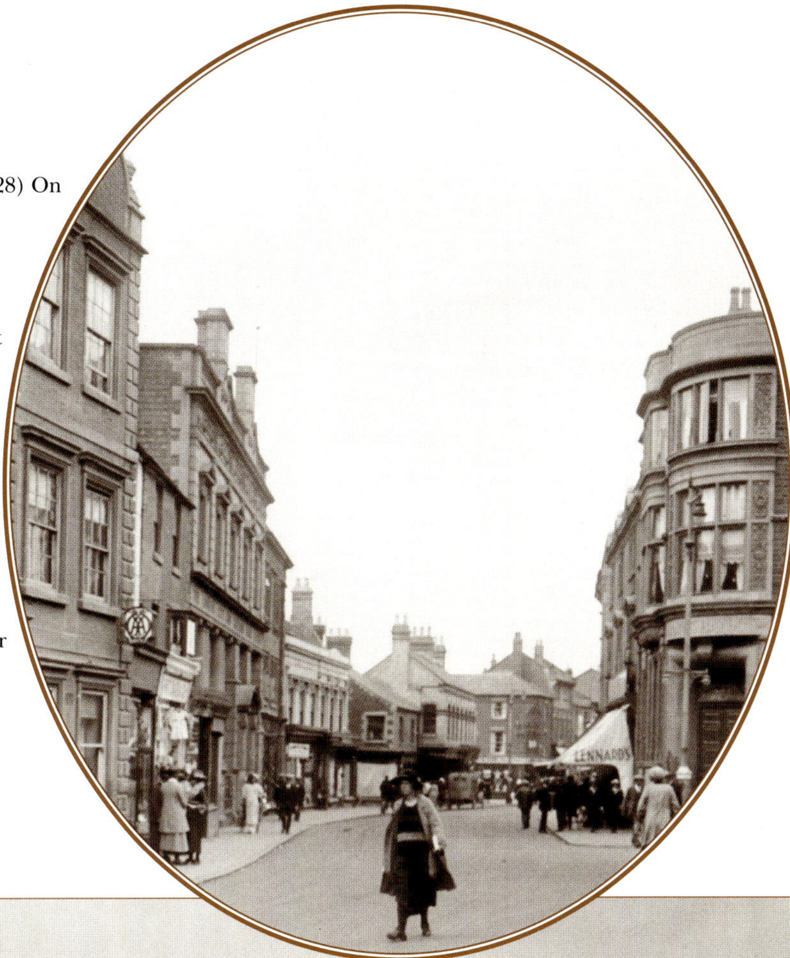

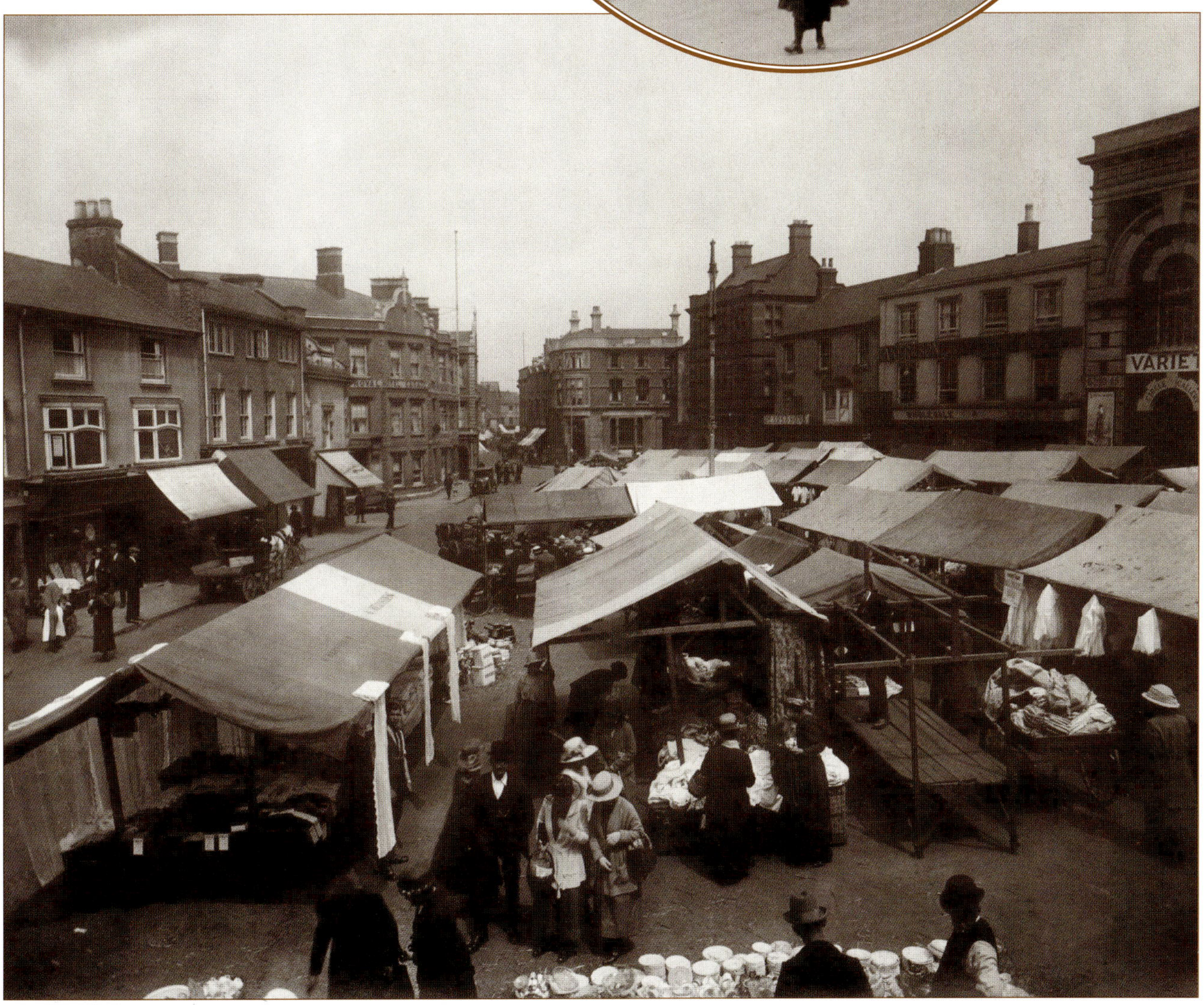

MARKET HARBOROUGH, close to the infant River Welland, 'is and always was a dull place'. So wrote Sir Richard Phillips in the early 1800s. He went on to say that he regretted that the poor were not like potatoes - to be buried in winter and dug up in summer. Fortunately, his views were not universally held, and many travellers have enjoyed the delights of this pleasant little market town - including its sizeable corset factory.

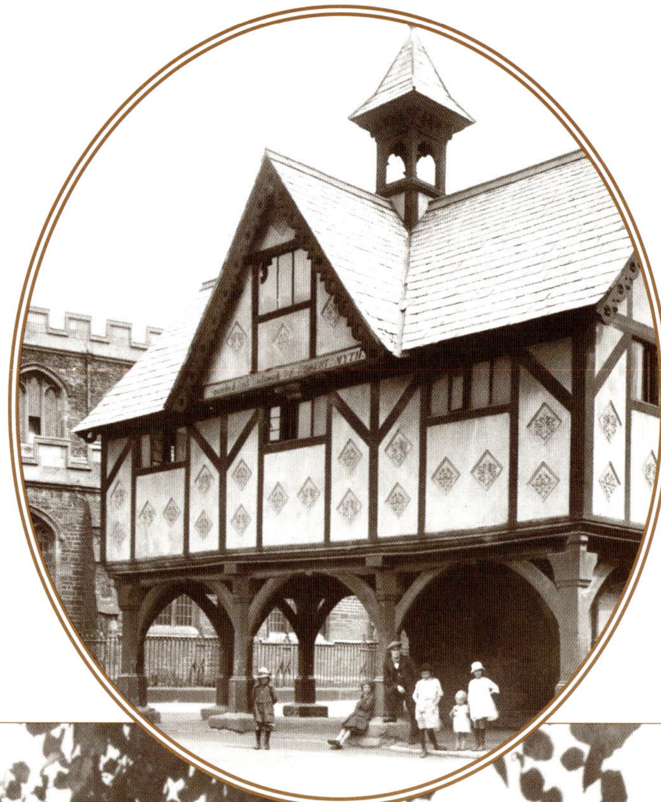

Right: The Old Grammar School, Market Harborough, 1922 (72269) Founded in 1613, this curious half-timbered building stands on broad, oaken pillars. While the boys studied Latin in a dark room on the upper floor, the much jollier butter market went on in full flurry below.

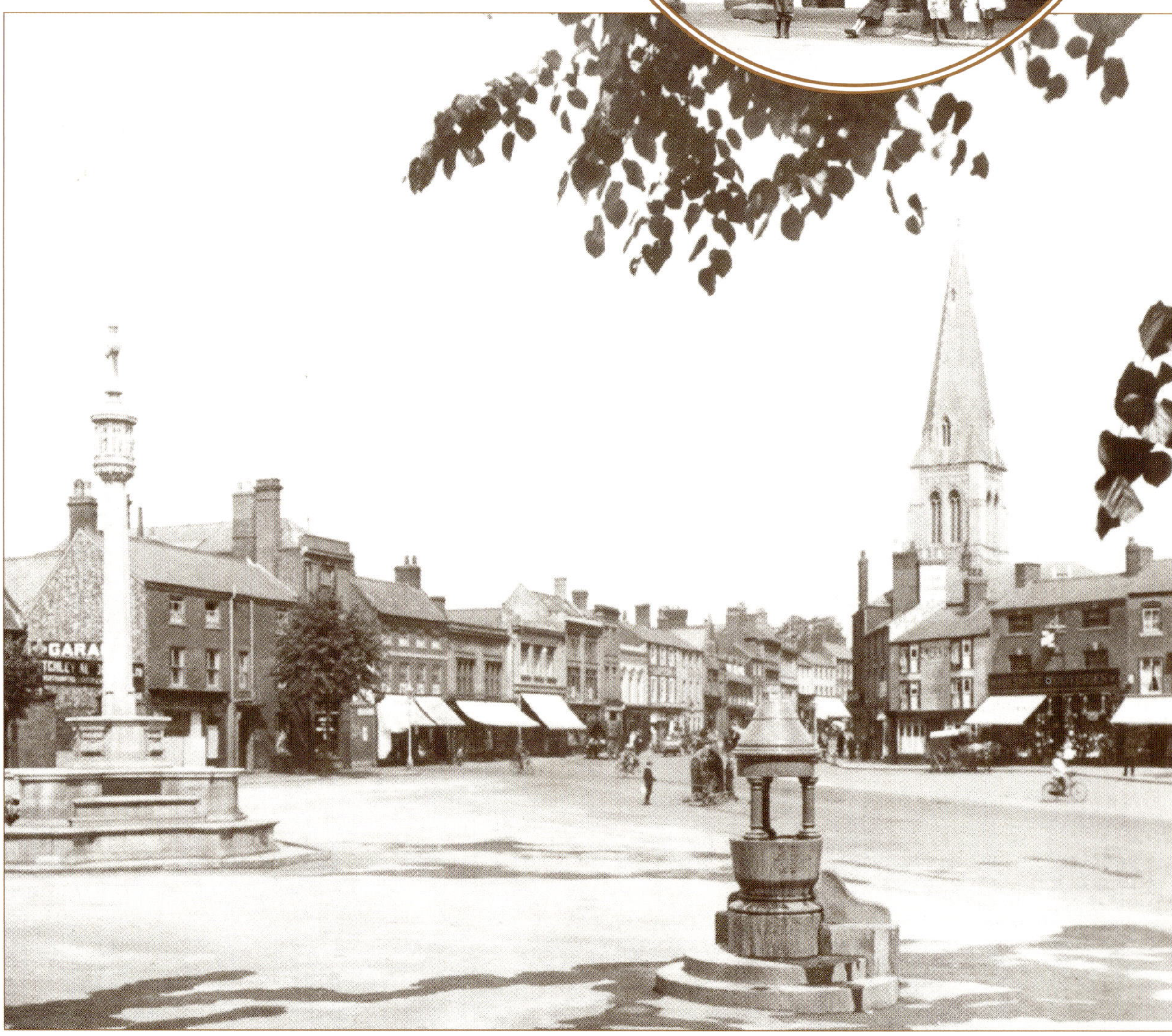

Above: The Market Square, Market Harborough, 1922 (72263) Although built primarily of red brick, a few of the old buildings in the square are of warm, yellow stone. On the left is the Northampton Brewery stores, and in the foreground the public water fountain. 'Market 'Arborow' was the setting for Whyte Melville's rambling hunting tales. The town is surrounded by rich grazing country.

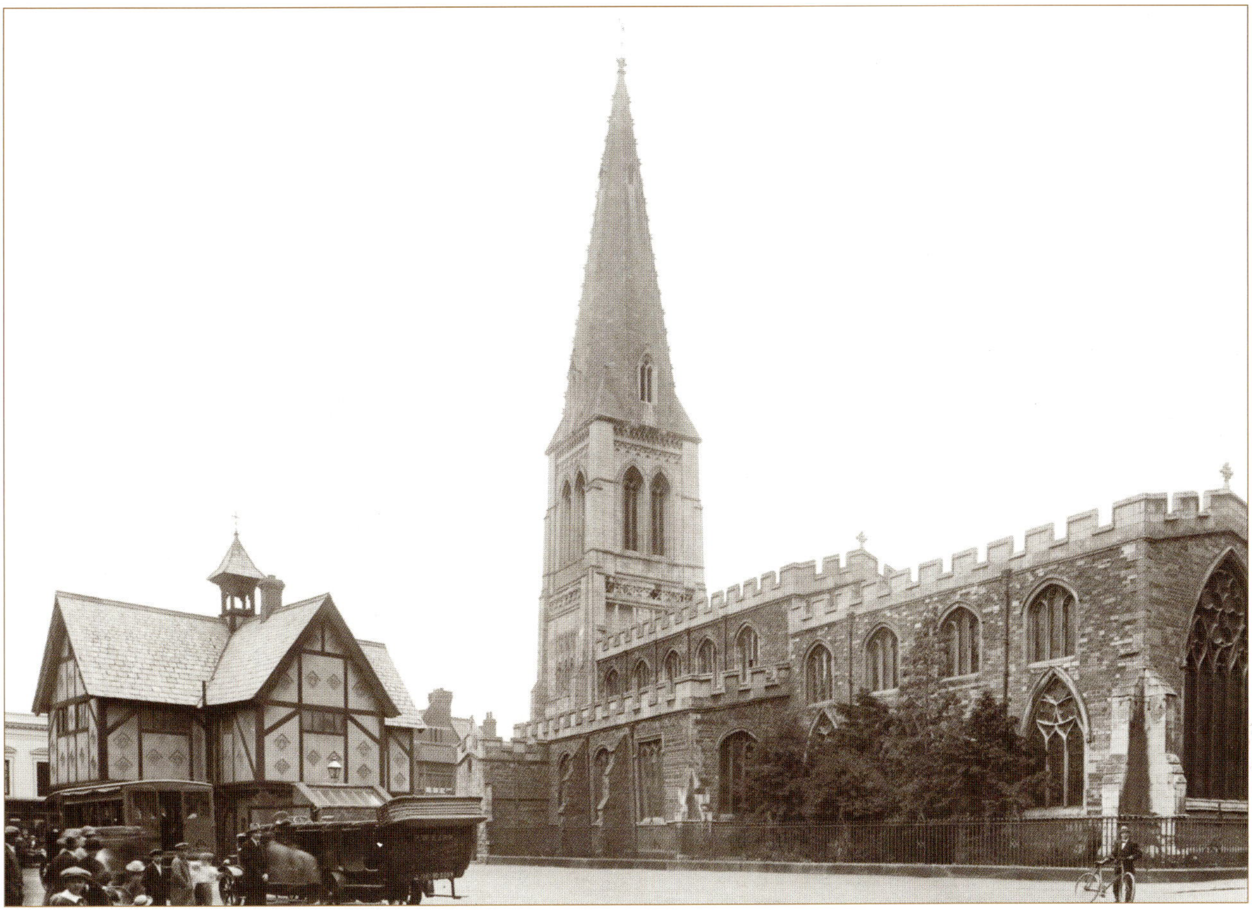

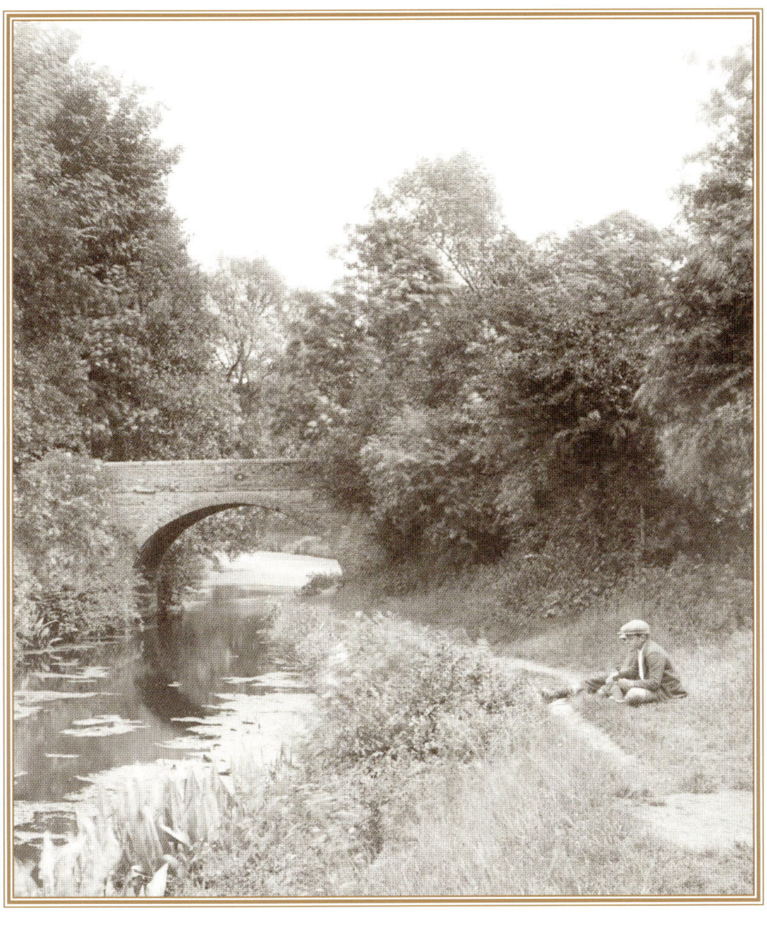

Above: Parish Church, Market Harborough, 1922 (72267) Huge and stately, the church of St Dionysius has one of the finest broach spires in England. The bells are rung every November in memory of a traveller who lost his way on the Welland marshes in the 16th century and was rescued by the townspeople. The ringers are rewarded with 1/- for beer. On the left, P W Kerr's charabanc and bus are waiting to carry the country people back to their farms and villages.

Left: The Canal Bridge, Market Harborough, 1922 (72272) Just a few miles from the town centre is an impressive run of ten canal locks, carrying barges and narrow boats to the Market Harborough Basin from the Grand Junction Canal. Even in the busiest and most populated industrial regions the canals offer welcome peace and quiet. The water drifts gently by and the overhanging trees are reflected in the sunlit depths.

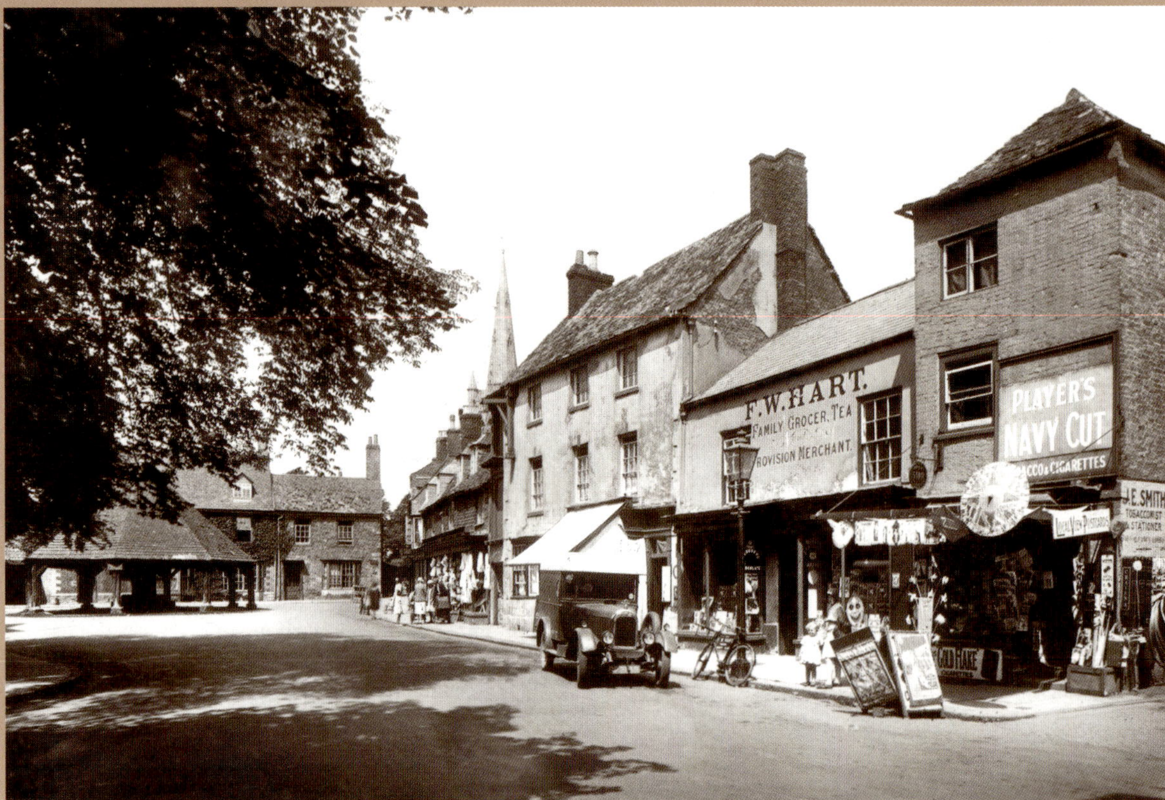
F.W.HART.
FAMILY GROCER, TEA
PROVISION MERCHANT.
PLAYER'S
NAVY CUT
J.E.SMITH

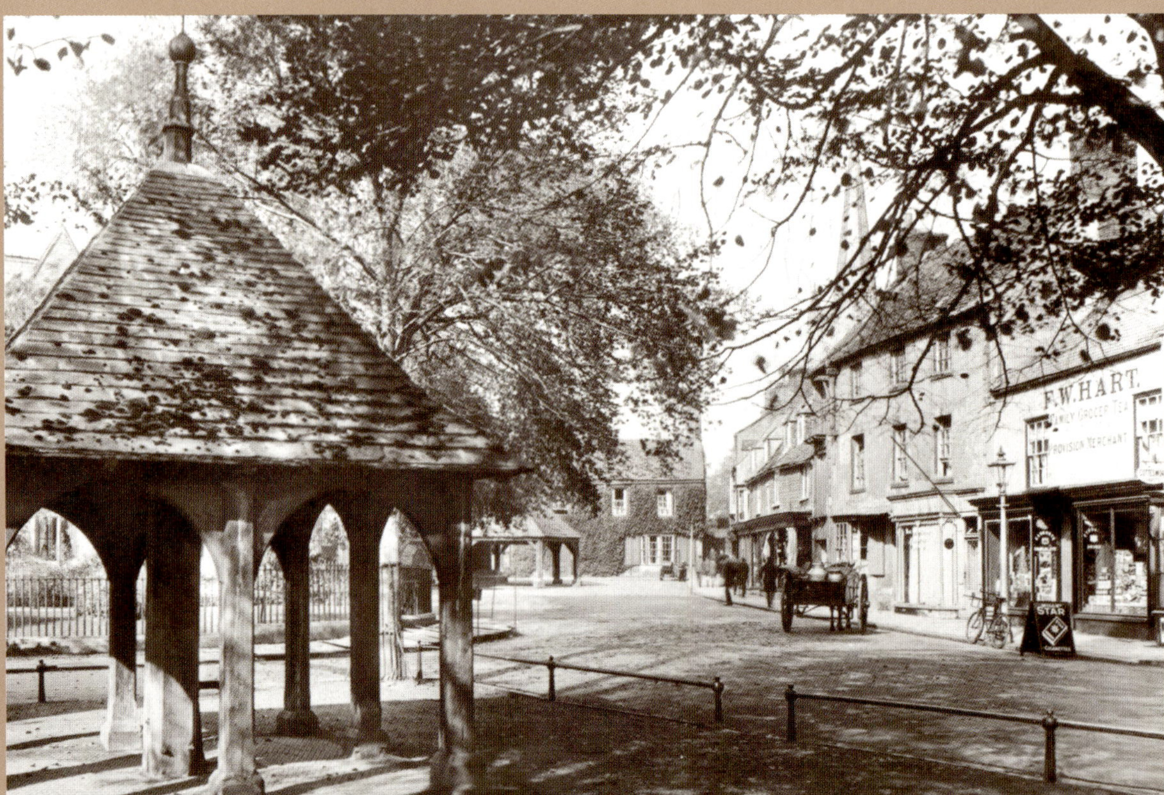
F.W.HART.
PROVISION MERCHANT
STAR

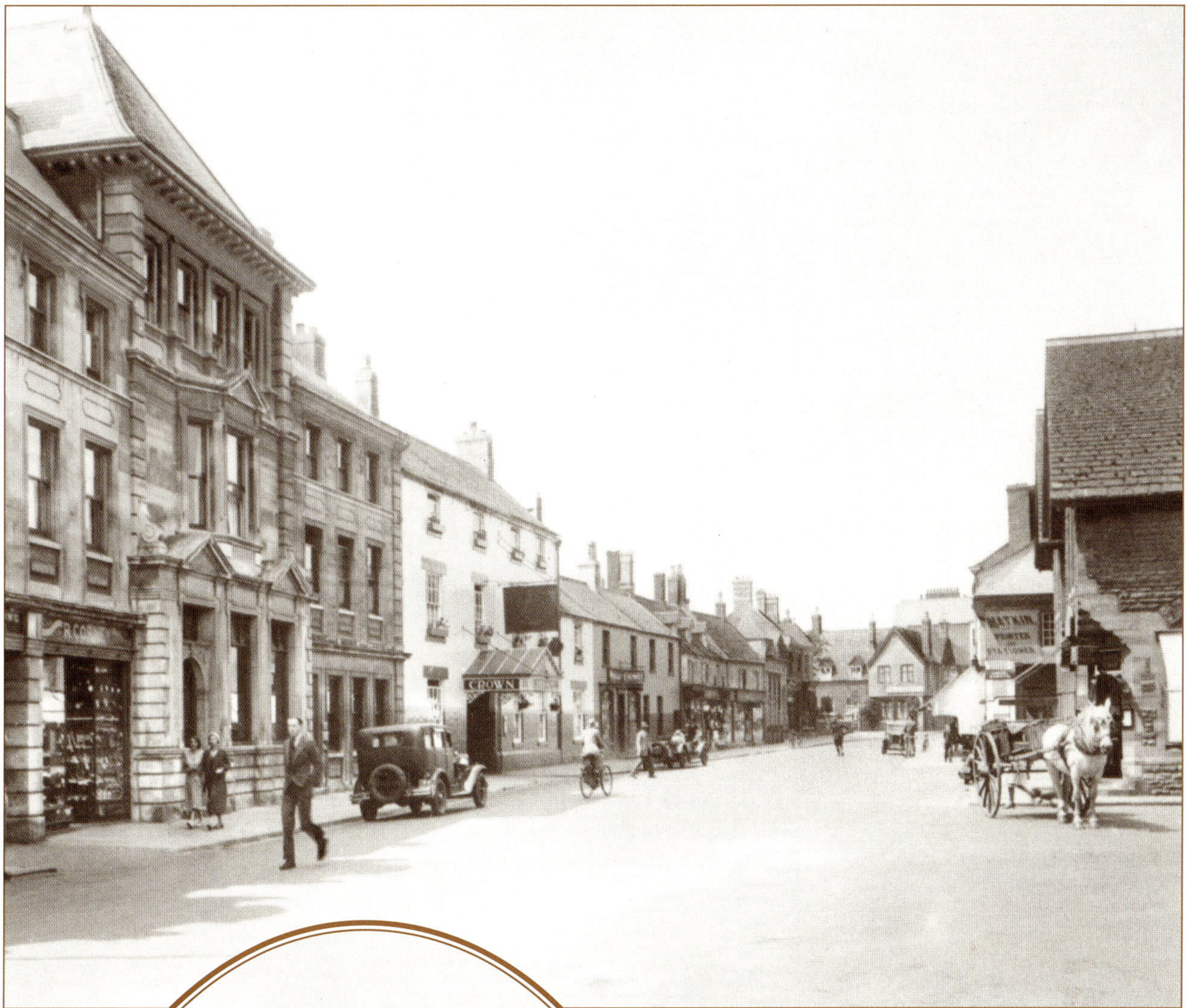

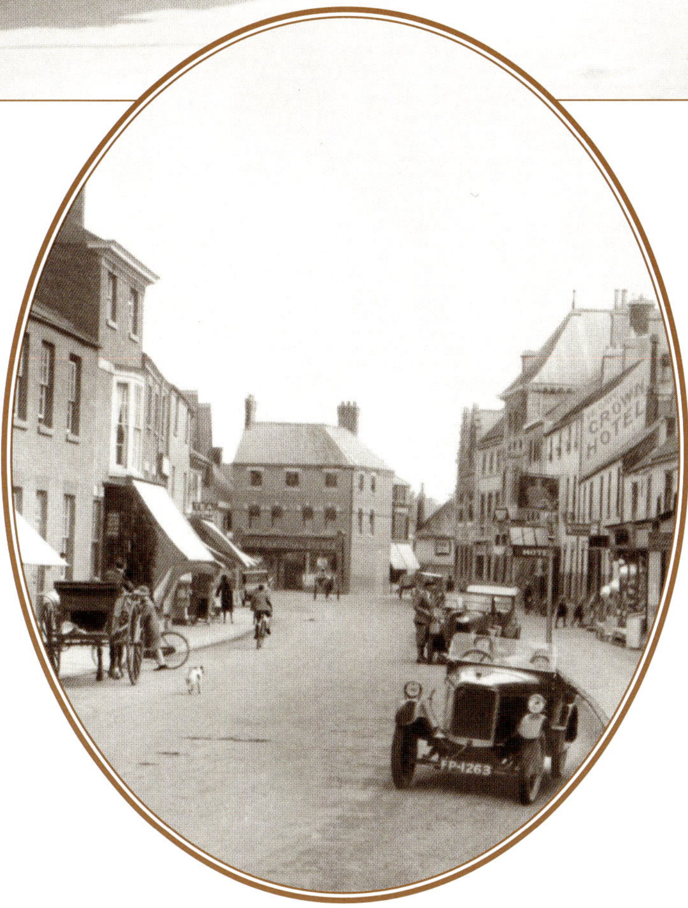

Opposite top: Market Place, Oakham, 1932 (85151) This pleasing little market town was once the capital of Rutland, England's tiniest county. Now absorbed into Leicestershire it has had to forfeit its status. In this peaceful scene we see F W Hart's family grocer business. Outside is a display board of local postcards - many doubtless from Frith & Co - and a range of items to keep the children happy, including hoops, clowns' masks and Chivers jellies.

Opposite below: Old Pump and Buttercross, Oakham, 1928 (80279) In the foreground is the town pump, and in the background the steep tiled roof of the Butter Cross, housing the stocks. Here rough and ready village justice was dispensed to disturbers of the peace.

Top: High Street, Oakham, 1932 (85149)

Left: High Sreet, Oakham, 1928 (80284)

MELTON MOWBRAY has long been the capital of hunting country in the county of Leicestershire. And it has suffered for it. In Victorian times it was the haunt of 'roaring blades' and 'Melton bloods'. Wine flowed freely, the atmosphere was rowdy and the talk was all of foxes, hacks, and broken bones. Townspeople were attacked at midnight by young bucks, who rode steeplechases through the midnight streets, with nightshirts over their hunting jackets. The town still lives by hunting, but life is mercifully more sedate.

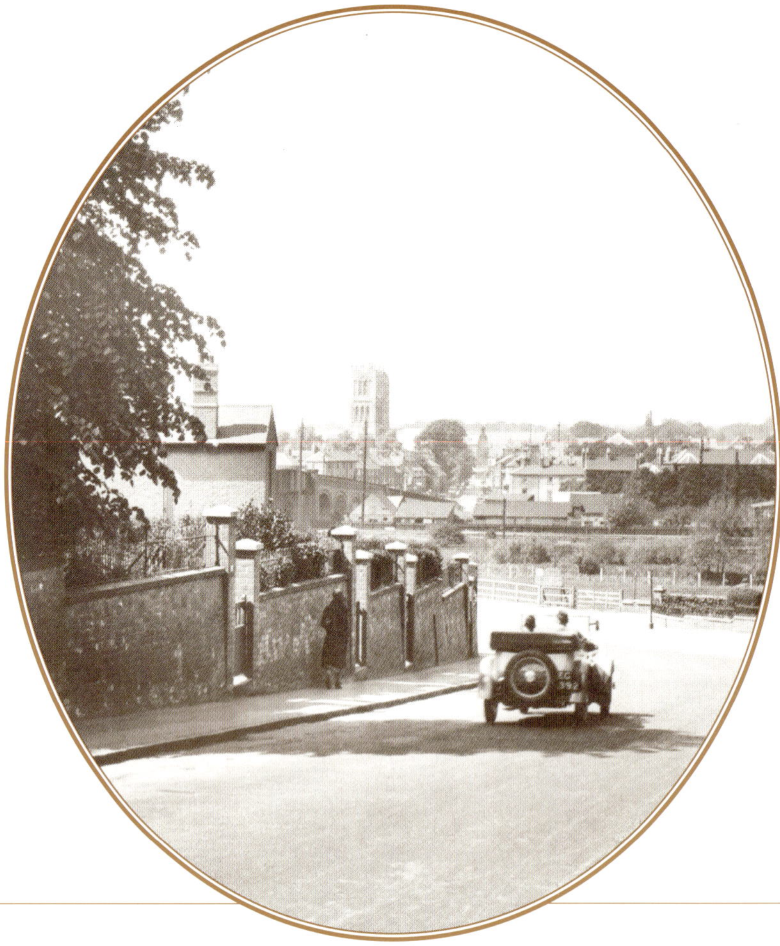

Right: Melton Mowbray, 1932 (85176) The parish church tower rises over the roofs.

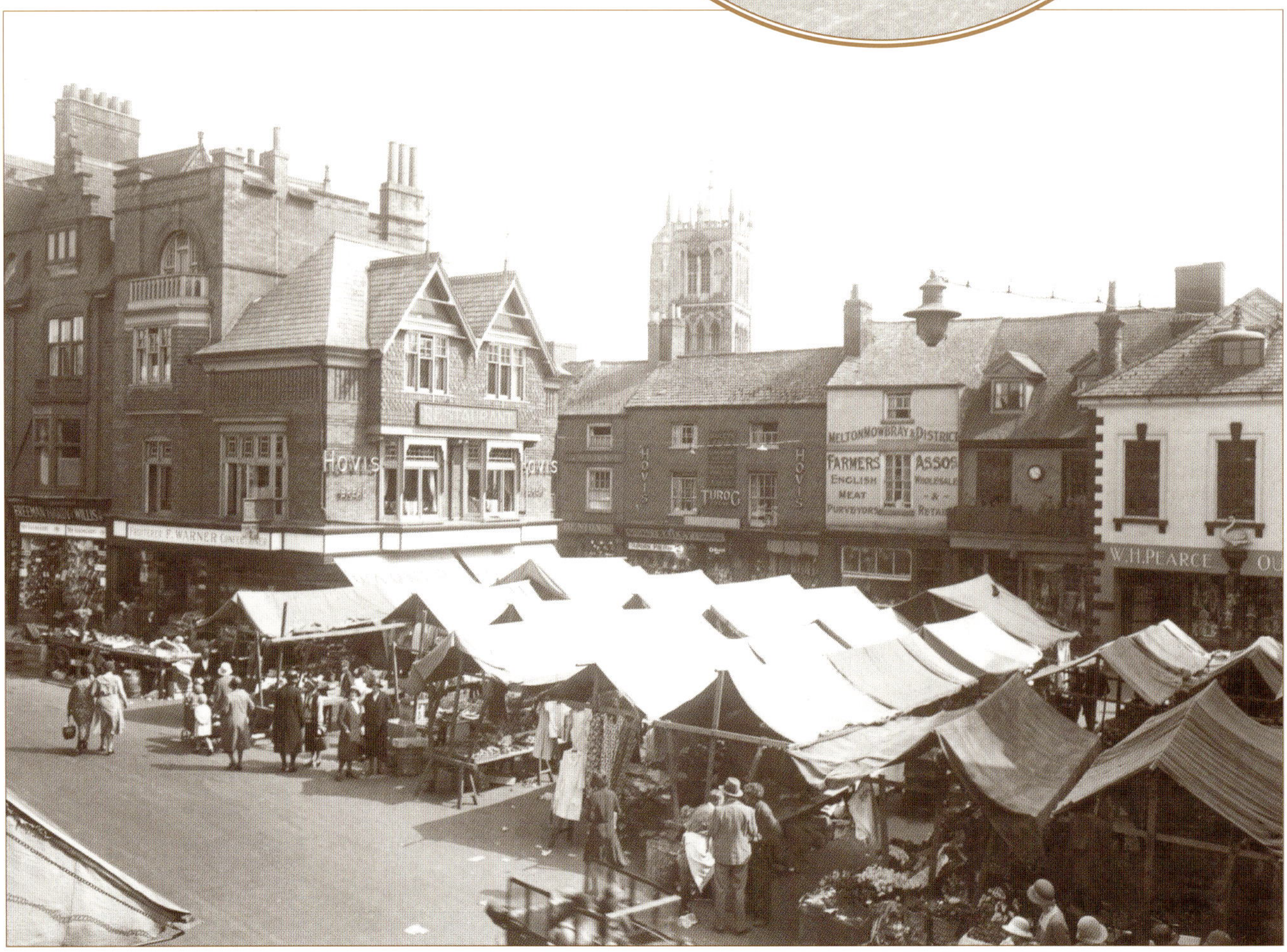

Above: Market Place, Melton Mowbray, 1932 (85169) While the huntsmen roared about the countryside, the town went about its daily life. Here, the market is in full swing. In the background is the headquarters of the Melton Mowbray Farmers' Association, wholesaling and retailing local meat. Note the old gilt Hovis signs above Warner's the fruiterer.

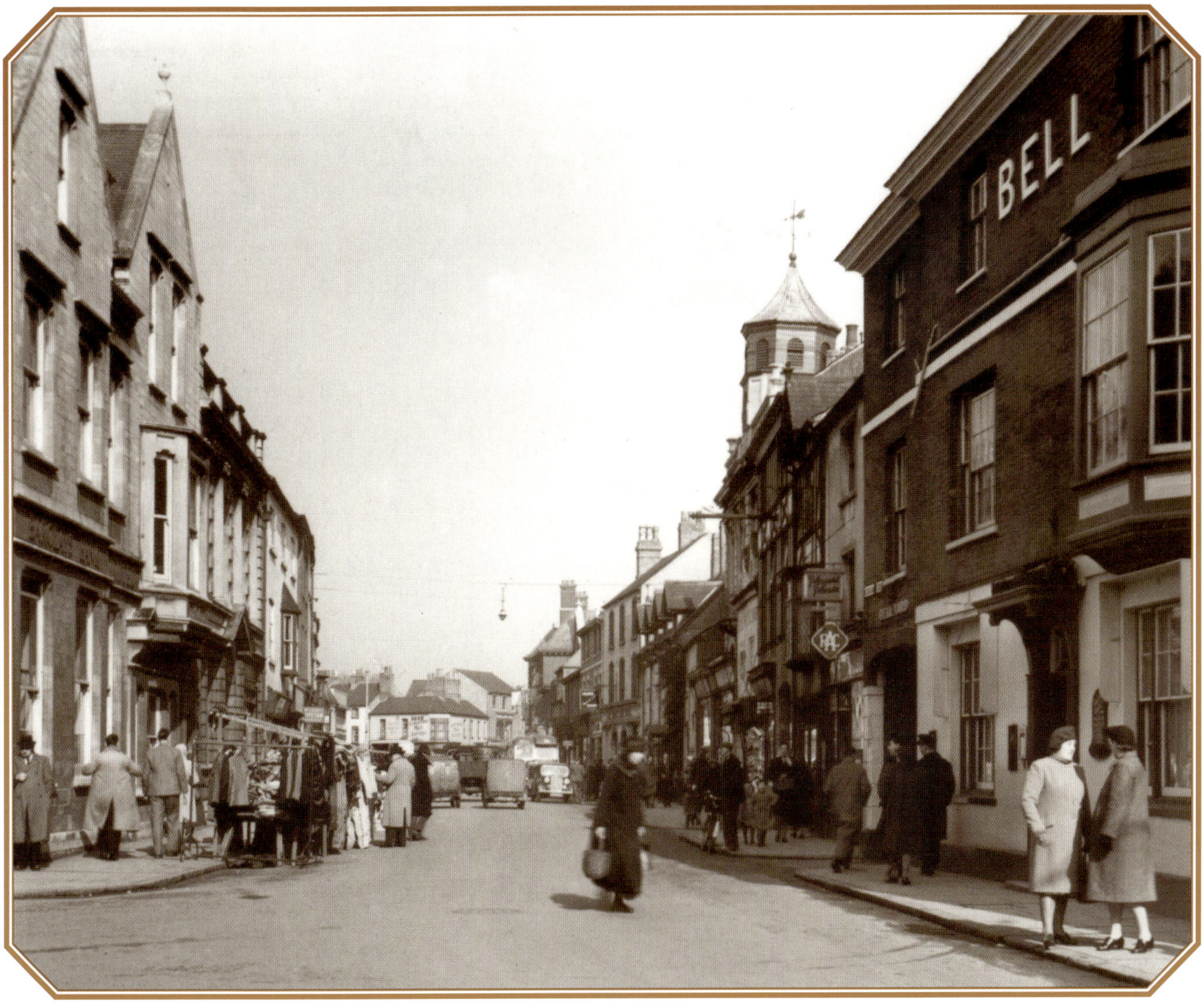

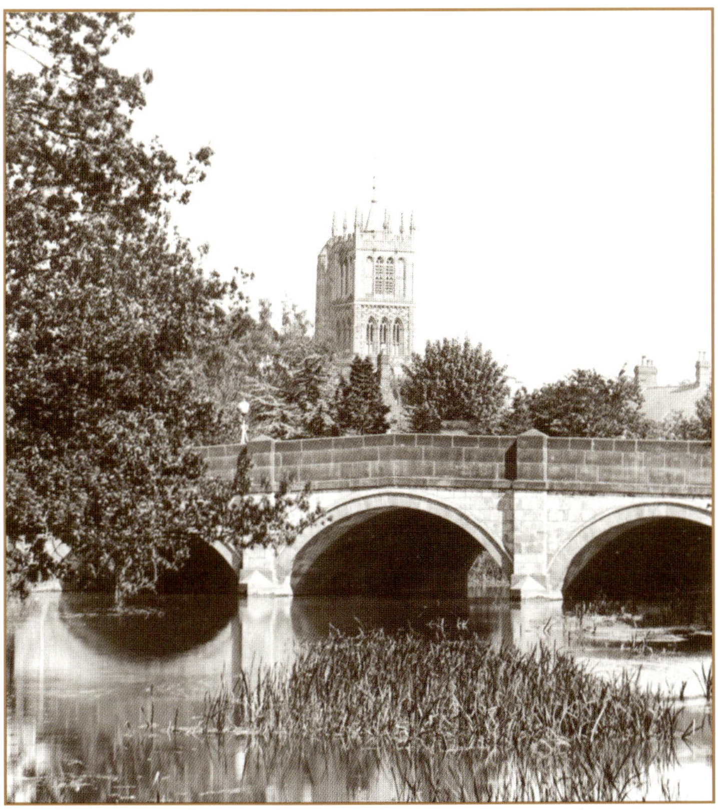

Above: Nottingham Street, Melton Mowbray, c1955 (M60031) On the right is the Bell Hotel. 'Nimrod', the hunting writer, notes how when he first visited the town there was only one inn, ' and that a very bad one'. Soon others sprung up. But none could match the opulence of the 'Old Club', where the members of the Quorn Hunt put their feet up and swapped tales of memorable runs, good fellowship and the open air life. 'Everything was as good as a first-rate man-cook can produce, and the wine of the best quality'.

Left: The Bridge and Church, Melton Mowbray, 1932 (85170) Leicestershire folk claim Melton's church is the most beautiful in England. It is like a cathedral in miniature, cruciform in shape, and with a lofty central tower. The River Wreake flows placidly under the town bridge.

LEICESTER. This thriving, prosperous and progressive city sits at the hub of rich farming country. Although we think of it as a major engineering centre, Leicester has a long history extending back to Roman times, and boasts the Jewry Wall, a massive brick and stone construction dating back to the second century AD. Many of the streets are narrow, cramped and crowded, confirming the city's great antiquity.

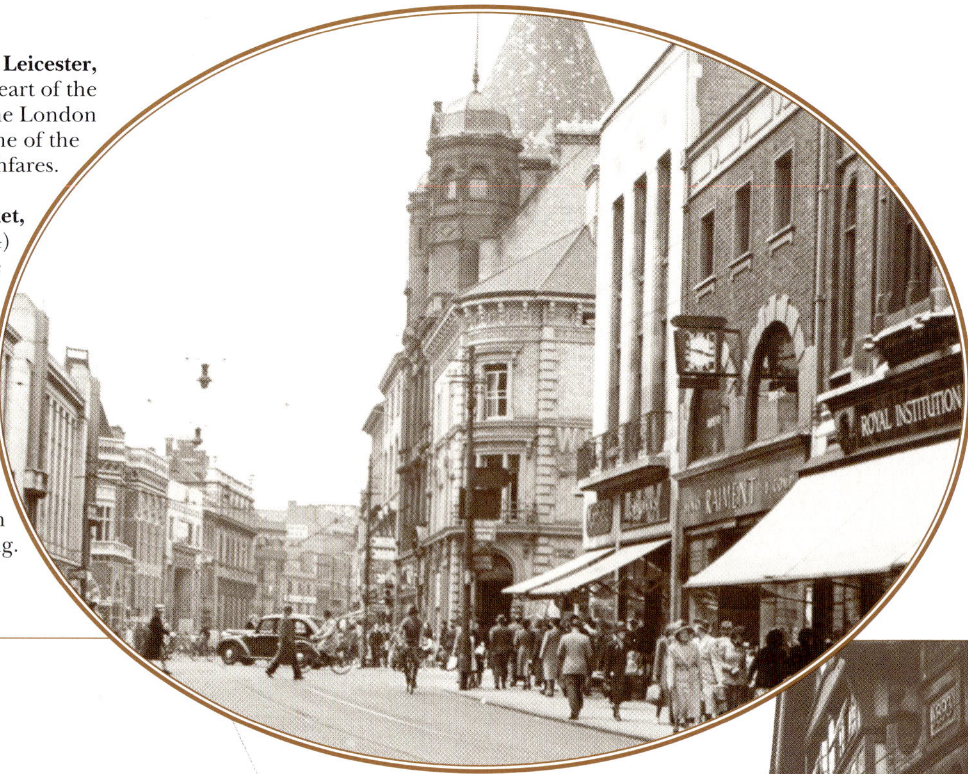

Right: Granby Street, Leicester, 1949 (L144032) In the heart of the city, leading off from the London Road, Granby Street is one of the main shopping thoroughfares.

Below: The Haymarket, Leicester, 1949 (L144034) Here is the city's theatre and the George Hotel. Note the overhead lines for the trolley buses. Timothy Whites' script name across the first floor would not be approved of by conservation societies today, but is nevertheless a splendid piece of sign making.

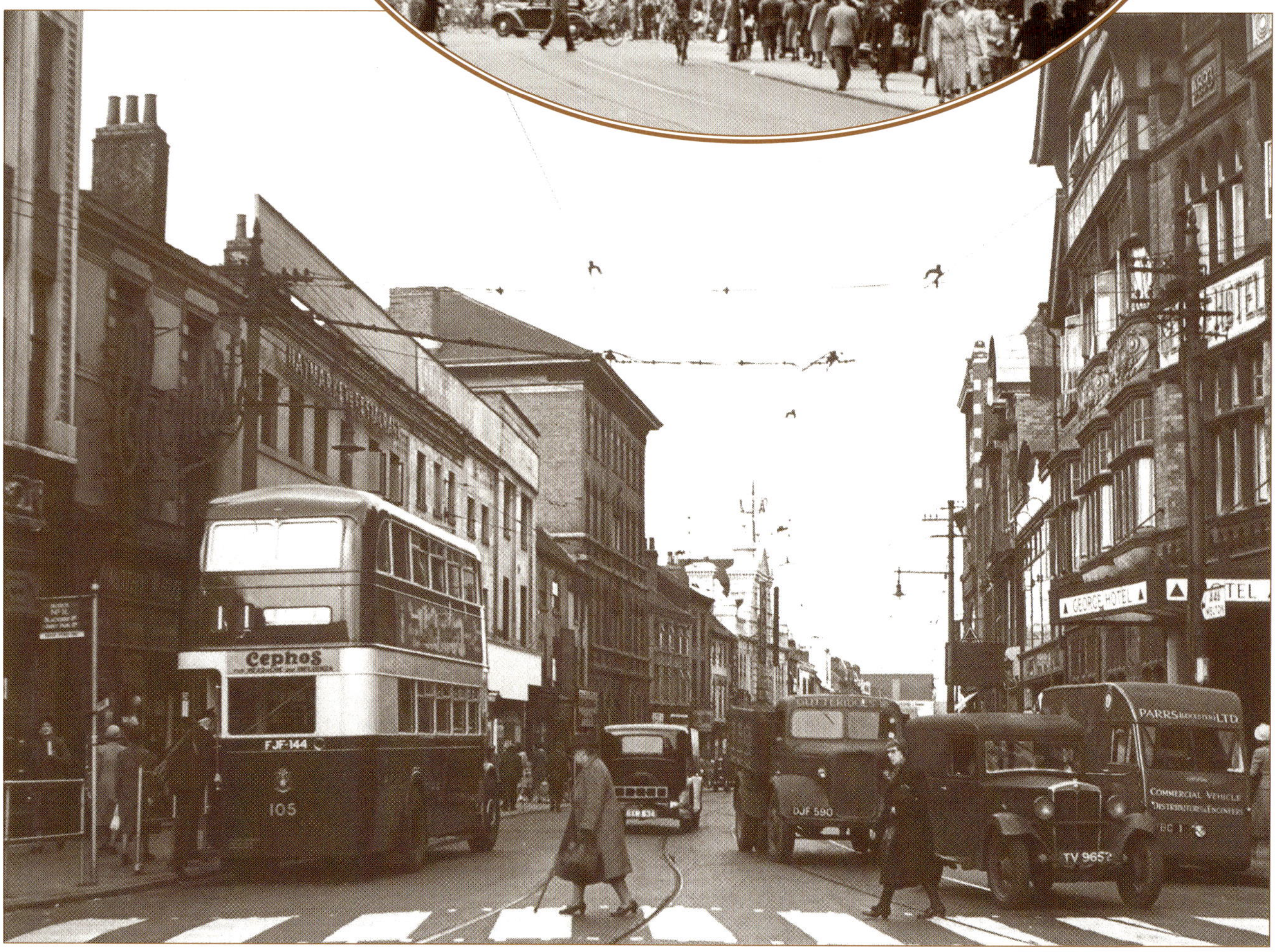

Opposite: The Clock Tower, Leicester, 1949 (L144002) This magnificent Gothic clock tower was constructed in 1868 to commemorate Simon de Montfort, William Wyggleston, Sir Thomas White and Gabriel Newton, noted benefactors of the town. The city must have always been very civic-minded: it was described in 1640 by John Taylor, the Water Poet, as 'so well paved and kept so clean of dunghills, filth or soil, that in the hottest and foulest weather, a man may go all over the town in a pair of slippers and never wet his feet.'

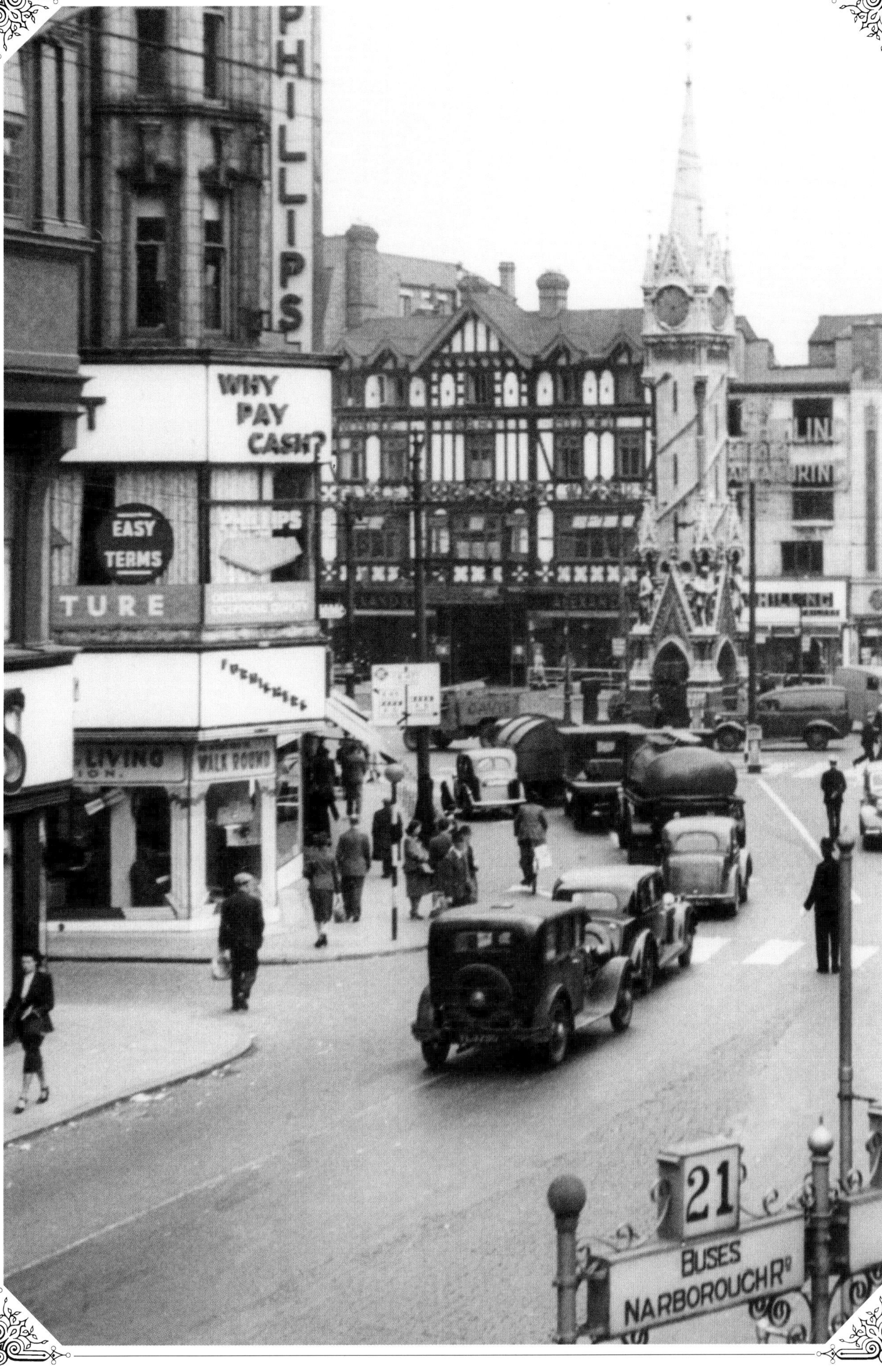
PHILLIPS
WHY PAY CASH?
EASY TERMS
TURE
LIVING
WALK ROUND
21
BUSES
NARBOROUGH Rd

LOUGHBOROUGH. In Victorian times Loughborough was little more than a village. Then John Taylor's world-famous bell foundry moved here from Oxford. The exploitative cottage framework knitting industry developed into a major factory industry and, very quickly, businesses of all kinds set up.

Right: Market Street, Loughborough, c1950 (L197028) On the left is Emerson's the house furnishers, who have been so successful they have expanded into several buildings along the street, all joined together by a single added frontage.

Below: Loughborough, c1955 (L197003) This photograph shows how Loughborough has rapidly expanded in recent years. The large modern shops, such as Harris's, contrast with the tiny shops (Coppock's, Martin's and Hilton's). Around the turn of the century most of the shops would have been as small as these. In their enthusiasm, Boots have given themselves a bigger than normal shopfront, cutting into the upper windows.

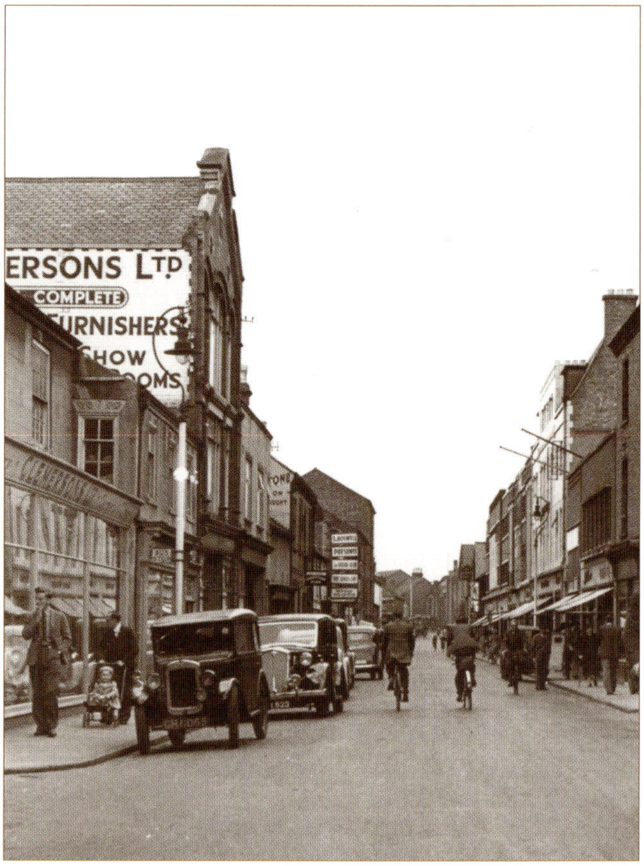

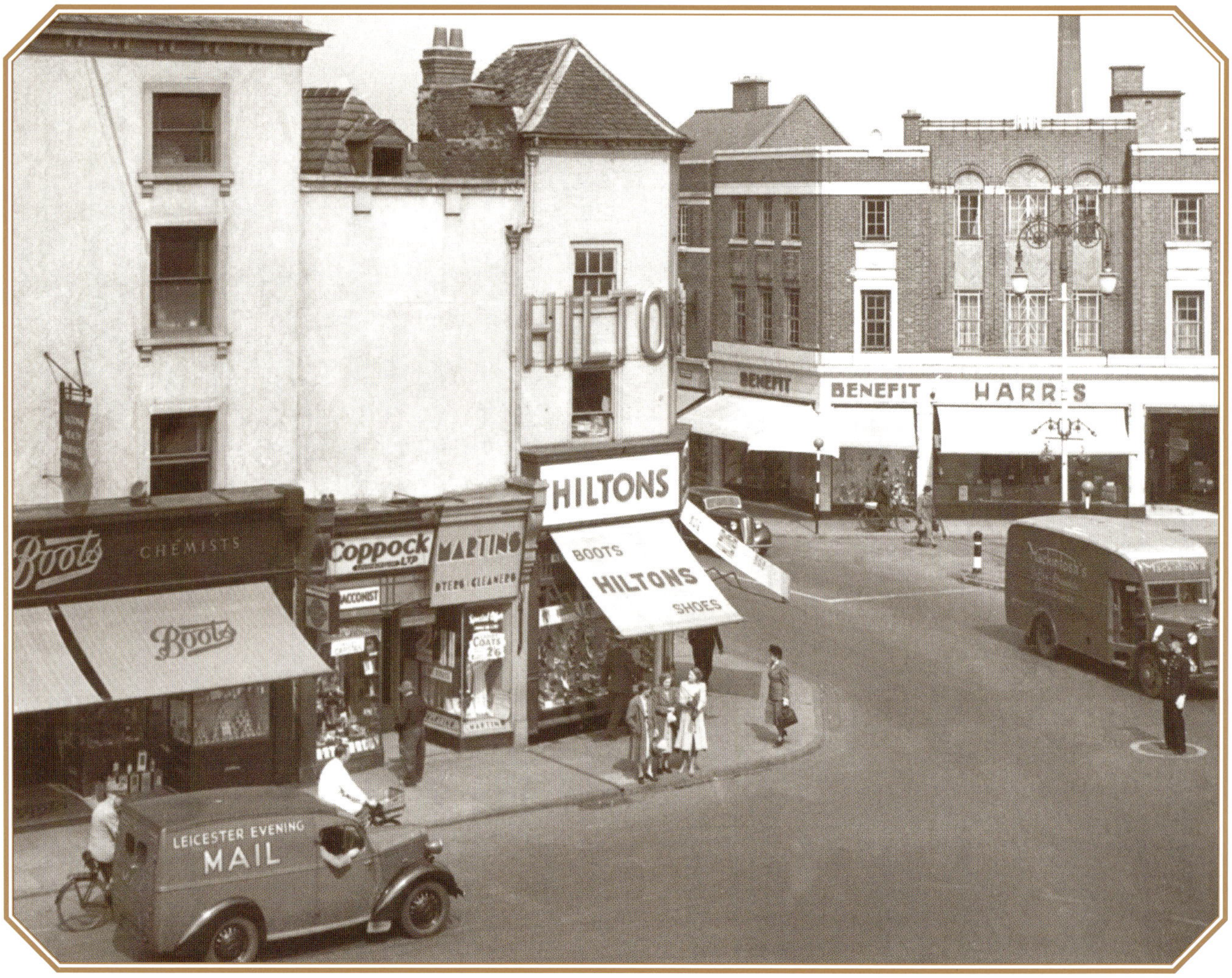

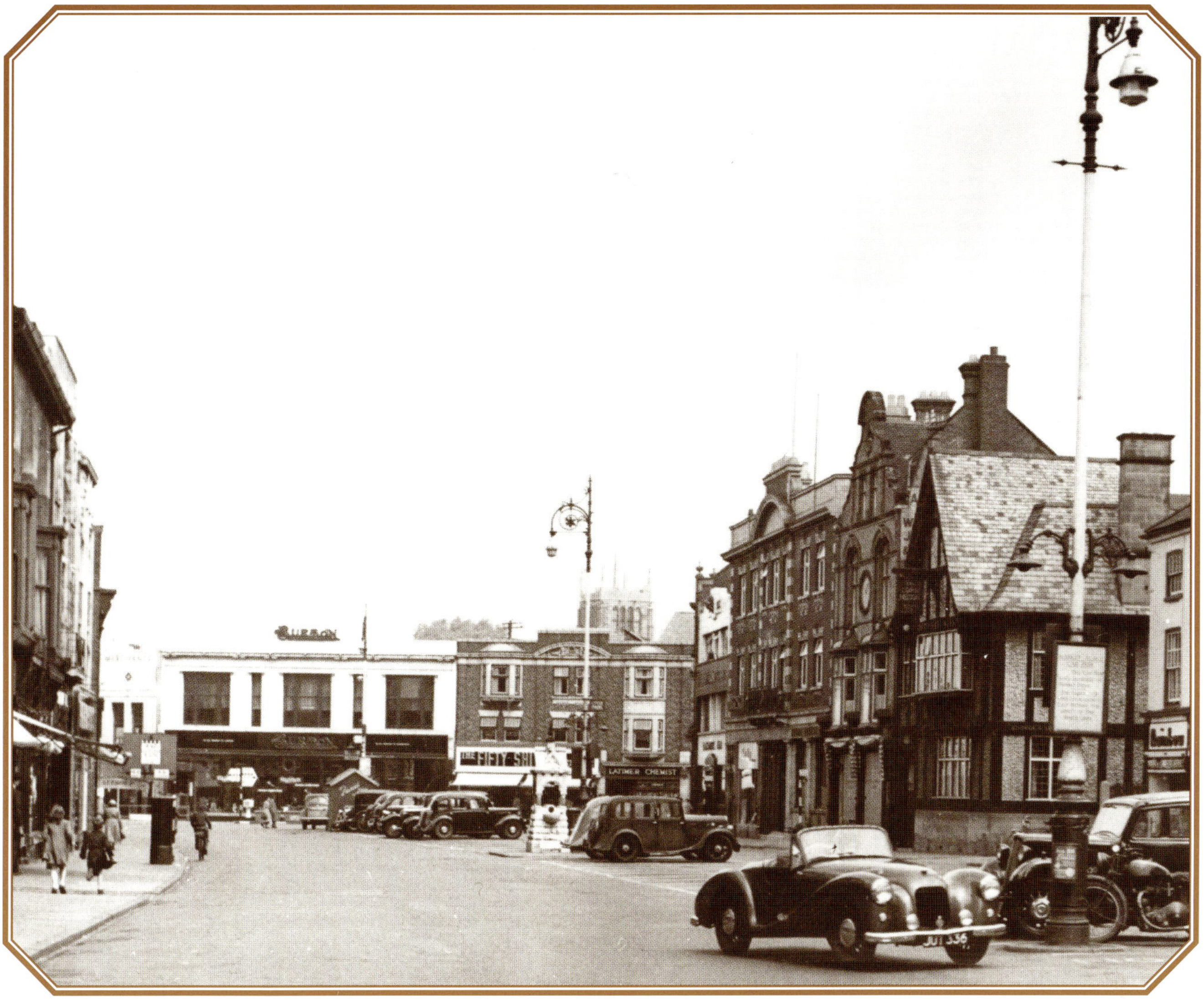

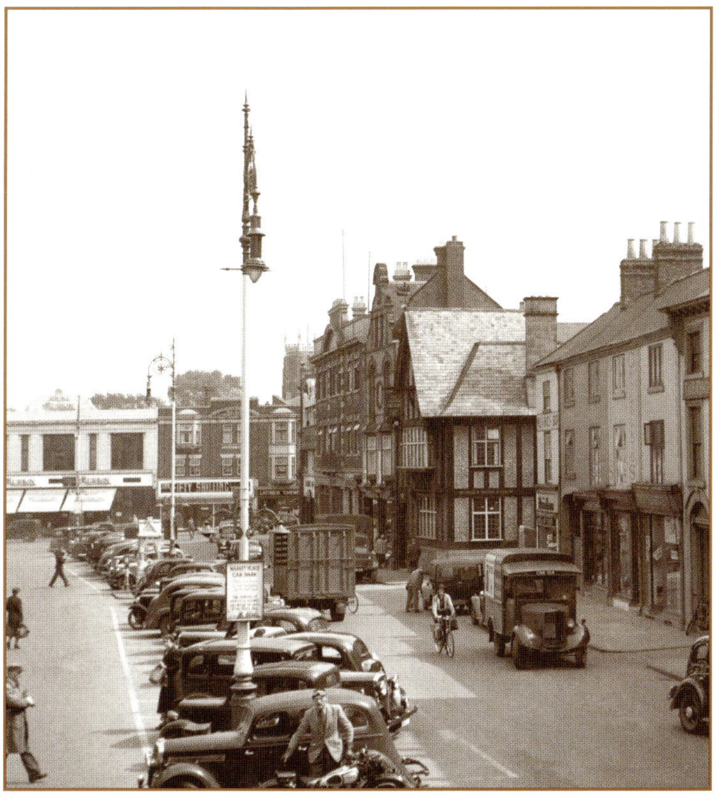

Above: Market Place, Loughborough, 1954 (L197050) Commentators have not been kind to Loughborough. One has said that it has lost almost all vestiges of antiquity, which have been 'ruthlessly swept away from the square'. Moreover, 'the Market Place has not size enough to be imposing, and the Town Hall is commonplace'. He was rather hard on the Town Hall, however, which is a pleasant building with a double bellcot. The Thursday market has been held here since 1206.

Left: Market Place, Loughborough, c1955 (L197019) On the right is the Midland Bank with its ornate columned porch, and just beyond, Keightley's Ironmongers and Seedsmen.

COVENTRY. In 1940, a single air-raid destroyed almost all of the historic heart of this great city. Famed for more than Lady Godiva, for centuries its clockmakers and silk weavers were supreme at their trade, until foreign competition led to a decline during the Victorian era. The city had to search for other routes to prosperity. In 1896, Daimler and Humber opened up factories, and Coventry quickly became an engineering and industrial centre, making cars, sewing machines, bicycles and the machinery of war. In this was its downfall. Its factories were a vital target for the Luftwaffe.

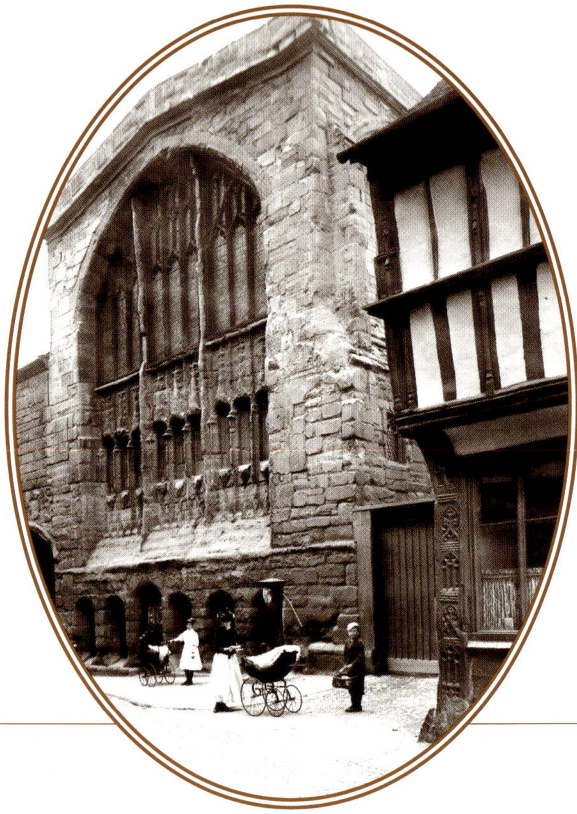

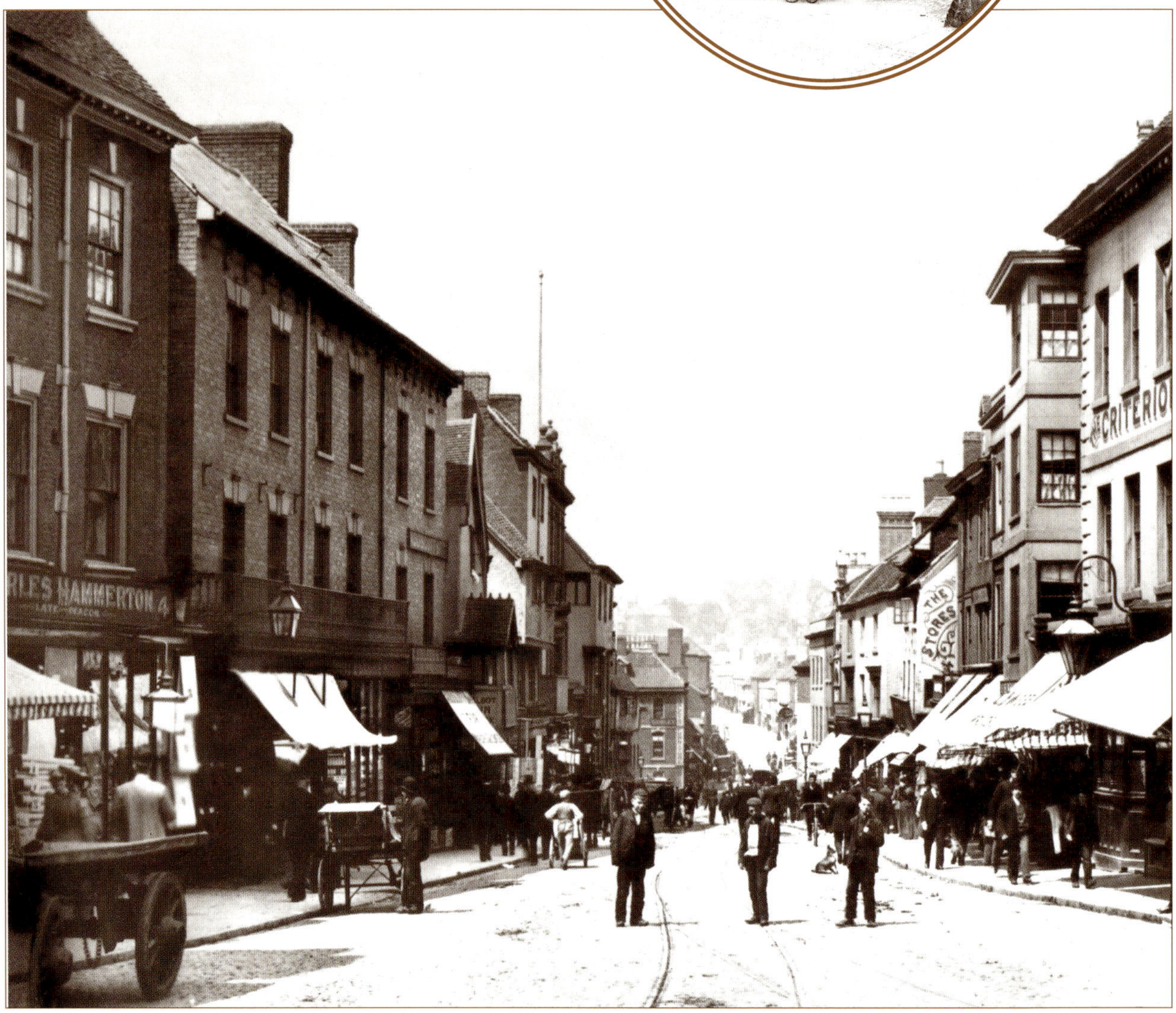

Top: St Mary's Hall, Coventry, 1892 (30929) This lovely old red sandstone building, much weathered and worn, was once the Guildhall. The city was very affluent in medieval times, the Merchants' Guild powerful and influential. St Mary's possesses some excellent early stained glass and a magnificent tapestry four centuries old, woven locally. **Above: Bishop Street. 1892** (30914) A bustling shopping thoroughfare leading northwards out of the city towards the canal basin.

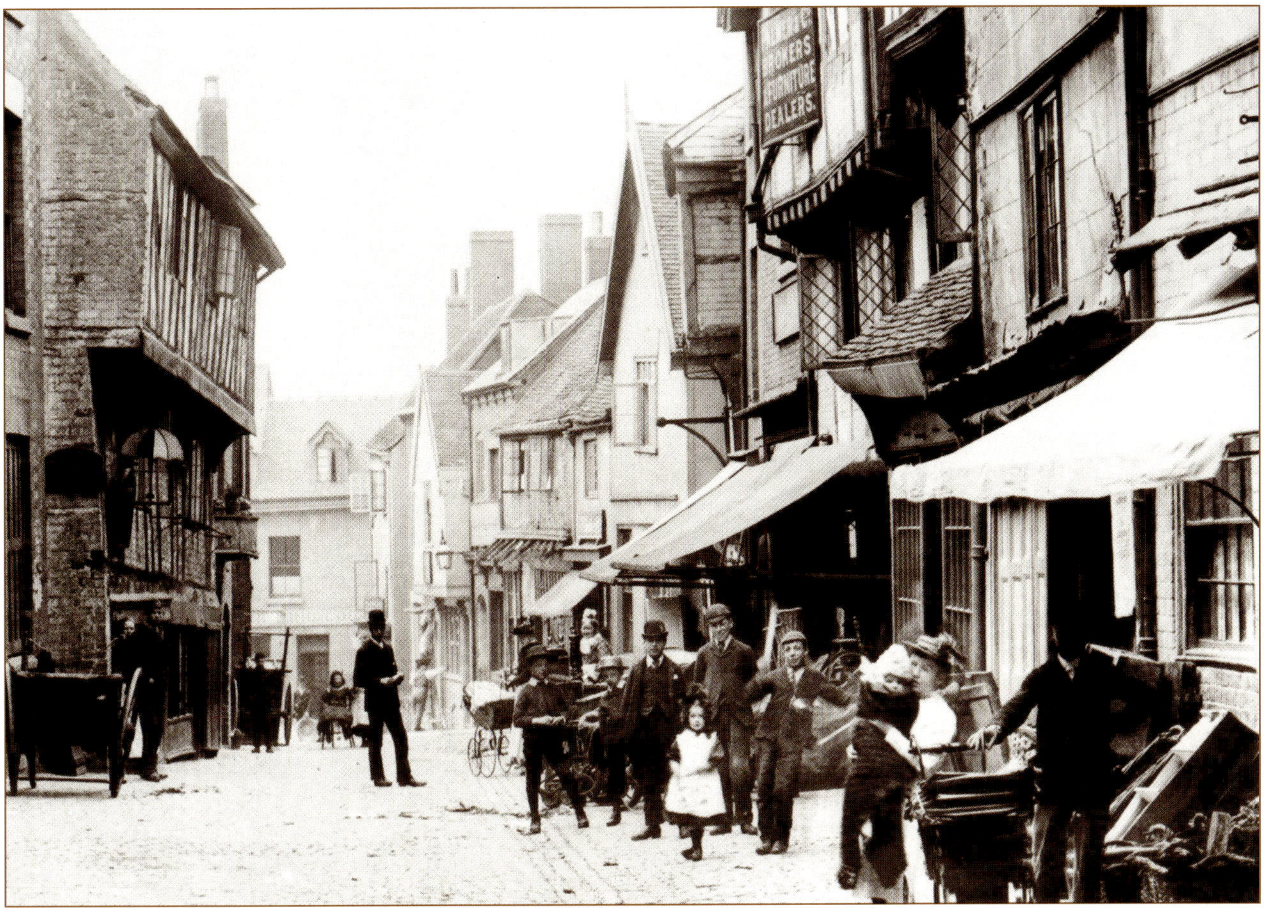

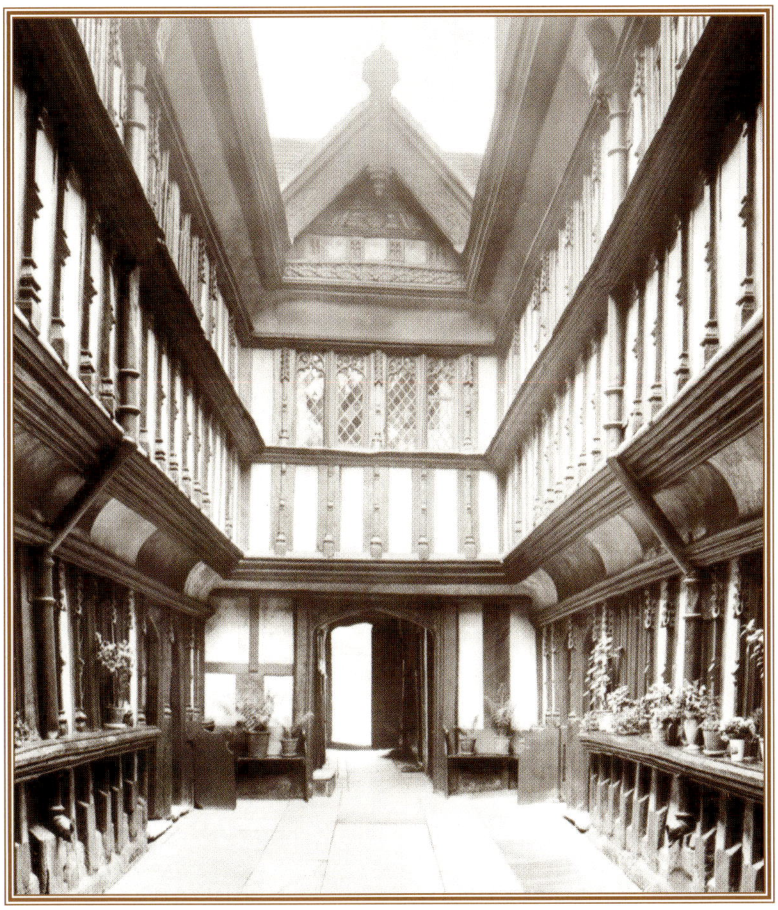

Above: Butcher's Row, Coventry, 1892 (30916A) A beautiful cobbled medieval street of jettied buildings. It gives a very clear impression of how most of Coventry would have looked a few hundred years ago. The buildings are of all shapes and sizes, yet combine to create a harmonious prospect. Note the tiny shops - on the left there is a barber's pole and, just beyond, an umbrella shop. Goods and furniture are heaped up on the right. Could it be an eviction? Is that the bailiff in the middle of the street serving his summons?

Left: Ford's Hospital, Coventry, 1892 (30918) Behind Greyfriars Lane is this exquisite Tudor timbered building with its richly-carved archway, founded by William Ford in 1529. Its history is picked out on barge boards over the courtyard windows, describing how the almshouses were 'for five men and one woman each given 5d a week'.

BIRMINGHAM. Britain's second city prospered as a result of the Industrial Revolution. Factories and workshops sprang up making everything from buttons to steam engines. Civic pride was fostered, too, and during the Victorian era the city became studded with great churches, galleries and public buildings.

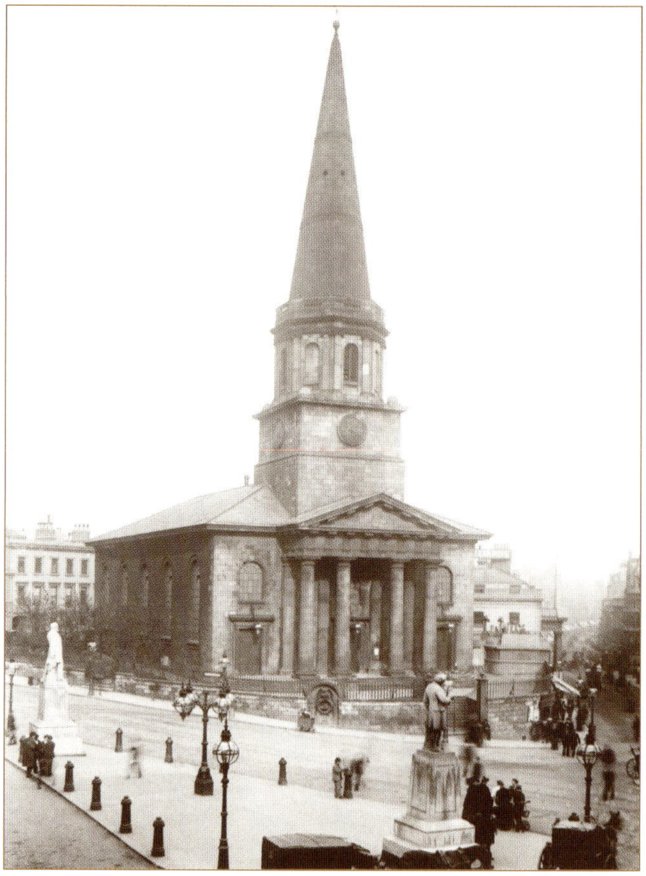

Right: Christchurch, Victoria Square, Birmingham, 1896 (37276) This superb 18th-century city church graced the broad open space at the corner of Colemore Row and New Street. By the end of Victoria's reign it had became redundant, unable to muster a big enough congregation. It was finally demolished in the 1890s. The area is now part of Victoria Square. Queen Victoria still stares regally down on passers by.

Below: Paradise Street, Birmingham, 1896 (37274) The canal wharf ran up close to this street until the 1920s. Here were the old Birmingham Medical School and the Midland Institute.

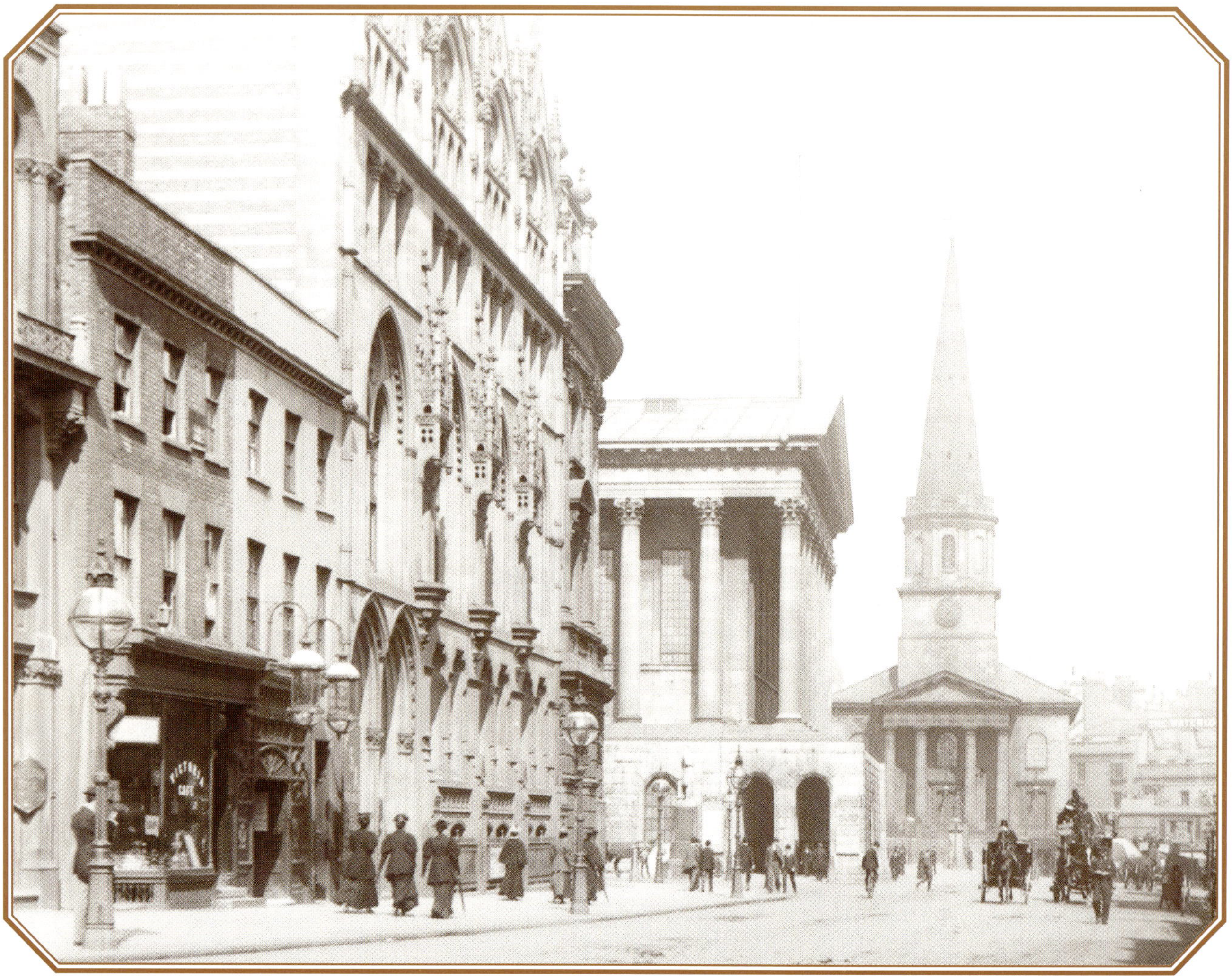

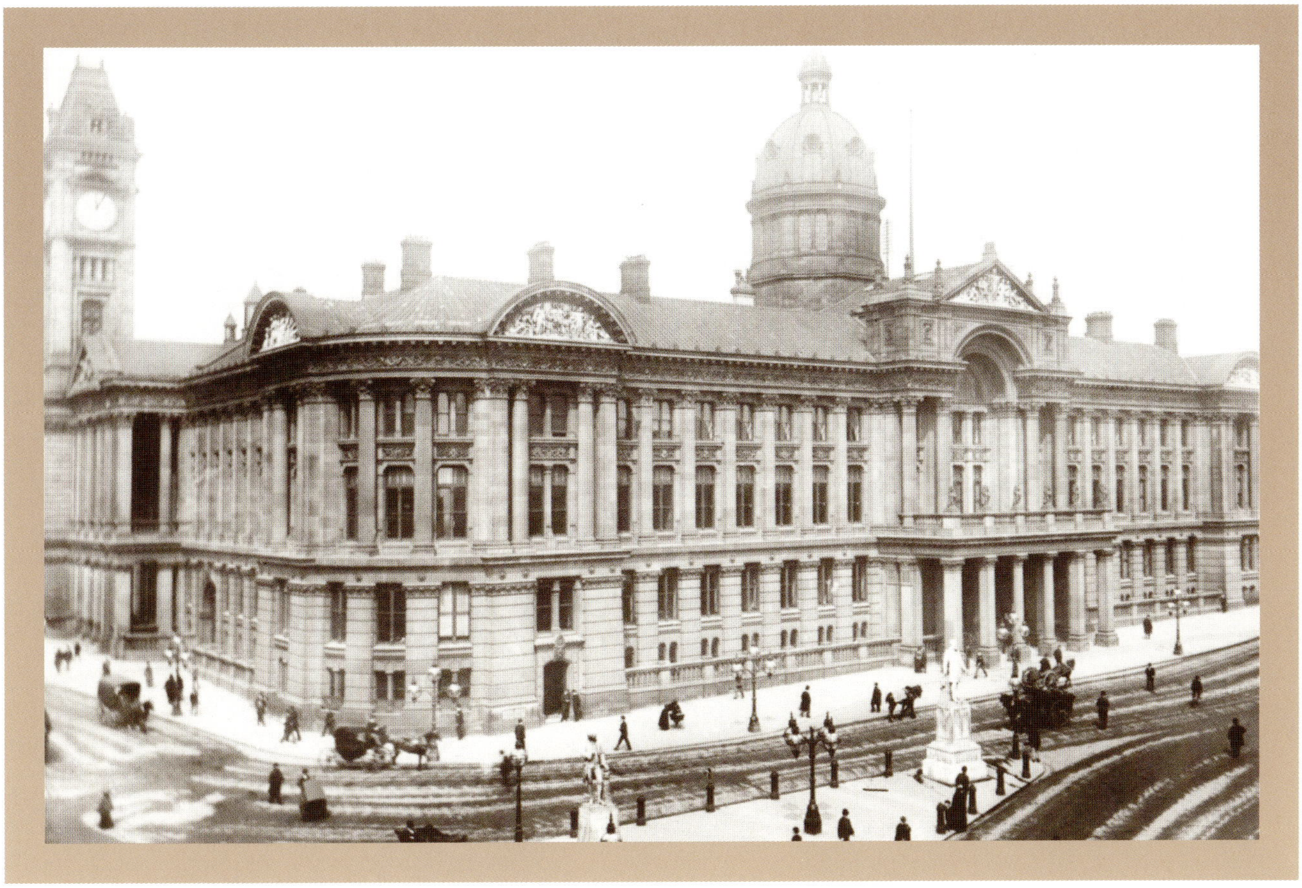

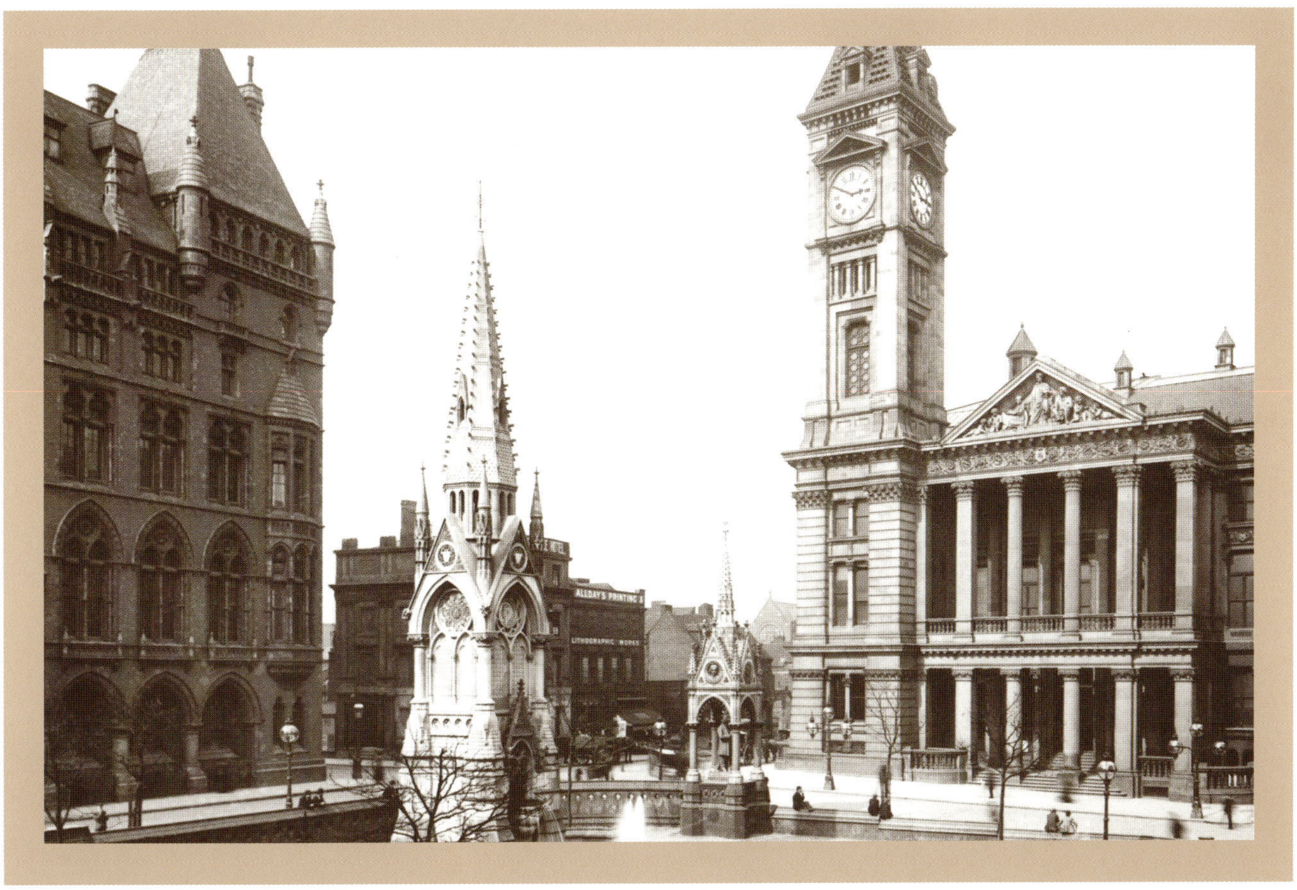

Top: Council House, Birmingham, 1896 (37277) Carriages clatter by the Council House's elegant facade and dome, built in 1879 at a cost of £84,000. The tower of the Art Gallery with its clockface known affectionately as 'Big Brum' rises up over the city behind. **Above: The Art Gallery, Birmingham, 1896** (37279) Built in 1885, this grand building houses a fine collection of Pre-Raphaelite paintings, including canvases by Rossetti, Holman Hunt. Ford Madox Brown and Millais.

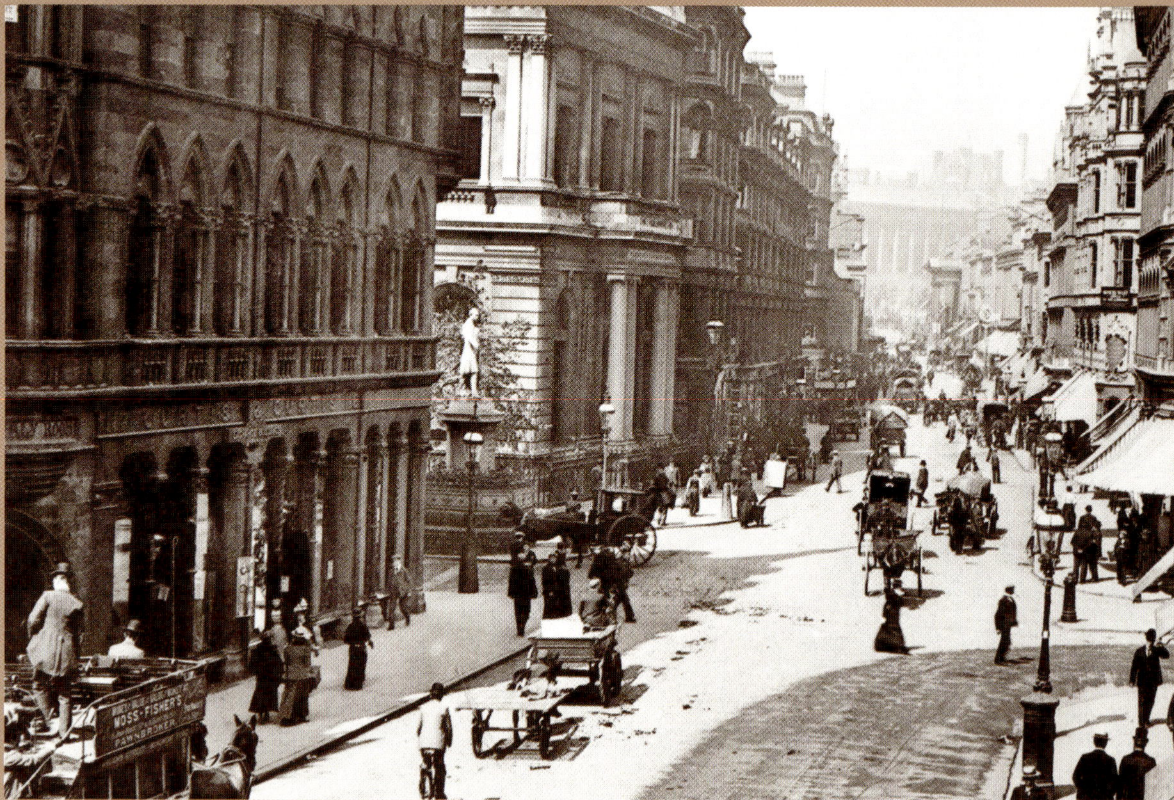
MOSS-FISHER'S
PAWNBROKER

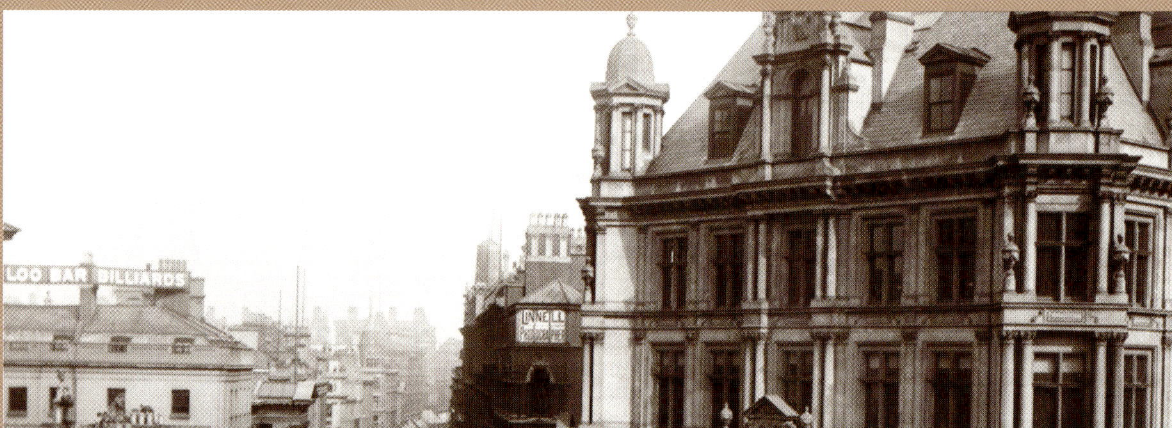
LOO BAR BILLIARDS

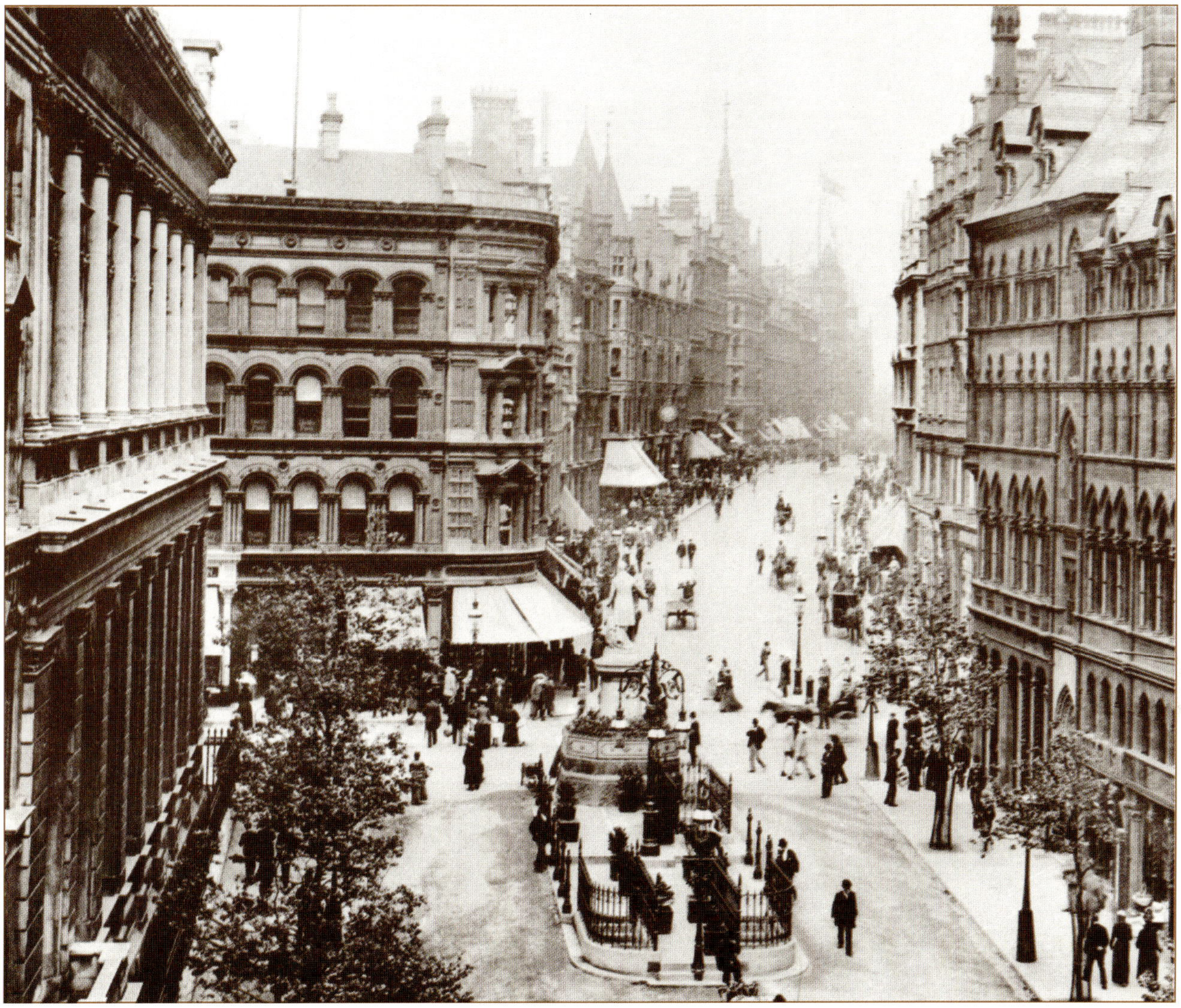

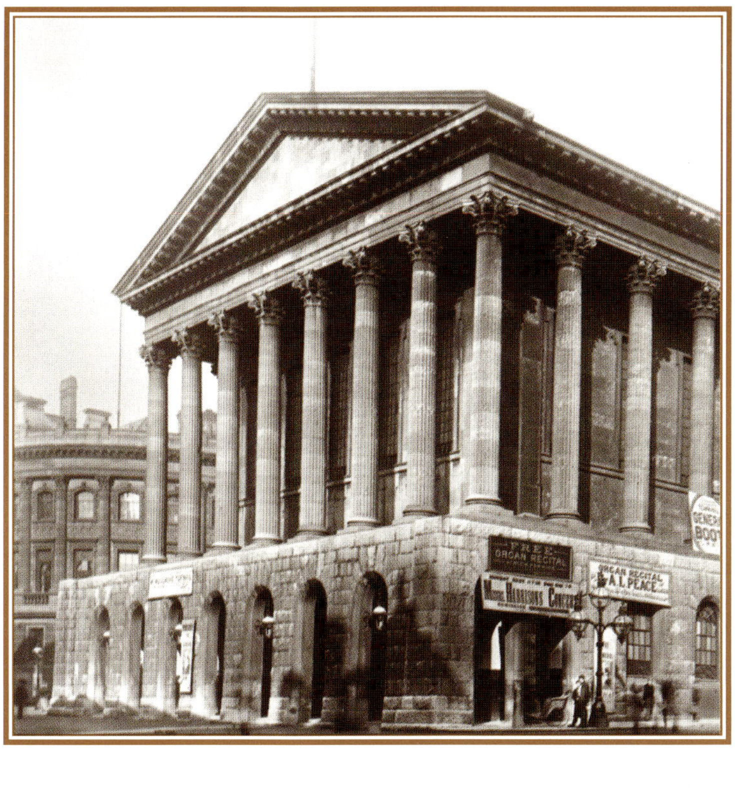

Above: Corporation Street, Birmingham, 1890 (B100002) A street of prestigious Victorian office and public buildings, reflecting the city's growing prosperity and influence.

Left: Town Hall, Birmingham, 1896 (37275) Hugh Miller described driving up New Street in 1845 and seeing this stately building for the first time: 'A noble building of Anglesea marble, of which Athens in its best days might not have been ashamed'.

Opposite top: New Street, Birmingham, 1890 (B100001) A horse-drawn bus threads its way through the city's streets. The fare to New Street Station was 1d. It is advertising Moss-Fisher's pawnbroking business, which offers 'Money-Value-Money-Value'.

Opposite below: New Street, Birmingham, 1896 (37270) Photographed from the Town Hall (pictured left), this picture shows Sir Robert Peel's statue before it was demolished by a lorry in the 1920s. On the right is the Post Office.

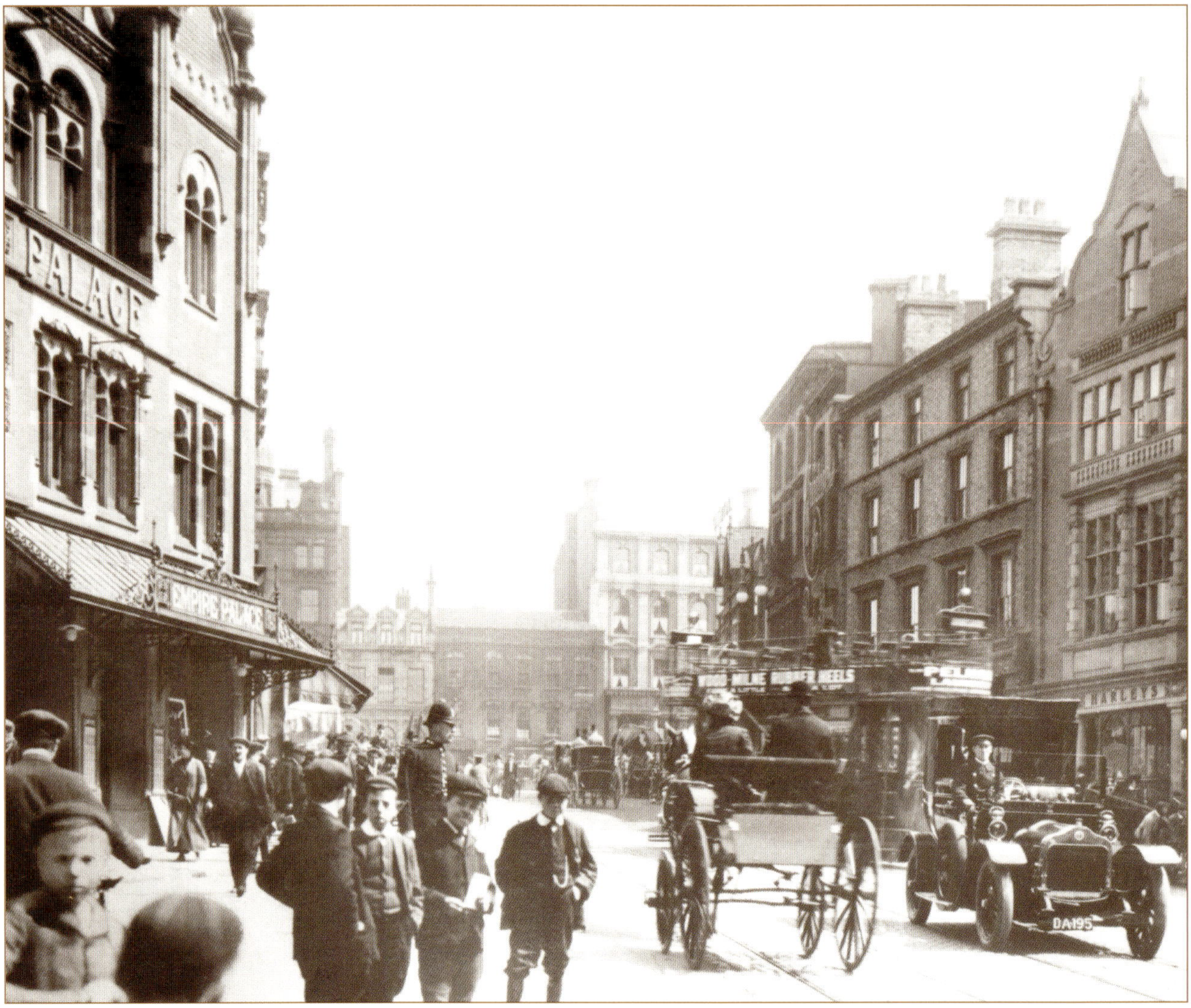

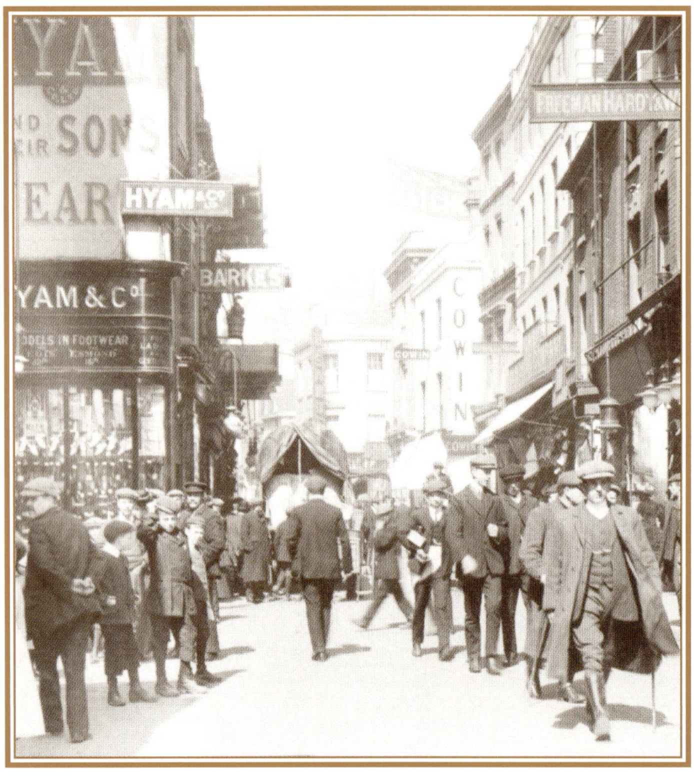

Above: Queen Square, Wolverhampton, c1910 (W285002) On the left is the Empire Palace. A policeman glances across at the chauffeur-driven car to see which dignitary has turned up on his patch.

Left: Dudley Street, Wolverhampton, c1900 (W285007) Hyam and Co are offering 'Three Models in Footwear' to wealthy clients: The Esmond 16/6, the Eric 10/6 and the Denis 12/6. The man striding along in boots and overcoat has the air of a gentleman farmer.

Opposite top: Queen Street, Wolverhampton, c1900 (W285001) Two uniformed, top-hatted coachmen drive by each other without a sideways glance, mindful of their dignity.

Opposite below: Victoria Street, Wolverhampton, c1910 (W285005) John Grant has packed the pavement in front of his imposing showrooms with rolls of linoleum and carpet.

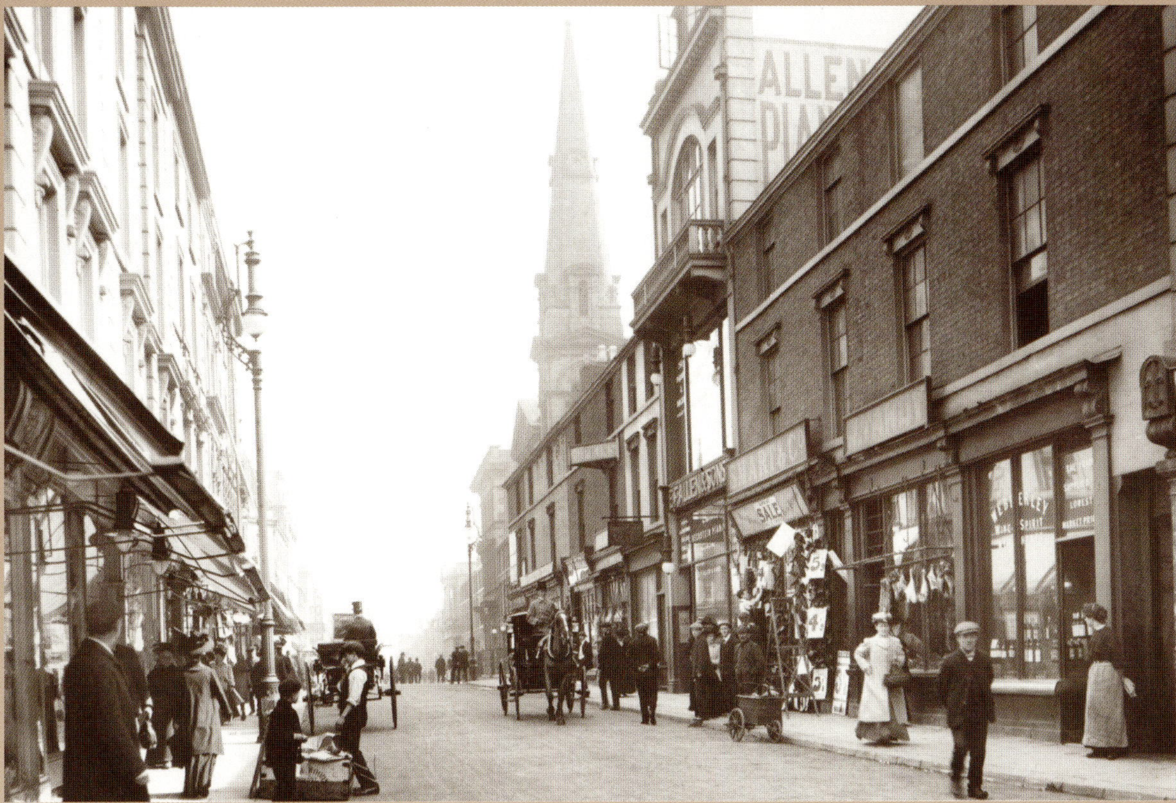
ALLEN
SALE

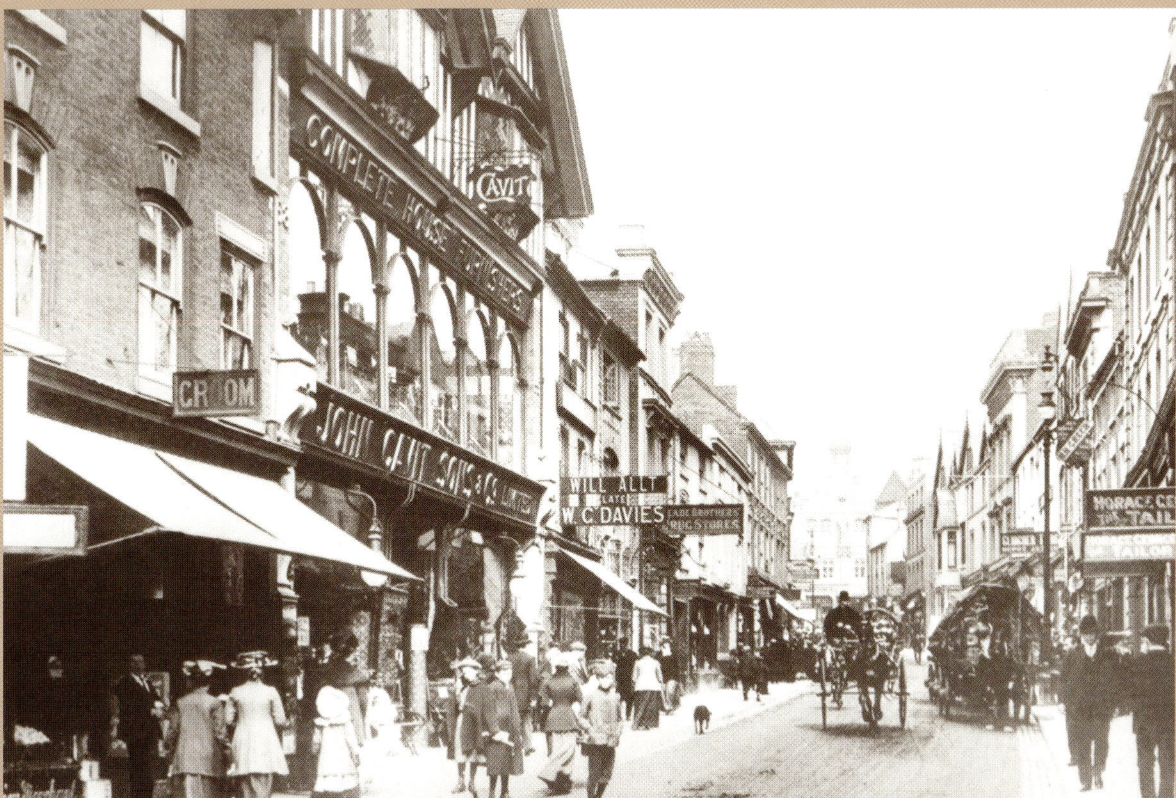
COMPLETE HOUSE FURNISHERS
WILL ALLT
LATE
W.C. DAVIES

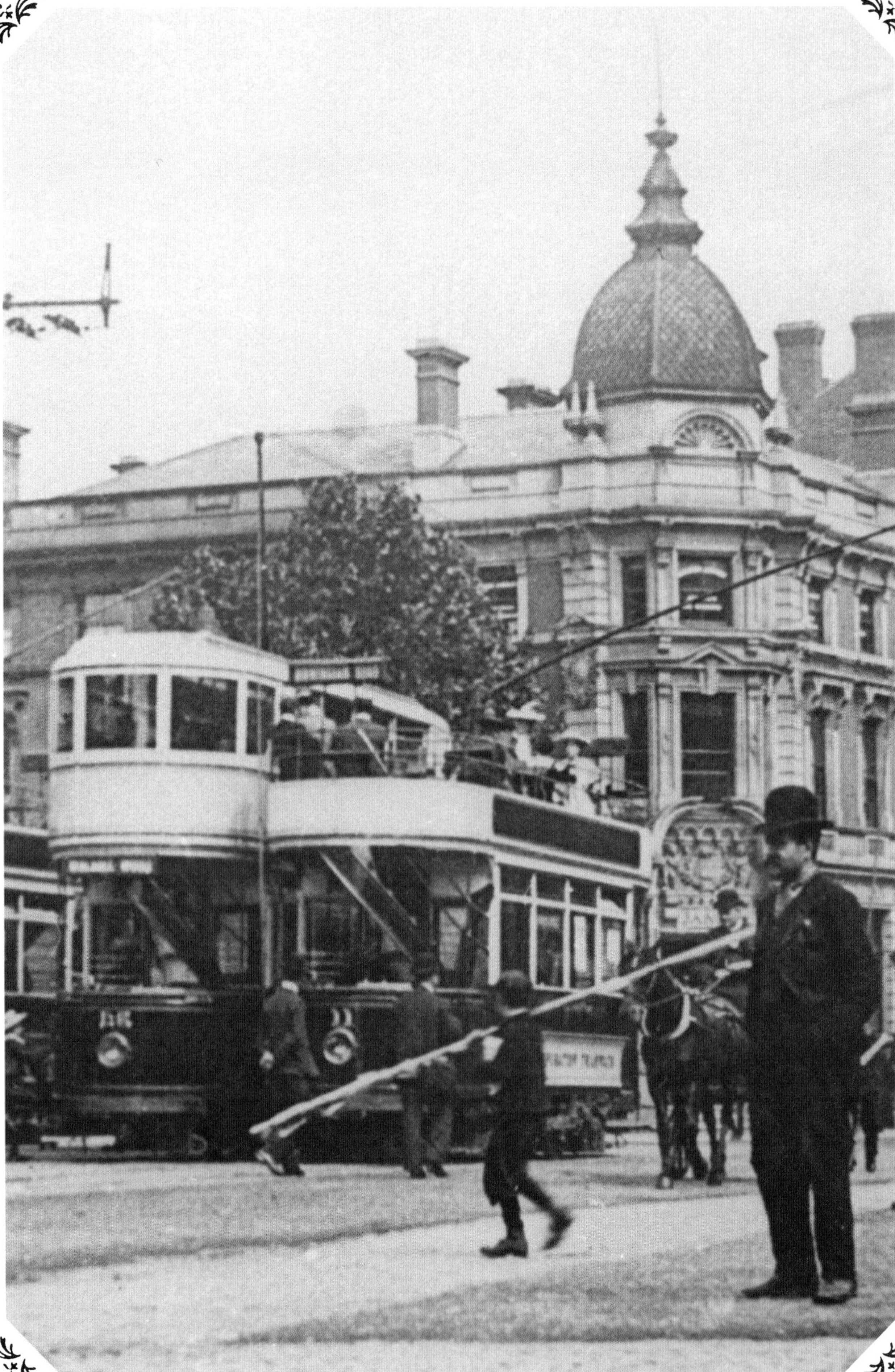

Opposite: The Bridge, Walsall, 1908 (W161001) Tagged 'The Town of a Hundred Trades', including the working of leather, Walsall was the birthplace of the writer Jerome K Jerome. Here the trolley buses unravel their connections to the overhead lines. A small boy is carrying the pole that is used to transfer the lines over. The Bridge is the heart of Walsall town, and is the home of a statue to Dorothy Pattison, who was nicknamed Sister Dora. A staunchly public-spirited Victorian lady, she looked after the the town poor, many of whom had suffered accidents in the factories, long before the days of health and safety legislation and industrial insurance.

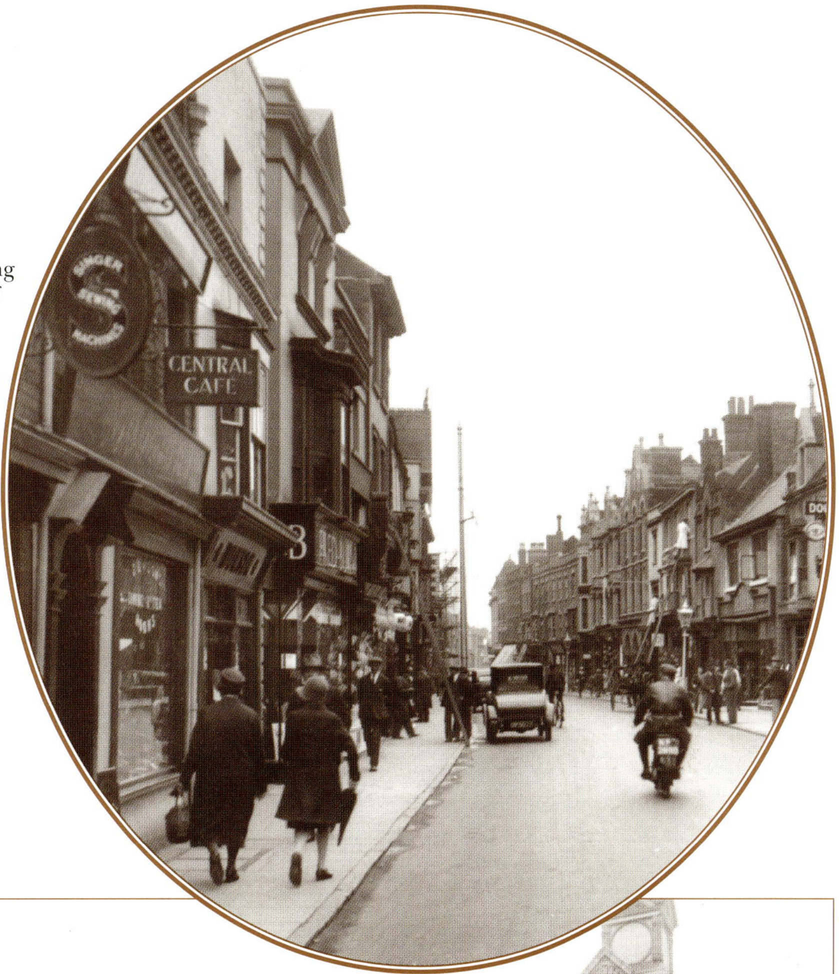

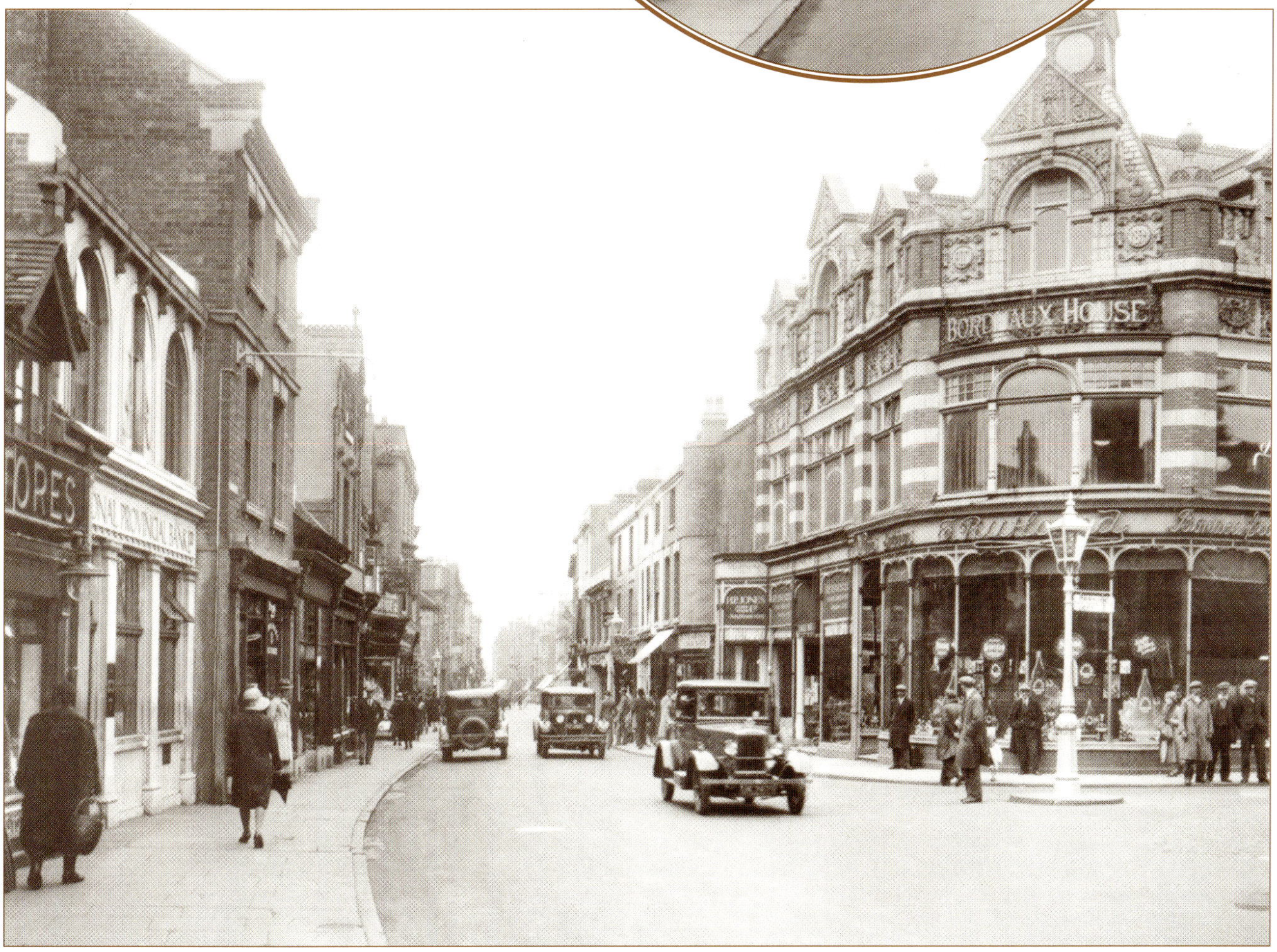

Top: High Street, Stourbridge, 1931 (84688) This thriving and pleasant industrial town on the edge of the Black Country is famous for its many industries, including glassmaking, engineering, ironworks, brick and tile making and tanning. Its weekly market was established far back in the 14th century. **Above: High Street, Stourbridge, 1931** (84685)

LICHFIELD. From whatever direction the traveller approaches the city, his first sight will be the beautiful 'Ladies of the Vale', the three soaring spires of the cathedral. Dr Samuel Johnson was born here, and his statue stands in the Market Place with that of his friend and biographer, James Boswell. With its six royal charters, its own sheriff, and its rich heritage of fine Tudor and Georgian buildings, Lichfield's reputation as a handsome city is richly deserved.

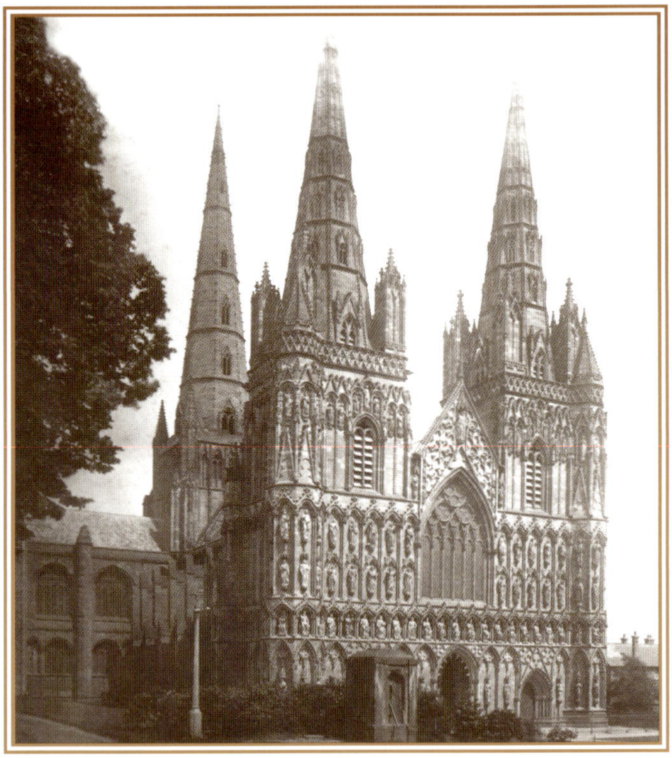

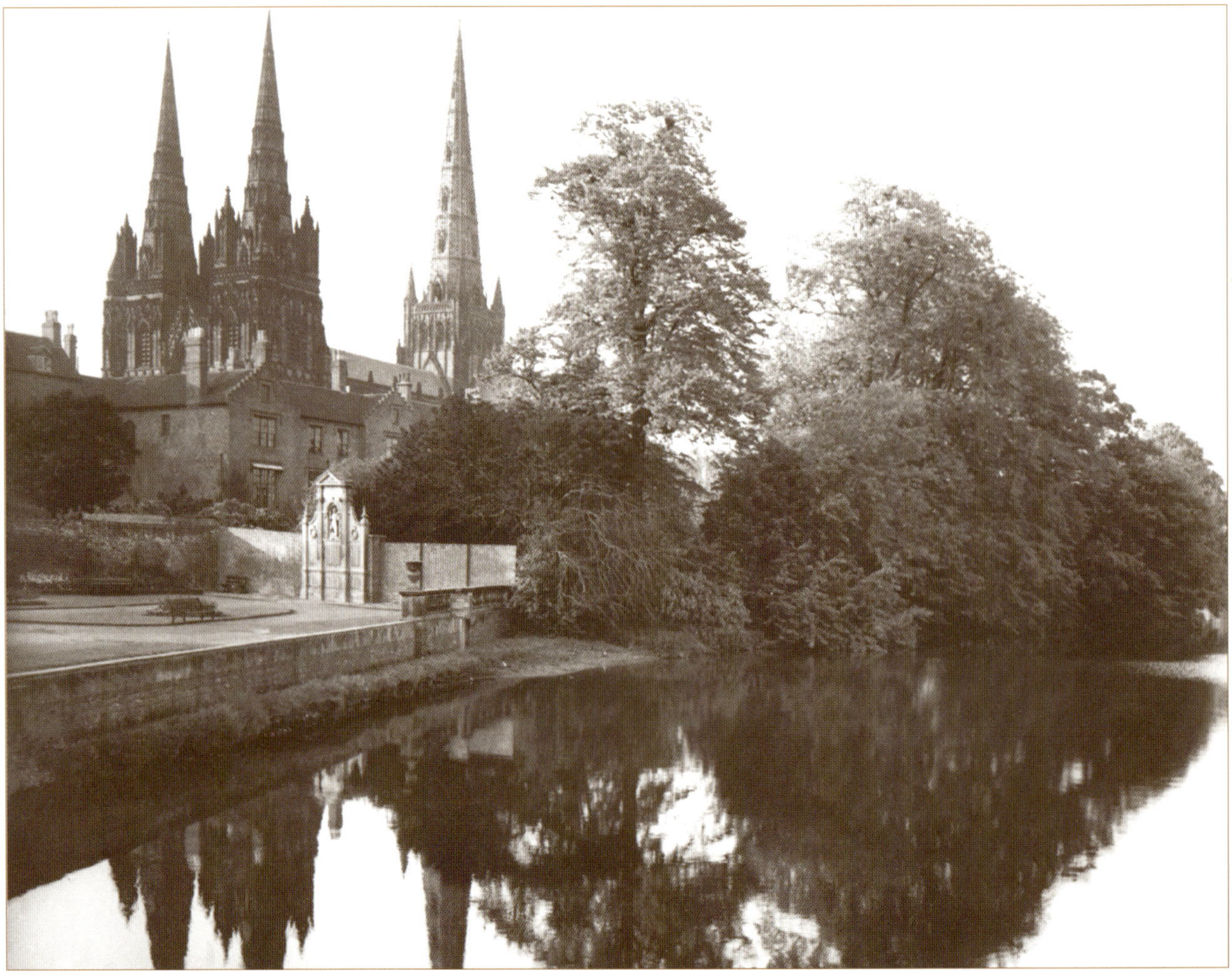

Top: The Cathedral, Lichfield, 1887 (20219) This historic red sandstone cathedral, with its three lofty spires, is the mother church of the Midlands. Since 700 AD, when the first holy building was built here, Lichfield has been a place of pilgrimage. The spectacular west front is richly decorated with more than a hundred statues, as well as arcading, trefoils and cinquefoils, and a beautiful geometric stained glass window. **Above: The Cathedral from the Minster Pool, 1969** (L45064) This magnificent prospect of the south side of the cathedral offers glimpses of the gardens of the buildings in the Close.

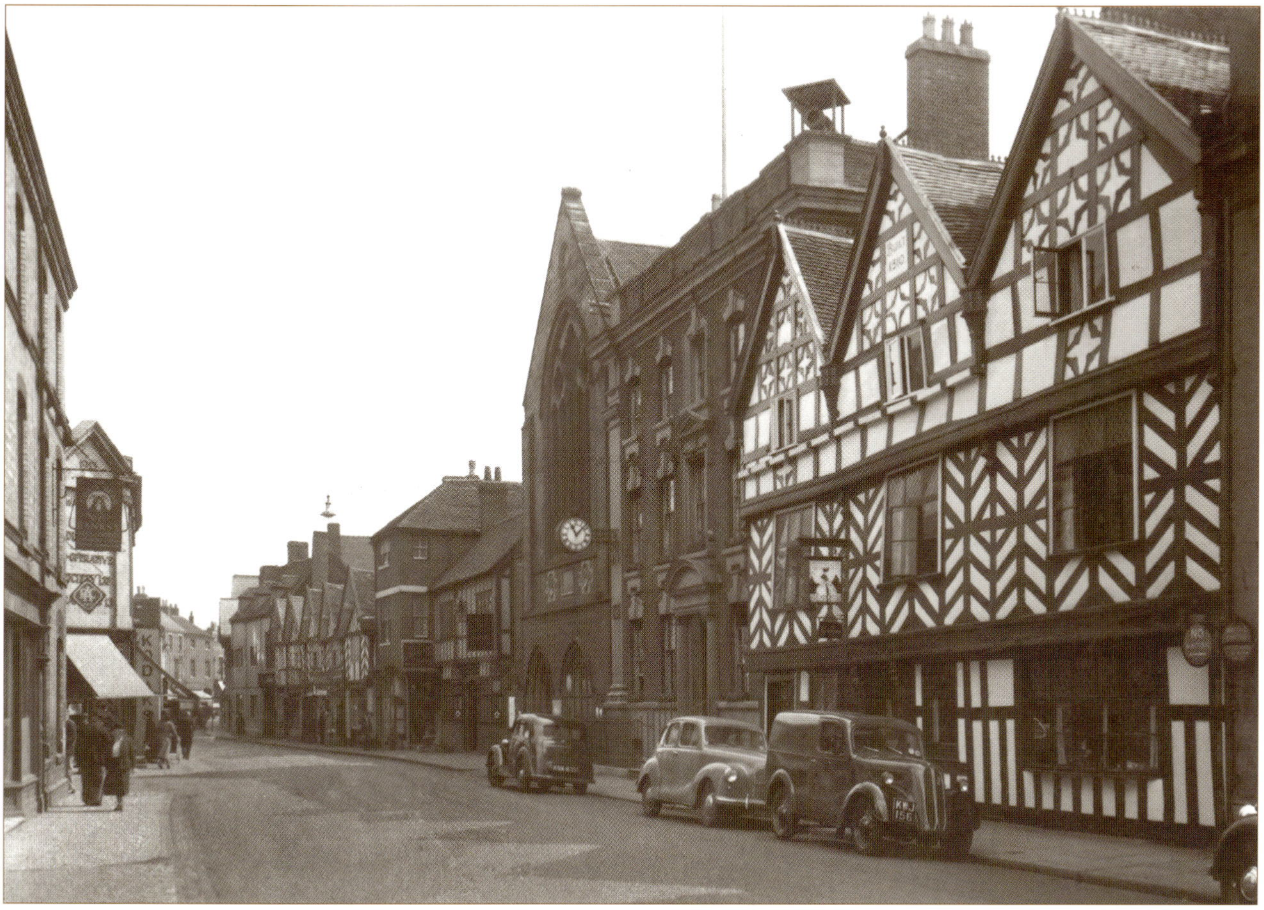

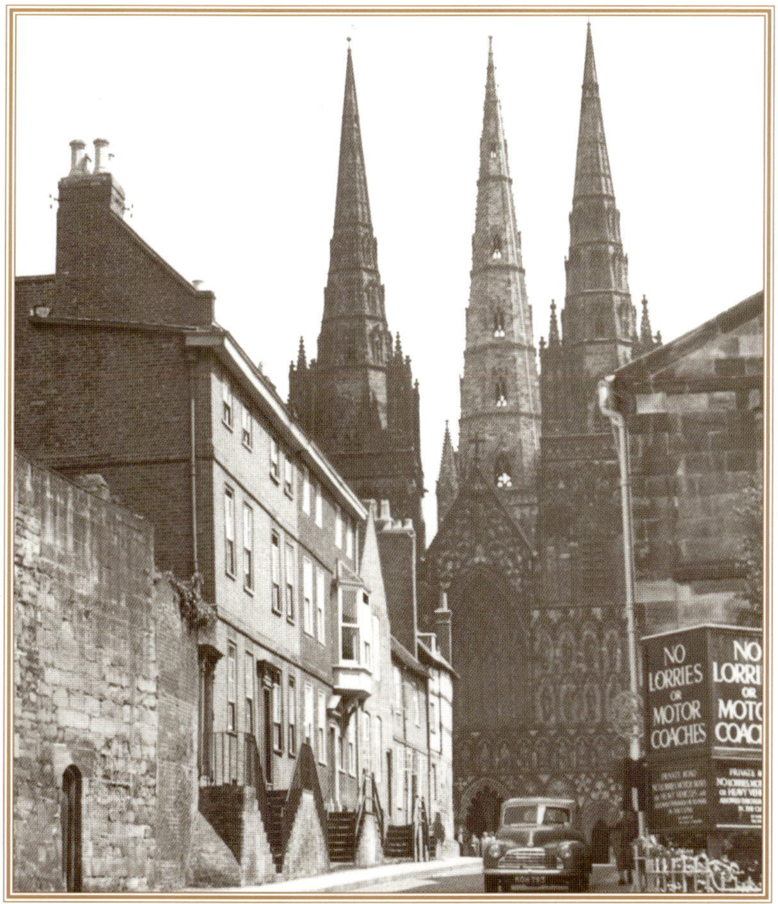

Above: Bore Street, Lichfield, c1955
(L45049) Leading out of the Market Place, Bore Street has many fine old buildings. On the right is the early 16th-century jettied and gabled Tudor cafe, a tour de force of decorative half-timber work. Beyond it is Donegal House, an imposing Georgian town house with a pedimented porch and stone window dressings. Next to this is The Gothic Hall, built in 1846. On the left is the Goat's Head Hotel.

Left: The Cathedral, Lichfield, c1955
(L45059) Although one of the smallest of our cathedrals, Lichfield's spires soar 200 feet over the roofs of this tiny city. The central spire is a replacement for one that was destroyed during the Civil War. Here we are looking up towards the Close. The harmonious street line displays a mixture of houses of all shapes and sizes, some with steep steps and railings to their front doors.

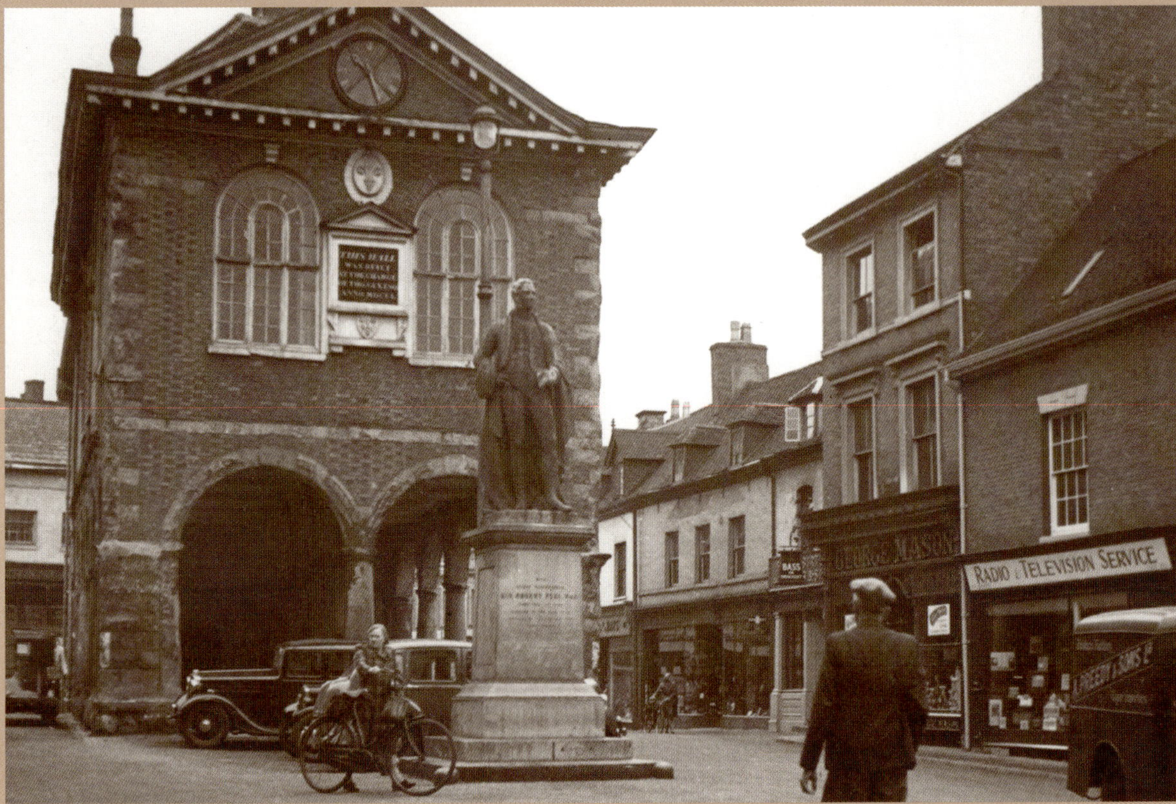
GEORGE MASON
RADIO & TELEVISION SERVICE

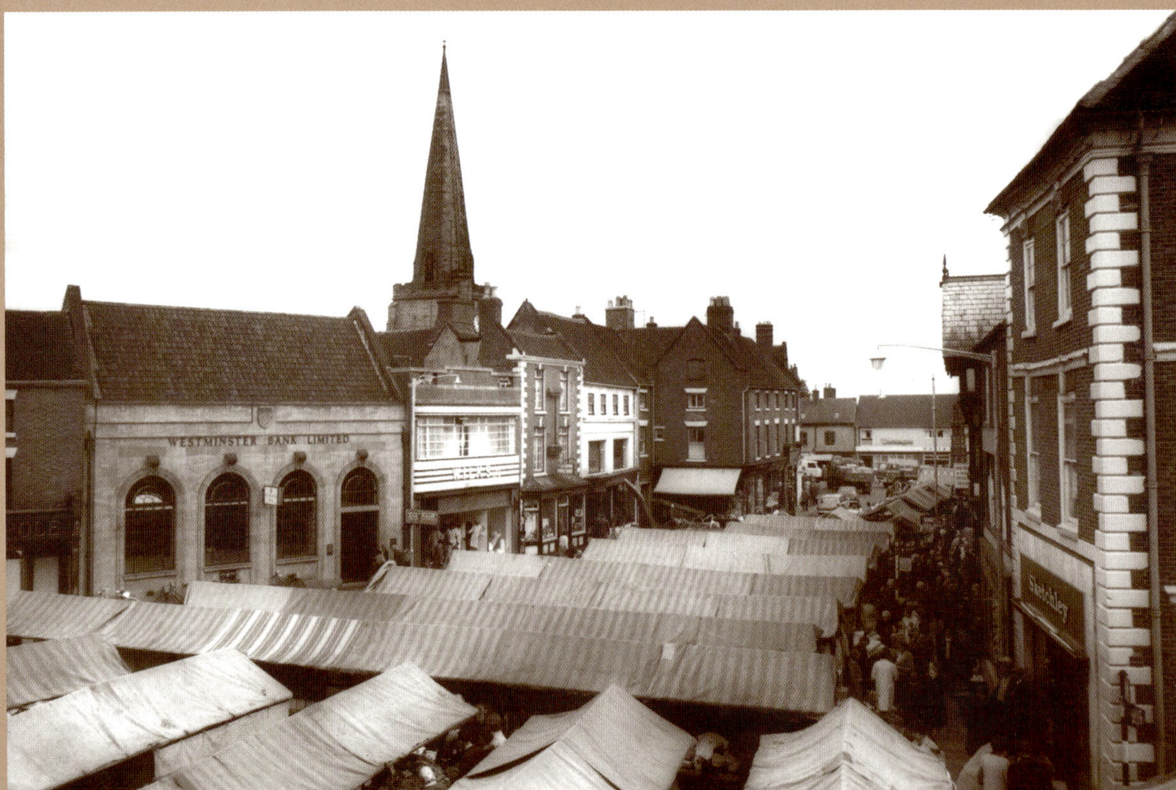
WESTMINSTER BANK LIMITED

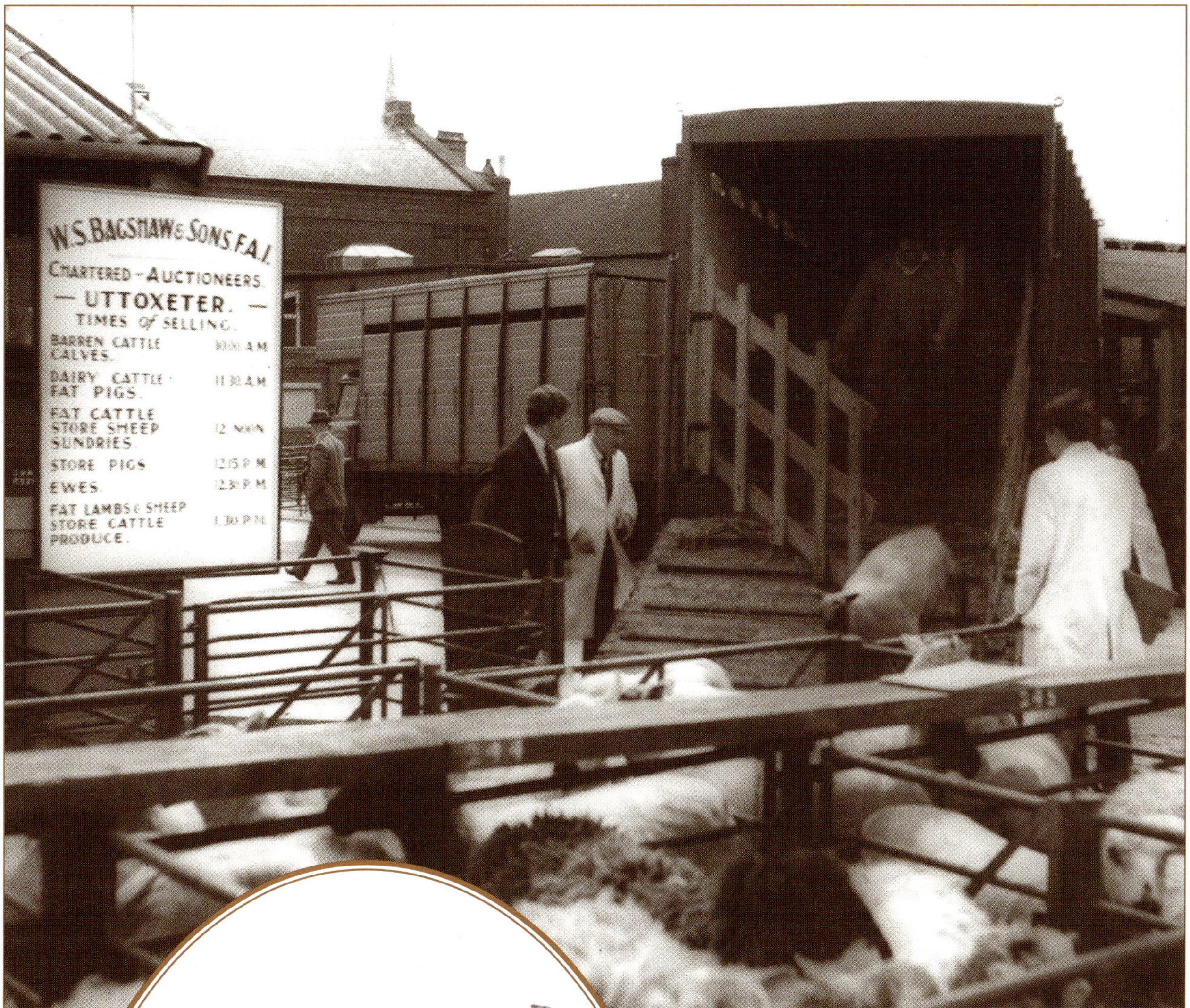

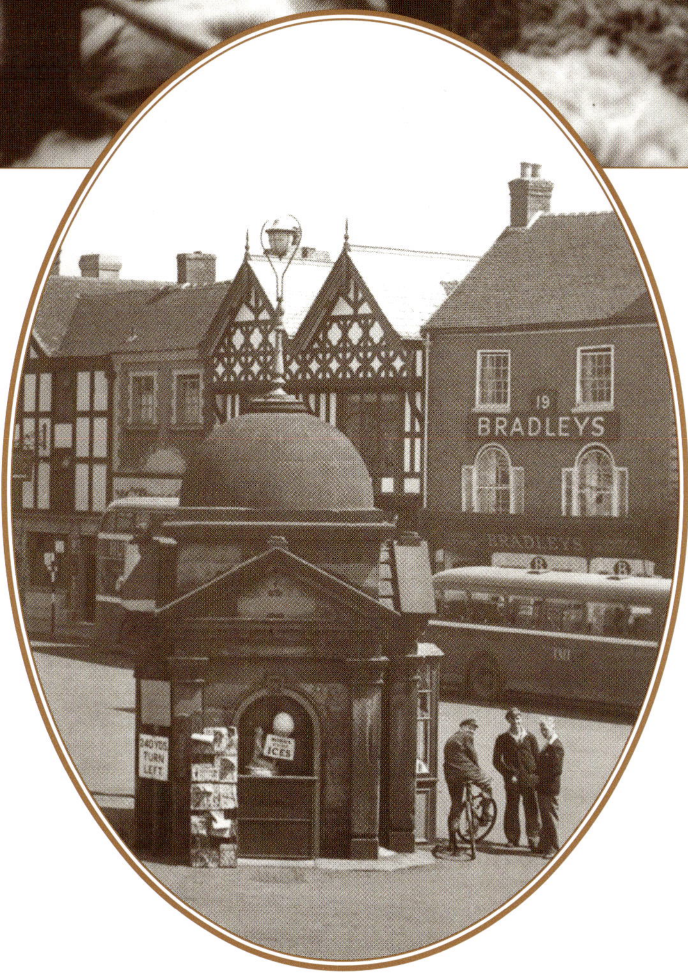

Above: The Cattle Market, Uttoxeter, c1955 (U29077) Bagshaw & Sons are the auctioneers. Pigs are being unloaded ready to be driven into the sale ring.

Left: Market Place, Uttoxeter, c1955 (U29012) In front is the miniature domed classical Weighing House of 1854.

Opposite top: The Town Hall, Tamworth, c1955 (T157011) This elegant building, with its cupola and arched Tuscan columns, was built in 1701 by Thomas Guy, founder of Guy's Hospital in London. Sir Robert Peel watches over the local people from his lofty pedestal.

Oppsoite below: The Market, Uttoxeter, c1965 (U29080) This pleasant market town, renowned for its racecourse, is set on the border of Staffordshire and Derbyshire. Here we look across a sea of awnings at the market place, which is formed of two irregularly shaped squares.

Right: Bent's Brewery, Stone, 1900 (46190)
We are in brewing country here. Up at Burton on Trent the monks were making beer in the Middle Ages. Bent's was a Liverpool brewery, who were keen to capitalise on the exceptionally fine quality of water in the Trent valley. They brewed pale ales here from 1889. Bent's was taken over by Bass in 1967, and brewing finally came to a halt in the 1970s. Stone was also the home of Joule's Old Brewery, established in the High Street in 1785.

Below: High Street, Stone, 1900 (46171)
This pleasing old town sits beside the River Trent. Peter de Wint, one of the very greatest of landscape painters, was born here, and was doubtless inspired and influenced by the countryside around, with its flat windswept fields, heath and woodland. The High Street curves gently round. On the left is the handsome Crown Hotel with its delicate shallow bays, designed by Henry Holland in 1778. Here, too, are other places for the weary traveller: on the right is the Fountain Commercial Inn, and at the end of the street, the Temperance Hotel.

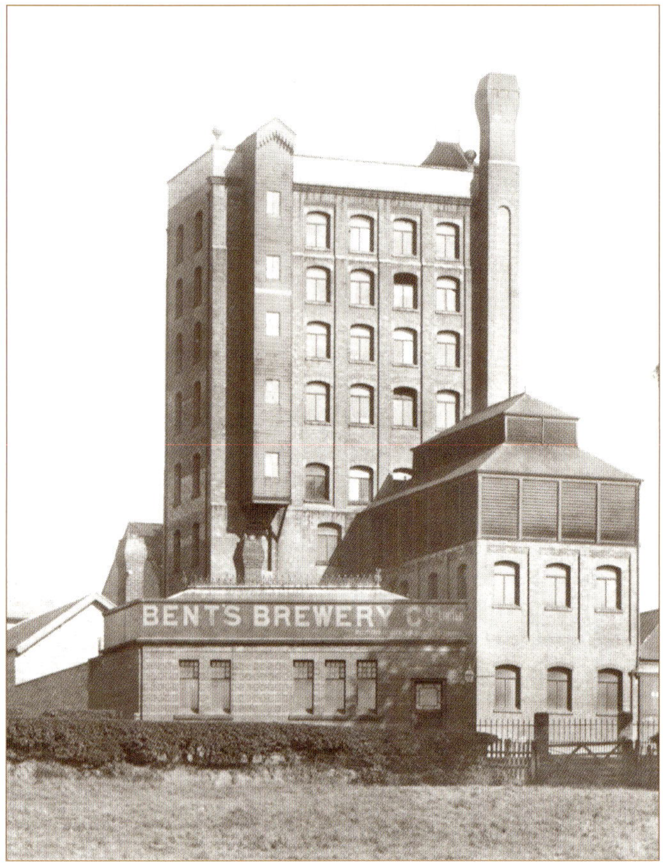

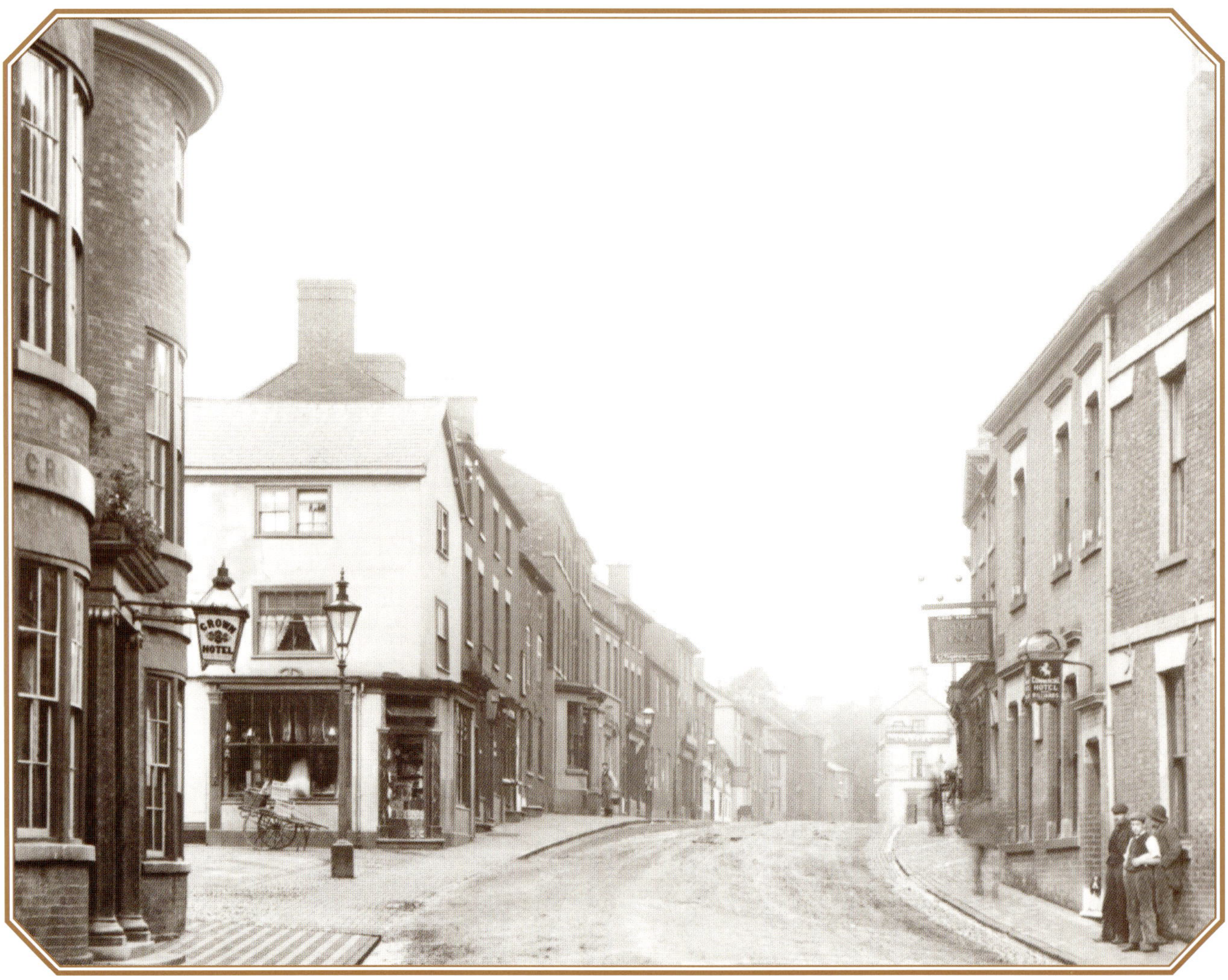

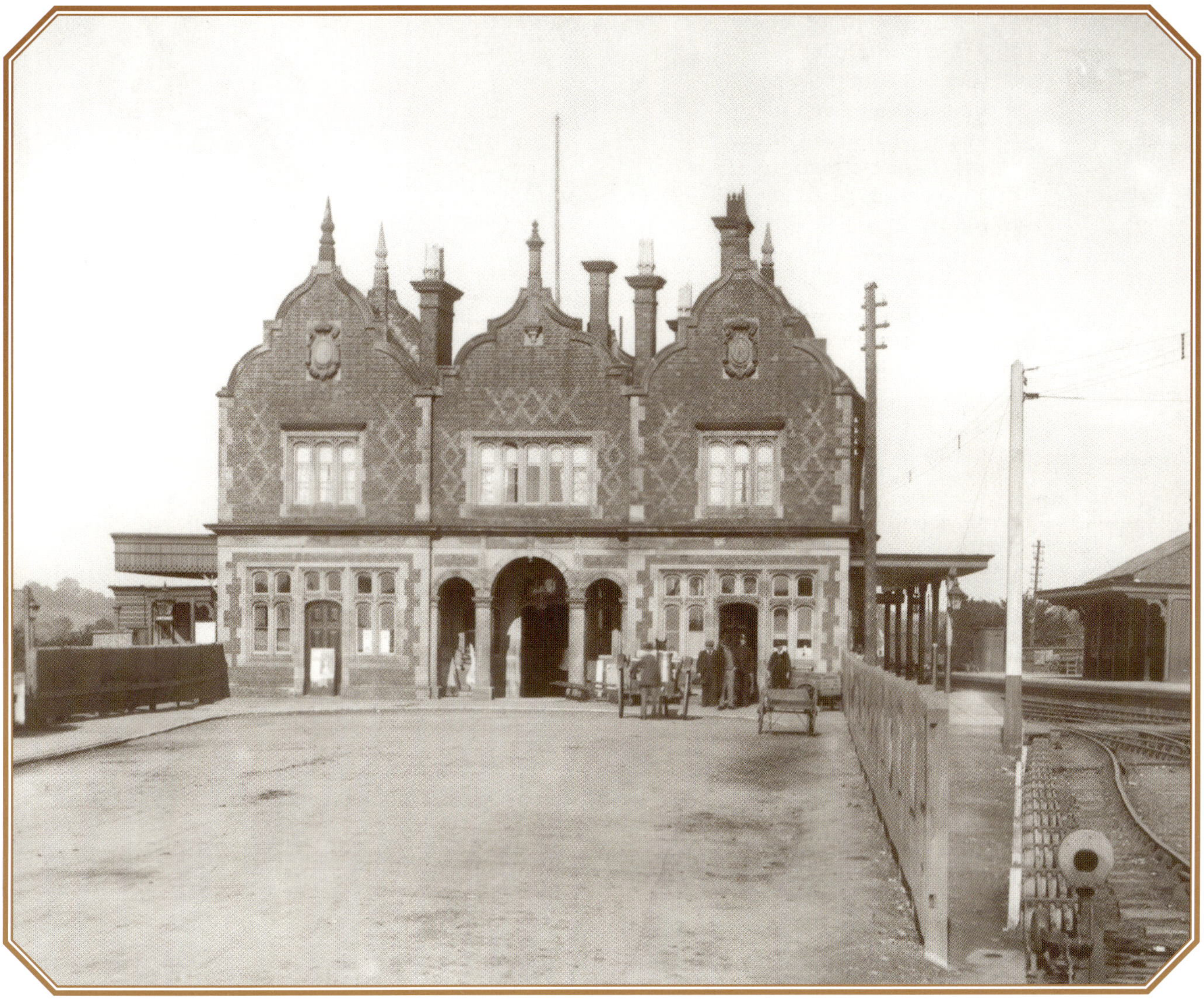

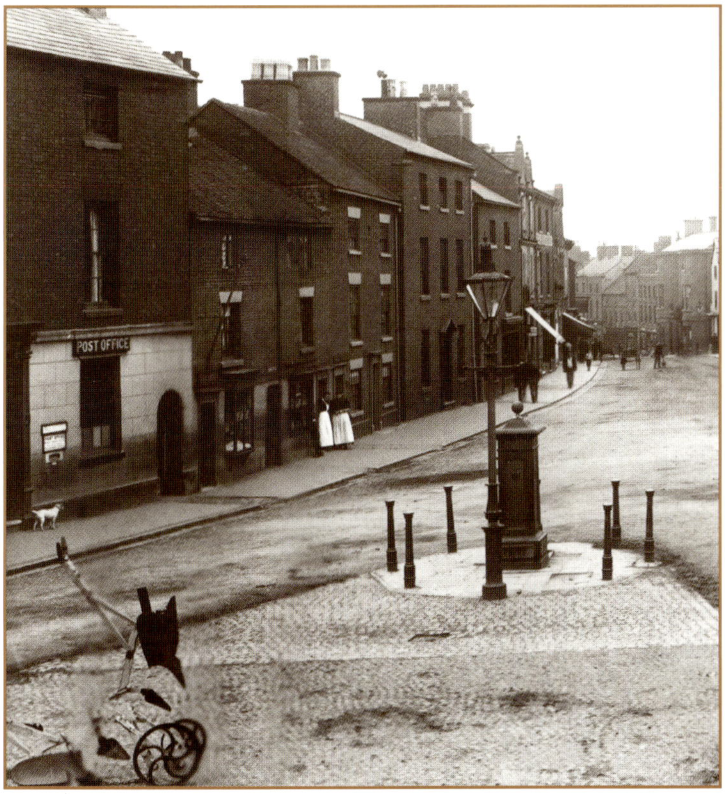

Above: The Railway Station, Stone, 1900 (46175) This exquisite Jacobean-style building, with its three gables topped with spikes, decorative brickwork and stone arcading, offers a sophisticated welcome to travellers on the North Staffordshire Railway. Stone is the junction where the NSR lines branch off for Stafford and Colwich. Standing by the door are the stationmaster and porter, taking delivery of milkchurns from a dairy cart. On the platform, Epps's are advertising their cocoa.

Left: High Street, Stone, 1900 (46170) In the foreground is a complicated-looking hand plough, its share and coulter pointing to the sky overhead.

STAFFORD. This ancient county town still has its medieval street pattern, surrounding the market square. Stafford offered a hearty welcome to visitors: George Borrow visited the town in 1825 and recalls the 'infinite life and bustle' of the inn where he stayed. Whenever he was melancholy, he 'called up the time I spent there, and never failed to become cheerful from the recollection'.

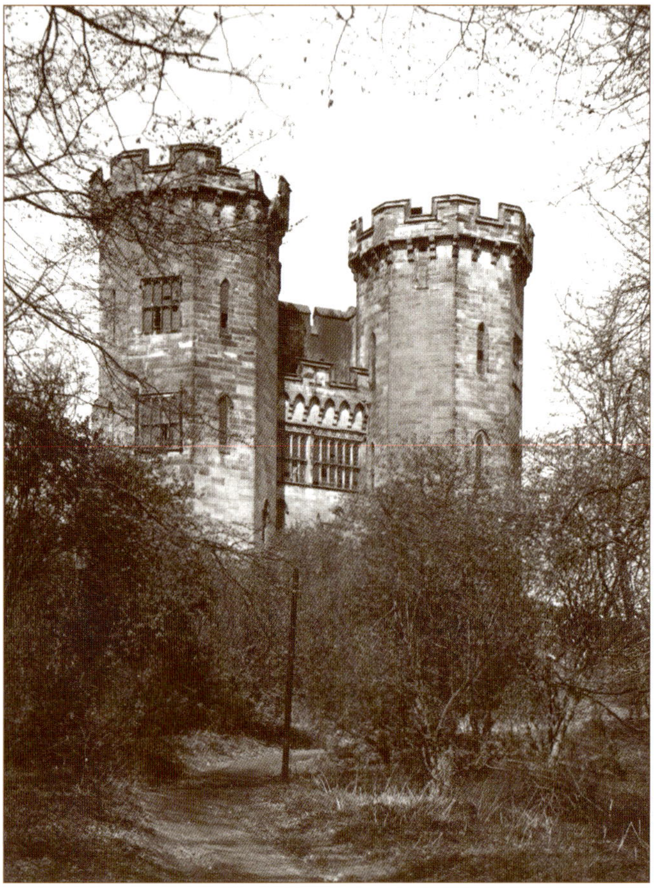

Right: The Castle, Stafford, c1955 (S411002) Robert de Stafford's imposing castle squats on a low wooded hill looking down on the western edges of the town. The old Norman castle is long gone, and the castellated version we now see was rebuilt in 1812 by Sir George Jerningham.

Below: Greengate Street, Stafford, c1955 (S411084) A panoramic view of Stafford's main thoroughfare, which has a wealth of fine Georgian and Regency buildings. The exquisite Norman church of St Chad is tucked away between the shops. Izaak Walton, England's most famous fisherman, was born in Eastgate Street in 1593.

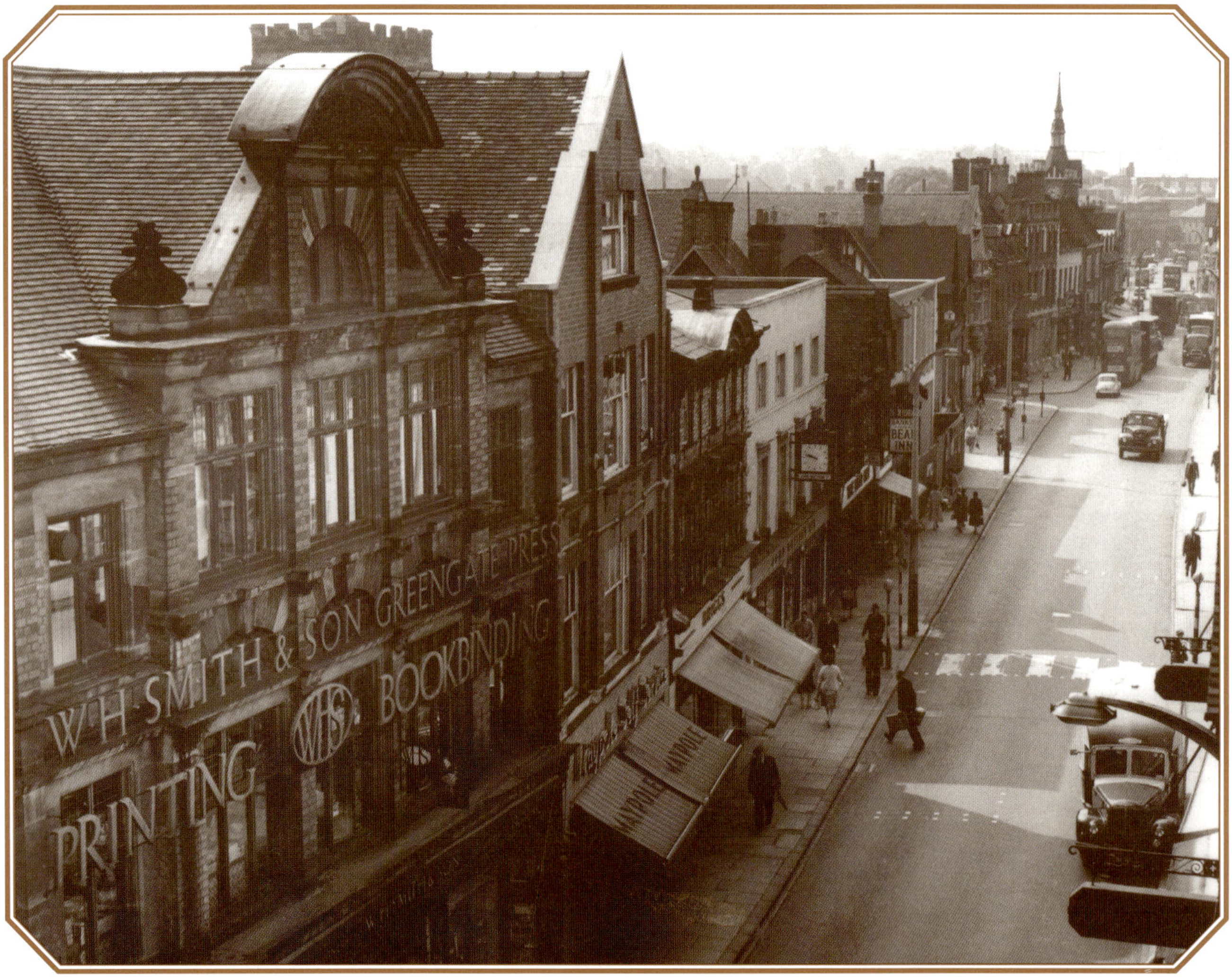

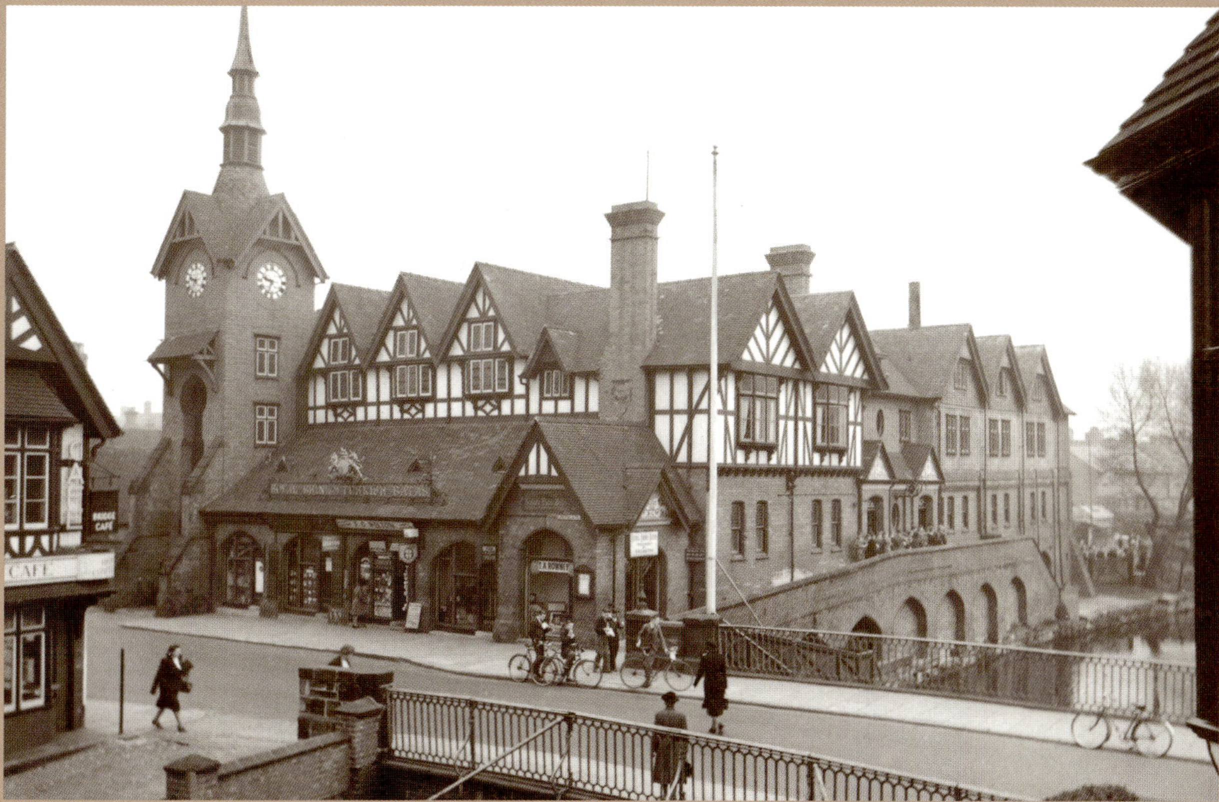

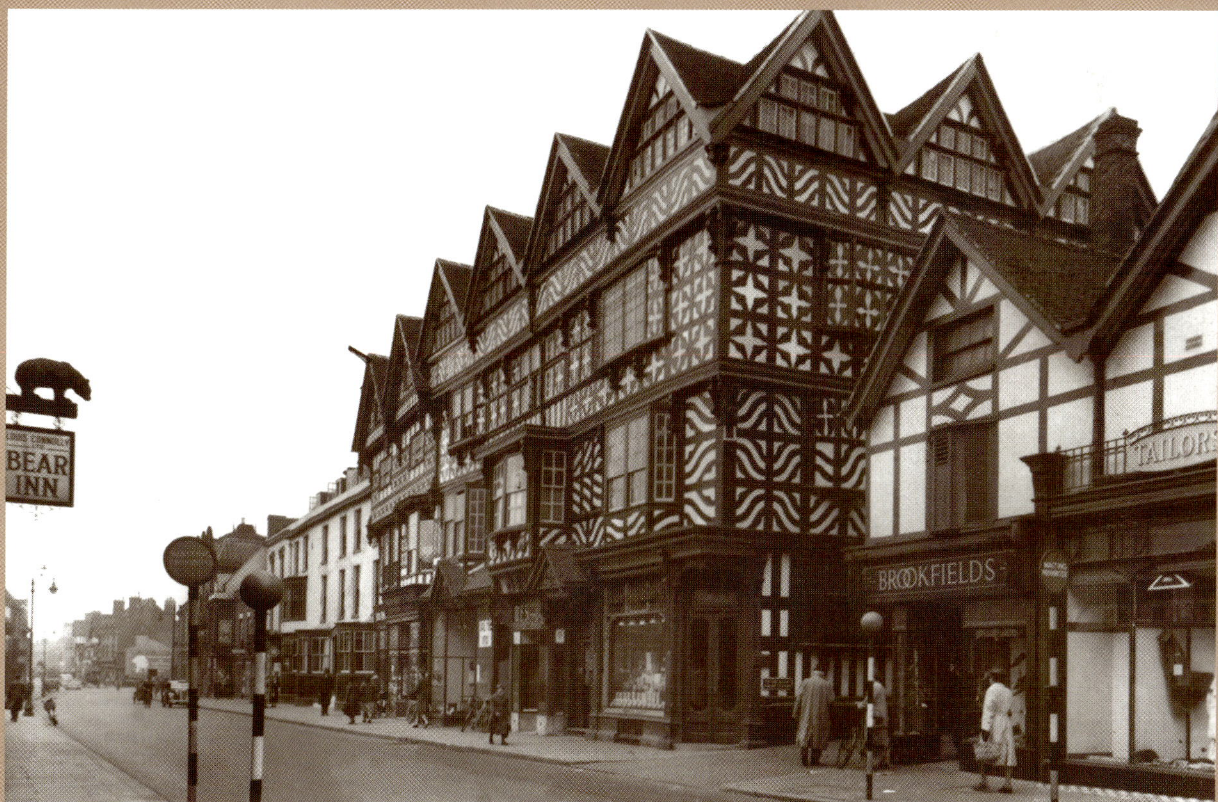

Top: The Royal Baths, Stafford, c1955 (S411004) The Victorians were very keen on taking health-giving waters. Stafford must have been delighted when salt deposits were discovered deep under the town's streets. The prestigious timbered baths opened in 1892, and here you could enjoy swimming in brine and a Turkish bath to finish off with. **Above: The Ancient High House, Stafford, 1948** (S411010) This splendid, four-storey timbered masterpiece was host to Charles I when he visited the town on a recruiting mission.

Right: St Edward Street, Leek, c1955 (L379009) This renowned silk weaving and textile town with its mills and chimneys is set below the wild expanse of moorland that stretches out towards Buxton in the north. St Edward Street is considered the most distinguished street in Leek, with many fine Georgian houses. On the corner of Brook Street is the Unicorn Inn.

Below: Market Place, Leek, c1955 (L379003) This cobbled square has seen markets for many hundreds of years. On the north side is a splendid Georgian building, Foxlowe House. The blinds are down - it is a scorching day. Lewis Bros's ice cream van must be making a killing.

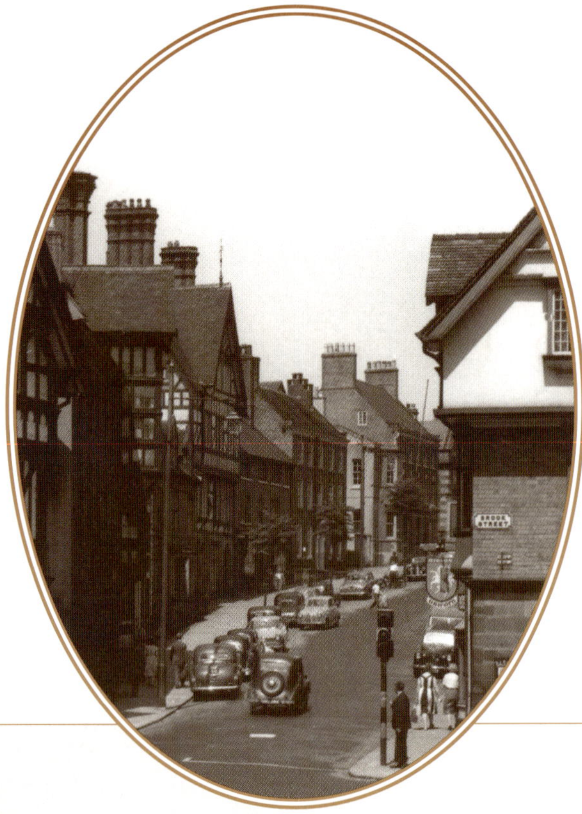

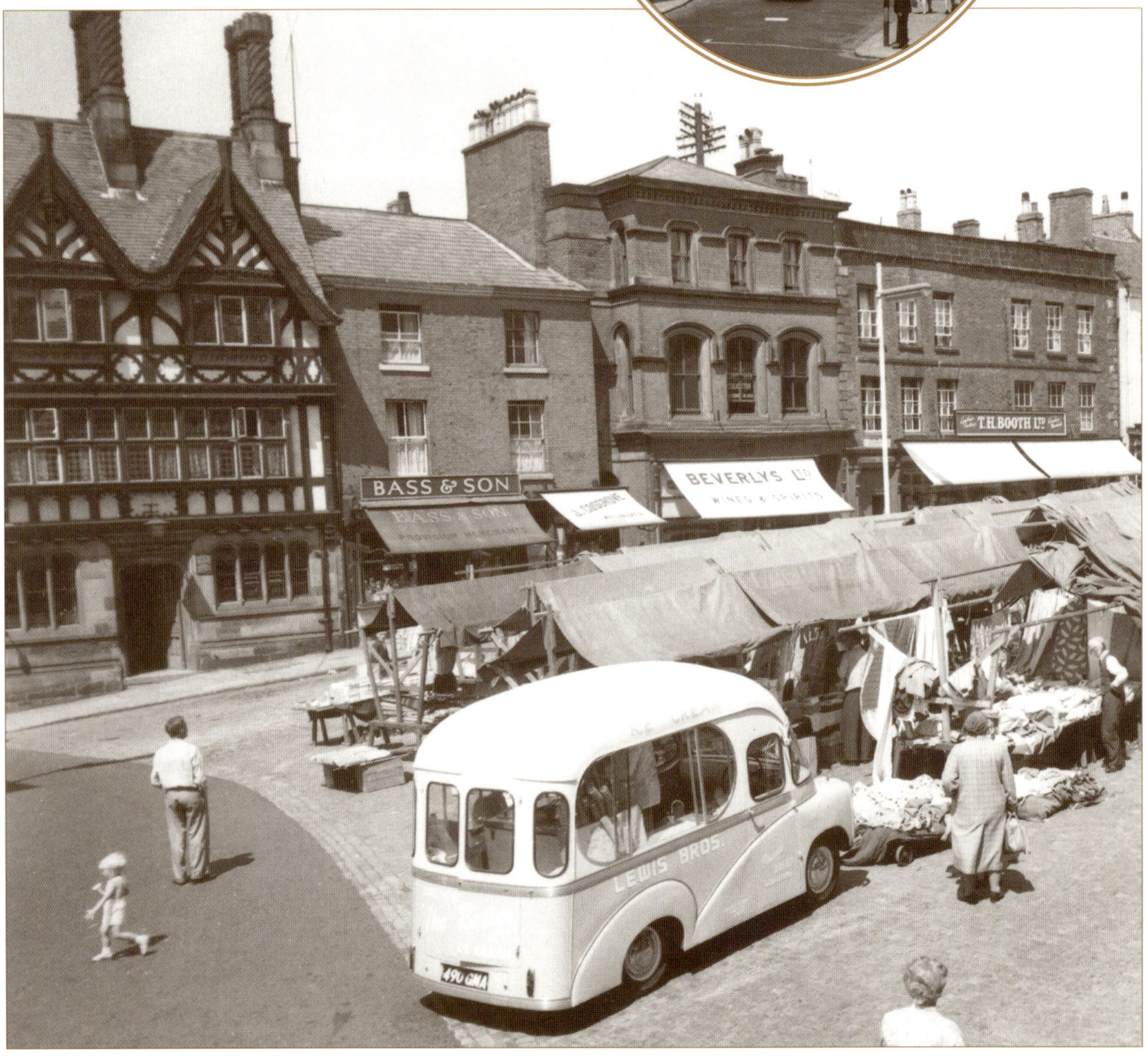

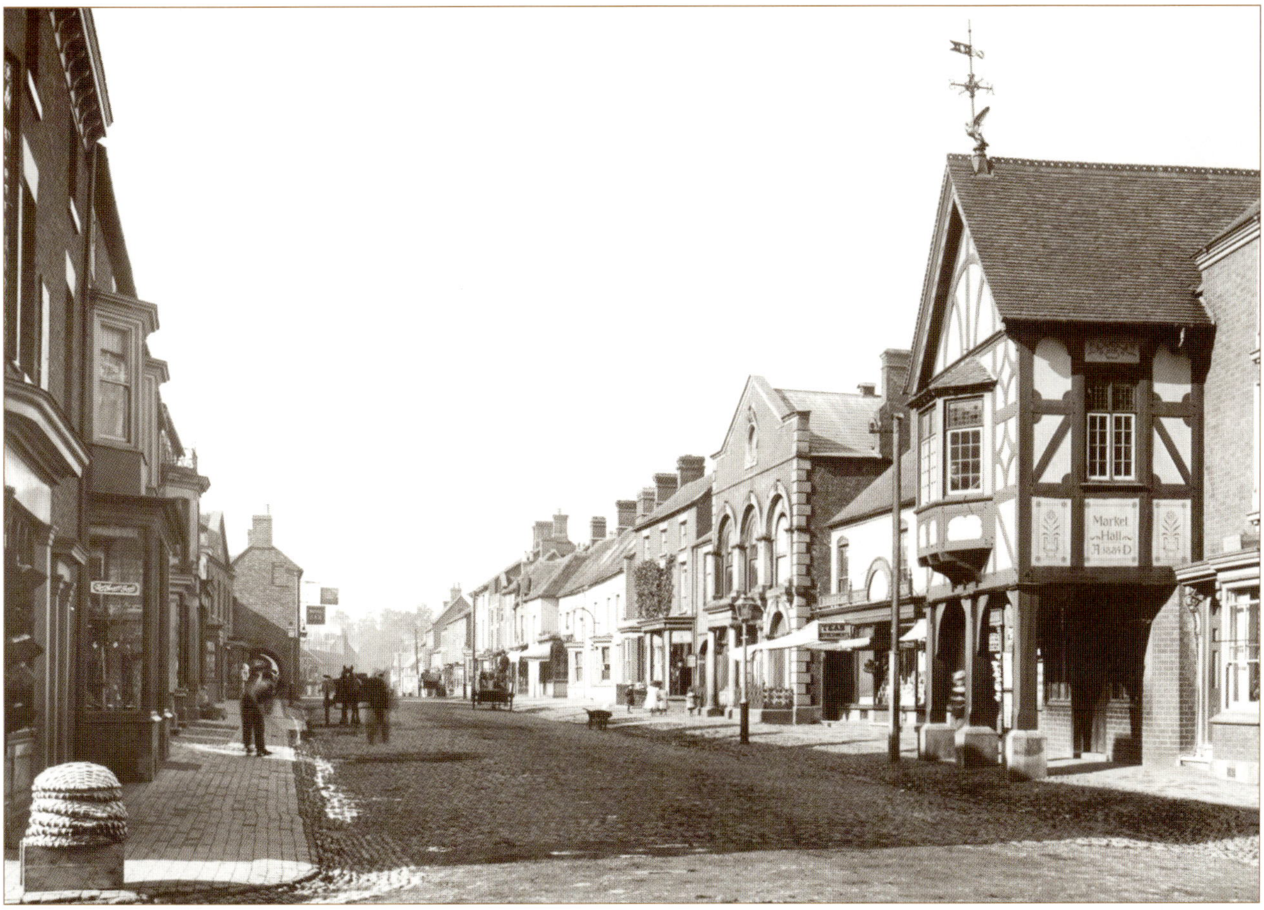

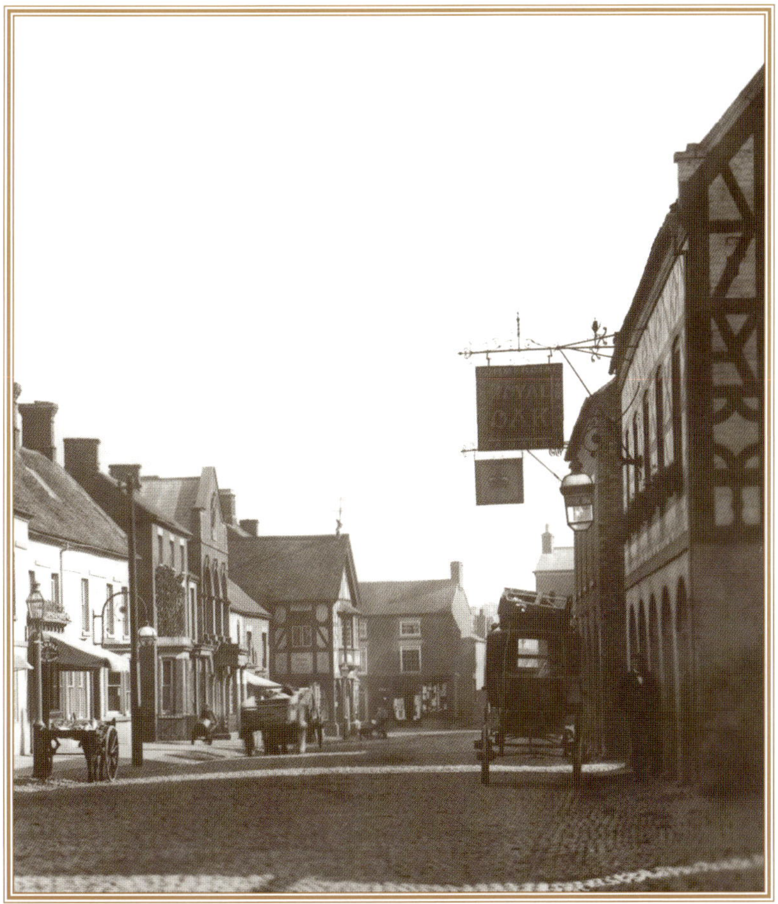

Above: High Street, Eccleshall, 1900
(46156) This small market town, set in wooded country, is the resting place of no fewer than six bishops of Lichfield. The market square is rich in Georgian houses, as well as the fine timbered Market Hall, built in 1854. There is a stack of shallow upturned baskets on the left and a tree of brooms hanging from the shop fascia behind. The buildings, in a variety of styles and sizes, create a harmonious blend - a classic example of the small English town at its very best.

Left: High Street, Eccleshall, 1900
(46158) The prospect from the other end of the market place, with the cobbled main street deep in shadow. On the right is the Royal Oak Hotel, with its decorative timbered gable end.

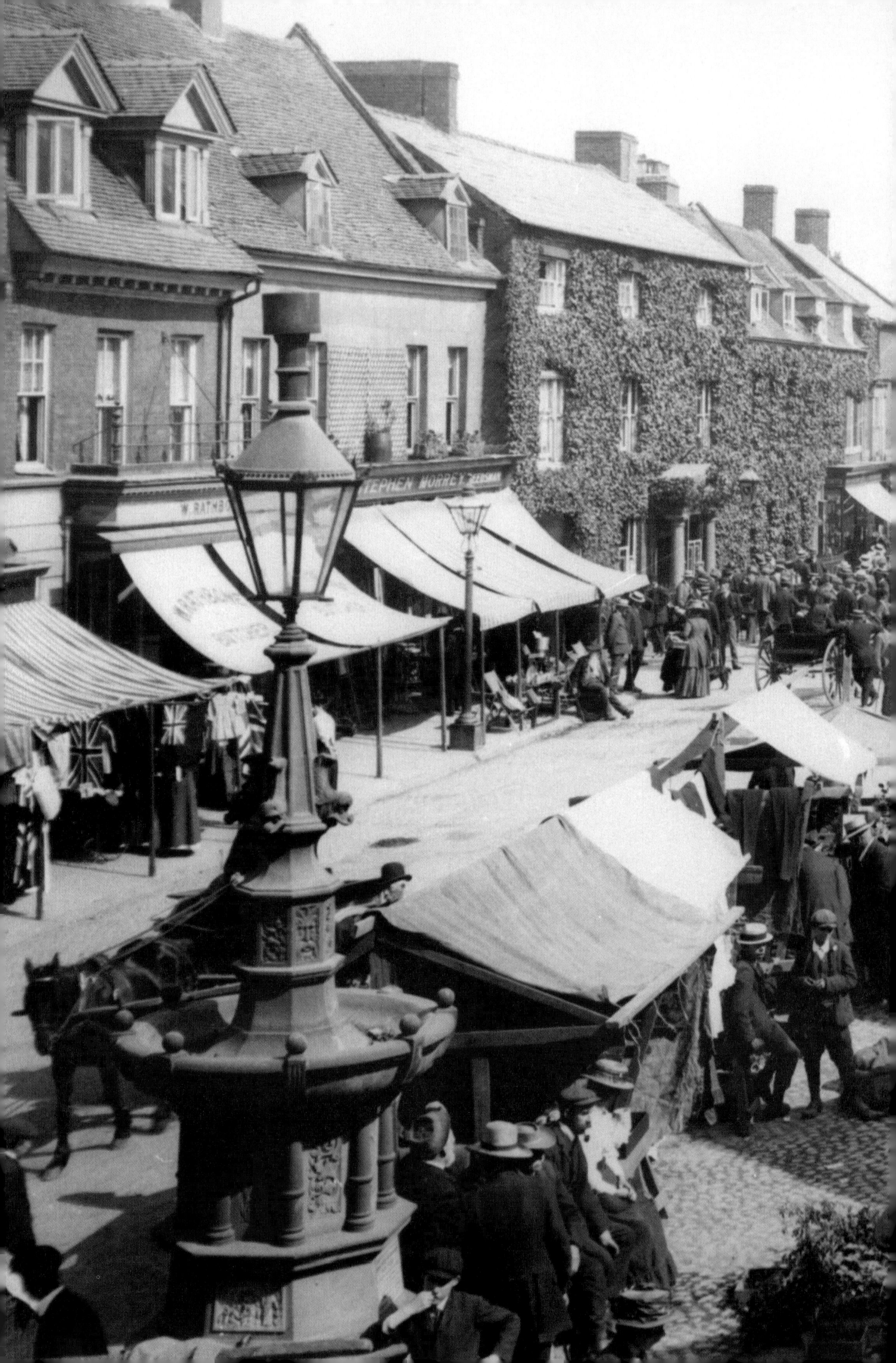

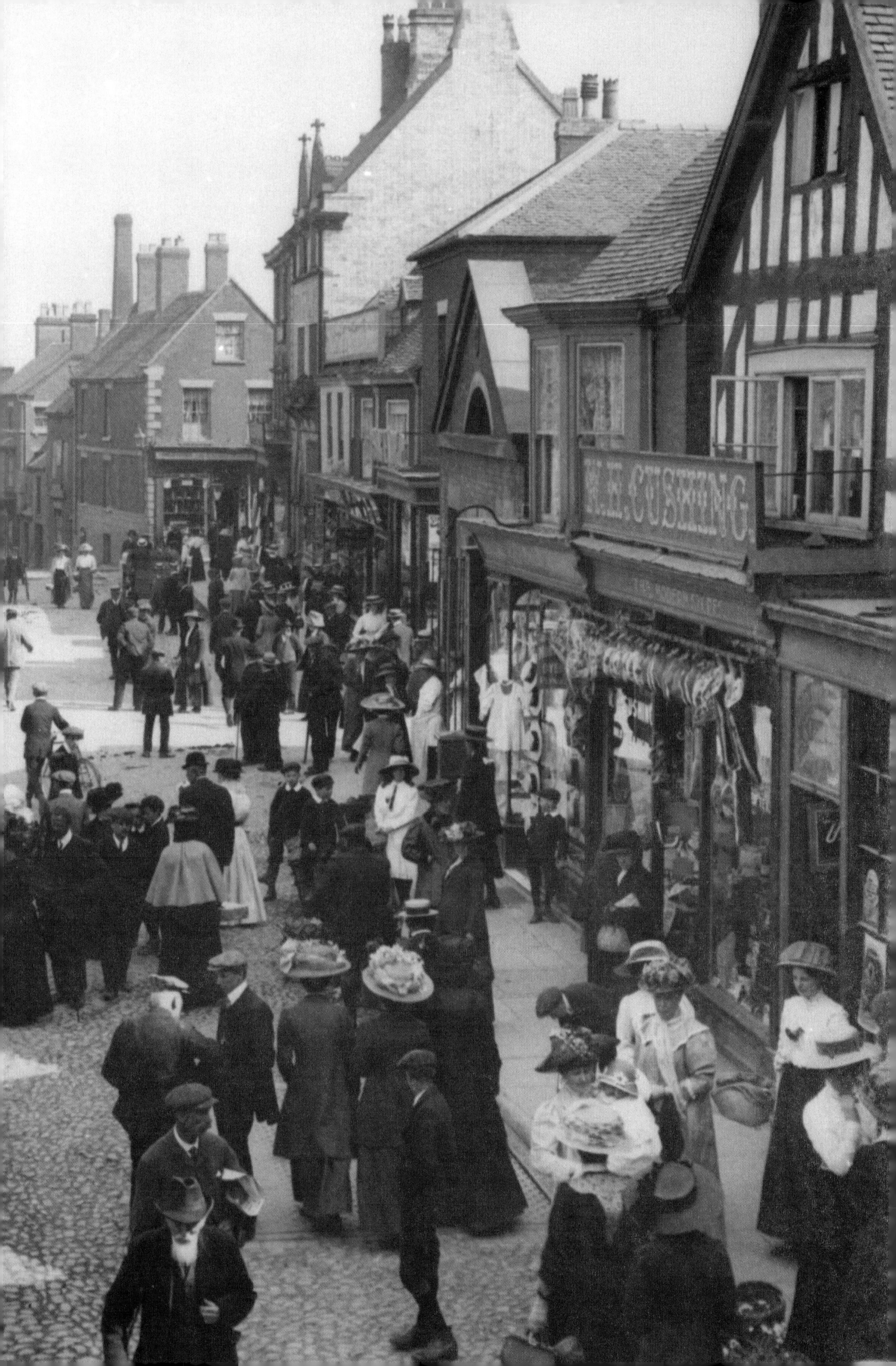
CUSHING

MARKET DRAYTON. With its market, broad streets, ancient Butter Cross, and fine 18th-century houses, Market Drayton has all the atmosphere of a vanished England. Close to the borders of Staffordshire and Cheshire, it sits in the midst of rich farming country. Robert Clive (Clive of India) ran wild as a schoolboy at the Old Grammar School, and his old desk, cut with his initials, is still there.

Previous pages: Market Day, Market Drayton, 1911 (63338) This magnificent photograph shows all the excitement of shopping old-style, the market place jammed with traders and keen customers. There are no cars, and the area is given over to the serious business of buying and selling. A later view shows the cobbles gone, the shops on the left demolished, and the market place little more than a through-way for traffic.

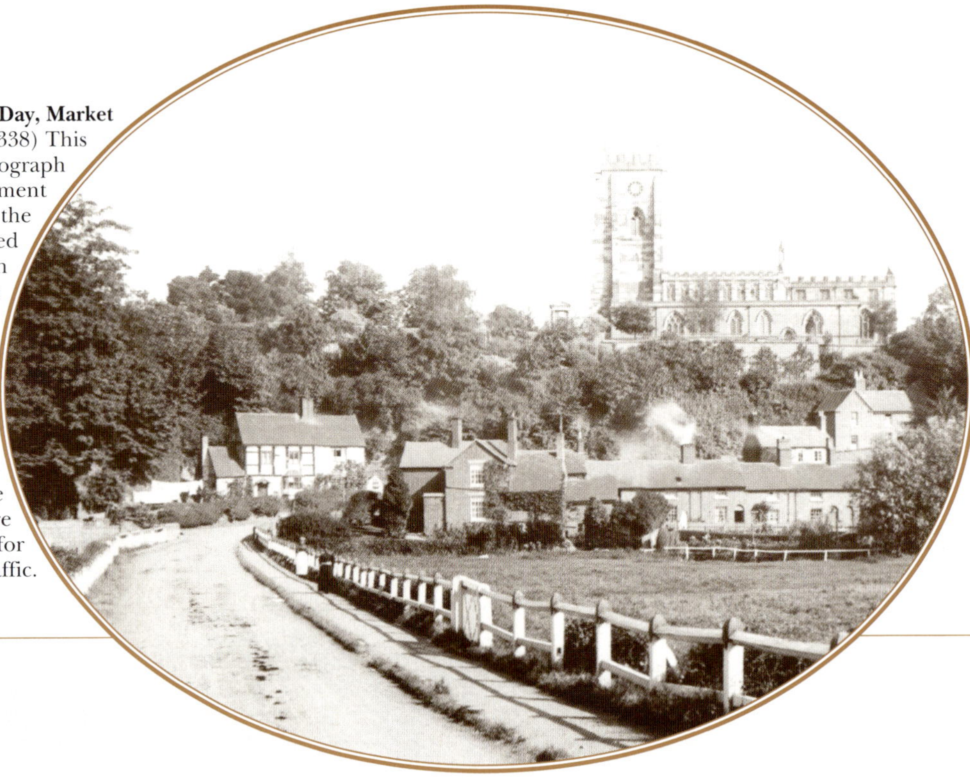

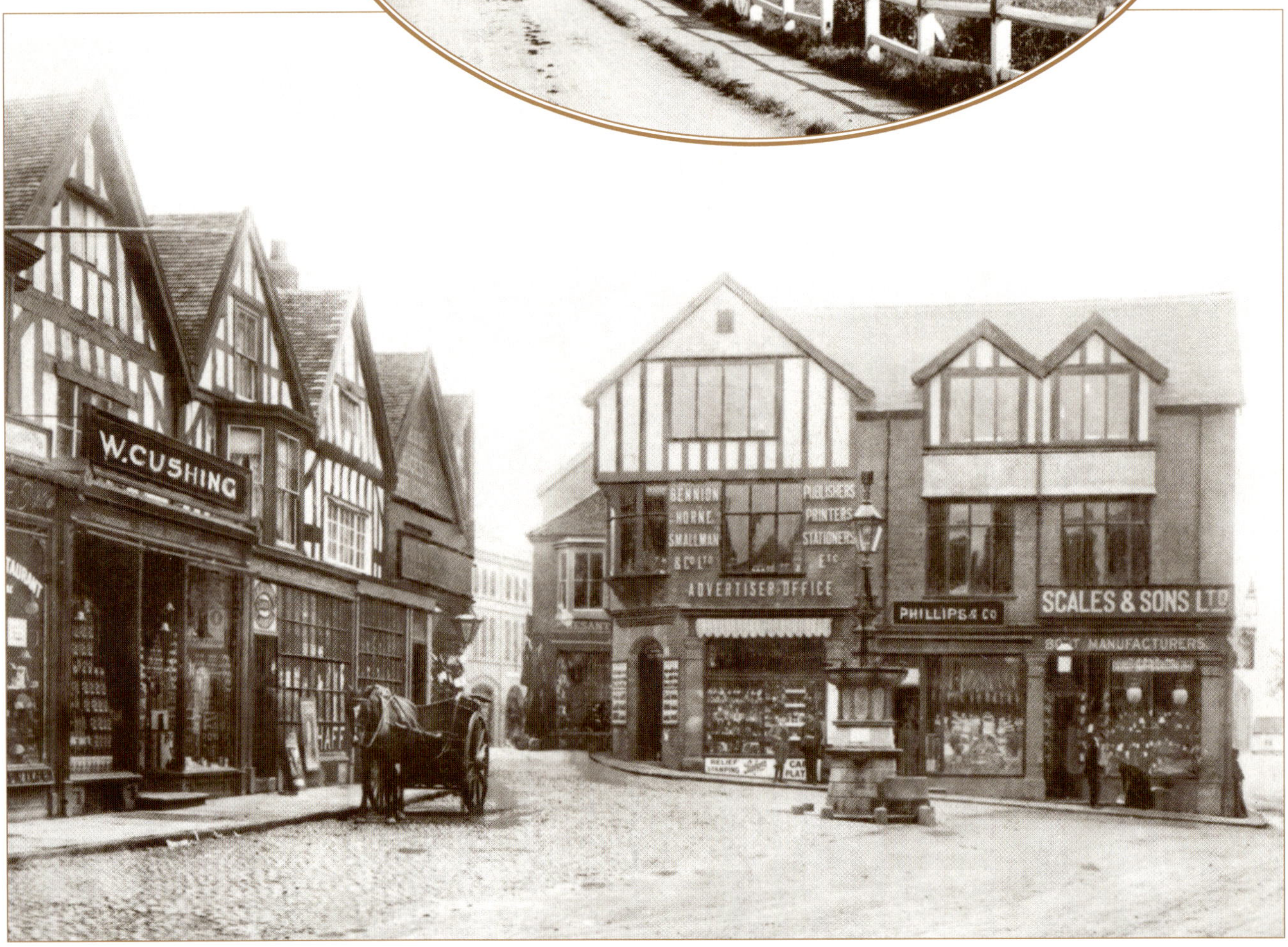

Top: Market Drayton from the South(42198) **Above: High Street, Market Drayton, 1903** (50717) Here we see Cushing's Stores (on the right in the picture on the previous page). The many-paned windows are jammed with stacked tins and other foods. It would have needed a massive staff to keep the display looking at its most seductive. In the centre is the Advertiser Office. A market has been held in the town every Wednesday since Edward I granted the town's charter almost 700 years ago.

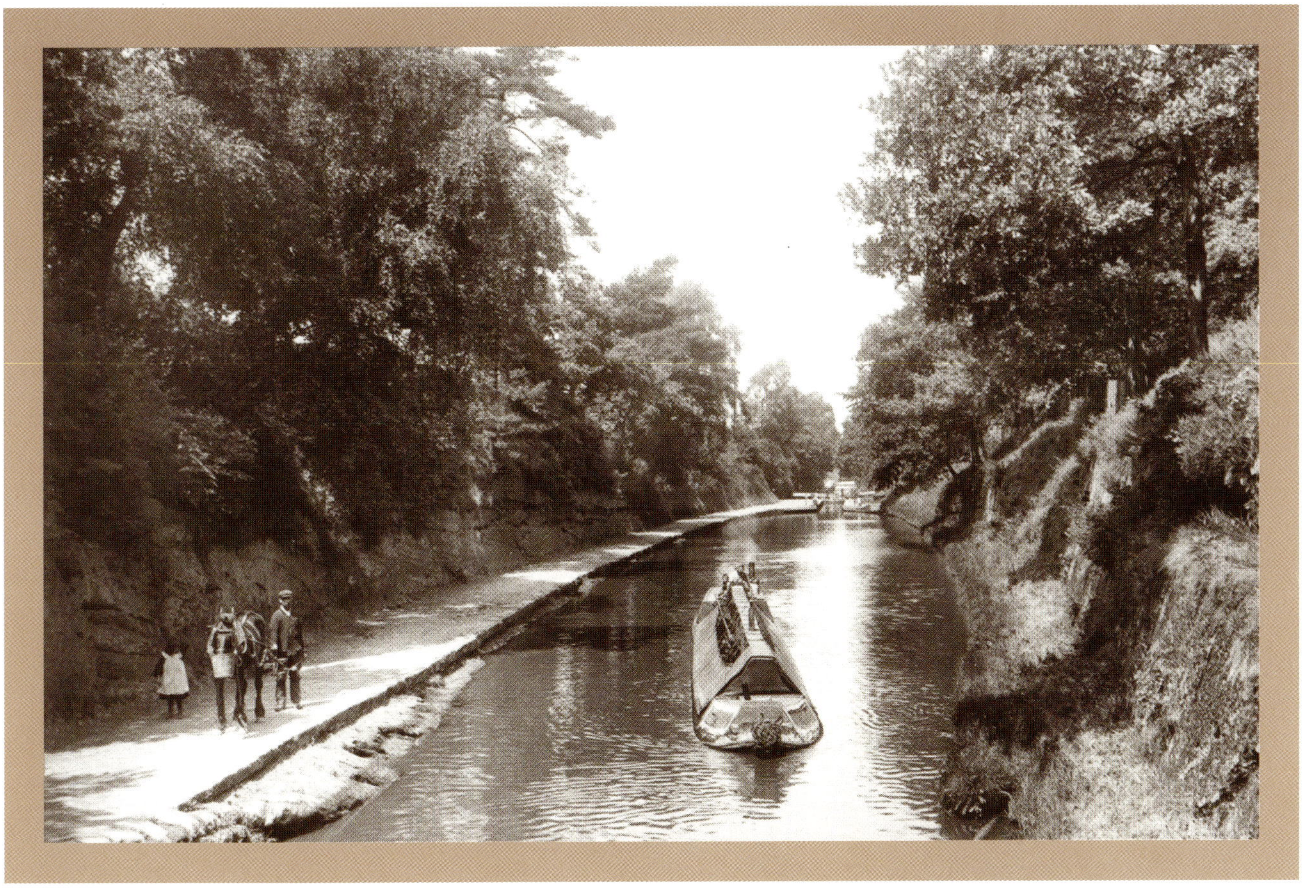

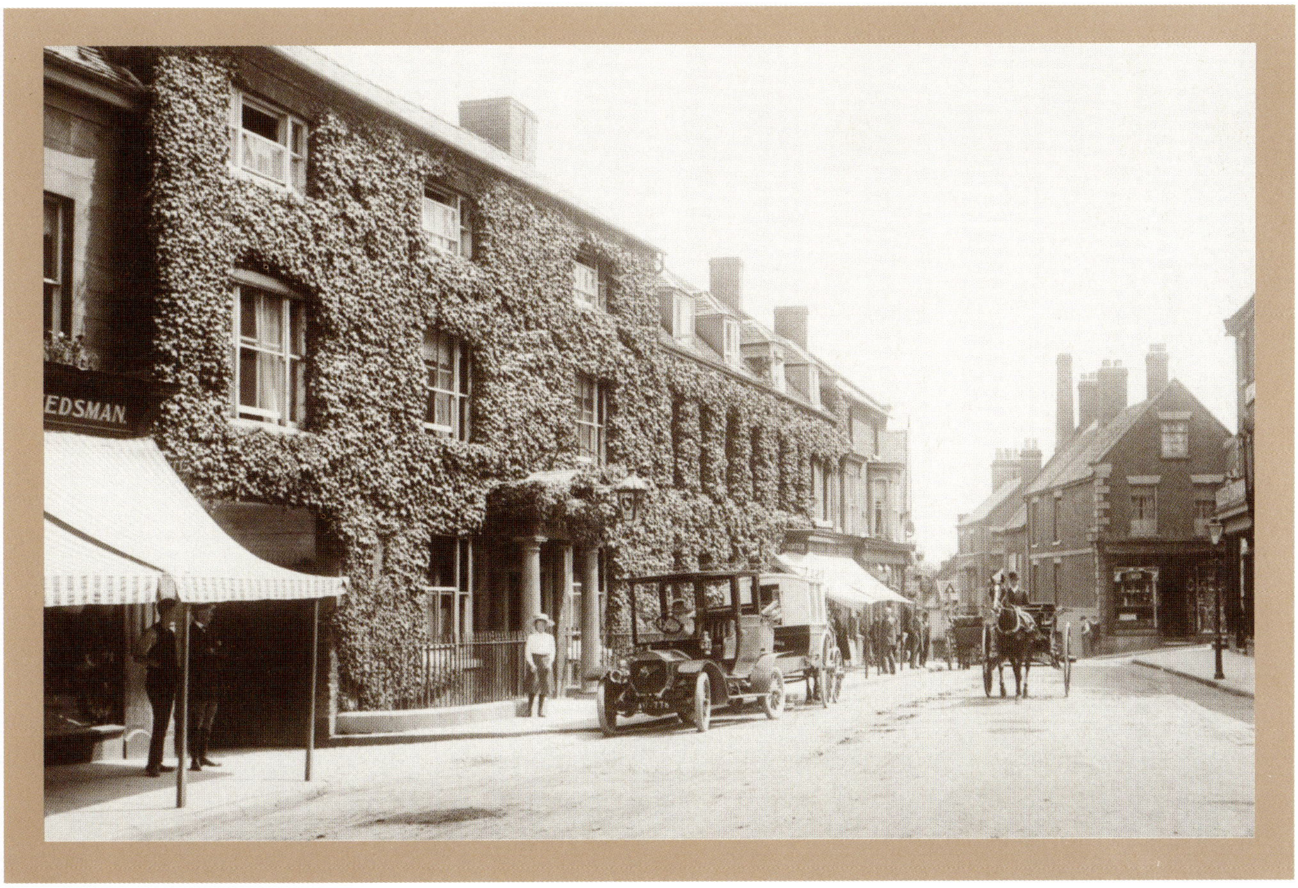

Top: Tyrley Locks, Market Drayton, 1911 (63346) The Birmingham and Liverpool Junction Canal was better known as the Shropshire Union Canal, and was planned by Telford and opened in 1835. Here a thin canal horse grabs some welcome sustenance from its nosebag. The locks are in the distance. The bargewoman sits at the back with her little boy alongside. **Above: The Corbet Arms Hotel, Market Drayton, 1911** (63336) A chauffeur in a luxurious Napier automobile awaits his employer, who is lunching at the hotel.

Right: Shropshire Street, Market Drayton, 1899 (44432) The fine timber building at the corner, with its shuttered windows, is smothered in announcements for Herbert Bowdler's great summer sale. Along the pavement there are newspaper hoardings for *The Golden Penny* and the *Liverpool Daily Post*, among others.

Below: High Street, Whitchurch, 1901 (47183) This quiet little mellow stone town stands on a hill surrounded by rich dairy country. On the right is J Walker's grocer's shop with the inevitable Hovis advertisement in the window. Children stand and stare, carrying their market baskets. On the left is a barber's pole reaching high over the pavement. Whitchurch has a surprising number of industries: there are dairies and creameries, and makers of iron and steel goods, clocks and corsets.

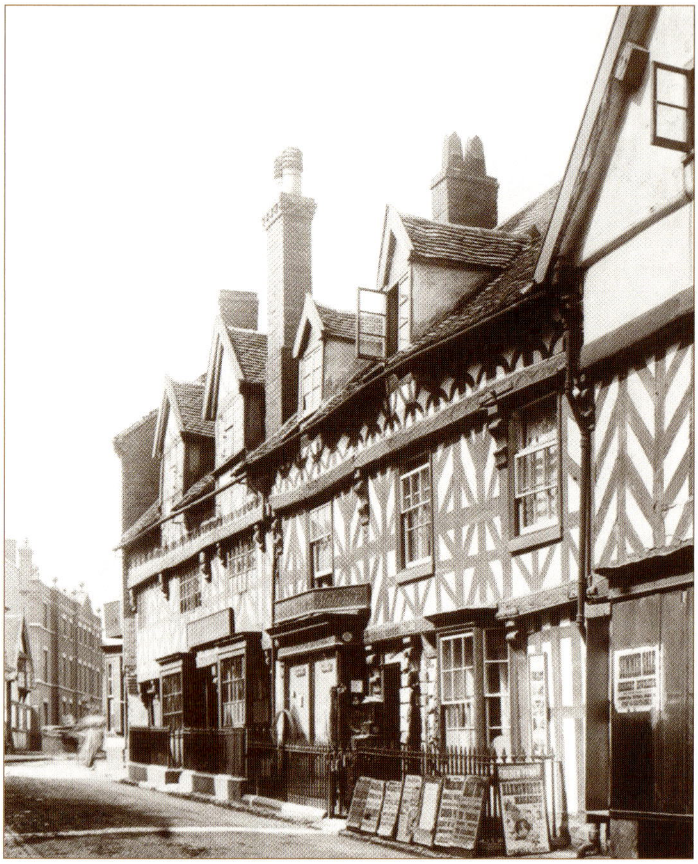

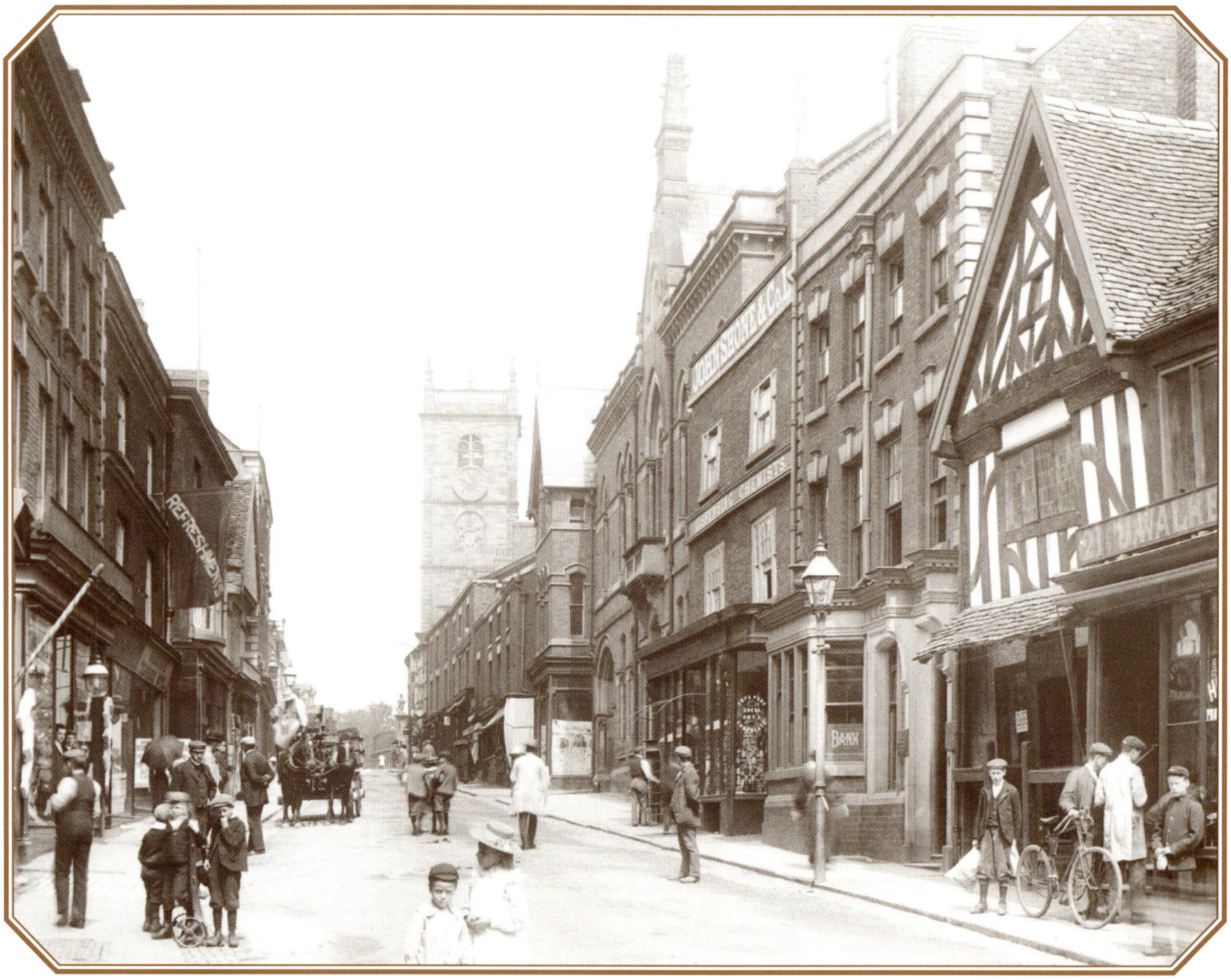

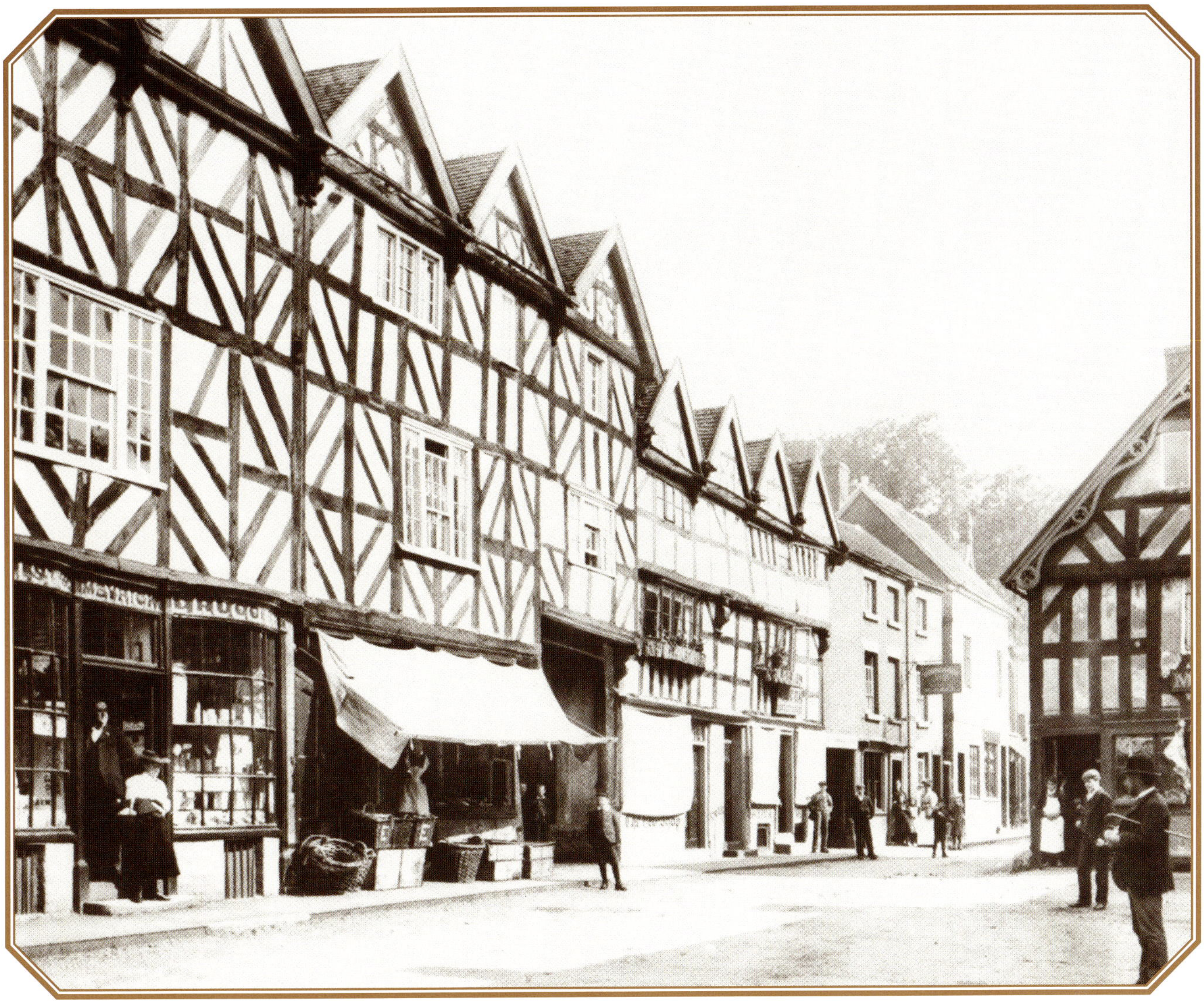

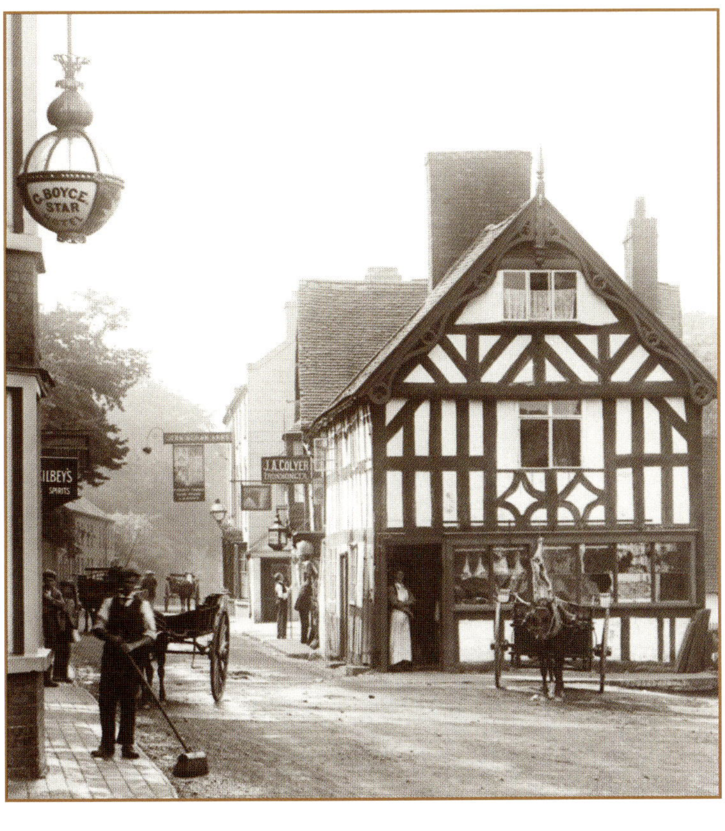

Above: Market Place, Shifnal, 1898 (41818) This very old coaching and posting town has some charming houses, and was a favourite of Dickens. He gives an account of it in "The Old Curiosity Shop". The old timbered shop on the left with its shallow bay windows is quintessentially Georgian, its name neatly painted on the fascia above.

Left: Market Place, Shifnal, 1899 (44150) Once a stopping place for coaches on the road to Holyhead, Shifnal is steeped in history, and this is reflected in its lovely architecture. One commentator has spoken of its 'timbered eaves and gables burdened with age'. In this photograph is Mason's the butcher's, with one of the staff in a long apron to his boots standing at the door. A little further on to the right is The Jerningham Arms.

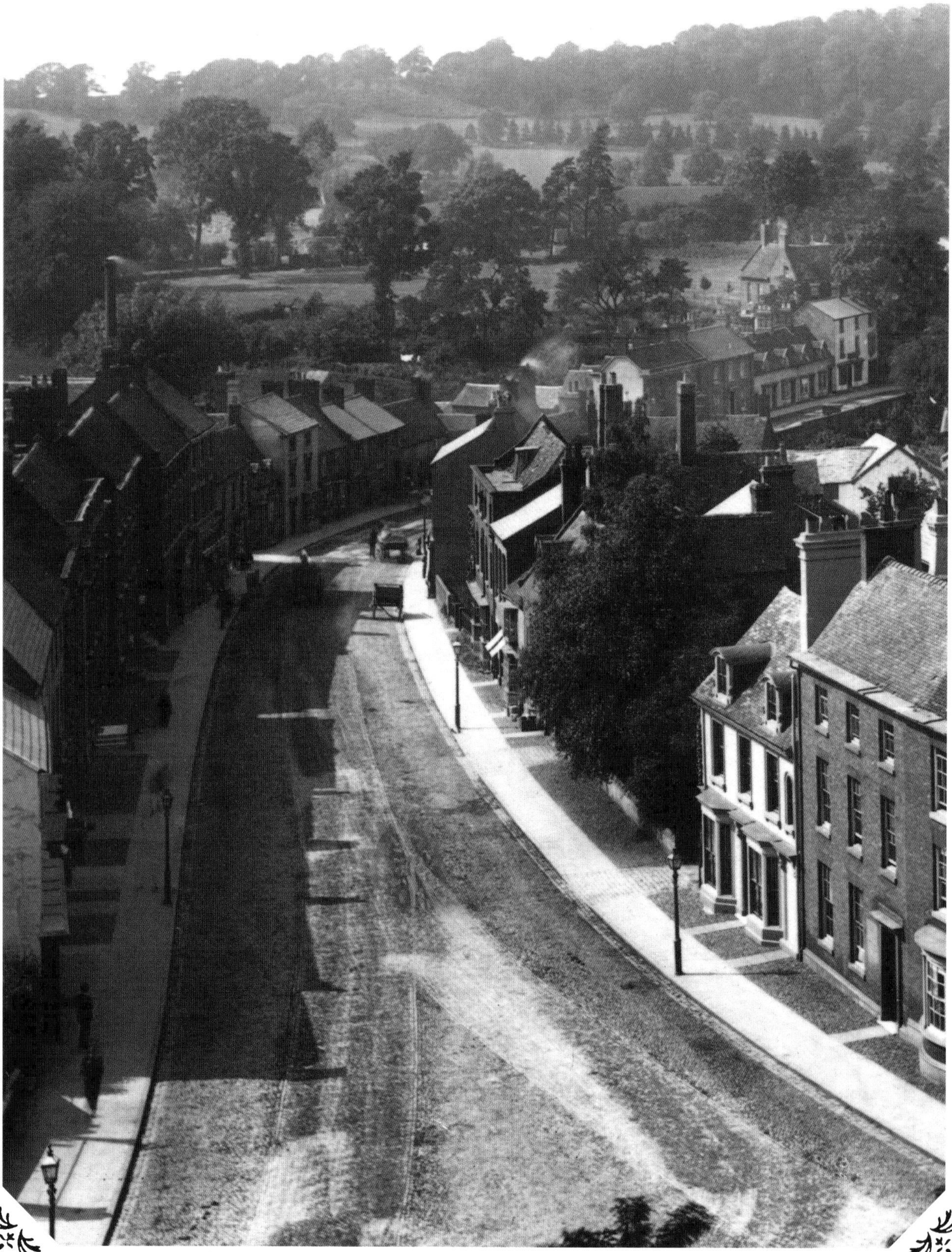

Opposite: Newport from the Church Tower, 1893 (41976) This little market town is on the busy main road from the Midlands to Chester, but you would never think so from this peaceful scene photographed from the tower of the old church of St Nicholas, which sits firmly on an island in the middle of the road. It was taken, of course, just before the first cars were to be seen in England's streets.

Right: The Castle Car Works, Hadley, near Ironbridge, 1902 (48814) Workers pour out of the factory. Ironworking has been, with coal, the vital industry in the Severn gorge around Coalbrookdale and Ironbridge ever since Abraham Darby pioneered the large-scale smelting of iron in 1708. In 1859 there were thirty-seven furnaces and fourteen ironworks, with factories turning out a wide range of engineering parts.

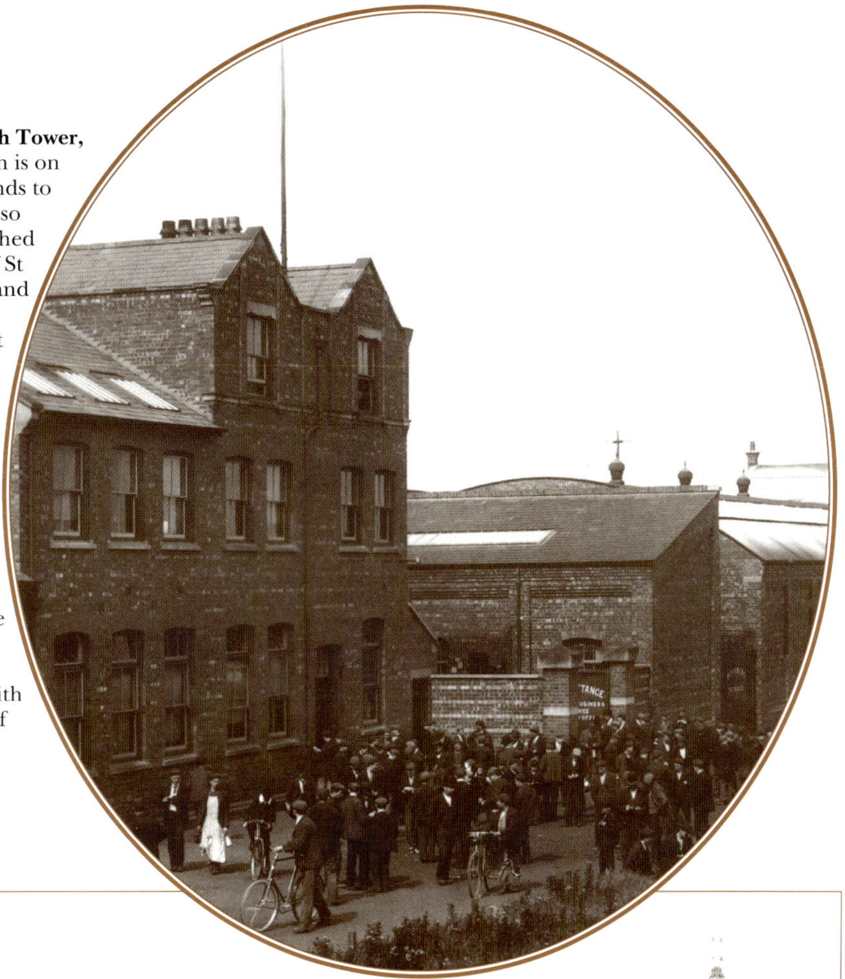

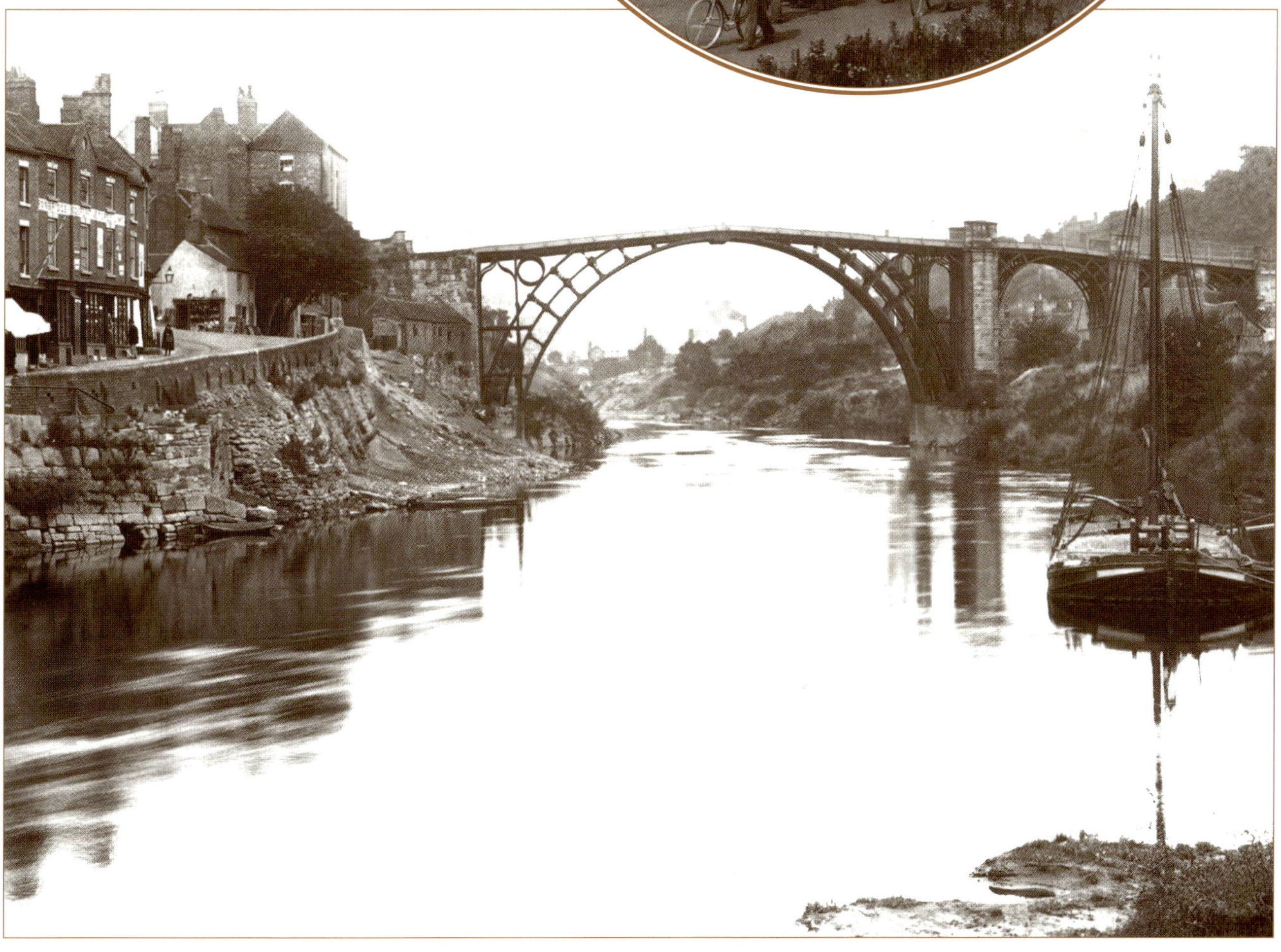

Above: Iron Bridge, 1892 (30891) The River Severn churns its way through the deep gorge. The little town looks down as it clings to the steep limestone slopes. This magnificent bridge, a pioneering achievement of engineering, was built by Abraham Darby of Coalbrookdale in 1777. The huge single central span is 100 feet. On the right is one of the flat-bottomed sailing barges that carried the products of the blast furnaces.

SHREWSBURY. Cradled in a loop of the River Severn, this imposing county town, with its narrow streets and tortuous winding passages, has a long history and a wealth of grand buildings, including a ruined castle. Charles Darwin was born here, and the writer William Hazlitt heard Samuel Taylor Coleridge preach such a stirring sermon at the Unitarian Chapel that he became a lifelong disciple of the poet on the spot.

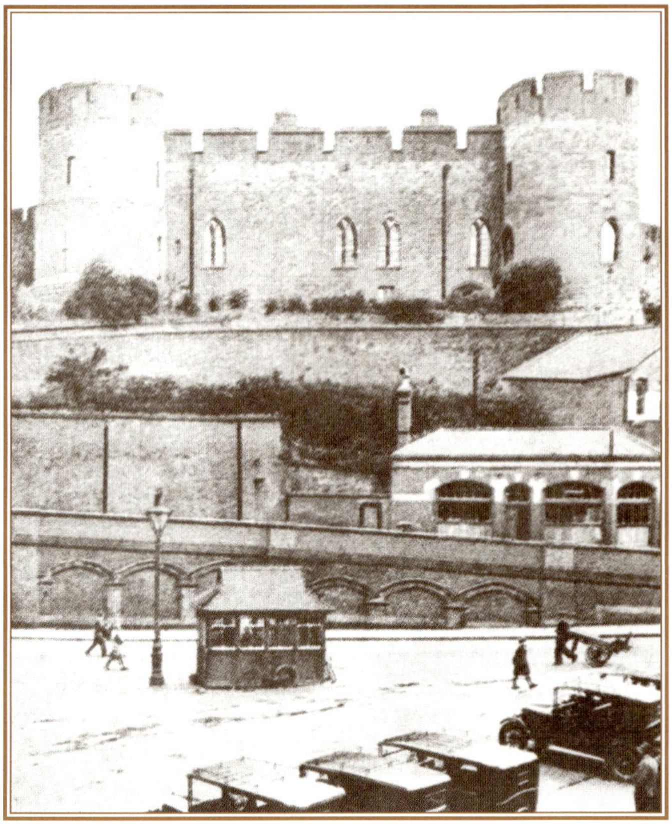

Right: The Castle, Shrewsbury, 1923 (73815) Perched on a low hill above the railway station, the castle has been knocked about and rebuilt over the centuries since Norman times. The tubby twin towers are 13th century. In 1790, the engineer Thomas Telford converted part of the ruins into a house for Sir William Pulteney and built a tower for Laura, his wife.

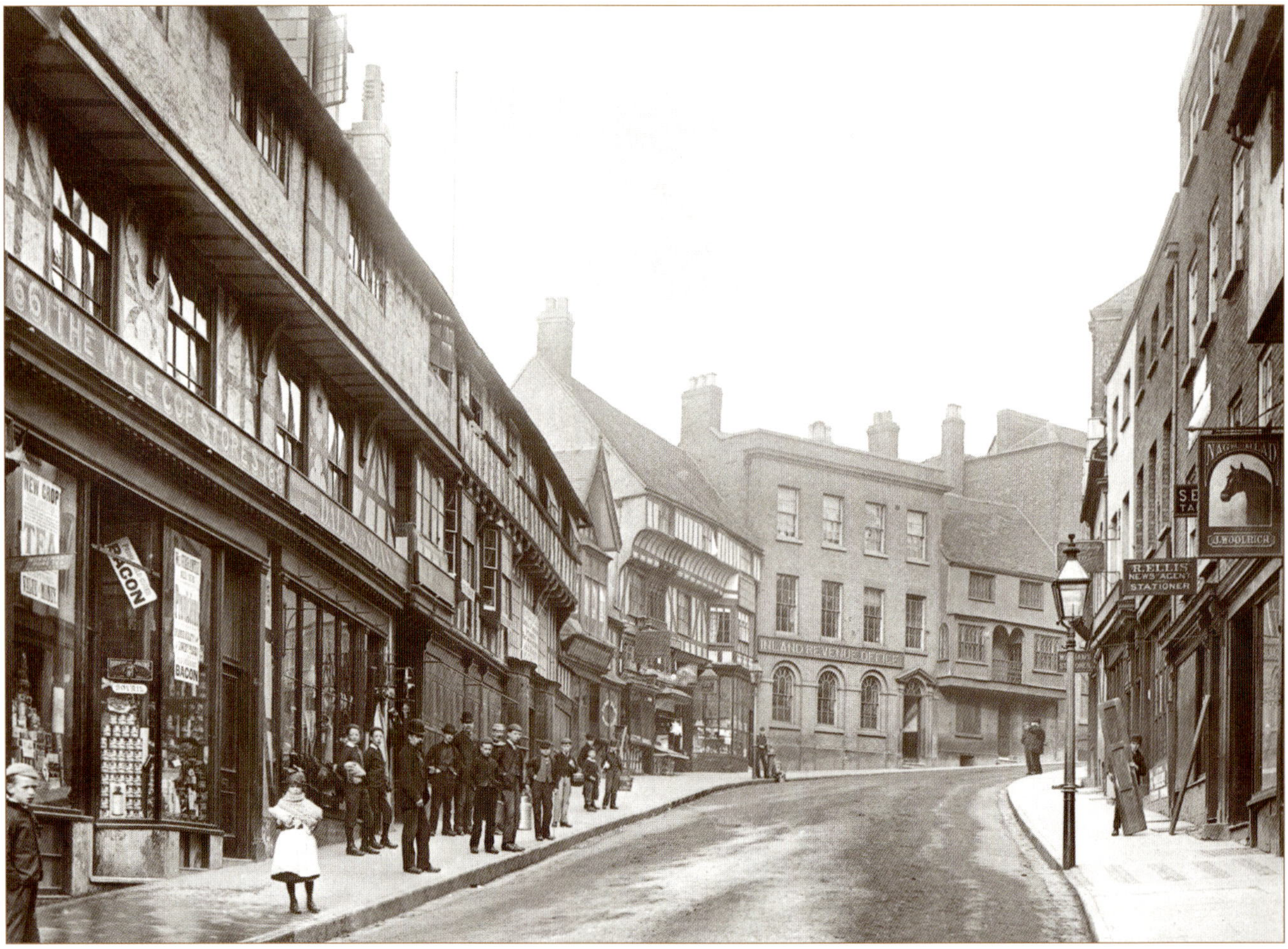

Above: Wyle Cop, Shrewsbury, 1891 (28910) The Nag's Head is on the right and at the top of the street is the Inland Revenue building. In those days you had to grit your teeth, enter the door and make your payment direct! On the left is the Wyle Cooperative Stores and a group of men and boys waiting for the carrier's cart. A young lad is putting up the shutters on Ellis's newsagents. **Opposite: Milk Street, Shrewsbury, 1911** (63227) The Old Post Office Inn, on the left, was once the home of the Proud family.

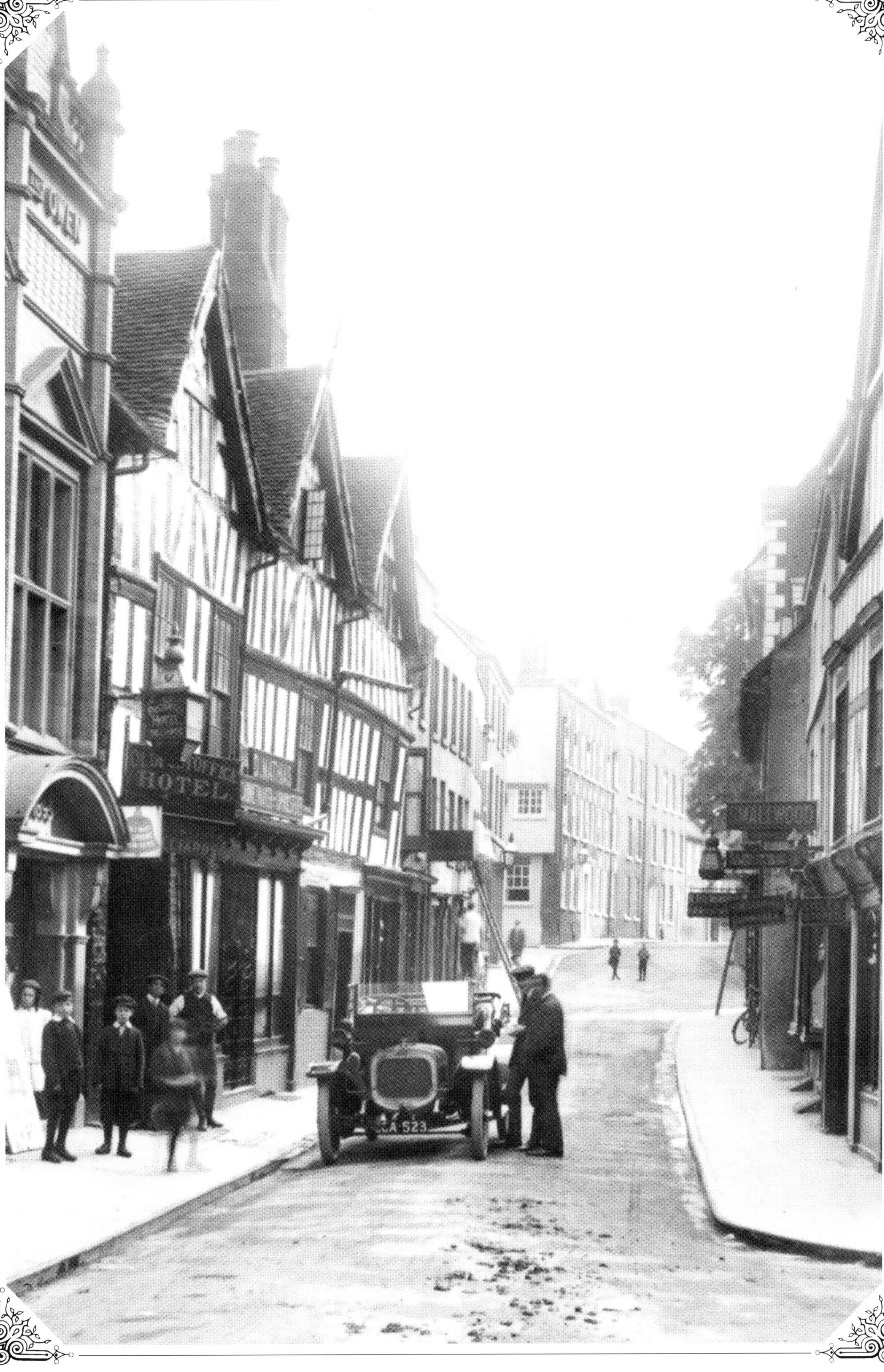
OWEN
HOTEL
SMALLWOOD

Right: The Church, Atcham, near Shrewsbury,1891 (28960) Swathed in ivy, the church of St Eata sits close to the banks of the lively Severn. Such an invasion of nature would never be allowed today. The Victorians were very different from us. They loved their grand buildings but they also had a deep feeling for the romantic, for untamed nature. In picture after picture in the Frith archive there are creeper-covered ruins where you could experience sublime and poetic emotions. This old tower is banded with ornament, and at its foot there is a Norman doorway with white stone shafts surmounted by leaves.

Below: Much Wenlock, 1936 (87402) Close to majestic Wenlock Edge, this graceful market town has seen few changes over the years. Here we see humble cottages lining the street and, in the distance, rising above the timbered houses, the church.

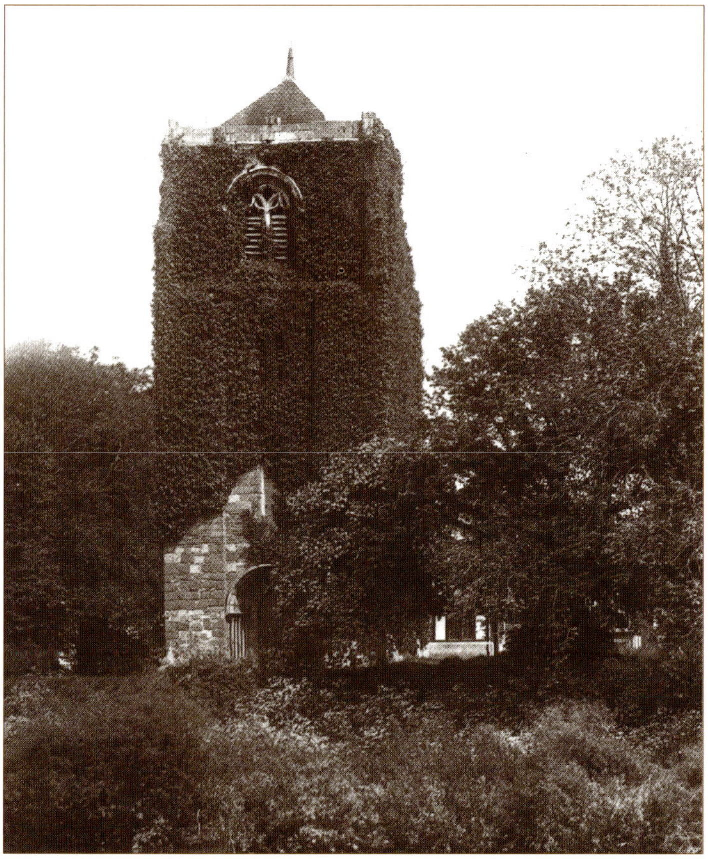

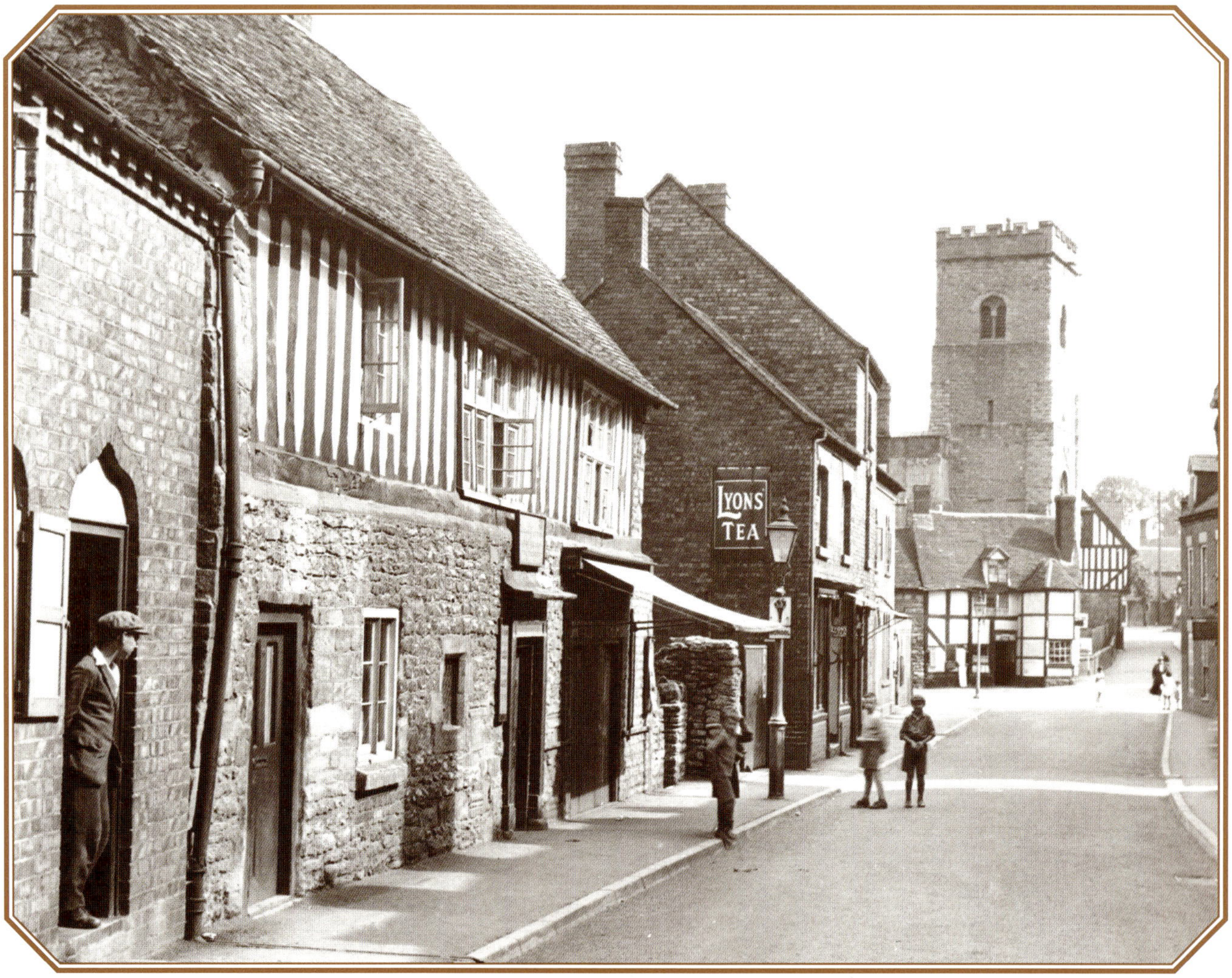

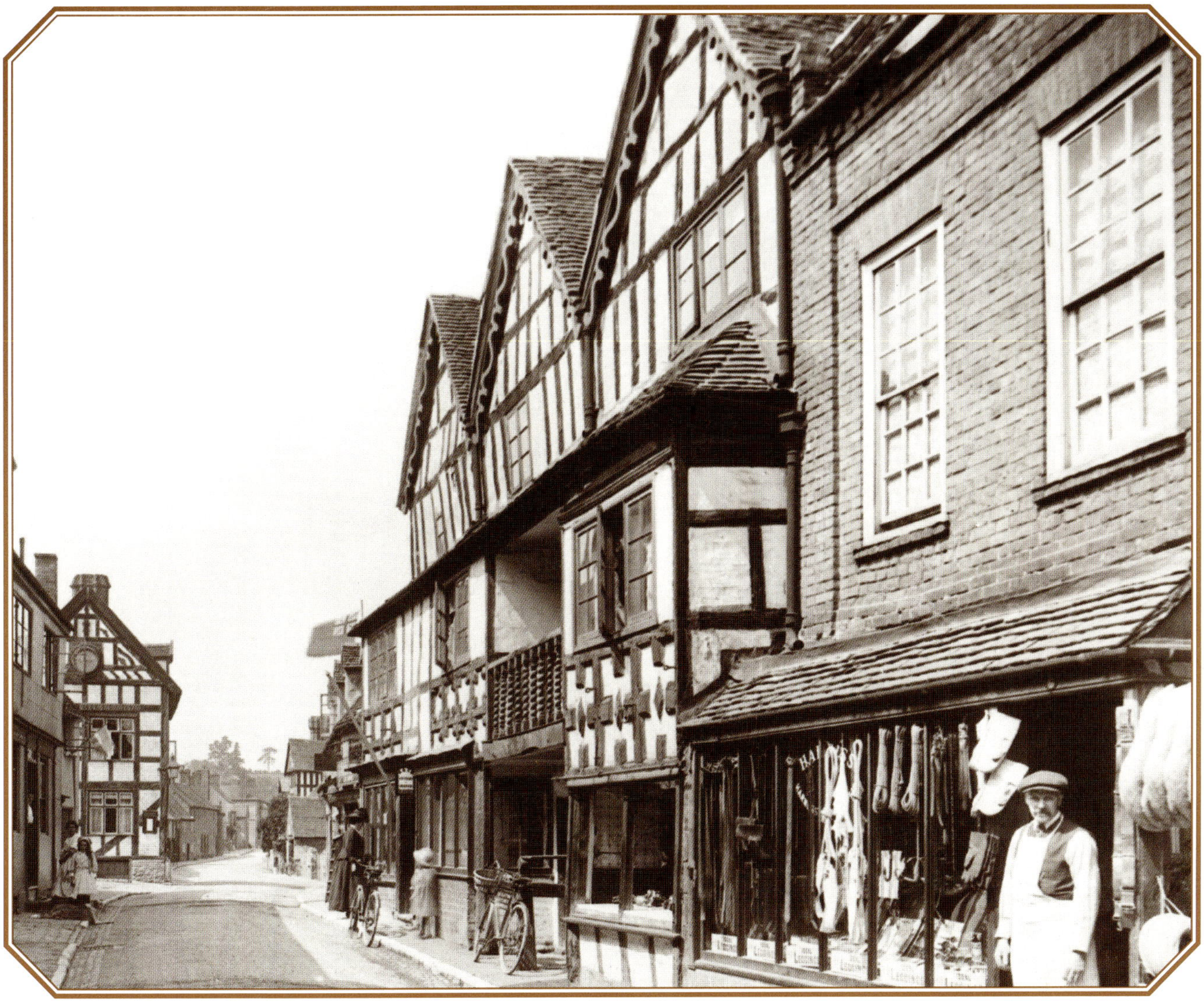

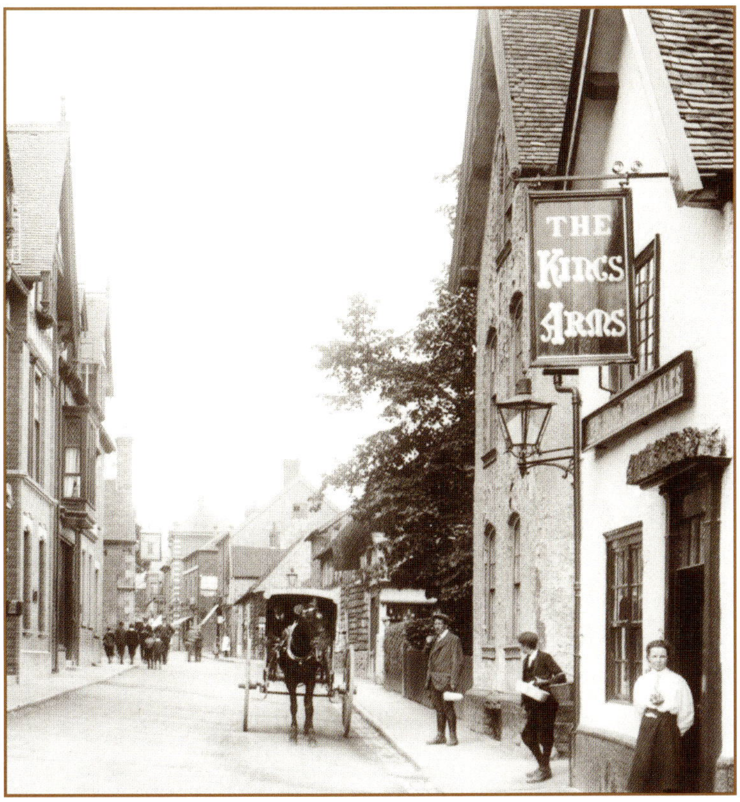

Above: High Street, Much Wenlock, 1911 (63266) The old Guildhall rests on the oaken arches of the butter market. It is said that its timber frame was erected in two days! Upstairs is the council chamber and court. Here, too, are kept the old stocks, which are on wheels so they could be rolled around the town to dispense justice where it was needed. The shopkeeper on the right has a window display of ropes and cordage.

Left: High Street, Church Stretton, 1910 (62721) Across the Caradoc hills from Much Wenlock, Church Stretton winds through a green valley. It was a favourite resort for the Victorians, who enjoyed the especial freshness of its air. On the right is The King's Arms.

Overleaf: The Caradoc Hills, 1910 (62728) These rugged hills lie to the east of Church Stretton. Up on the windy summit are the ramparts of Caer Caradoc's ancient fortification, built, some say, by Caractacus.

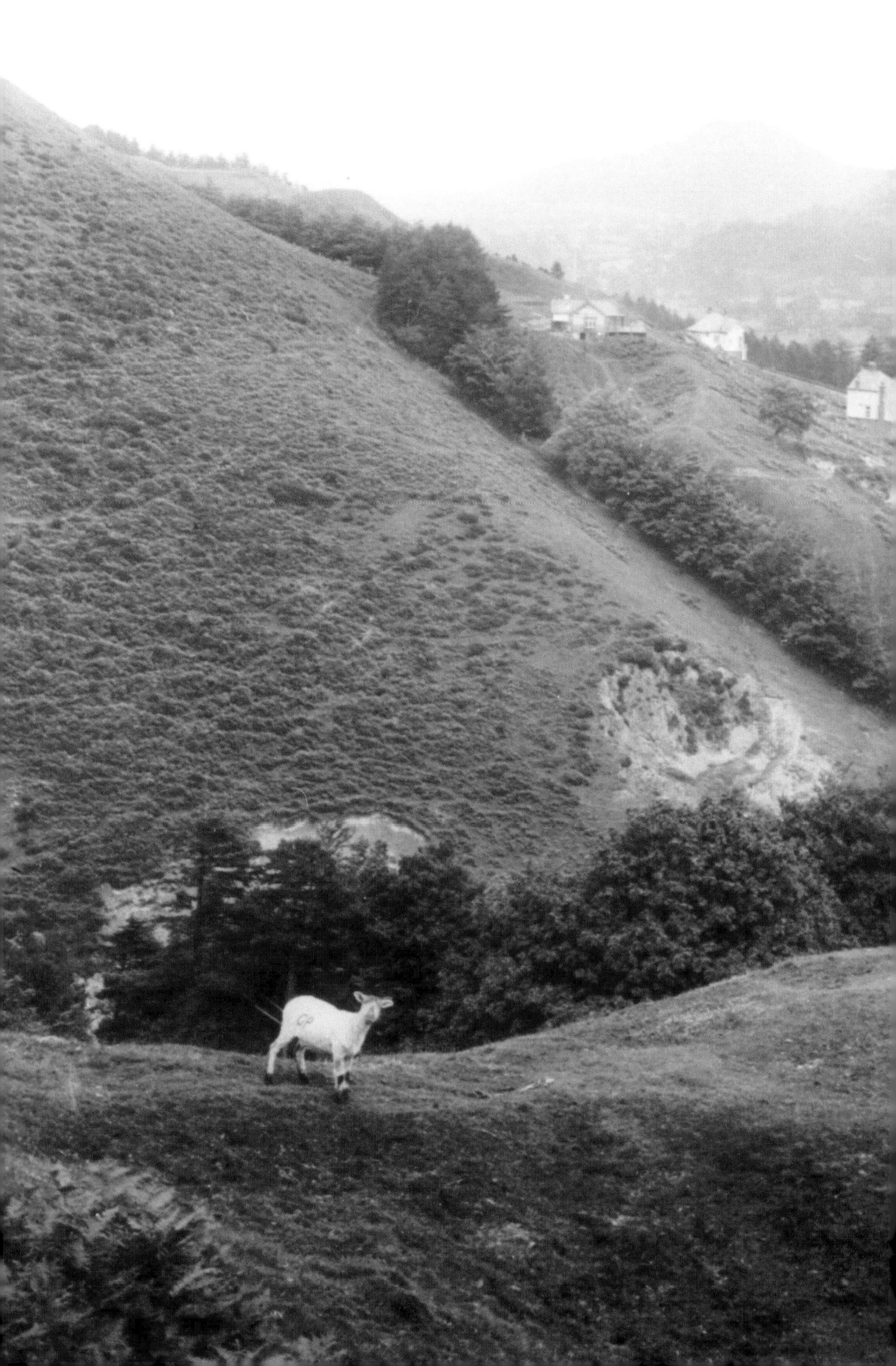

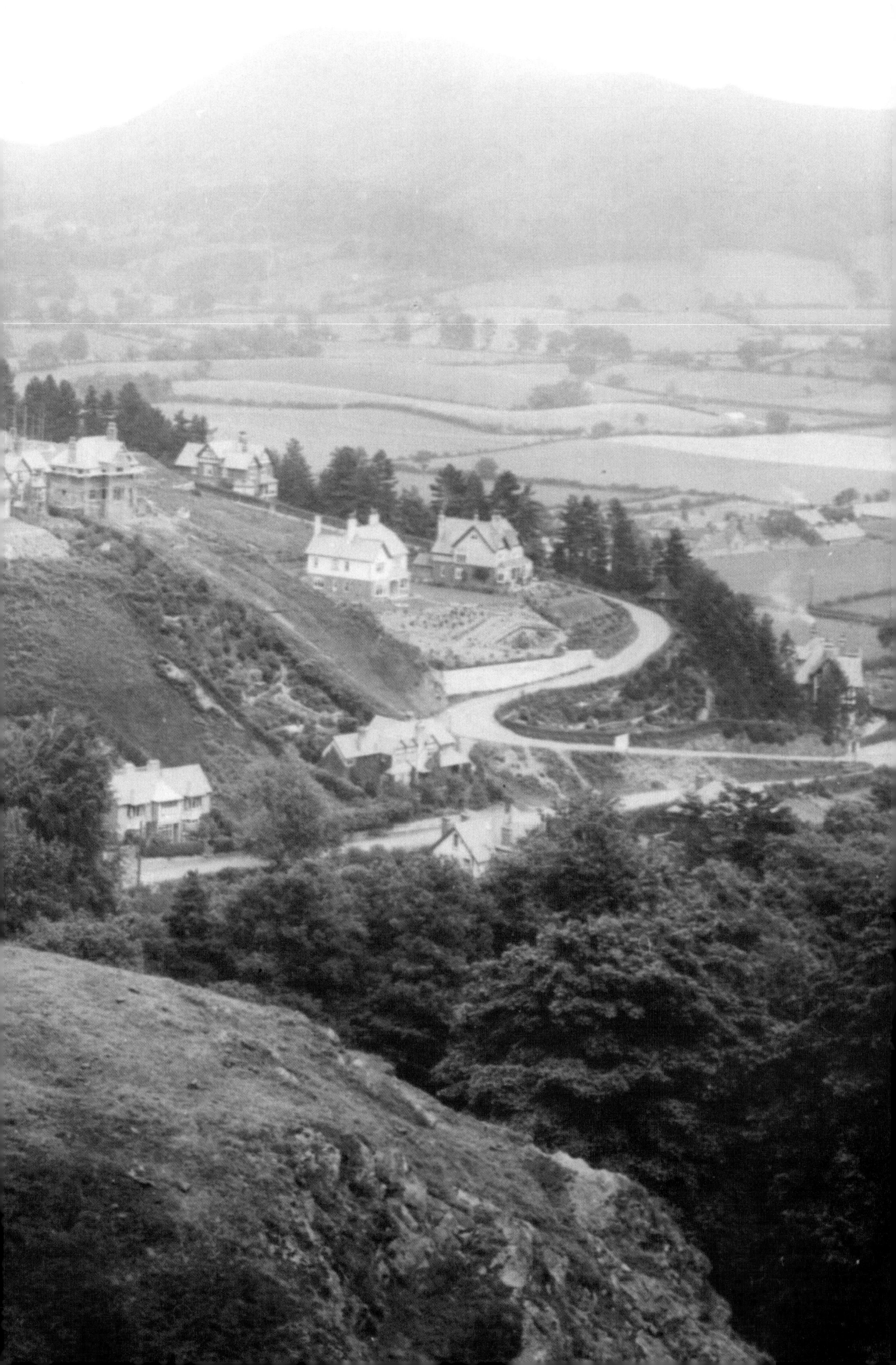

BRIDGNORTH. This historic town by the Severn is divided into two distinct halves, High Town and Low Town, connected by a graceful bridge, a steep cable railway and some tortuously winding alpine passages. It is said that the two towns kept themselves to themselves, the genteel inhabitants of High Town looking down their noses at their Low Town neighbours, whose wharfside work and rough and ready ways were a little too much for their refined tastes.

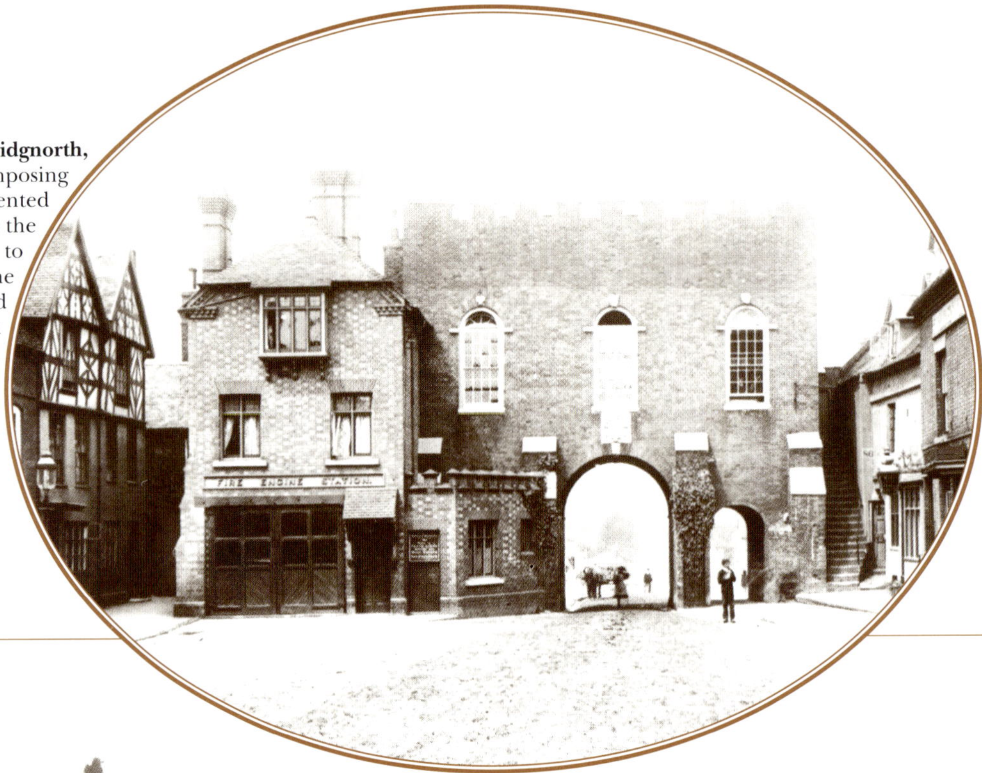

Right: Northgate, Bridgnorth, 1896 (38127) This imposing sandstone battlemented arch commands the northern approaches to Bridgnorth, and is the sole survivor of the old fortified town, which was rebuilt in the 12th century. Next to it is the Fire Engine Station.

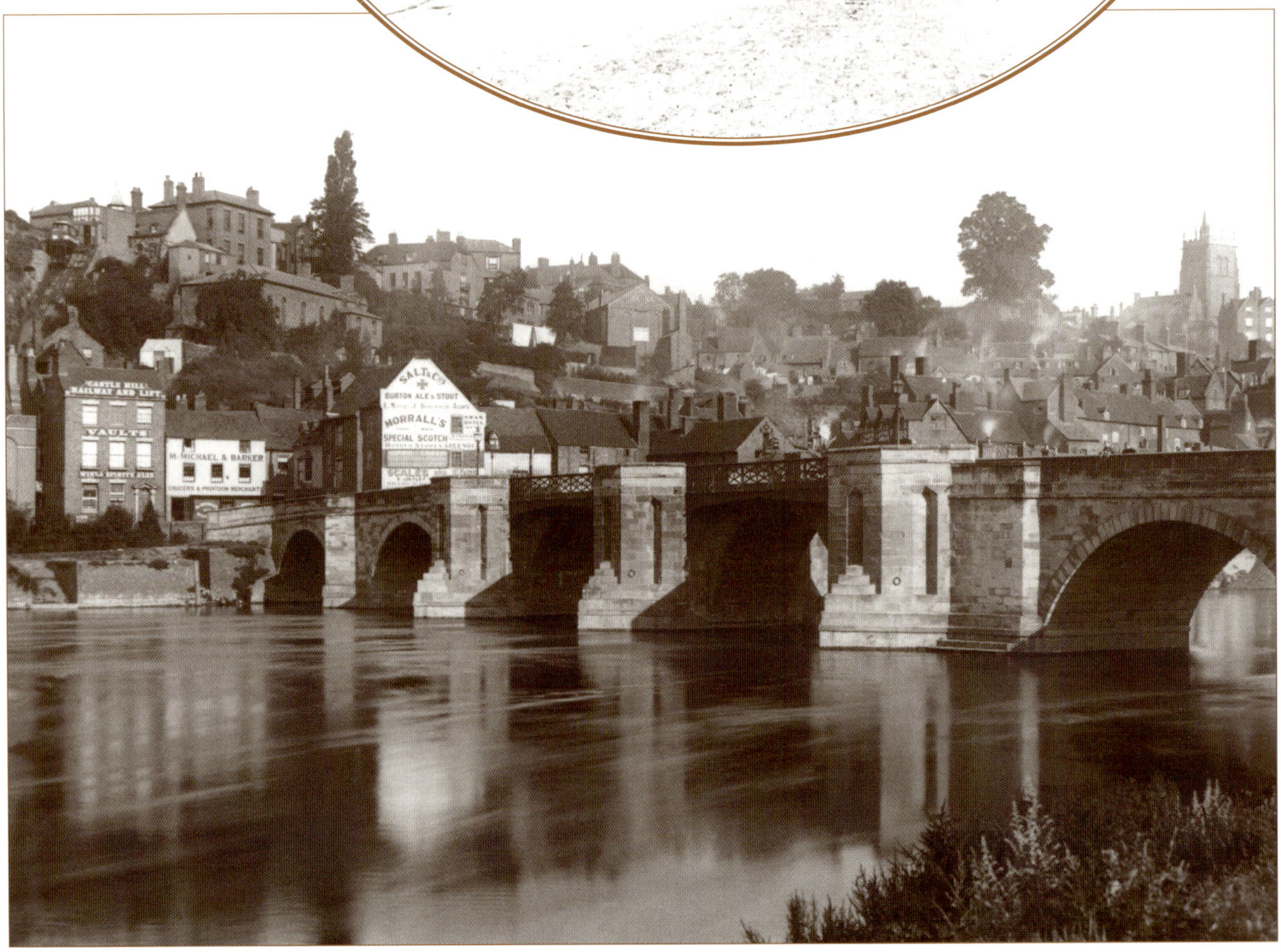

Above: Bridgnorth from the River, 1898 (42624) This grandiose six-arched bridge straddles the fast-flowing River Severn. The roofs of the town rise in tiers above the sandstone cliff. It is no wonder that Cotman and Turner came here to paint such a fine prospect. On the left is the Castle Hill railway lift, with its gradient of two in three, which transports the traveller to the High Town. Coracles once wound their uncertain course along the river, and flat-bottomed barges called trows used to ply their trade.

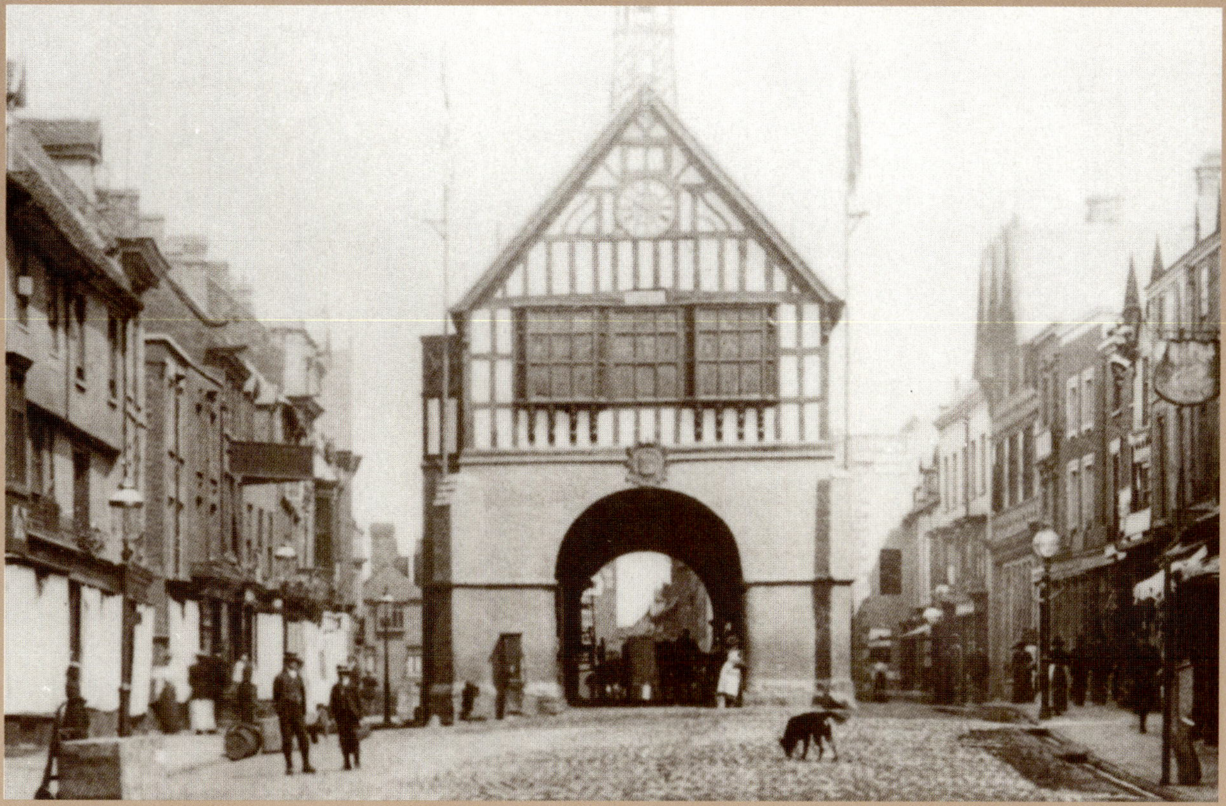

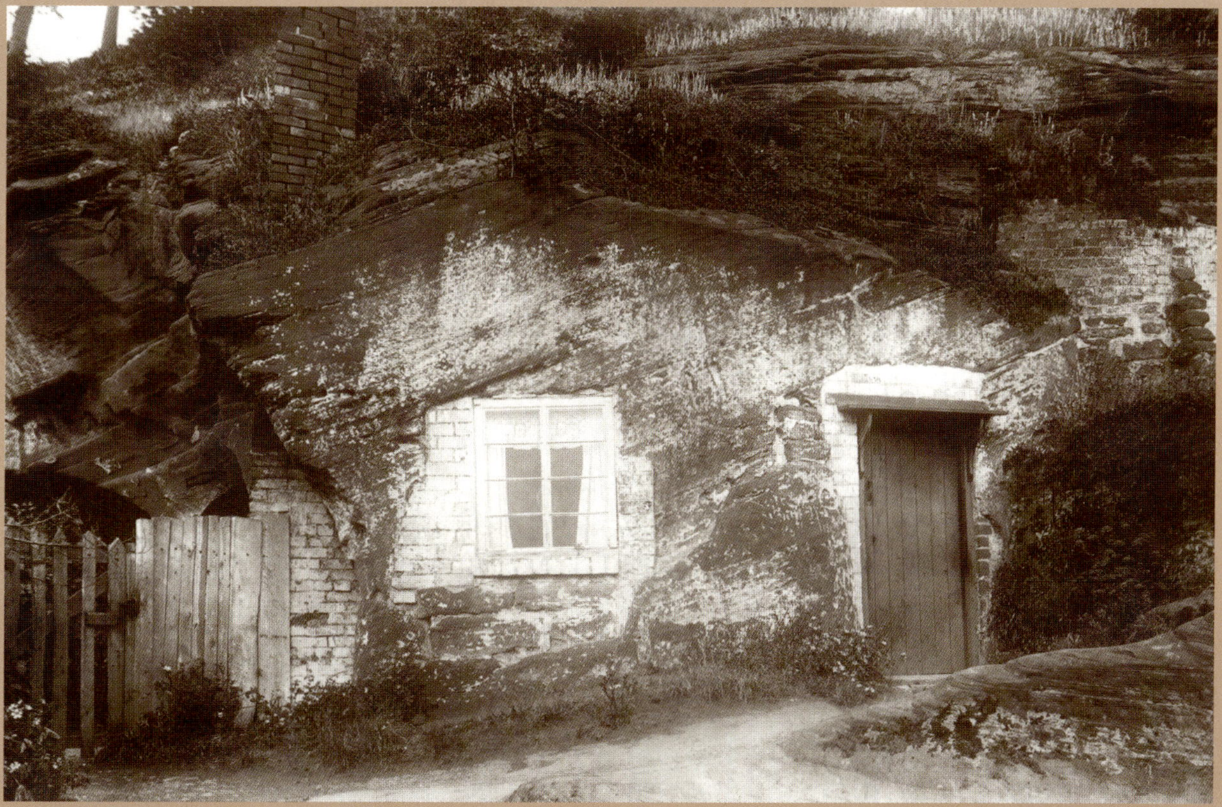

Top: The Town Hall, Bridgnorth, 1896 (38126A) It is said that this handsome building started out its life as a barn, and was carried here from Much Wenlock and re-erected on solid stone arches. On the top is an ornate lantern. **Above: Rock House, Bridgnorth, 1896** (38136) These caves, on the Cartway, which leads down from the High Street, were carved out of solid sandstone. In Victorian times, as we see here, local people lived in them. Although they have all the trappings of normal houses, including simple windows and plank doors, they must have made damp, dark homes. They were later converted into storehouses.

LUDLOW. This beautiful hilltop border town was once the capital of the Welsh Marches. Encircled by rivers, and with its ancient castle, mediaeval gate and wealth of historic buildings, it transports the visitor instantly back down the centuries. It has many old inns, including the Angel Hotel, the Rose and Crown and the Feathers. Close by is much spectacular scenery to explore - the Long Mynd, the Clee Hills and Wenlock Edge.

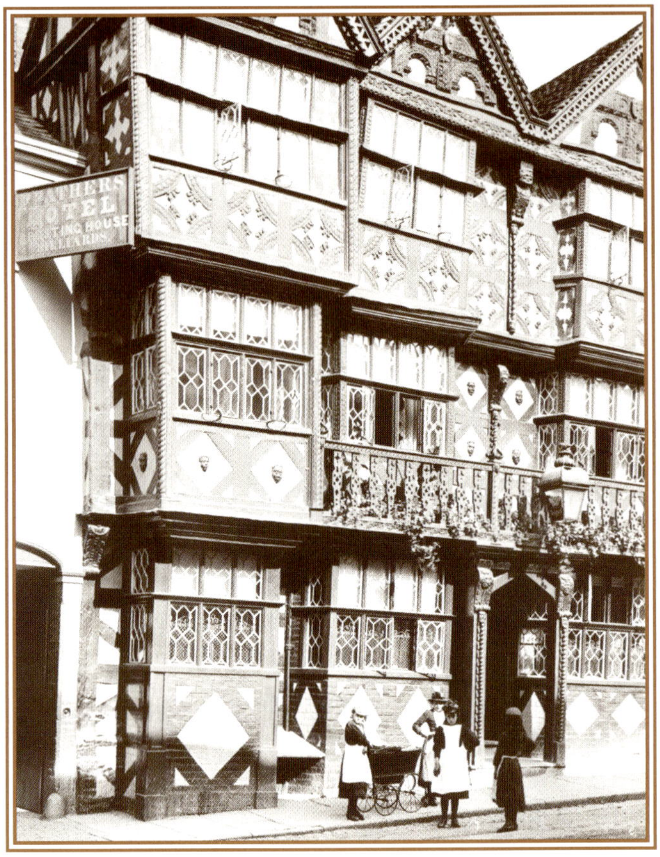

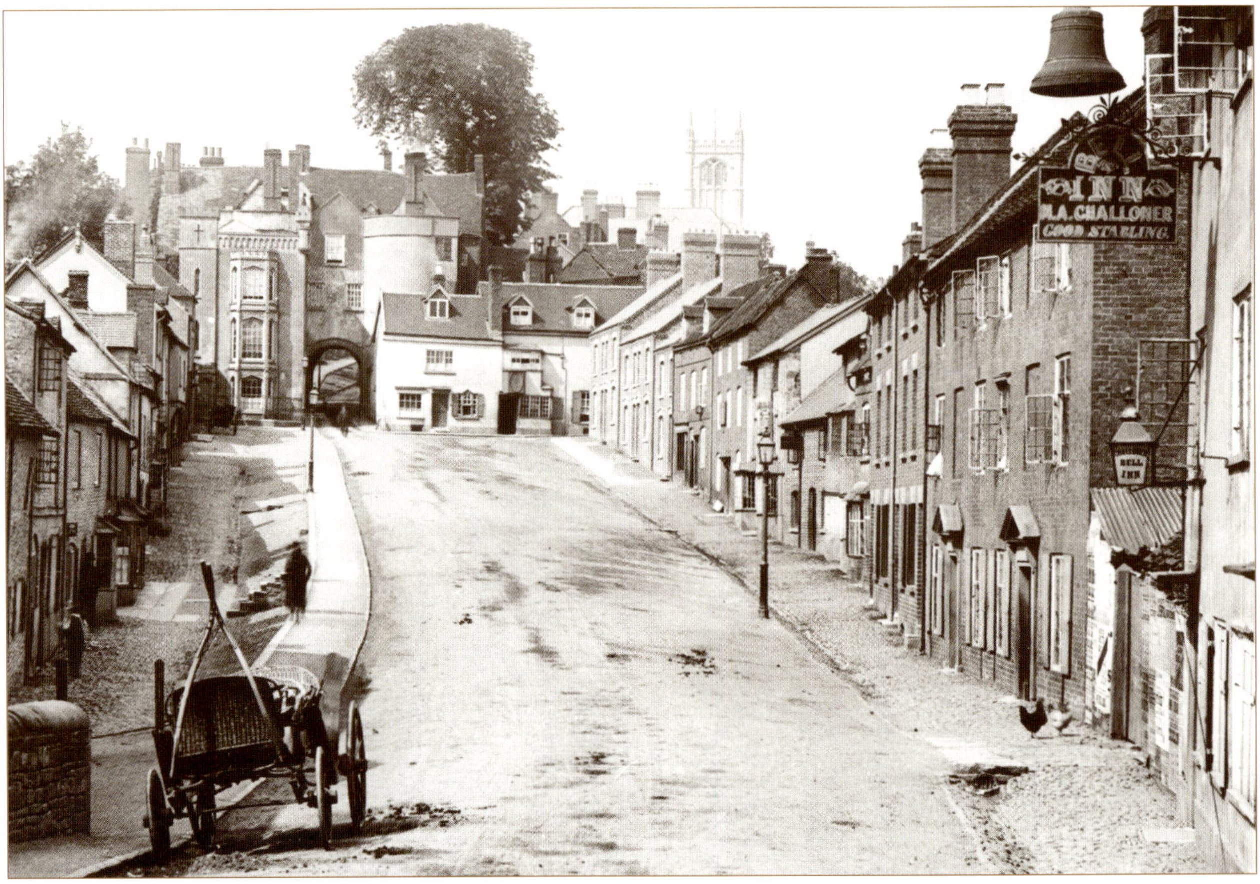

Top: The Feathers Hotel, Ludlow, 1892 (30829) This flamboyant timbered building stands in the Bull Ring at the top of Corve Street. It has looked after travellers' needs since 1521. With its twisted timbers, intricate balconies, diamond motifs and carved dolphins, it offers an overwhelming glimpse of another age. **Above: Broad Street, Ludlow, 1892** (30825) At the top of this steep, winding street is the old Broad Gate, with its portcullis grooves, the town's only surviving medieval gateway. Many of the houses here date from the 15th century.

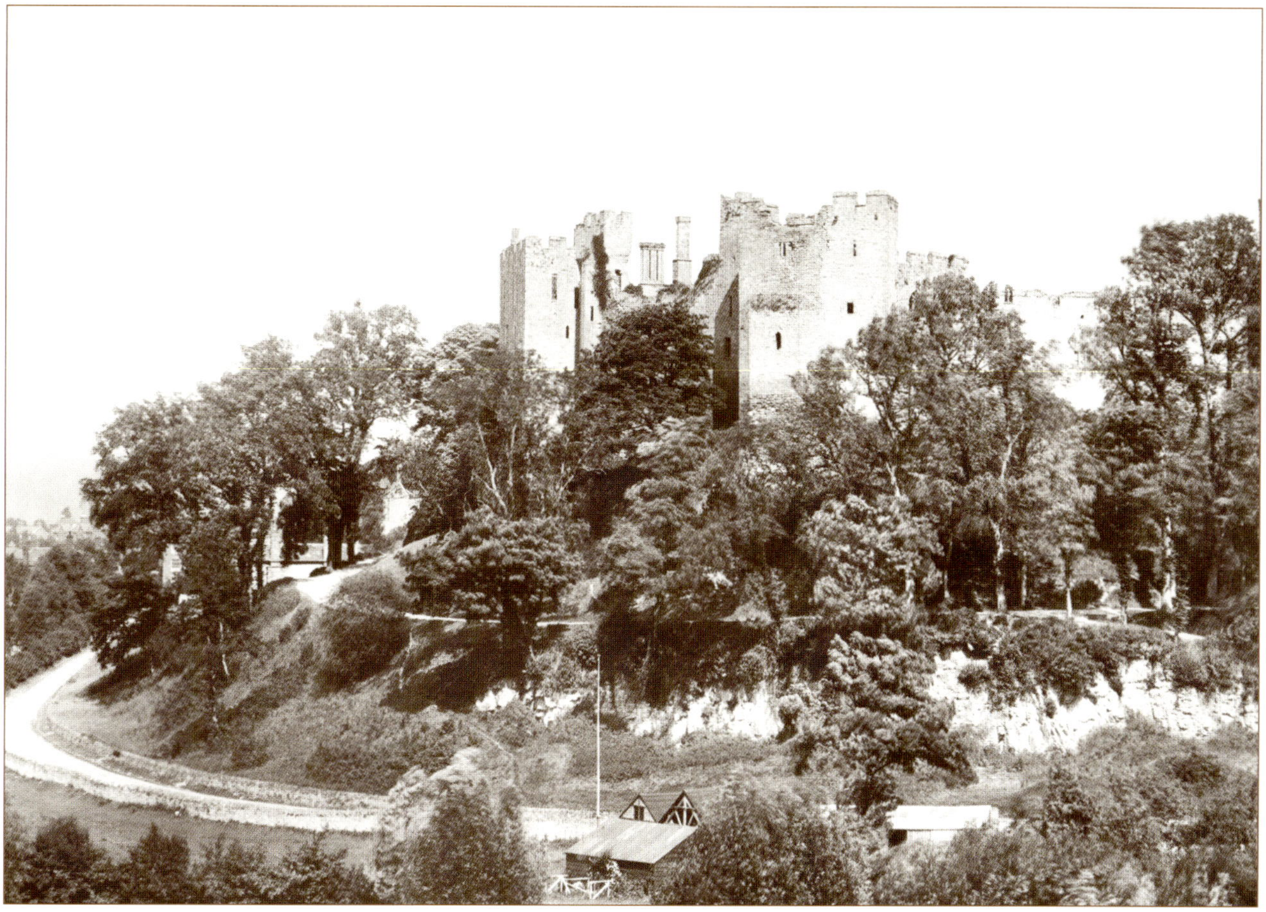

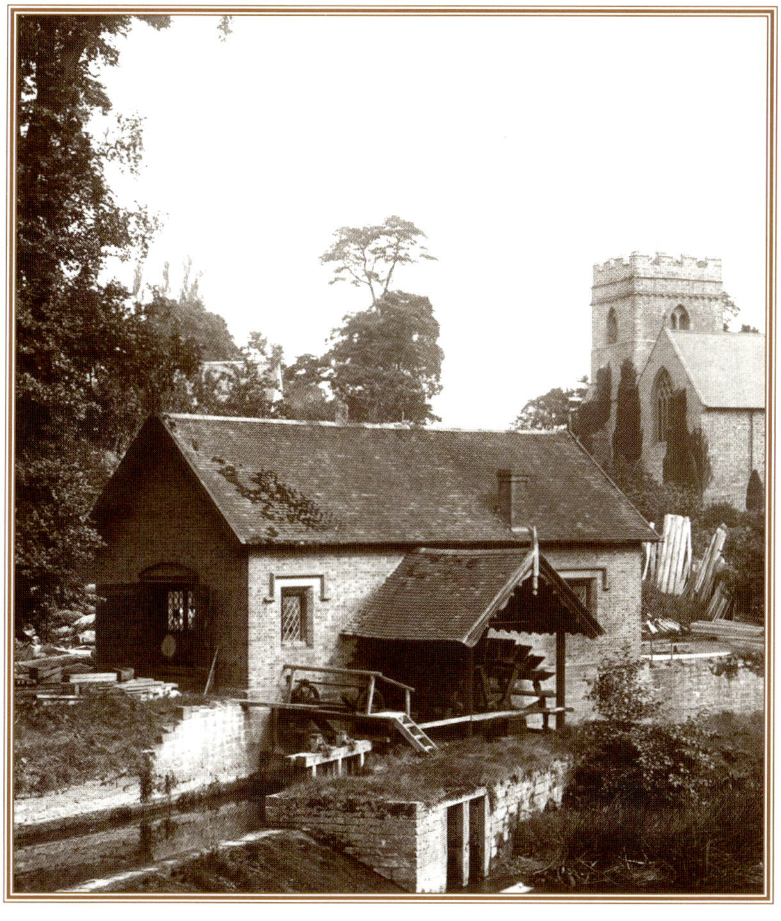

Top: Ludlow Castle, 1896 (38149) This majestic red stone ruin crowns the hill on which historic Ludlow perches, and looks down on the romantic wooded valley of the River Teme below. Here we see the massive walls and towers of the outer bailey. Ludlow Castle was one of a long string of fortifications lining the frontier that maintained the peace between England and Wales. Henry Tudor shrewdly extended the old Norman keep and courtyard. During Richard III's reign, it was from Ludlow Castle that the two young princes set out on their final journey to the Tower of London to be heartlessly murdered.

Left: The Mill, Bromfield, near Ludlow, 1892 (30842) This simple millhouse, with its porch over the mill wheel and leaded windows, is close by the banks of the River Teme. Its garden is in use as a woodyard. In the background is the medieval parish church.

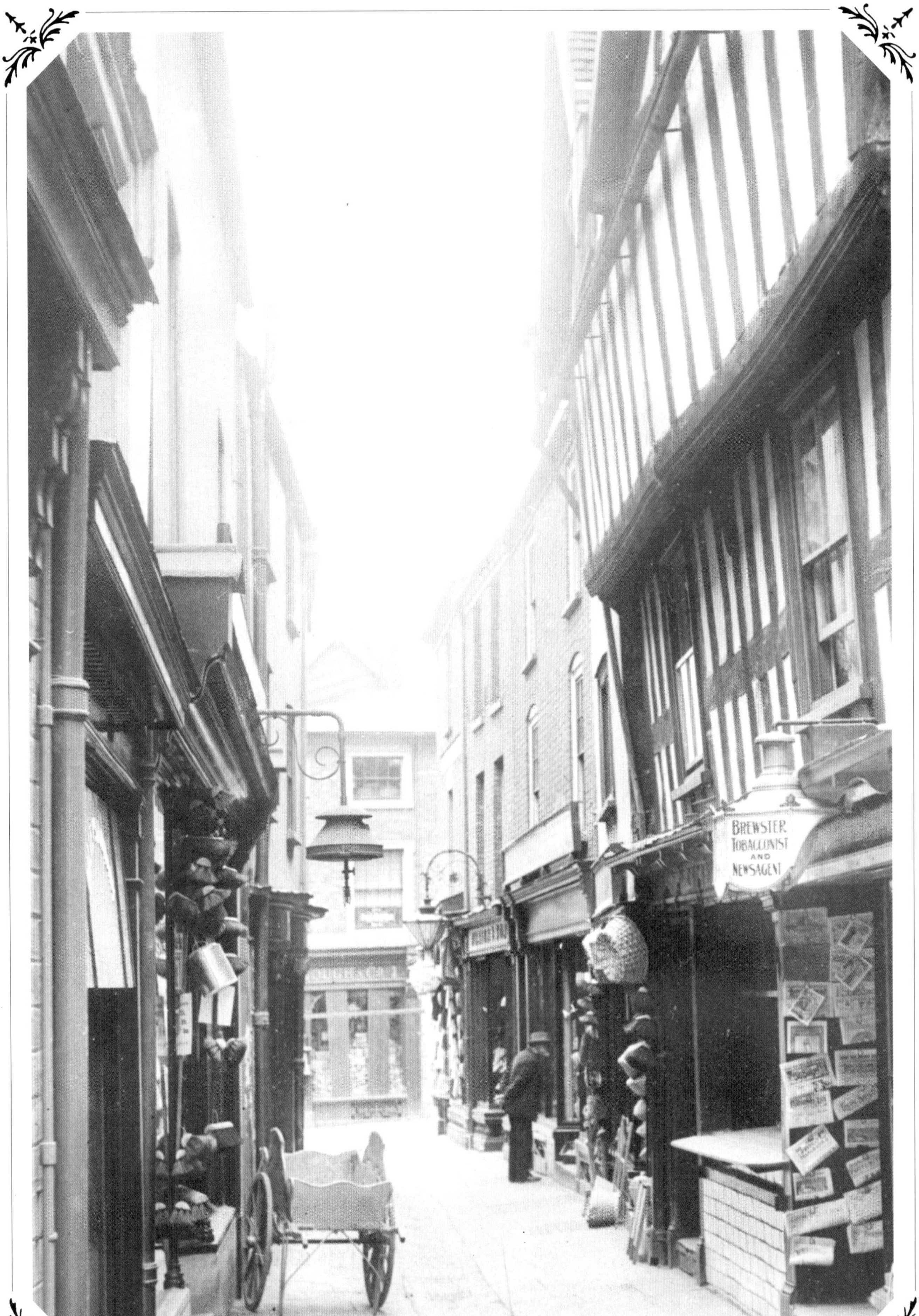
BREWSTER
TOBACCONIST
AND
NEWSAGENT

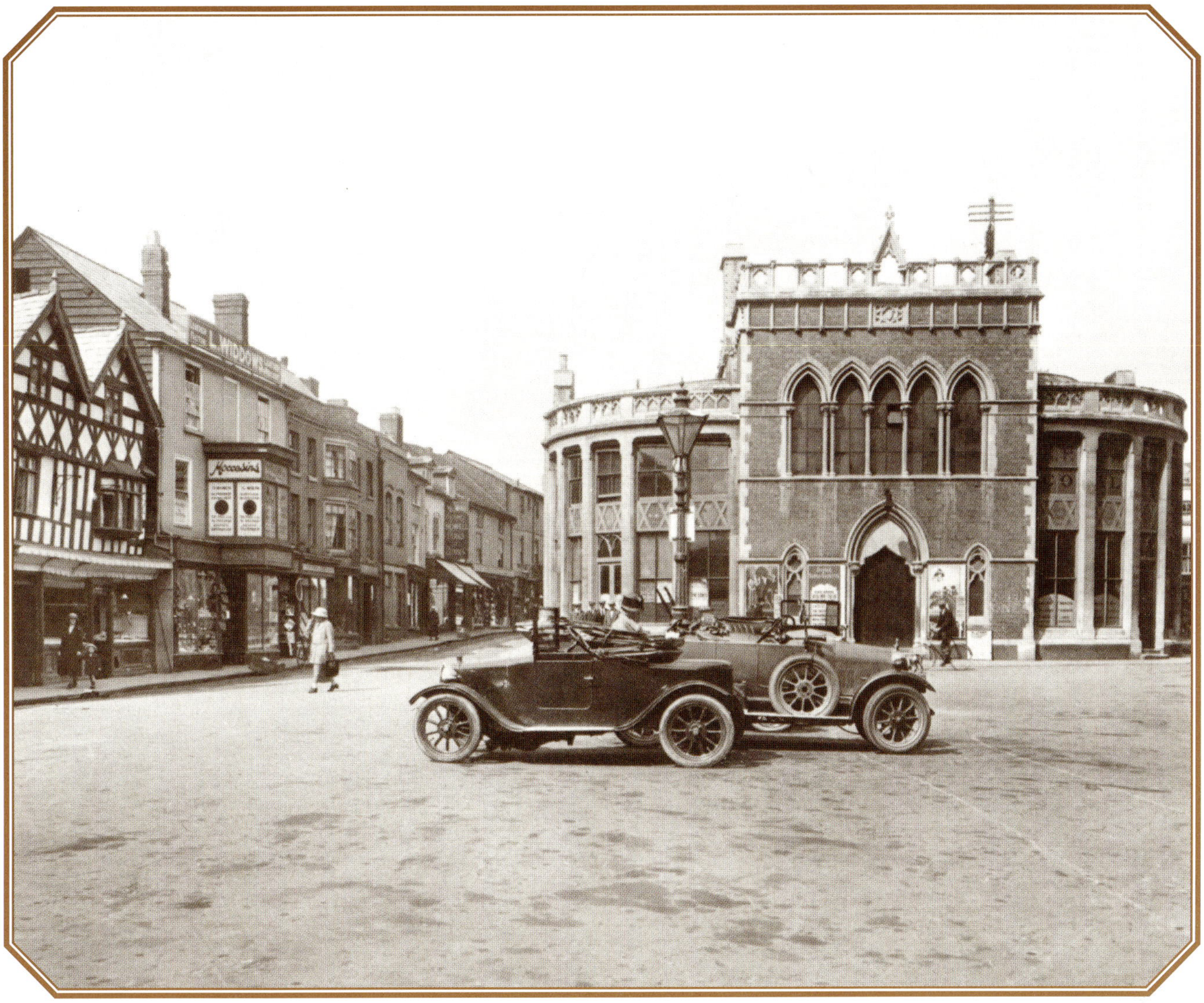

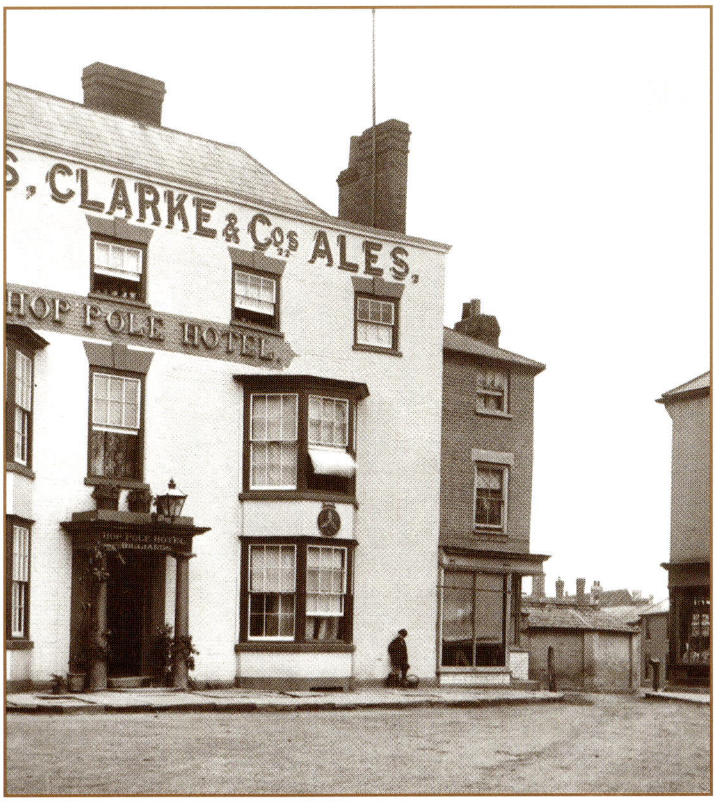

Opposite: Drapers Lane, Leominster, 1904 (51922) This historic town is second only to Hereford in importance in the county. Its narrow ways and passages display its medieval origins. The gables of the handsome old timbered building topple forward so that the inhabitants could almost shake hands with those opposite. Brewster's Newsagents is selling a formidable range of comics and magazines, including *Photo Bits*, *Big Budget* - and the *Police News*!

Top: The Corn Square, Leominster, 1925 (76929) The town once boasted the finest wool market in England. The florid Victorian Italianate Town Hall hardly harmonises with the timbered buildings surrounding the rest of the square, yet adds a touch of grandeur to their more rustic simplicity.

Left: The Hop Pole Hotel, Bromyard, 1906 (54302) This hotel is aptly named - the town is set in orchards and hopfield country.

HEREFORD. This ancient cathedral city on the banks of Wye still has the atmosphere of a market town, and on Wednesdays farmers converge here to buy and sell their cattle. The poet Thomas Traherne was born here, the son of a shoemaker, and must have experienced his mystic vision of 'immortal wheat' during his childhood in the fields surrounding the city.

Right: The Cathedral and Bridge, Hereford, 1885 (4831) A loop of the Wye nudges the southern edges of the city, crossed by this graceful medieval bridge. In the foreground is a fleet of punts and skiffs from which visitors can enjoy the prospect from the river. Soaring over the roofs is the majestic red sandstone tower of the cathedral, dating from 1400.

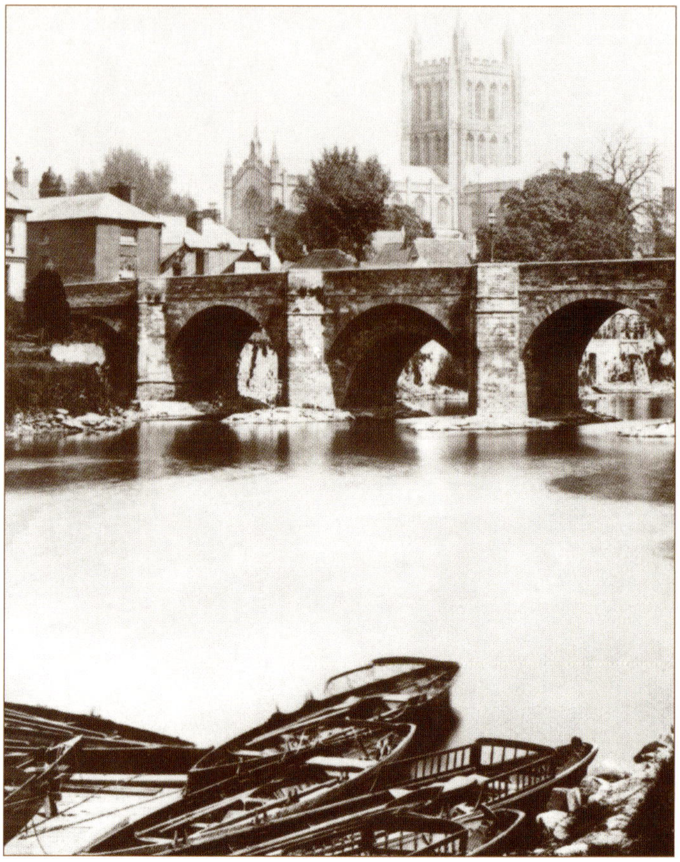

Below: High Town, Hereford, 1891 (29285) A busy scene in the heart of the old city. In the background is the Old House. Here, carts and cabs ply the streets. Is it possible that these two ladies can enjoy the sunshine, swathed as they are in heavy, dark dresses, and sheltering under an even darker sunshade?

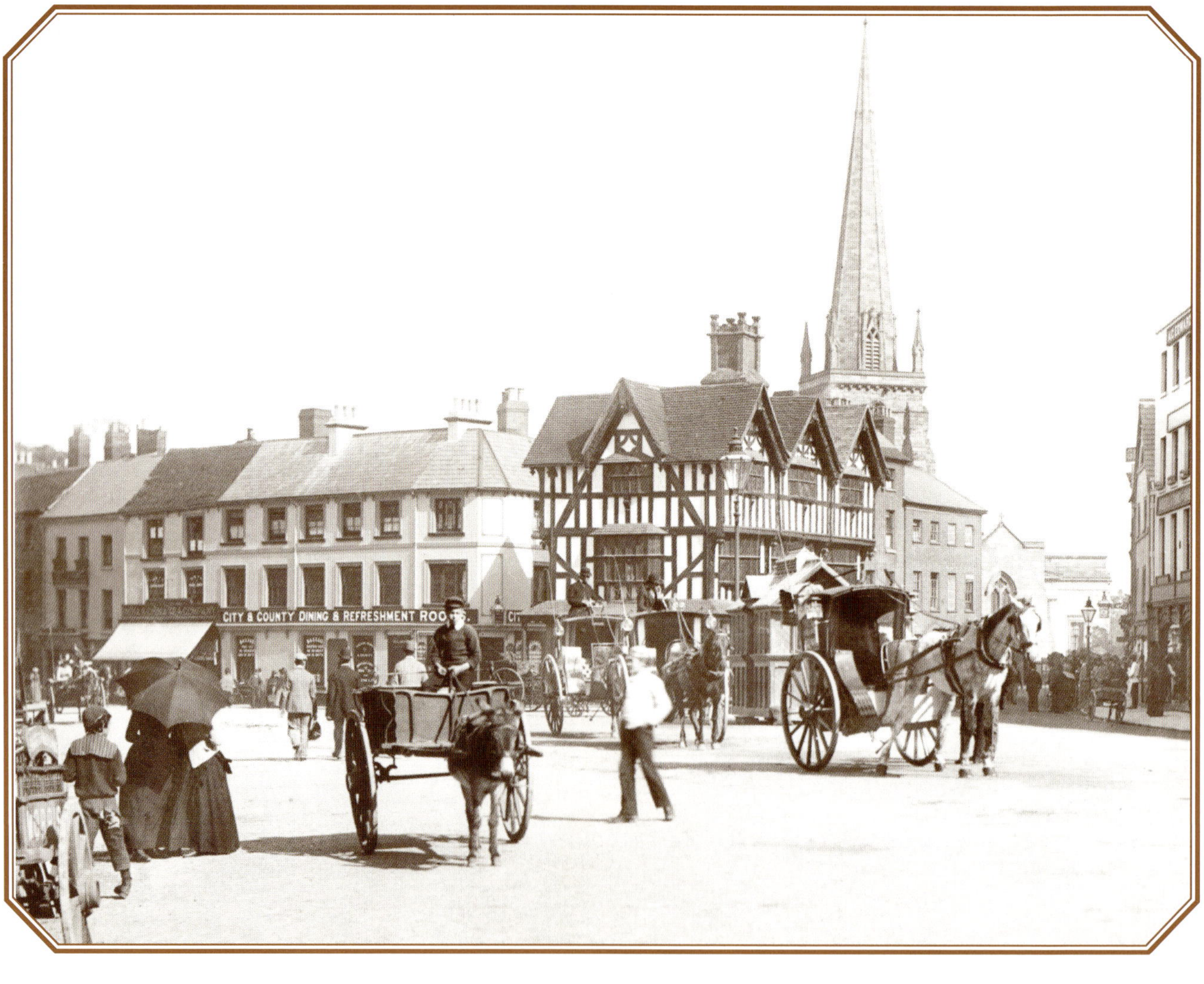

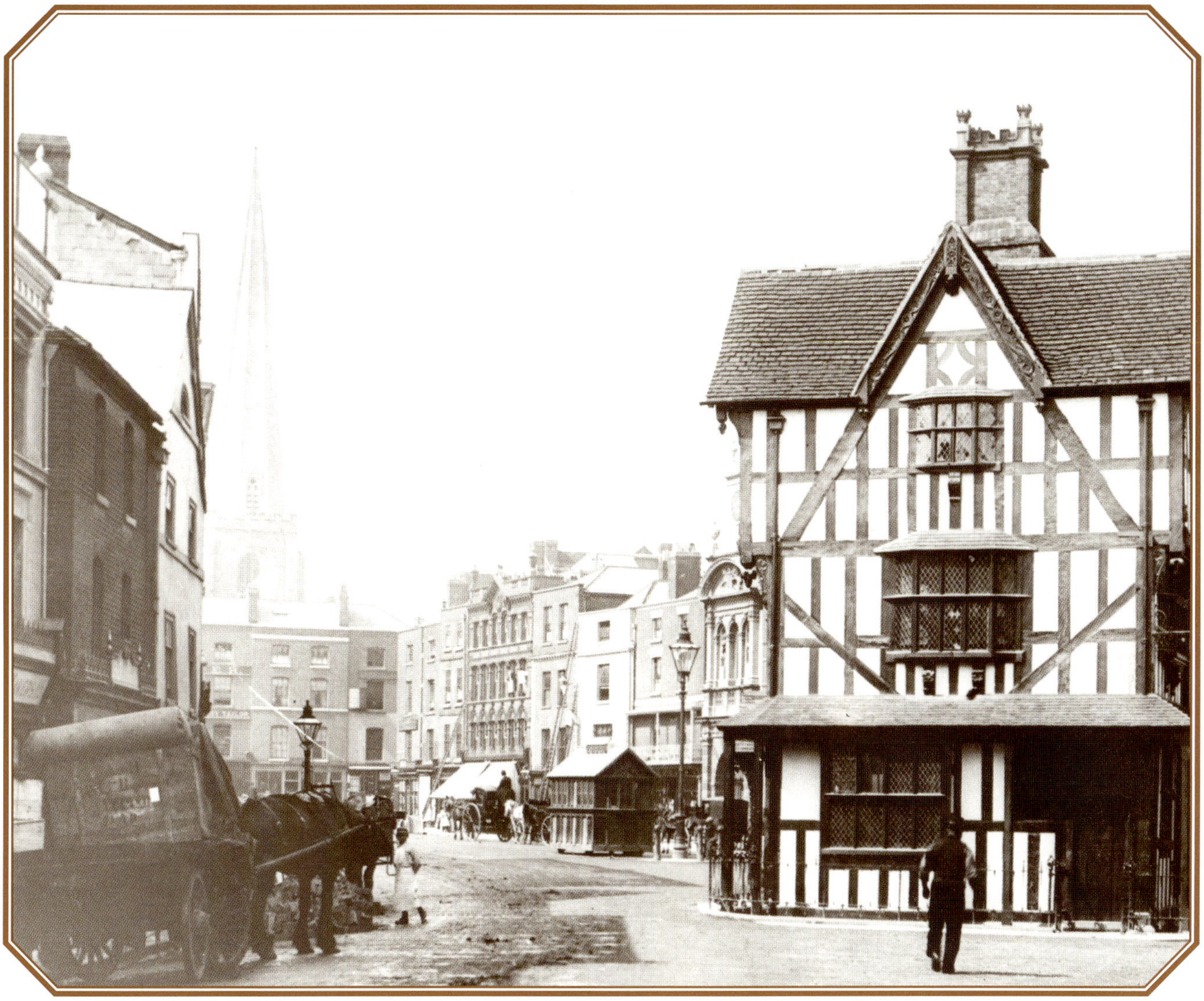

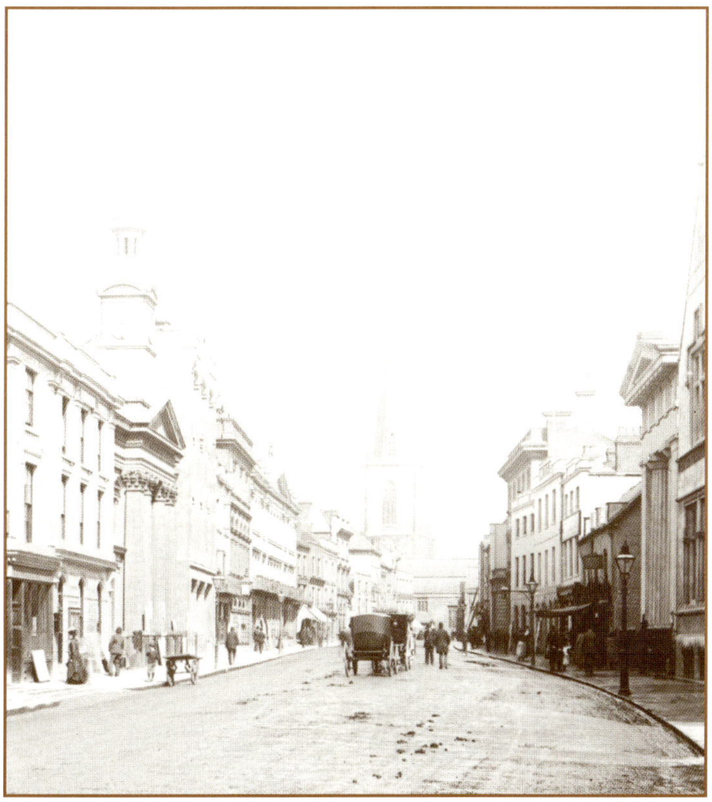

Above: The Old House, High Town, Hereford, 1891 (29286) This Jacobean, timber-framed building is one of the treasures of the city. It was built for the Butchers' Guild in 1621, and is now a museum of Elizabethan furniture. On the left, men are unloading a huge packing case from the back of a waggon. In the centre of the view is the cab rank office, conveniently mounted on wheels.

Left: Broad Street, Hereford, 1891 (29284) This spacious street runs towards the cathedral. In the distance is All Saints' church, with its somewhat twisted spire. Here are the Victorian Gothic public library and the City Museum and Art Gallery.

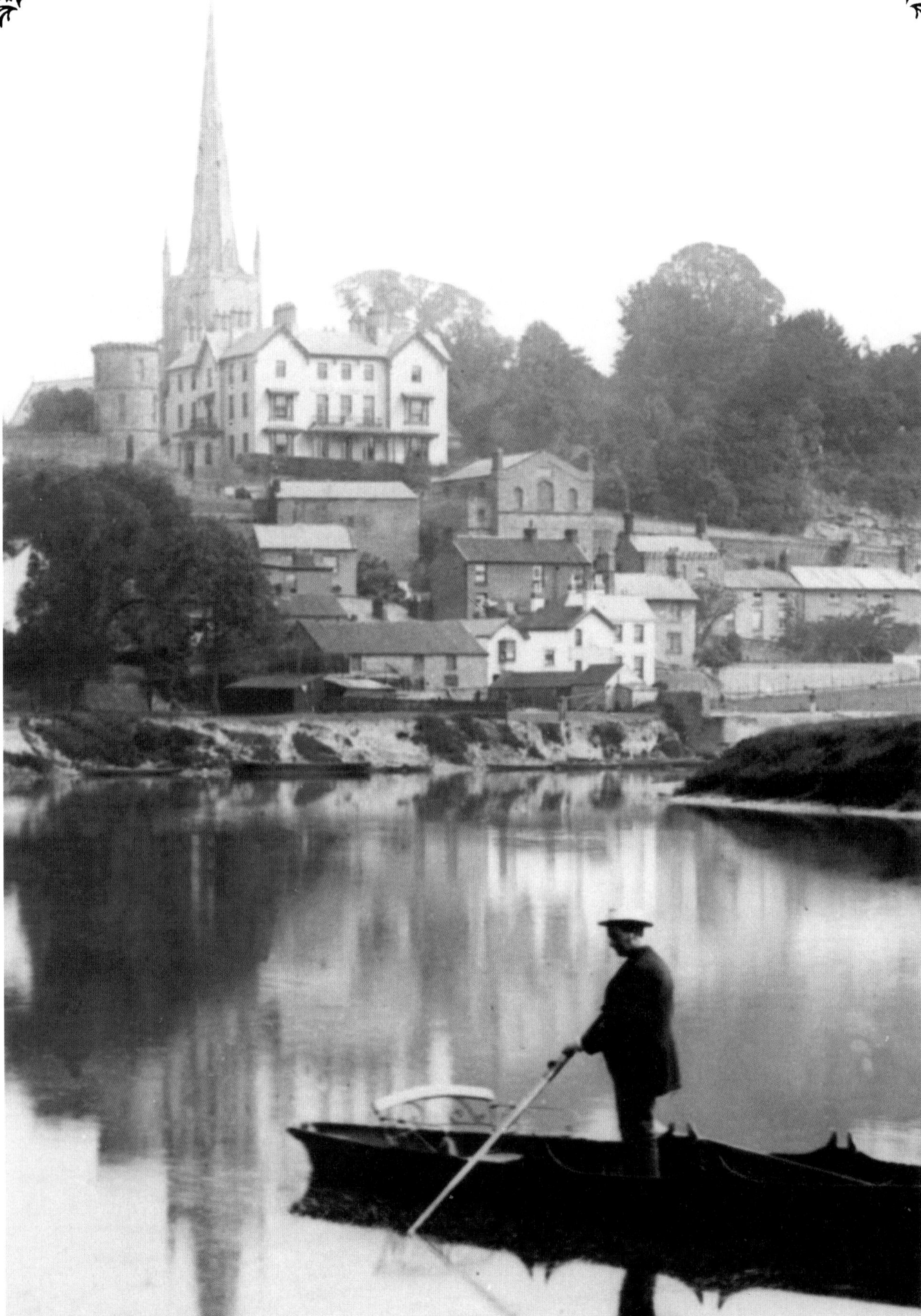

Opposite: Ross on Wye, from the River, 1893 (32423) This breathtaking prospect of Ross and its ancient church is from the shaded banks of the Wye. The spire soars above the roofs and is reflected in the placid water below. The boatman has dropped his oar and is content to stand and stare. He has probably ferried the Frith cameraman along the river to this perfect spot for taking a photograph.

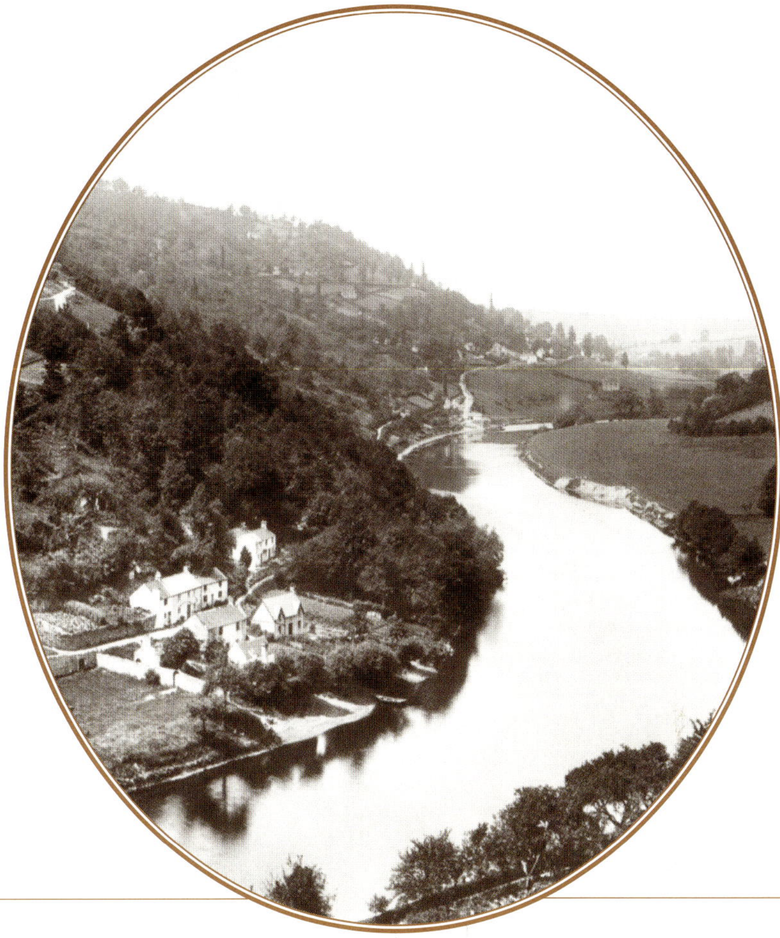

Right: Symonds Yat, near Ross, 1893 (32441) This wooded, majestic gorge has long been a favourite with visitors. The Victorians flocked here to experience wild nature, peering through their telescopes at the great rock of Symonds Yat that rears up 500 feet above the Wye.

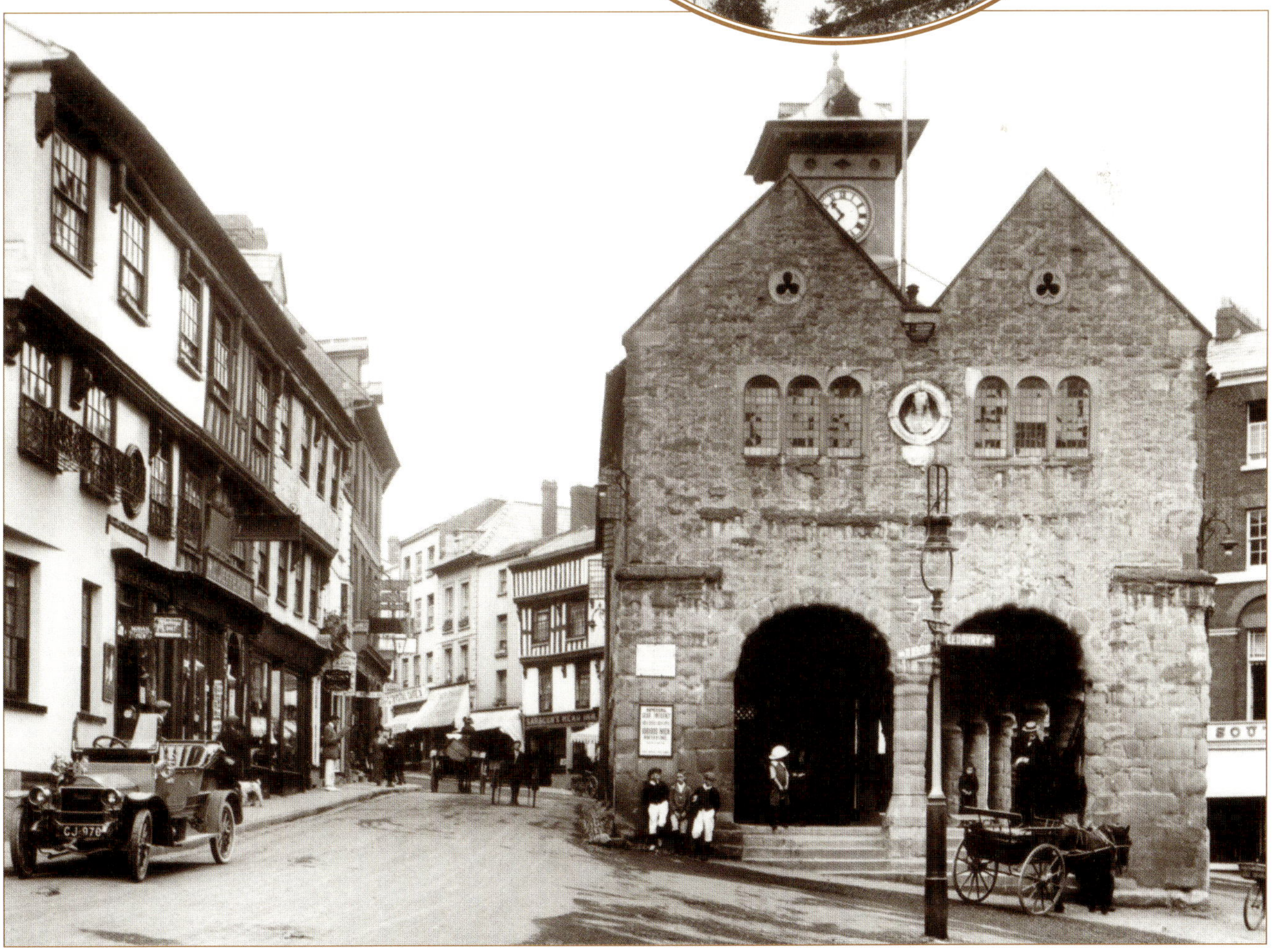

Above: The Market House, Ross, 1914 (67700) This ample 17th century Market Hall is supported on fourteen arches. It is 1914 and a time of war. A poster on the wall announces the 'special grave emergency. 100,000 men wanted at once'. On the left is a shop specialising in selling moccasins. In the distance is the timbered Saracen's Head Inn.

GREAT MALVERN. This hugely popular spa town nestles below the Malvern Hills. It is an almost entirely Victorian creation - until its curative waters had been discovered and thoroughly marketed, it had been a tiny village that grew up around a Benedictine Priory. Then hotels like the luxurious Coburg and Foley sprang up, and its steep streets were soon filled with a pleasing hotch-potch of buildings in a wild range of styles from Italianate to Grecian.

Right: The Beacon from Wyche Cutting, Great Malvern, 1936 (87357) This breezy and commanding summit was a favourite of the Victorians, who trekked up to it on foot or were carried there on the backs of donkeys. The effort was well worth it - they could enjoy the fresh air and marvel at the view. Even Edward VII made a special trip up there in his royal Daimler.

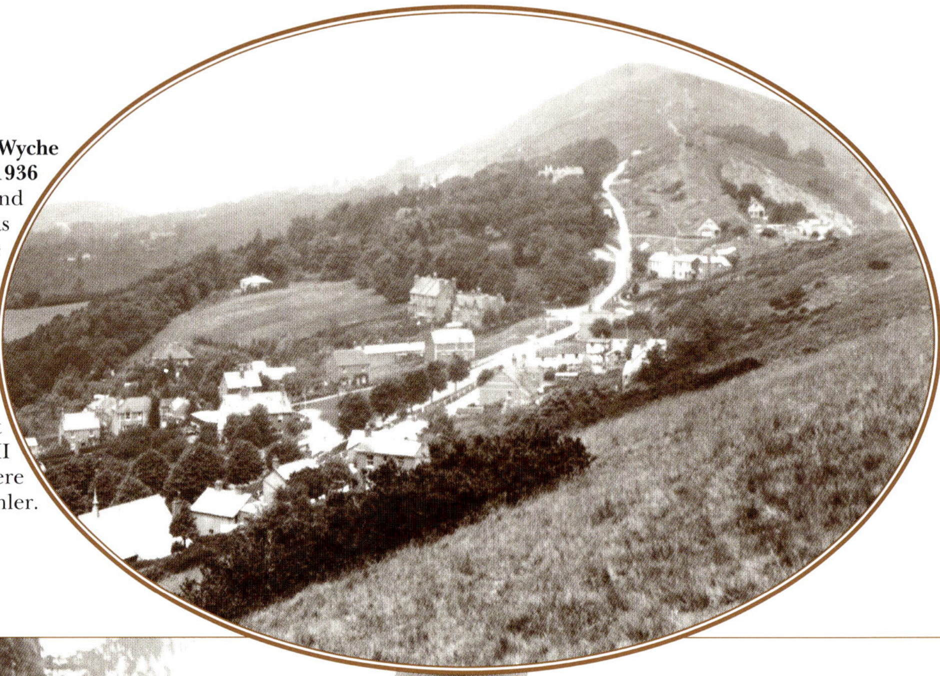

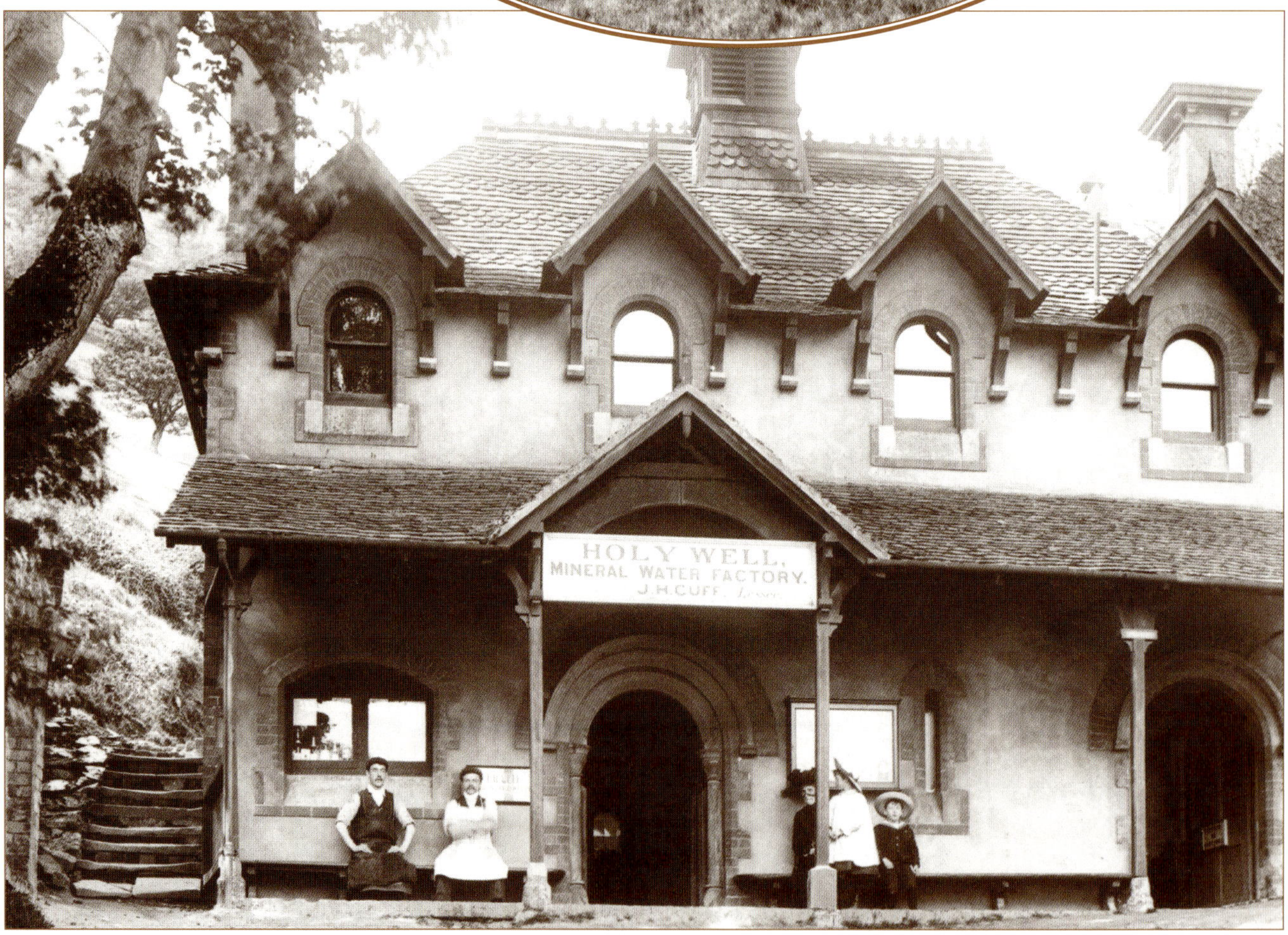

Above: Holywell, Great Malvern, 1904 (51153) Staff take their break at J H Cuff's Mineral Water Factory. The wells at Malvern had long been famous for their curative properties, and earlier in the century Doctors Wilson and Gully had set up a hydropathic establishment where patients underwent a spartan regime of cold baths and icy douches. It wasn't just the gullible who endured it - Gladstone, Dickens and Florence Nightingale tried it, too. However, the really smart patients stuck to drinking Mr Cuff's particularly pure mineral water - with a sizeable tot of whisky added, of course.

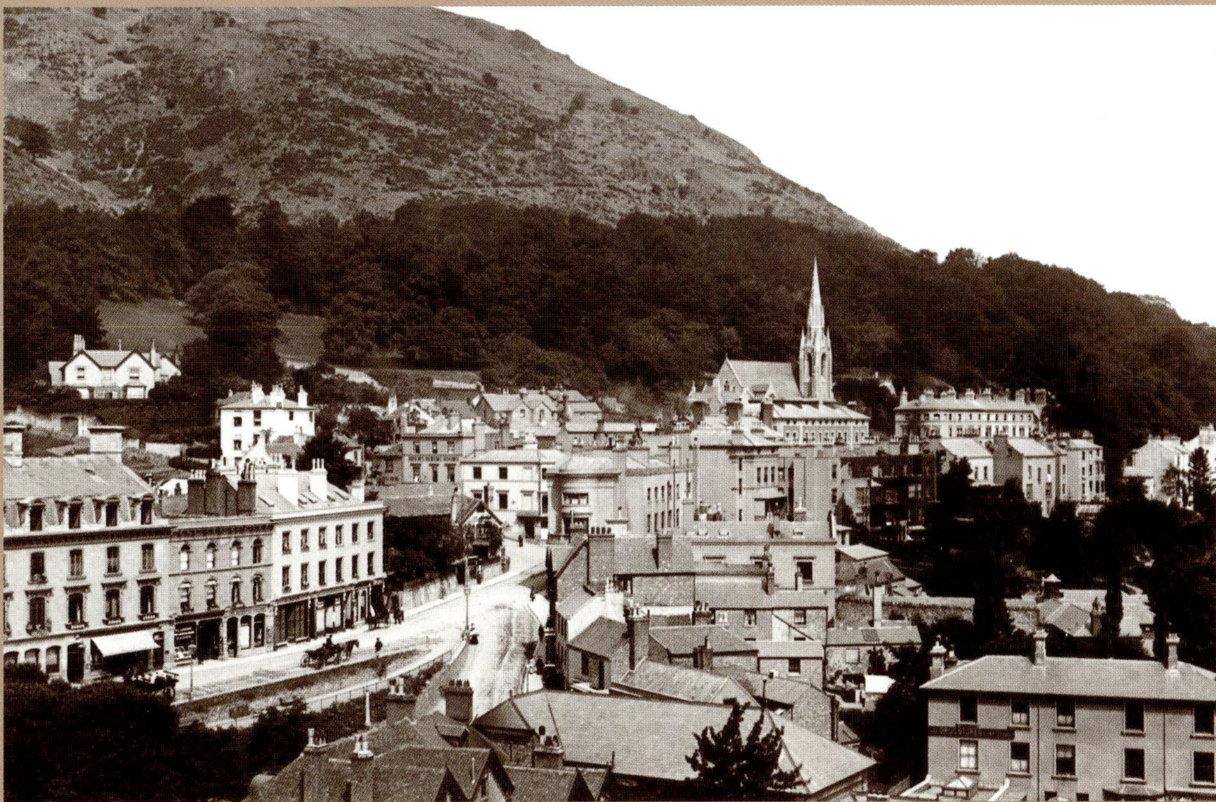

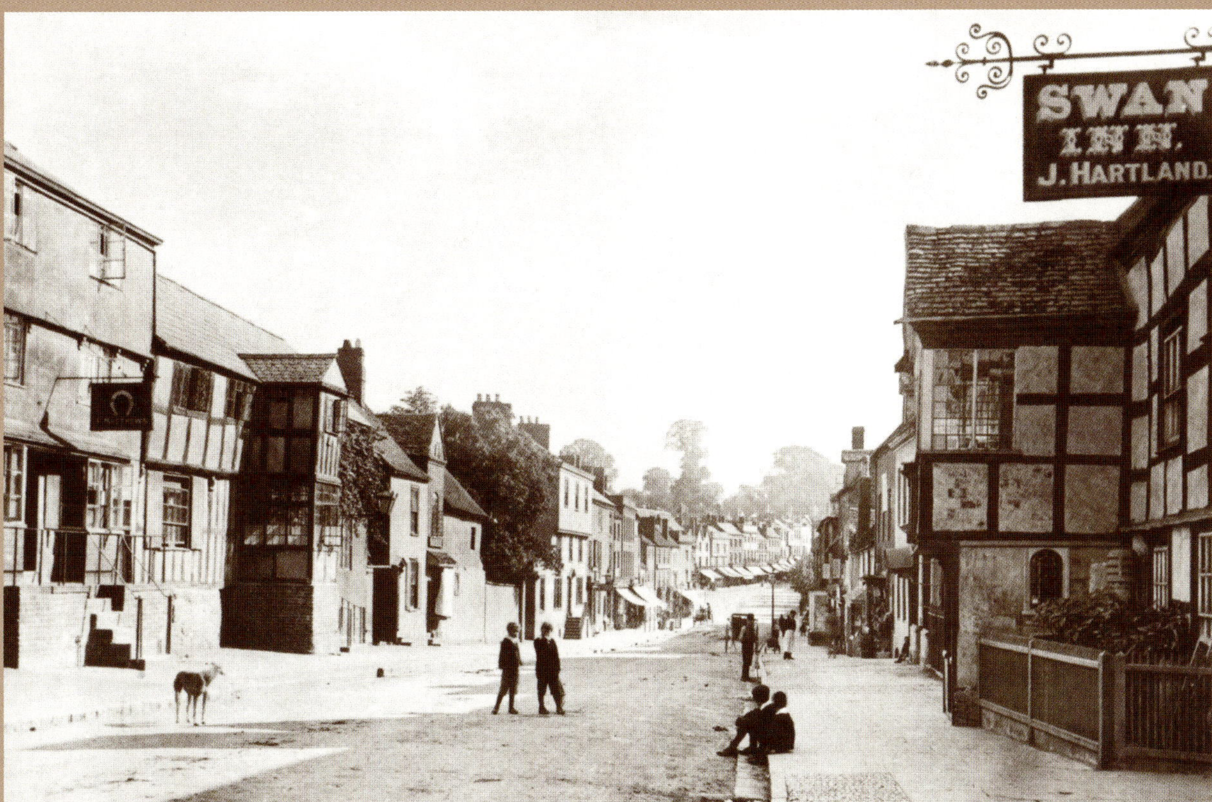

Top: Great Malvern, 1893 (32387) A superb panoramic view. In the streets the hills are ever-present, the great crags leaning heavily on the town. **Above: The Homend, Ledbury, 1870** (L132002) The mile long High Street in this gem of a town is lined with almost perfect half-timbered houses with overhanging upper stories, many now refronted in brick.. On the right is the Swan Hotel, with its wrought iron bracketed signboard.

EVESHAM. This historic market town is at the heart of orchard and fruit-growing country. Set in a broad vale of fertile soil, perfect for market-gardening, it is bordered on three sides by a long loop in the River Avon. Evesham grew up around the Benedictine Abbey founded in 701, but there are few fragments of this remaining. There are some fine buildings, notably the Dresden House and the Booth Hall.

Right: The Three Spires, Evesham, 1892 (31089) Three little girls play close by Abbot Lichfield's grandiose Abbey bell tower, the medieval spire of All Saints and the tower of St Lawrence. These three elevated landmarks jostle each other in the same churchyard.

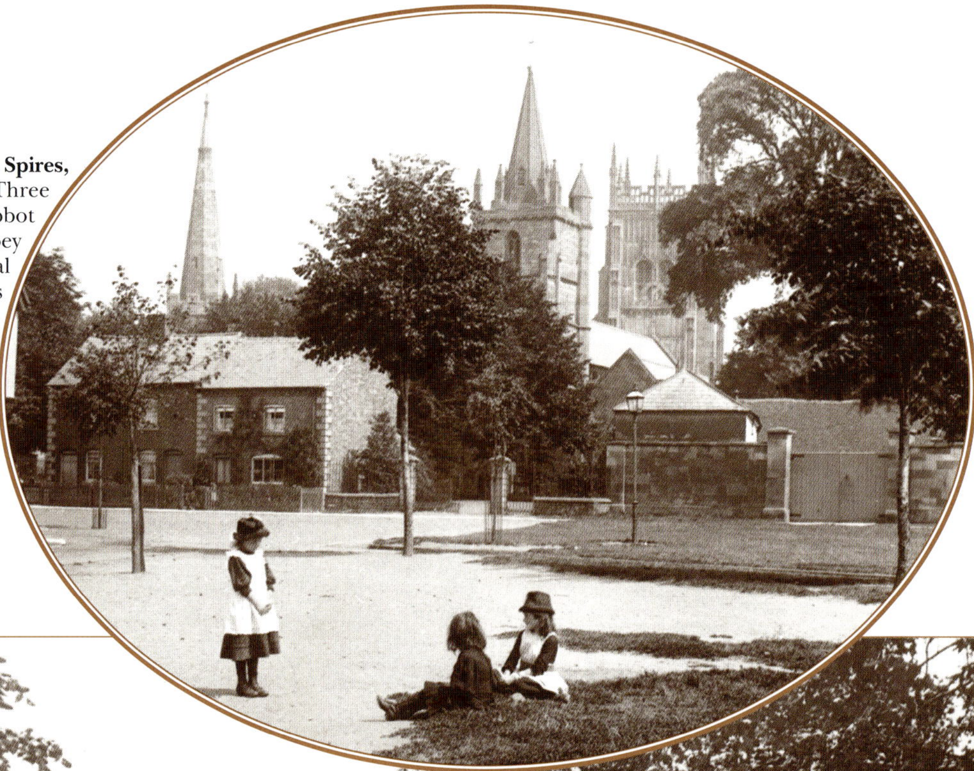

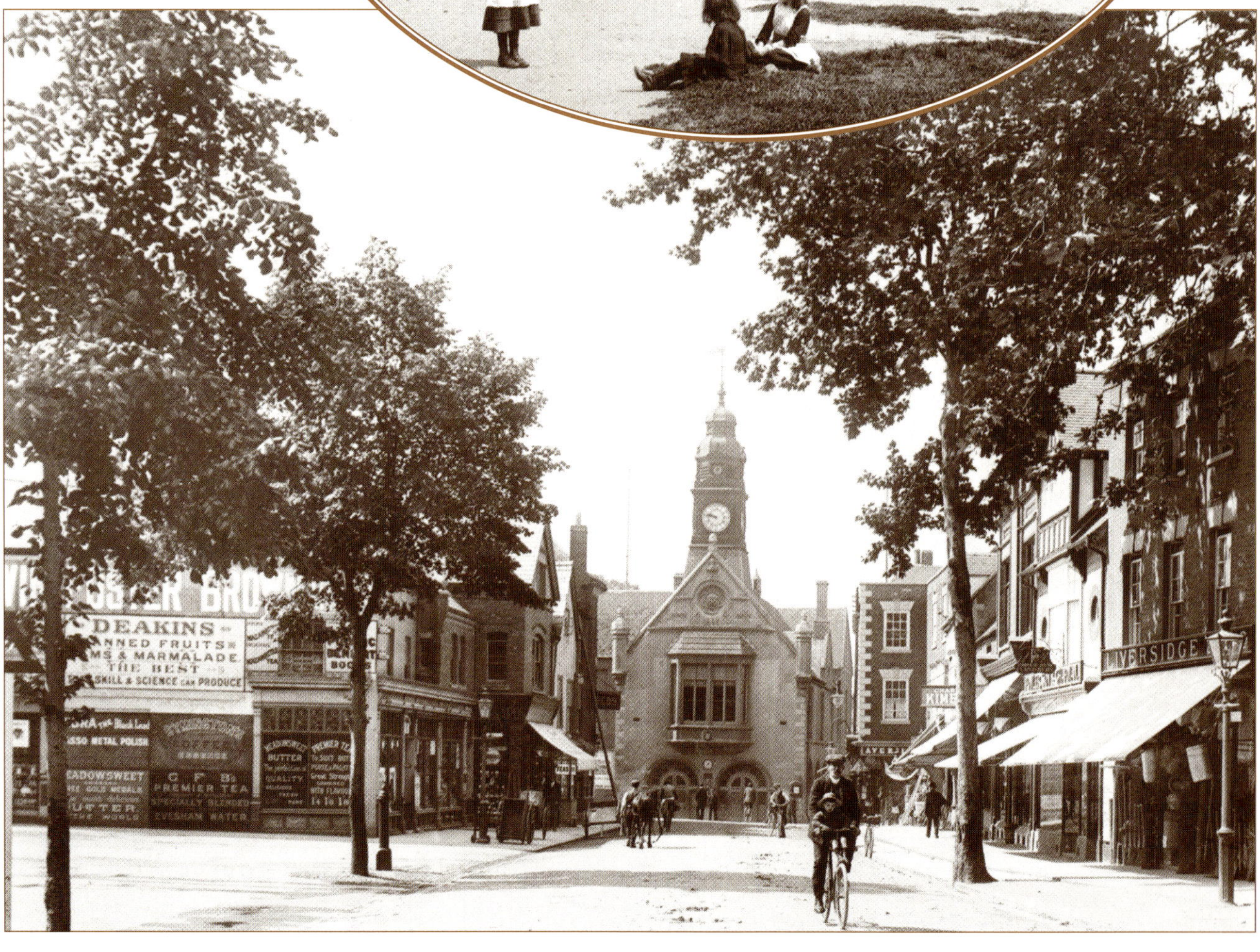

Above: High Street, Evesham, 1910 (62339) On the left, Deakin the grocer is offering 'the best that skill and science can produce'. He particularly recommends his 'meadowsweet butter to suit both purse and palate'. On the right is The Twine Warehouse, where you could buy hemp and onion twine, jute twist and hay cord. A young boy sits on the crossbar of his father's bike. **Opposite: Bridge Street, Evesham, 1892** (31106) Local children pose for the camera. This narrow, pleasing street leads to the river.

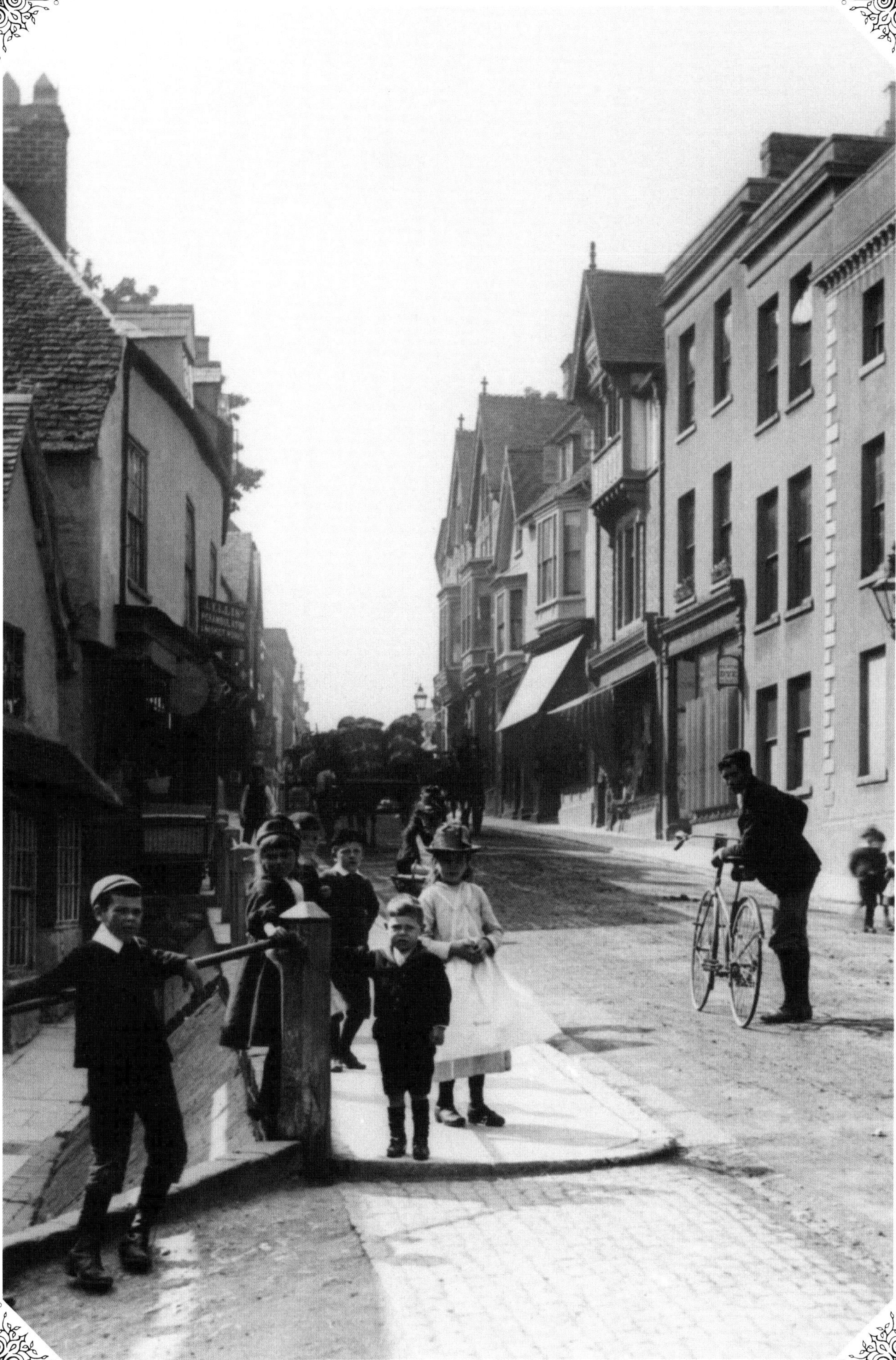

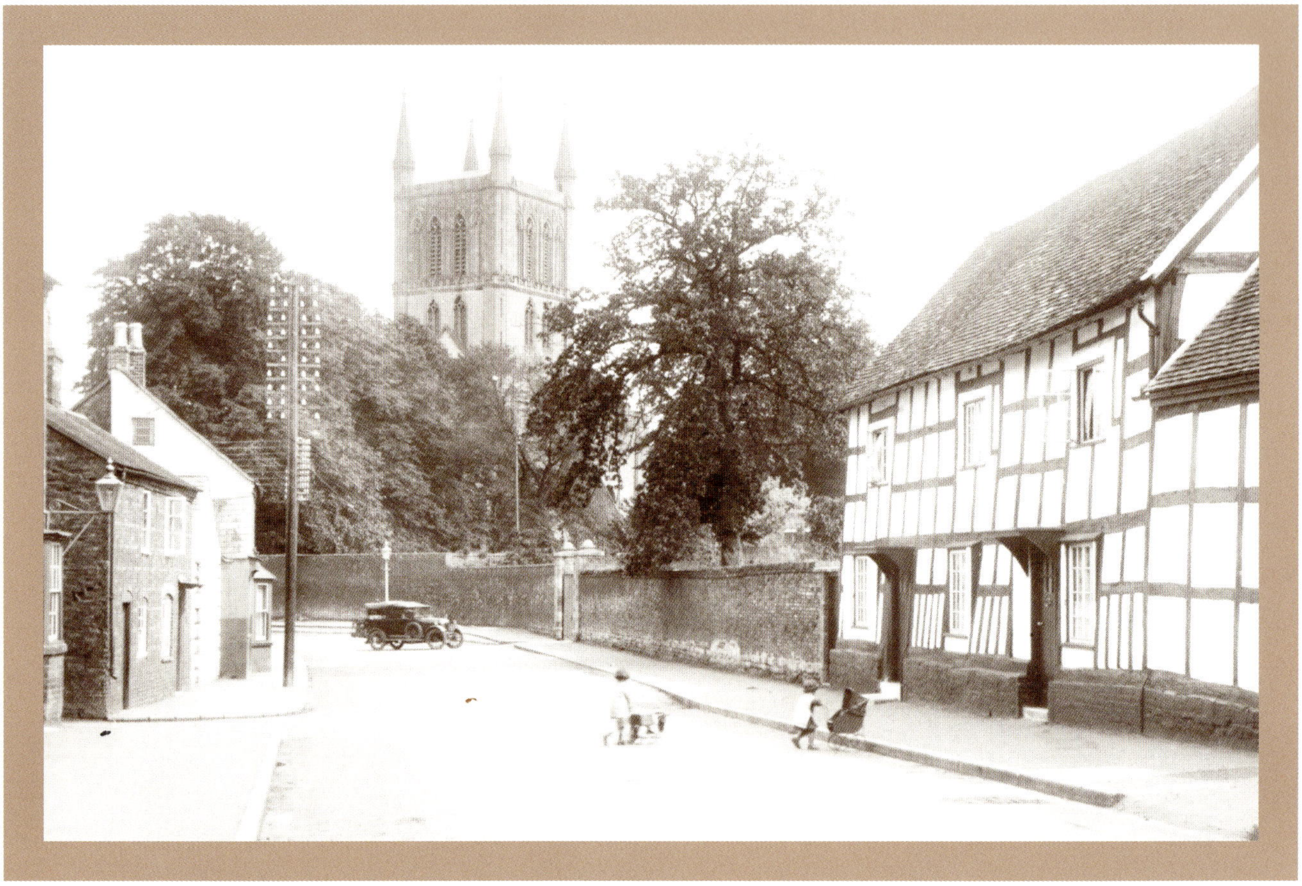

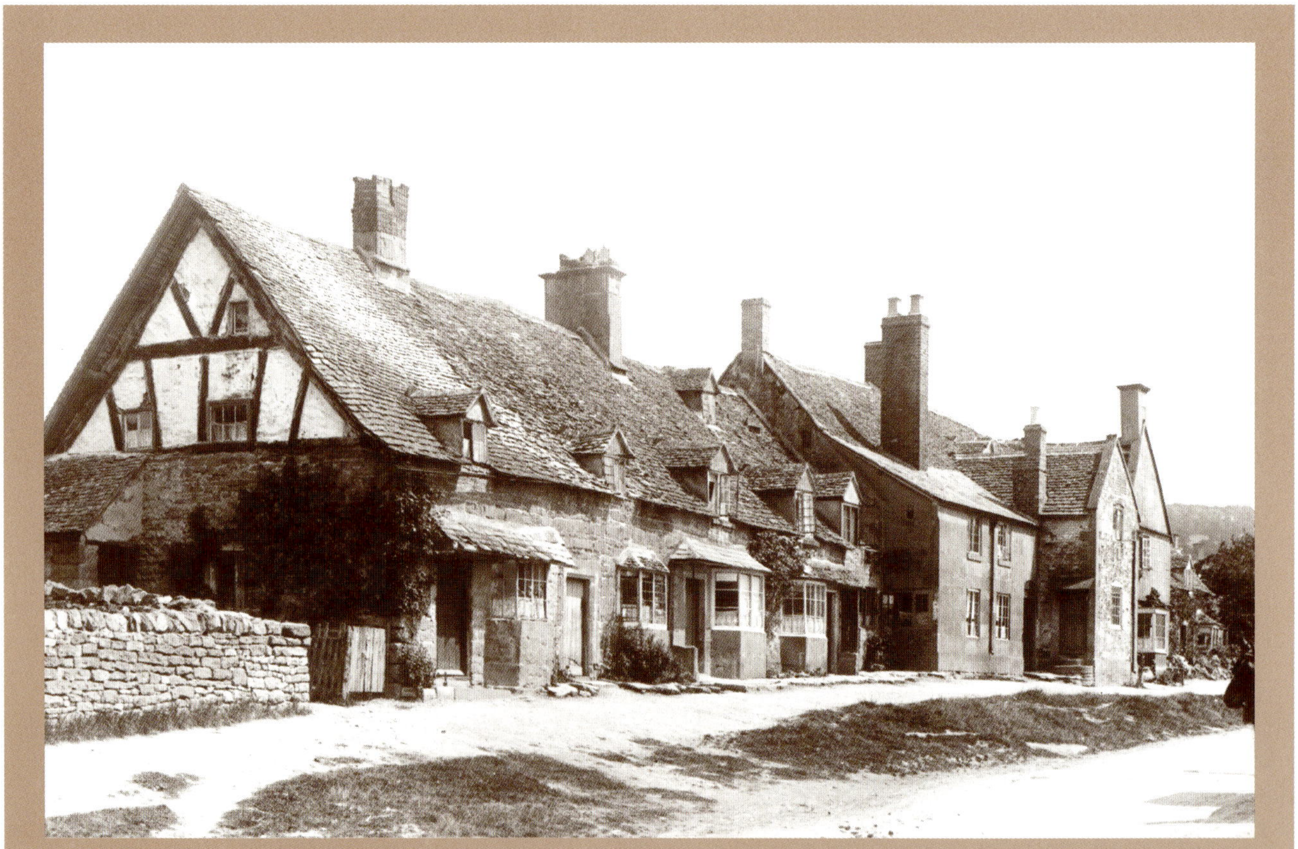

Top: Lower Newlands, Pershore, 1931 (84675) Famed for its plums, and set inside a loop in the Avon, Pershore is a perfect old market town with the remains of an ancient abbey. Here we see an old timbered house, its walls twisted and distorted and, in the background, the magnificent lantern tower of the old Abbey, with its corner turrets. **Above: Broadway, 1899** (44113) Believed by many to be the most beautiful village in England, the long street is fringed with architectural treasures in golden Cotswold stone.

WORCESTER. This historic city, surrounded by rich farming country, is famed for its sauce, fine china and glove-making. It is dominated by its beautiful cathedral. Francis Kilvert gives an unforgettable account of a visit to Worcester and experiencing its overpowering presence. 'The deep soft muffled tones were still echoing the grand pealing of bells from the lighted tower, and the dark night was all in a tremble from the sweet vibration.'

Right The Cathedral from the River, Worcester, 1891 (29298) The Severn laps the edges of this historic cathedral, with its lofty tower of 1374. Here, among other buildings, are the remains of the old monks' dormitory, and terraced paths and gardens. The river is not always so placid and peaceful - it has flooded these lower levels on many occasions.

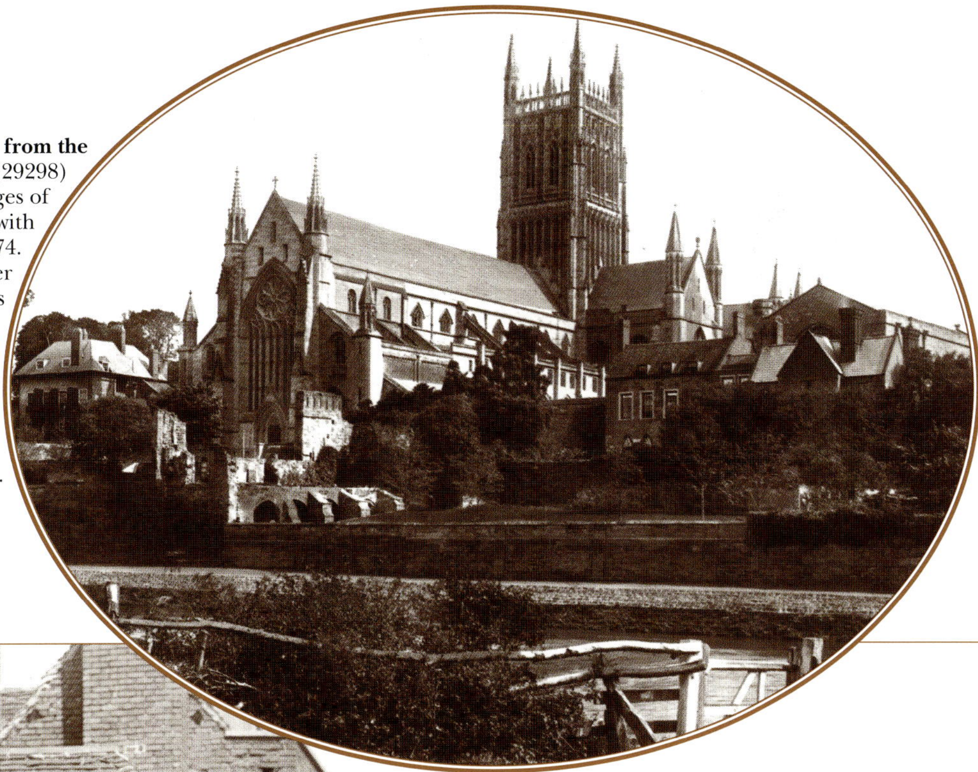

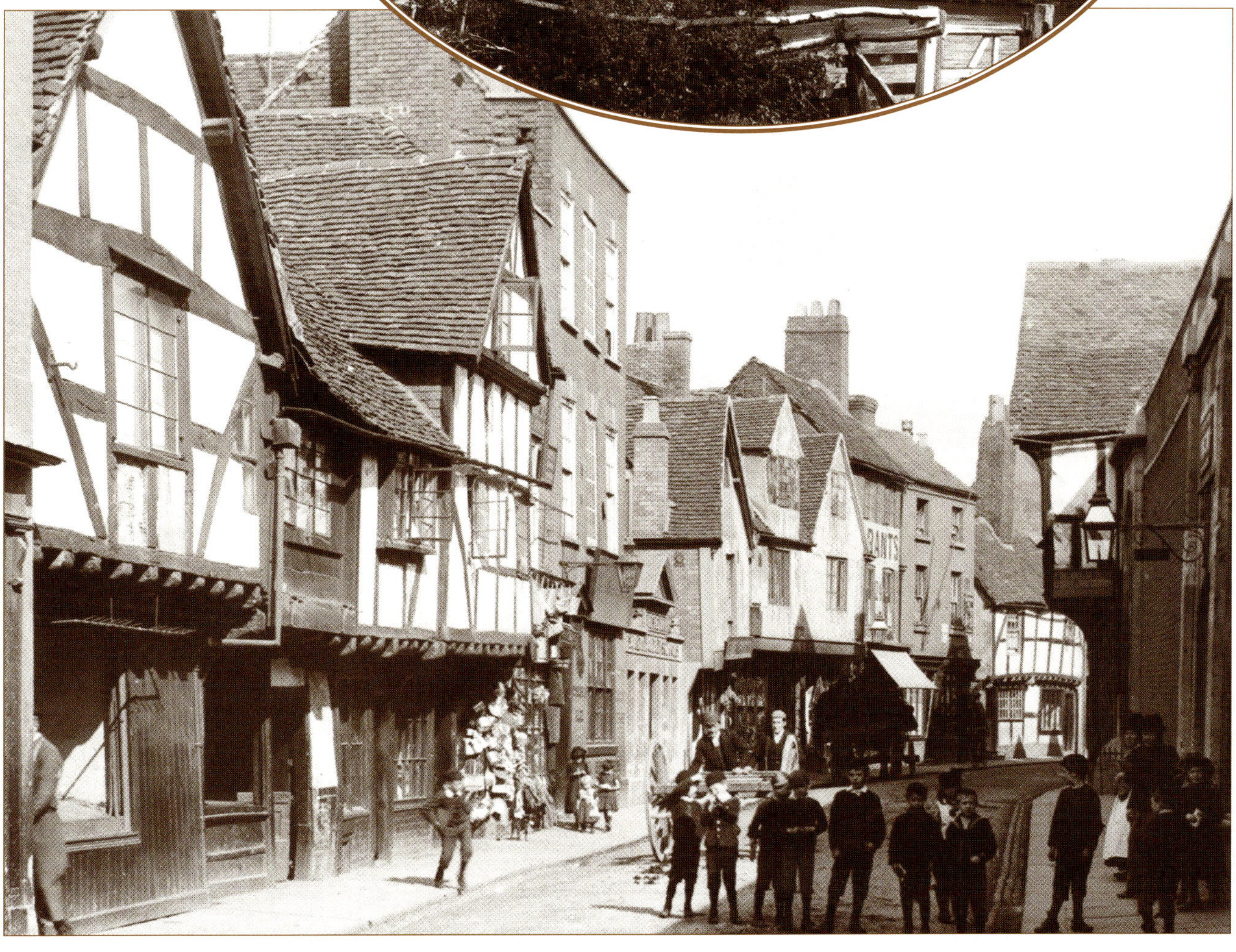

Above: Friar Street, Worcester, 1891 (29321) This is one of the ancient streets of this great city. Here you will find the 14th-century timber-framed lodging of the Franciscan priory, and many other handsome houses of the 15th century, some now converted to shops. They create a unique and lovely harmony, with their medley of gables and overhanging stories, and the patterns of timber-framing.

Right: The Cross, Worcester, 1899 (44010) This panoramic prospect shows Worcester's greatest thoroughfare, which begins close by the cathedral and heads north through the city, first as the High Street, then the Cross and Foregate, and finally the Tything. It is rich in imposing Georgian buildings, including the Gothic Revival House.

Below: The Bull Ring, Kidderminster, 1931 (84609) This town by the River Stour has been a major cloth weaving centre since medieval times. Here in the Bull Ring is the statue of Richard Baxter, the 17th-century clergyman, who stands high on his pedestal like a stone traffic policeman. In the background is the Victorian church of St Mary.

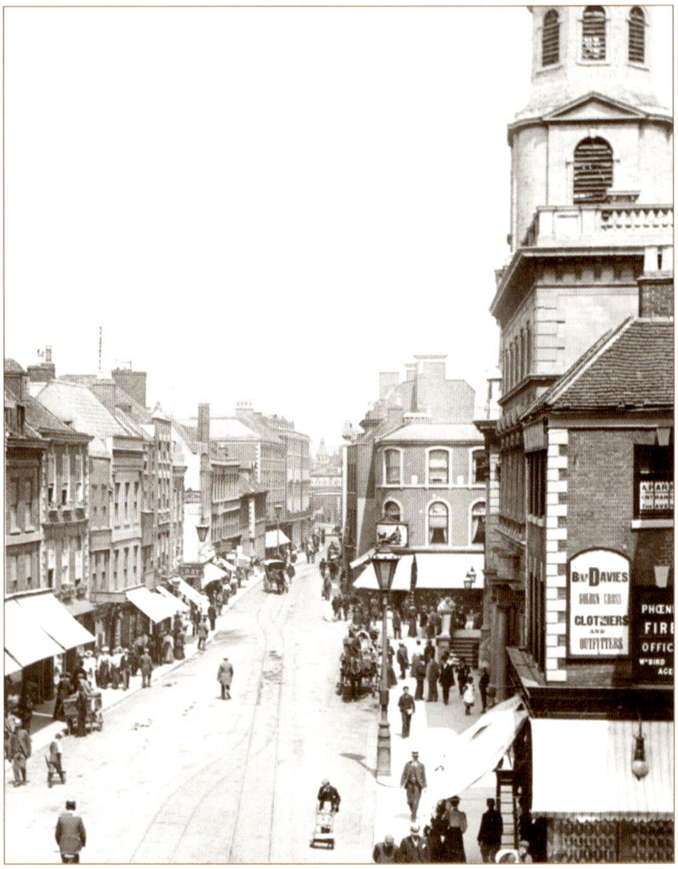

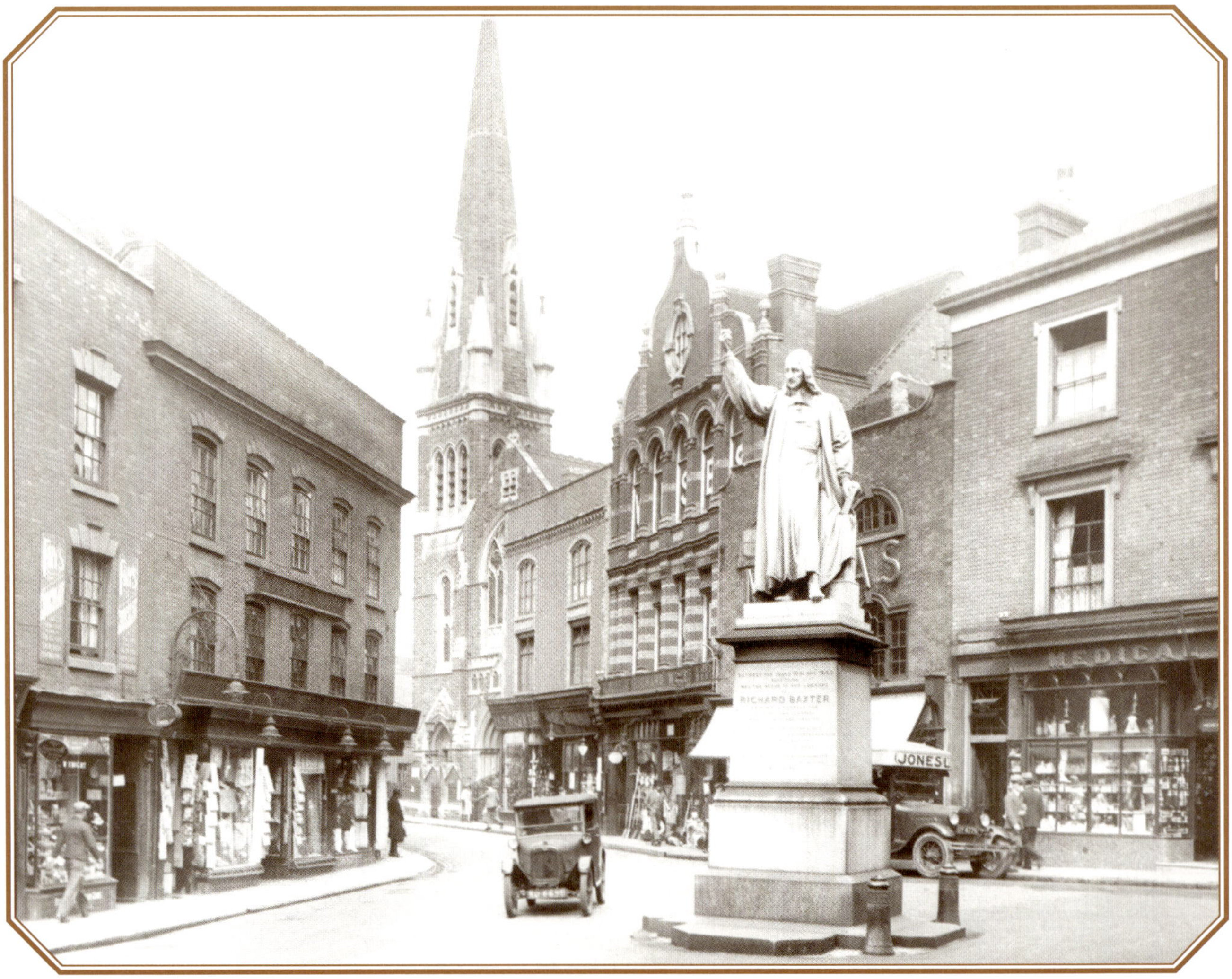

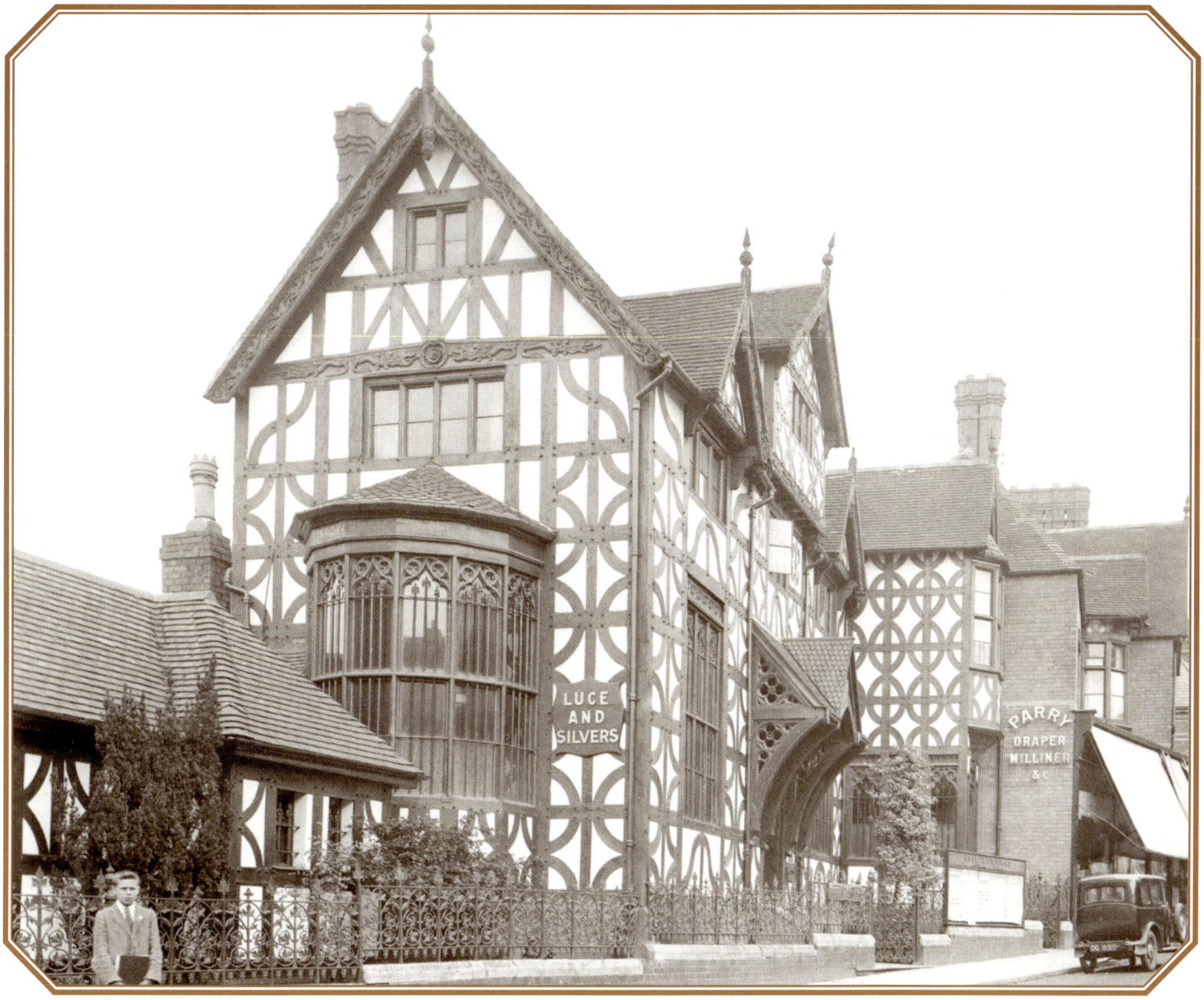

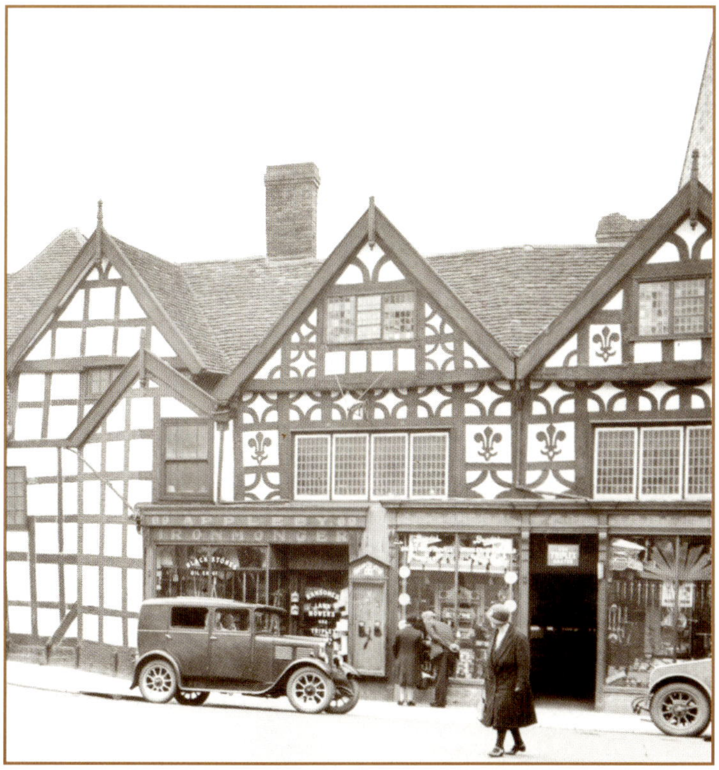

Above: The Tudor House, New Road, Bromsgrove, 1931 (84651) Leland described the town nearly 400 years ago as 'all in manner of one street, very long, standing in a plaine ground'. It is now renowned mainly for its manufacture of nails. This picture shows the elegant old Hop Pole Inn of 1572, which was moved here from its original position in the High Street.

Left: St John's Street, Bromsgrove, 1931 (84649) Appleby the ironmonger is fortunate to have his shop in this lovely timbered building, with its fleur de lys decorations under the gables and multi-paned leaded windows.

Overleaf: Droitwich, 1904 (51938) A classic scene of old English town life. On the corner, Mr Target has a wonderful display of straw hats, two delivery boys are setting out with a basket-woven cart from George Wythe's wines sellers and, in the background, the tower of St Andrew's church looks down over the town.

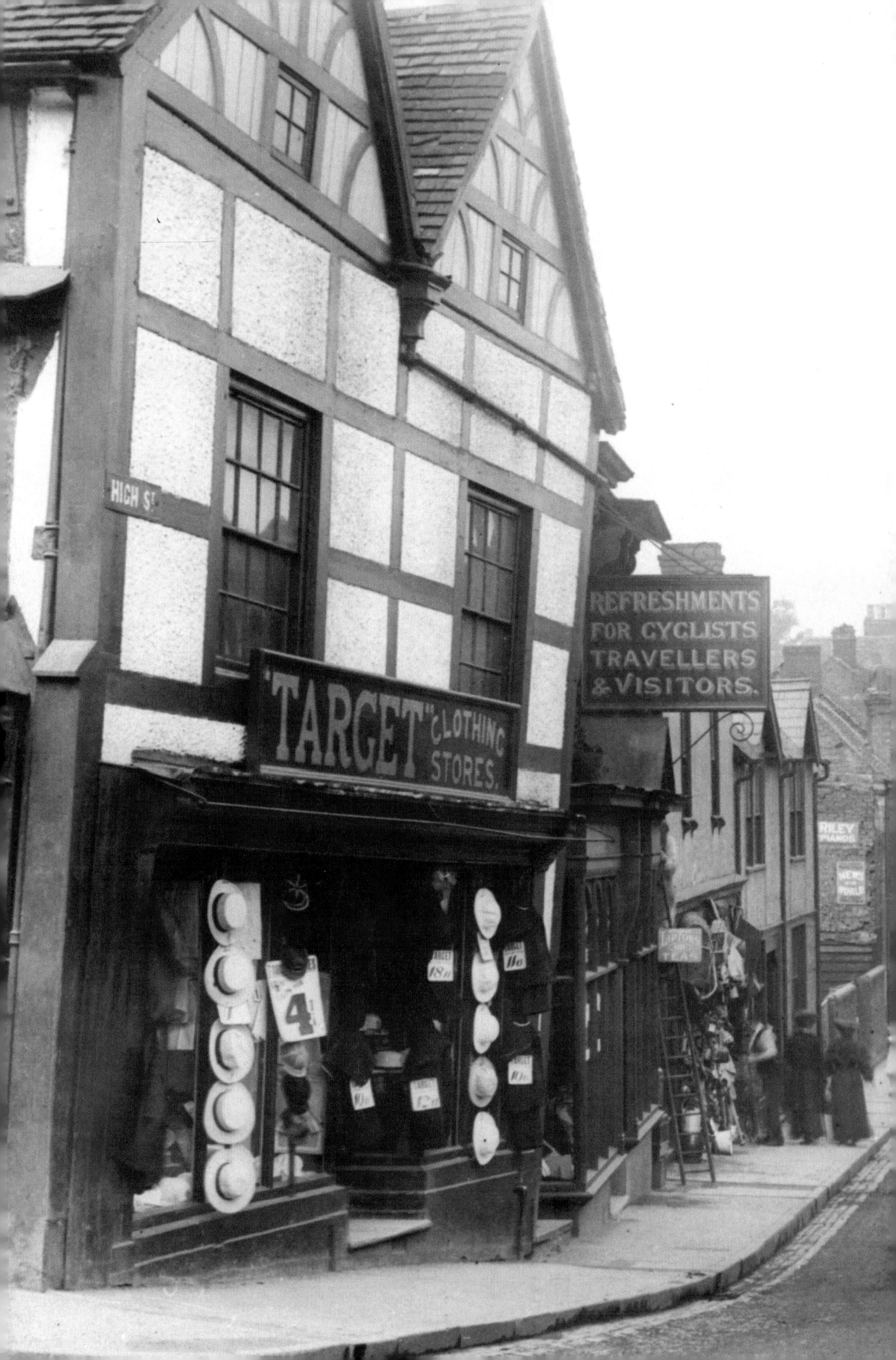
HIGH St
"TARGET" CLOTHING STORES.
REFRESHMENTS FOR CYCLISTS TRAVELLERS & VISITORS.

Index

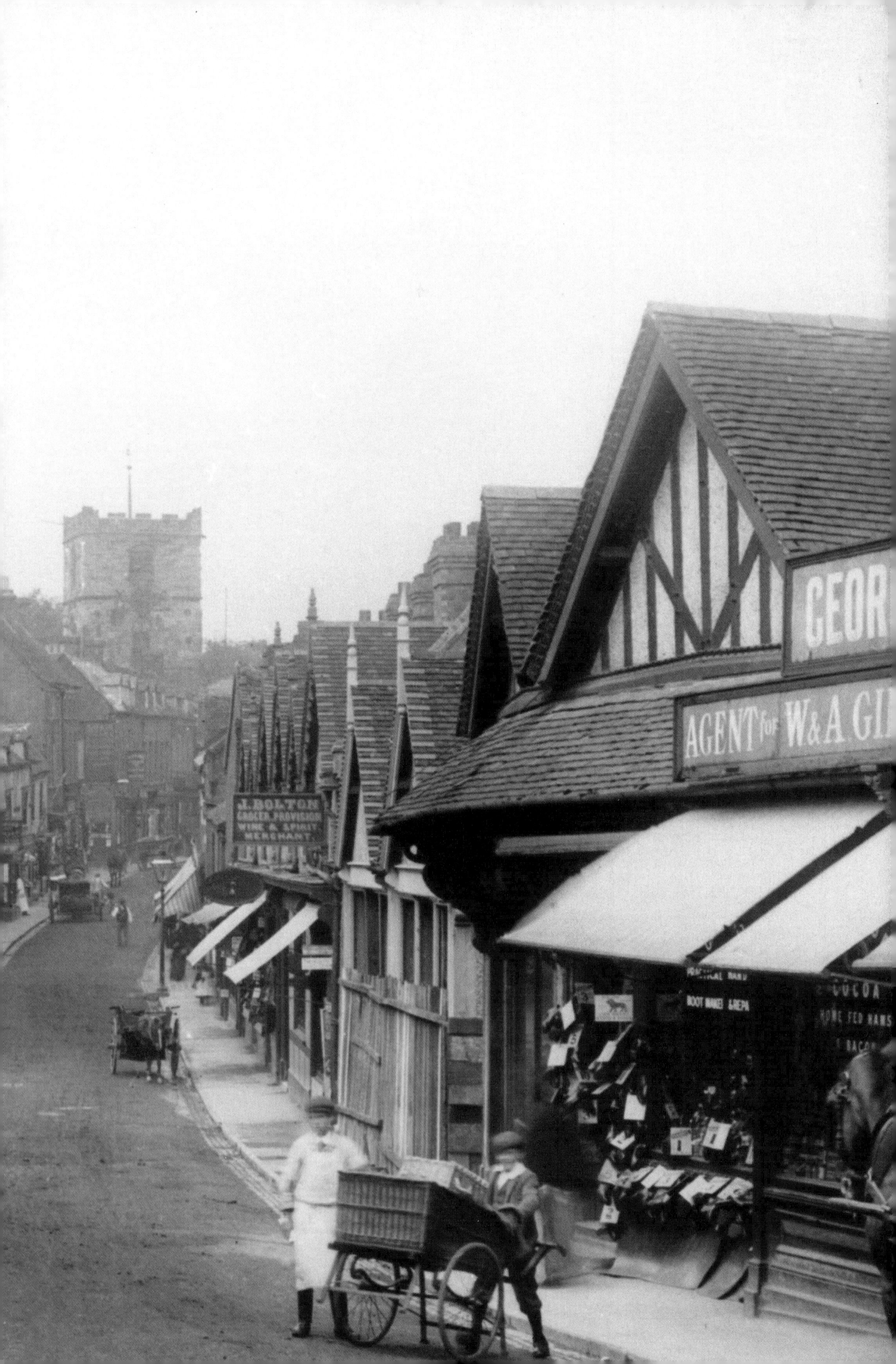
GEOR
AGENT for W&A GI
J. BOLTON
GROCER, PROVISION
WINE & SPIRIT
MERCHANT
COCOA
HOME FED HAMS
BOOT MAKER & REPA